PRICING CORPORATE SECURITIES AS CONTINGENT CLAIMS

PRICING CORPORATE SECURITIES AS CONTINGENT CLAIMS

Kenneth D. Garbade

The MIT Press
Cambridge, Massachusetts
London, England

© 2001 Massachusetts Institute of Technology

This book was set in Times New Roman in 3B2 by Asco Typesetters, Hong Kong and was printed and bound in the United States of America.

Library of Congress Cataloging-in-Publication Data

Garbade, Kenneth D.
  Pricing corporate securities as contingent claims / Kenneth D. Garbade.
    p.   cm.
  Includes bibliographical references and index.
  ISBN 0-262-07223-8 (hc. : alk. paper)
  1. Securities—Prices—Mathematical models. 2. Investment analysis—Mathematical models. I. Title.
  HG4636 .G365 2001
  332.63'2—dc21
                                                                    2001044153

for Daniel J. Kevles, Gregory C. Chow, and William L. Silber

Contents

About the Book ix

1 Introduction, Overview, and Assumptions 1

I BASIC CONCEPTS 19

2 The Contingent Value of Debt and Equity 21

3 Senior and Subordinated Debt 63

4 Institutional and Empirical Characteristics of Bankruptcy 79

5 Bankruptcy Costs and Violations of the Absolute Priority Rule 111

II SECURITIES WITH CALL AND CONVERSION OPTIONS 125

6 Callable Debt 127

7 Early Redemption of Callable Debt 143

8 Convertible Debt 149

9 Conversion Forcing Calls of Convertible Debt 179

10 Warrants 187

III PAYMENTS TO CREDITORS AT DIFFERENT TIMES 209

11 Multiple Debt Securities 211

12 Coupon-Bearing Debt 233

13 Pay-in-Kind Bonds 249

IV DIVIDENDS AND OTHER DISCRETIONARY DISTRIBUTIONS TO SHAREHOLDERS 271

14 Dividend-Paying Stock 273

15 Optimal Dividend Policy 283

16 Empirical Characteristics of Corporate Dividend Policy 291

17 Leveraged Recapitalizations 315

18 Spin-offs 335

V   **ASSESSING THE METHODOLOGY**   365

19   **Empirical Tests of Contingent Value Models**   367

20   **Managerial Discretion and Implicit Management Options**   377

        References   389
        Index   409

About the Book

Participants in securities markets spend a large fraction of their work day thinking about prices and values. The most talked-about issue is whether the price of a particular security or group of securities is more likely to rise or fall. Additionally market professionals spend a significant amount of time on a variety of other valuation topics, such as the following:

· What *is* the current price of a security; that is, at what price can it be bought or sold?

· How can the risks of a security or portfolio of securities be quantified?

· Is a security cheap or expensive compared to other similar securities with comparable risks?

· How can the risk of fluctuations in the price of a security be hedged (or mitigated)?

This book addresses these other topics in the context of the markets for corporate securities.

A quarter of a century ago, Fischer Black and Myron Scholes (1973) and Robert Merton (1973) pointed out that securities issued by a corporation can be priced as claims whose values are contingent on the value of the enterprise as a whole. The notion of corporate securities as contingent claims is important in its own right, and also because it integrates a variety of otherwise loosely related topics, including equity risk, credit risk, seniority and subordination, early redemption of callable debt, call and conversion of convertible debt, and dividend policy. This book examines the pricing, hedging, and risk assessment of corporate securities as contingent claims.

Chapter 1 provides an overview of the concept of contingent value and its uses.

Part I (chapters 2 to 5) explores the basic principles of contingent value analysis, including the description of the dynamic evolution of the value of the firm as a random walk and the idea that different classes of corporate securities are claims with different priorities. We show how the priority of debt relative to equity, and the priority of senior debt relative to subordinated debt, affects the prices of those securities. We also describe the institutional characteristics of bankruptcy in the United States, and we show how bankruptcy blurs the stated priorities of different claims.

Part II (chapters 6 to 10) examines securities with embedded call and conversion options, including callable debt, convertible debt, and warrants. We show how an option can enhance or diminish the value of a security, depending on whether the right of exercise rests with the holder or with the issuer. We also review empirical evidence bearing on the question of whether contingent value models reflect correctly the decision of a firm to call conventional debt for early redemption or to force conversion of convertible debt.

Part III extends the basic framework to firms capitalized with multiple debt issues (chapter 11) and coupon-bearing bonds (chapters 12 and 13). Part IV (chapters 14 to 18) extends the analysis further, to firms capitalized with common stock that pays dividends and that may make other distributions to shareholders.

Part V (chapters 19 and 20) reviews empirical evidence bearing on the validity of the contingent value methodology. The evidence suggests that contingent value models provide only a rough description of the cross-sectional structure of corporate securities prices and that they systematically understate the value of common stock relative to more senior corporate claims. The pricing errors can be attributed, in part, to a failure to specify correctly the circumstances and consequences of default and bankruptcy, as well as to a failure to allow for fluctuations in yields on default-proof fixed income securities. However, the errors may also be due to a failure to recognize implicit management options, including the ability of the firm to undertake mergers and acquisitions, divestitures, spin-offs and recapitalizations, and the value of control over the exercise of such options.

Two Pedagogical Notes

This book examines structural models of corporate securities prices of the type proposed by Black and Scholes (1973) and Merton (1973) and does not address reduced-form pricing models.[1] This reflects our interest in pricing common stock and equity-linked securities (e.g., convertible debt and warrants) as well as conventional debt, and our interest in examining decisions to exercise embedded and managerial options (e.g., options to call debt for early redemption and to distribute cash and securities to common shareholders).

The exposition of contingent claims analysis is here phrased in terms of discrete time binomial processes, commonly called binomial trees, rather than partial differential equations or stochastic integrals derived from continuous time Gaussian processes. This choice makes the material accessible to a larger audience and establishes with greater clarity the locus and characteristics of decisions such as whether to call debt for early redemption,

---

1. Reduced-form models have been proposed by Jarrow and Turnbull (1995), Jarrow, Lando, and Turnbull (1997), Cathcart and El-Jahl (1998), and Duffie and Singleton (1999).

convert debt into common stock, and pay interest on pay-in-kind debt in cash.[2]

Acknowledgments

The origins of this book can be traced to December 1992, when I was employed in Global Markets Research at Bankers Trust Company. In the wake of the 1990–91 recession the chairman of the board and chief executive officer, Charles S. Sanford Jr., became interested in developing better methods of avoiding or mitigating losses in the bank's loan portfolio. In particular, he was interested in whether the bank could reprice its loans to current market values on a regular basis (as a way of identifying deterioration in credit quality more quickly) and in whether the bank could actively hedge and otherwise manage its exposure to credit risk.[3] Contingent claims analysis was recognized as a potentially fruitful area of inquiry. I became involved in the project because of my experience with pricing, hedging, and assessing risk in the markets for U.S. Treasury and related fixed income securities (Garbade 1996).

I owe a substantial debt of gratitude to those who managed and participated in the research undertaken at Bankers Trust in the mid-1990s, including Alan Lerner and P. Daniel Borge (the managers of Global Markets Research), Garret Thunen (who coordinated the research on corporate securities and kept us focused on the important business issues), and my colleagues, Luca Celati, Craig Dibble, David Fite, Gene Guill, Richard Harmon, Howard Mason, Dan Mudge, Robert Munsey, Anish Shah, Robert Siegel, Marc Steglitz, Yoav Tamir, and Kenneth Weiller. Kenneth Abbott, Kenneth Baron, Tom Daula, and Clinton Lively were enormously helpful in developing the scope and depth of the analysis. I am equally indebted to the market participants who reflected on the research, including George Courtadon, Stephen Kealhofer, William Melton, Ehud Ronn, and Timothy Thompson, and to Tom Hyer, Alex Lipton and Dmitry Pugachevsky for their extremely helpful analysis of pricing and hedging passport options.

In January 1997 I joined the faculty of the Stern School of Business at New York University and began teaching a seminar in the contingent pricing of corporate securities. This book grew out of the lecture notes for that seminar. I am grateful for the interest and enthusiasm of the seminar

2. See similarly Andersen and Sundaresan (1996, p. 48) (model in discrete time has greater transparency).
3. These and related ideas are discussed in Sanford (1993).

participants, including especially Viral Acharya, Issac Chang, Paolo Pasquariello (who, among other contributions, had the insight to observe how pay-in-kind bonds provide a conceptual bridge between the fixed contractual obligations of conventional debt and the discretionary dividend payments of common stock), and Miriam Polyakov. My colleagues at NYU, including William Allen, Edward Altman, Jennifer Carpenter, N. K. Chidambaran, Ned Elton, Stephen Figlewski, Kenneth Froewiss, Kose John, Marcel Kahan, William Silber, Roy Smith, Marti Subrahmanyam, Rangarajan Sundaram, Lawrence White, and David Yermack, helped with comments and suggestions as I struggled to understand and exposit issues that arise at the interface between corporate finance and asset pricing. Yakov Amihud and Menachem Brenner were especially generous with their time and accumulated wisdom. Special thanks go to Martin Gruber and Anthony Saunders, the chairs of the Finance Department during my time at NYU.

In August 2000 I joined the staff of the Capital Markets Function in the Research and Market Analysis Group of the Federal Reserve Bank of New York. I am grateful to Paul Bennett and Christine Cumming for their support during the final months of editing and proofreading.

This book would never have seen the light of day without the interest, professionalism, and efforts of my editors at The MIT Press: Elizabeth Murry and Dana Andrus. It was a pleasure to work with two people who have such high standards.

My greatest debt is to the authors cited at the end of this book.

Although my debts are many in number and large in magnitude, the errors and shortcomings of this book are for my account alone. The views expressed in the book do not necessarily reflect the position of the Federal Reserve Bank of New York or the Federal Reserve System.

Finally, I am thankful for the times when Larissa Louise, Edward Arthur, and Rachel Rose were quiet, and for the times when they were rambunctious, as well as for the times when Bernice was somewhere in between. Their hugs are the best medium of exchange.

PRICING CORPORATE SECURITIES AS CONTINGENT CLAIMS

1 Introduction, Overview, and Assumptions

Consider a firm capitalized with N classes of securities, including common stock and debt of various maturities, seniorities, and coupon rates—where different classes of debt may carry options for early redemption or conversion to common stock. Let $V_i(t)$ denote the aggregate value of the ith class of securities at time t. The aggregate value of the firm, denoted $W(t)$, is the sum of the values of the securities that capitalize the firm:

$$W(t) = V_1(t) + V_2(t) + \cdots + V_N(t) \tag{1.1}$$

Suppose that there exists a set of functions $\{f_1, f_2, \ldots, f_N\}$, where each function has two arguments that vary over time: time itself and the value of the firm[1] such that the value of the ith security at time t can be computed as

$$V_i(t) = f_i(W(t), t), \qquad i = 1, 2, \ldots, N \tag{1.2}$$

Equation (1.2) says that at any point in time we can value each class of securities issued by the firm *contingent* on the contemporaneous value of the firm as a whole.

This book addresses the construction of the f_i "contingent value functions," or the identification of how the value of each slice of the corporation's capital structure varies as a function of time and the value of the firm.[2] We begin, in this introductory chapter, by pointing out some practical uses of contingent value functions, presenting an overview of the chapters that follow, and noting some important assumptions of the analysis.

1.1 Uses of Contingent Value Functions

Contingent value functions have four important uses: cross valuation, assessing relative value, hedging, and risk assessment.[3] We will describe each at a fixed point in time by writing equation (1.2) more simply as

---

1. A function may have additional arguments, but the value of any other argument is assumed to be constant (so the argument does not need to be noted explicitly), a function of time, or a function of the value of the firm.

2. The idea of pricing corporate securities as contingent claims was set forth explicitly in the seminal work of Black and Scholes (1973) and Merton (1973). The idea was developed subsequently by Merton (1974), Black and Cox (1976), Ingersoll (1976, 1977a), Brennan and Schwartz (1977, 1980), Geske (1977, 1979), Galai and Schneller (1978), and Ho and Singer (1982, 1984). Cox and Rubinstein (1985, pp. 375–415), Mason and Merton (1985) and Park and Subrahmanyam (1990) provide accessible expositions of the basic principles.

3. Contingent value analysis has also been used to estimate the likelihood of corporate default (Caouette, Altman, and Narayan 1998, ch. 11; Crosbie 1999) and to address issues in corporate capital structure, including the optimal choice of leverage and debt maturity (Brennan and Schwartz 1978, 1984; Kane, Marcus and McDonald 1984; Fischer, Heinkel, and Zechner 1989; Wiggins 1990; Leland 1994, 1998; Leland and Toft 1996).

$$V_i = f_i(W), \qquad i = 1, 2, \ldots, N \tag{1.3}$$

where it is understood that the value of the firm, the values of its securities, and the forms of the contingent value functions are "as of" the specified time.

Cross Valuation

Not every corporate security trades in a liquid public market. Bank loans, for example, trade infrequently and in private transactions among banks, mutual funds, and private investment funds.[4] This can present thorny problems in appraising the market values of such loans.[5] It may be similarly difficult to assess the values of privately placed securities and executive and employee stock options.[6]

On the other hand, the value of the common stock of most major and many midsized companies, and (in some cases) the value of a portion of their debt, can be identified readily from reported transactions in liquid public markets. Such public valuations can be used to "cross value" illiquid securities.

For example, suppose that we know the contingent value function for every security issued by a firm. Suppose also that we observe the market value V_j of the jth security, but that we cannot readily or reliably observe the market value of the kth security. From V_j we can impute the value of the firm as the value of $\hat{W}$ that satisfies the equation

$$V_j = f_j(\hat{W}) \tag{1.4}$$

We can then impute the value of the kth security as

$$\hat{V}_k = f_k(\hat{W}) \tag{1.5}$$

It is also feasible to impute the value of the firm from the observed values of the ith and jth securities (as the value of $\hat{W}$ that satisfies the equation $V_i + V_j = f_i(\hat{W}) + f_j(\hat{W})$), and then to cross-value a third security as in equation (1.5).

---

4. The market for bank loans is described in Carlson and Fabozzi (1992), Simons (1993), Gorton and Pennacchi (1995), Angbazo, Mei, and Saunders (1998), and Saunders (2000, pp. 648–62).

5. See "Fund Investors Worry Values May Be Off Base," *Wall Street Journal*, October 19, 1999, p. C1, and "Bank-Loan Funds' Valuation Questioned," *Wall Street Journal*, December 14, 1999, p. C33 (describing the problems of open end loan-participation funds in valuing thinly traded and illiquid loans to corporate borrowers).

6. The market for private placements is described in Zinbarg (1975), Zwick (1980), Hawkins (1982), Carey, Prowse, Rea, and Udell (1993), Kahan and Tuckman (1996), Amihud, Garbade, and Kahan (1999, 2000), and Kwan and Carleton (1999). Lambert, Larcker, and Verrechia (1991), Jennergren and Naslund (1993), Huddart (1994), Kulatilaka and Marcus (1994), Cuny and Jorion (1995), Rubinstein (1995), and Carpenter (1998) discuss the valuation of executive and employee stock options.

Assessing Relative Value

Every business day investors have to decide whether to buy, sell, or hold an enormous variety of corporate securities. An important practical aspect of any investment decision is assessing whether a particular security is cheap or expensive compared to other securities. For example, mutual funds, insurance companies, and hedge funds are active participants in the high-yield, or "junk," corporate bond market, as well as in the market for syndicated bank loans to corporate borrowers rated at less than investment grade. Their decision to purchase high-yield bonds or syndicated loans depends on their assessment of the relative values of the respective securities.[7] Similarly, before an investor decides whether to purchase the convertible debt of a company, she might examine whether the same risk is priced more attractively as a combination of the firm's straight debt and common stock.[8]

Contingent value functions can facilitate comparisons of relative value.[9] Suppose that we observe the market values V_j and V_k of the jth

7. See "Oversupply, Rising Rates Pinch 'Junk Loan' Market," *Wall Street Journal*, September 13, 1999, p. C24 (reporting the comment of one observer that "You have institutional investors arbitraging the two asset classes. Virtually every influence that impacts the high-yield bond market now impacts the leveraged-loan market.").

8. Issuers are also sensitive to the relative costs of capital in different markets. See "Cox Communications Sells $2 Billion of Securities, Continuing Growth in Issuance of Corporate Debt," *Wall Street Journal*, August 11, 1999, p. C21 (reporting that "issuers are turning to the [convertible bond market] instead of the high-yield market because it is less expensive"), "Internet Companies Revive the Market for Convertibles after Summer Slump," *Wall Street Journal*, September 27, 1999, p. B19E (reporting a "flood of Internet deals" in the convertible bond market, in part because of a "sickly" high-yield bond market), "Why the Fed Hasn't Fazed Big Borrowers," *Wall Street Journal*, March 22, 2000, p. C1 (observing that one company substituted mortgage debt for a planned junk bond issue because of a change in the relative costs of credit in the secured debt and junk bond markets), and "More Firms Launch Different Securities Simultaneously," *Wall Street Journal*, June 30, 2000, p. C20 (reporting the growing practice of combining common stock and convertible debt in a joint offering, where the offered amounts of the two securities are adjusted during the marketing period as a function of investor interest, to "tap two types of investors and play one against the other and maximize proceeds").

9. For practical and related examples of relative value analysis, see Ingersoll (1976) (income and capital shares of dual purpose closed end mutual funds), Brauer (1993) (two bonds of the same issuer that—outside of a minor difference in maturity date—differ only with respect to terms of a single restrictive covenant), McConnell and Schwartz (1986) (zero-coupon convertible debt and common stock), Jarrow and O'Hara (1989) ("primes" and "scores"), Titman and Torous (1989) (commercial mortgages), Rosenthal and Young (1990) and Froot and Dabora (1999) (closely linked pairs of common stock), Dammon, Dunn, and Spatt (1993) (different classes of debt issued by RJR Nabisco), and Brenner, Eldor, and Hauser (2001) (exchange traded and inalienable foreign exchange options). See also "Market Place: A G.M. Issue Has Created an Anomaly," *New York Times*, November 9, 1992, p. D4, "Market Place: Such a Deal: A Security That Thrilled Short-Sellers," *New York Times*, May 15, 1997, p. D1, "Heard on the Street: Ignored Stocks May Contain Surprise Deals," *Wall Street Journal*, September 28, 1999, p. C1, and "Market Place: MPS Stock: Class Warfare vs. Rationality," *New York Times*, August 2, 2000, p. C1.

and kth securities issued by the firm, and that we want to assess whether one security is cheap or expensive compared to the other. We can impute a value for the kth security from the observed market value of the jth security as $\hat{V}_k = f_k(\hat{W})$, where $\hat{W}$ is the value of the firm that satisfies the equation $V_j = f_j(\hat{W})$. If V_k is less than $\hat{V}_k$, we might conclude that the kth security is "cheap" relative to the jth security because the market value of the kth security is less than the value we would impute to that security based on the market value of the jth security. Conversely, we might conclude that the kth security is relatively expensive if V_k is greater than $\hat{V}_k$.

This methodology for assessing relative value is distinctly different from more traditional analyses that compare, for example, yields on bonds with similar terms and credit ratings issued by a *variety* of corporations, or price/earnings ratios for the common stock of a *variety* of companies. We are here comparing the values of different securities issued by a *single* firm.[10]

Hedging

Suppose that an investor holds a fraction h_j of the jth security of a company, where h_j is between zero and unity, and has decided to reduce his risk with respect to fluctuations in the value of that security. The simplest approach is to sell some of the security. However, he can also reduce his risk with an off-setting "hedge" in another security issued by the same firm.[11] His problem is to compute the size of the hedge position.

Let $f_j'(W)$ denote the derivative of the jth contingent value function evaluated at W. If the value of the firm changes from W to $W + \Delta W$, the values of the jth and kth securities will change by ΔV_j and ΔV_k respectively, where, to a first-order approximation,

10. Mason and Merton (1985, p. 25) observed that, "The traditional approach to the pricing of corporate liabilities is exemplified by the organizational structure of a typical, vintage corporate finance textbook: a chapter on the pricing of equity, a chapter on long-term debt, a chapter on preferred stock, a chapter on warrants and and convertible securities, etc. Each chapter employs a different valuation technique and rarely, if ever, are any attempts made to integrate the various components of the firm's capital structure as even a check on the internal consistency of these diverse valuation methodologies. In contrast, the [contingent claims] approach to the pricing of corporate liabilities begins with the firm's total capital structure and uses a single evaluation technique to simultaneously price each of the individual components of that structure. Thus, the [contingent claims] methodology takes into account the interactive effects of each of the securities on the prices of all the others and insures a consistent evaluation procedure for the entire capital structure."

11. See "Market Place: Valujet Stock: Short Sellers' Nightmare," *New York Times*, July 5, 1996, p. D1 (hedging the risk of a debt position by short selling the issuer's common stock), "Bond Hit at Morgan: $25 Million," *Wall Street Journal*, October 19, 1996, p. C1 (hedging the risk of a position in convertible bonds by short selling common stock and call options on the stock), and "Salomon Has Its Deal and Eats It, Too, Bailing out Holders of Comcast Bonds," *Wall Street Journal*, February 11, 2000, p. C1 (hedging the risk of a position in exchangeable bonds by short-selling the stock for which bonds are exchangeable).

$$\Delta V_j = f_j'(W) \cdot \Delta W \qquad\qquad (1.6a)$$

$$\Delta V_k = f_k'(W) \cdot \Delta W \qquad\qquad (1.6b)$$

Recall that the investor holds the fraction h_j of the jth security. Suppose that he hedges with a position in a fraction h_k of the kth security. The change in the value of his portfolio for given changes in the values of the securities will be

$$\Delta Q = h_j \cdot \Delta V_j + h_k \cdot \Delta V_k \qquad\qquad (1.7)$$

Substituting the expressions for ΔV_j and ΔV_k from equations (1.6a, b) into equation (1.7) gives

$$\Delta Q = h_j \cdot f_j'(W) \cdot \Delta W + h_k \cdot f_k'(W) \cdot \Delta W \qquad\qquad (1.8)$$

or

$$\Delta Q = [h_j \cdot f_j'(W) + h_k \cdot f_k'(W)] \cdot \Delta W \qquad\qquad (1.9)$$

Now define h_k^* as

$$h_k^* = -\frac{f_j'(W)}{f_k'(W)} \cdot h_j \qquad\qquad (1.10)$$

If the investor chooses his hedge position so that $h_k = h_k^*$, ΔQ will be zero (to a first-order approximation) regardless of whether the value of the firm rises or falls. If h_k is between zero and h_k^*, the investor will have reduced, but not eliminated, his exposure to fluctuations in the value of the firm.

Risk Assessment

Institutional investors, banks, and broker-dealers commonly own a variety of securities issued by a single corporation, including senior and subordinated debt, convertible debt and common stock, and sometimes encounter difficulty assessing their overall exposure to the issuer. For example, an institution may be uncertain whether to classify a convertible bond as debt or equity—or as some combination of debt and equity—and it may find it difficult to aggregate the credit risk on a bond with the equity risk on common stock.

Contingent value functions can be used to identify the aggregate risk of a position in a variety of securities issued by the same firm. Suppose that an investor holds a fraction h_i of the ith security of the firm, for $i = 1, 2, \ldots, N$. The change in the value of the investor's portfolio associated with a change in the value of the firm can be computed, to a first-order approximation, with a simple generalization of equation (1.9):

$$\Delta Q = \left[\sum_{i=1}^{N} h_i \cdot f_i'(W) \right] \cdot \Delta W \tag{1.11}$$

This shows how the change in the value of the investor's portfolio depends on his holdings of the various securities issued by the firm (the h_i's), the sensitivity of the value of each security to change in the value of the firm (the $f_i'(W)$'s), and the given change in the value of the firm (ΔW).

Suppose that we want to express the investor's exposure to fluctuations in the value of the firm as a "risk-equivalent" position in the kth security. Let h_k^e denote the fraction of the kth security in the risk-equivalent position. If the value of the firm changes by ΔW, the change in the value of the risk-equivalent position will be

$$\Delta Q^e = h_k^e \cdot f_k'(W) \cdot \Delta W \tag{1.12}$$

We choose h_k^e so that the change in the value of the risk-equivalent position is identical to the change in the value of the investor's portfolio regardless of the value of ΔW, that is, so that ΔQ^e in equation (1.12) is equal to ΔQ in equation (1.11) for every value of ΔW. Comparing equations (1.11) and (1.12) shows that we require

$$h_k^e \cdot f_k'(W) = \sum_{i=1}^{N} h_i \cdot f_i'(W)$$

so that

$$h_k^e = [f_k'(W)]^{-1} \cdot \sum_{i=1}^{N} h_i \cdot f_i'(W) \tag{1.13}$$

The aggregate risk of the investor's portfolio is, to a first-order approximation, equivalent to the risk of owning a fraction h_k^e of the kth security issued by the firm. Thus, for purposes of assessing risk, we have reduced the original portfolio to an equivalent position in a single security.

1.2 Overview

The nineteen chapters that follow are grouped into five parts.

Part I explores some basic concepts in the contingent valuation of corporate securities in the simple context of a firm capitalized with noncallable, nonconvertible zero-coupon debt and common stock that does not pay a dividend. Chapter 2 considers a firm capitalized with a single class of zero-coupon debt; chapter 3 extends the analysis to a firm capitalized with senior and subordinated debt.

The analyses in chapters 2 and 3 demonstrate the importance of bankruptcy in constructing contingent value functions. Chapter 4 surveys the institutional and empirical characteristics of bankruptcy in the United States and provides a critical assessment of the common assumptions that bankruptcy is costless and leads to distributions of cash and securities in accord with the "absolute priority rule" that senior claimants must be paid in full before more junior claimants get anything. Chapter 5 examines whether bankruptcy costs and violations of the absolute priority rule can be incorporated into the specification of a contingent value model.

Part II examines the contingent valuation of securities with embedded options, such as an issuer's option to call its bonds for early redemption or a holder's option to convert her bonds into common stock. Chapter 6 examines callable debt, and chapter 7 reviews the institutional and empirical characteristics of calls for early redemption. Chapter 8 examines convertible debt, and chapter 9 reviews the institutional and empirical characteristics of conversion forcing calls of convertible debt. Chapters 7 and 9 emphasize the practical difficulty of specifying accurately the circumstances under which a company will choose to call debt for early redemption. Part II concludes with a discussion of warrant pricing in chapter 10.

Part III extends contingent value analysis to firms capitalized with debt that promises to make payments to creditors at different times, including firms capitalized with multiple debt securities (chapter 11) and coupon-bearing debt (chapter 12). Chapter 13 examines a special category of coupon-bearing debt: pay-in-kind (PIK) bonds, where the firm has an embedded option to satisfy an interest obligation by issuing additional bonds instead of paying cash. PIK bonds are important because they provide a conceptual bridge between the fixed contractual obligations of conventional debt and the discretionary dividend payments of common stock.

Part IV extends the analysis further, to include dividends and other discretionary distributions to shareholders. Chapter 14 describes the contingent valuation of corporate securities when the dividend policy of the firm is known, and chapters 15 and 16 consider some of the practical problems associated with identifying the dividend policy of a firm. The following two chapters discuss more specialized distributions to shareholders: leveraged, or debt-financed, dividend payments (chapter 17), and spin-offs of subsidiary stock (chapter 18).

Part V concludes with two chapters assessing the methodology of contingent value analysis. Chapter 19 summarizes several quantitative appraisals of contingent value models of corporate securities prices. The empirical evidence supports the proposition that conventional models systematically undervalue common stock relative to more senior corporate claims or, equivalently, overvalue debt and other senior claims relative to common stock. We suggest in chapter 20 that one source of the bias is the absence from the models of much of the managerial discretion—including options to undertake mergers, acquisitions, divestitures, leveraged recapitalizations, and spin-offs—that contributes to the value of common stock.

1.3   An Assumption on the U.S. Treasury Yield Curve

A little reflection shows that corporate securities can not possibly be valued with functions as simple as those specified in equation (1.2).

Yields on U.S. Treasury securities reflect the cost of credit for a default-proof borrower. In general, corporate security values are not invariant with respect to fluctuations in Treasury yields. Holding the value of the firm constant, the yield on a corporate bond will vary with the level of Treasury yields: the bond will be more valuable the lower the level of Treasury yields and less valuable the higher the level of Treasury yields. Moreover, since we are holding the value of the firm constant, it follows from equation (1.1) that the value of at least one security issued by the firm must vary *directly* with the level of Treasury yields. However, Treasury yields do not appear as arguments in the contingent value functions of equation (1.2).

For expositional simplicity, we assume the yield curve for U.S. Treasury debt is flat and stationary through time.[12] This assumption justifies suppressing the level of Treasury yields as an explicit argument in the contingent value function for a corporate security. As a matter of notation we denote the continuously compounded yield per annum on Treasury debt as R_f, so the present value of a Treasury promise to pay F dollars in τ years is $F \cdot e^{-R_f \cdot \tau}$. For example, the present value of a Treasury promise to pay \$100 in 5 years when $R_f = 0.10$ (or 10% per annum) is \$60.65 ($60.65 = 100 \cdot e^{-(0.10) \cdot (5)}$).

12. It is possible, but notationally cumbersome, to relax the assumption of a flat and stationary Treasury yield curve by incorporating a model of yield curve evolution as proposed by Vasicek (1977); see also Longstaff and Schwartz (1995), Shimko, Tejima, and Van Deventer (1993), Cox, Ingersoll, and Ross (1985), Titman and Torous (1989), Acharya and Carpenter (1999), Ho and Lee (1986), Hull and White (1990), Brennan and Schwartz (1980), and Kim, Ramaswamy, and Sundaresan (1993).

1.4 An Assumption on the Evolution of the Value of the Firm

It is widely appreciated that we have to say something about the prospective evolution of the price of a stock if we want to value a conventional call option on the stock. The situation is not different if we want to value a corporate security contingent on the value of the firm: we have to say something about the prospective evolution of the value of the firm.

We will assume that (between payments to securities holders) the natural logarithm of the value of the firm evolves as a normal, or Gaussian, random walk with expected change μ per annum and variance σ^2 per annum.[13] Assuming the firm does not make any payments to securities holders between time t and time $t + \Delta t$ (time is measured in decimal years, so that $t = 1997.5$ denotes a point in time exactly halfway through 1997), the change in the log of the value of the firm can be written as

$$\ln[W(t + \Delta t)] - \ln[W(t)] = \mu \cdot \Delta t + \sigma \cdot \Delta t^{1/2} \cdot z \tag{1.14}$$

where z is a normally distributed random variable with mean zero and a variance of unity. We assume that μ and σ are fixed and known parameters. The model of equation (1.14) is commonly called a "lognormal random walk."[14]

From equation (1.14) we can compute the expected value of the change in the log of the value of the firm as

$$\text{Ex}[\ln[W(t + \Delta t)] - \ln[W(t)]] = \text{Ex}[\mu \cdot \Delta t + \sigma \cdot \Delta t^{1/2} \cdot z]$$

$$= \mu \cdot \Delta t + \sigma \cdot \Delta t^{1/2} \cdot \text{Ex}[z]$$

or since $\text{Ex}[z] = 0$,

$$\text{Ex}[\ln[W(t + \Delta t)] - \ln[W(t)]] = \mu \cdot \Delta t \tag{1.15}$$

It follows that, as stated, μ is the expected change per annum in the log of the value of the firm.

We can also compute the variance of the change in the log of the value of the firm:

---

13. At the time of a payment, the value of the firm will decline—in a discrete and discontinuous jump—by the amount of the payment. Discontinuous changes in value resulting from payments to securities holders are examined in chapters 11, 12, 13, and 14.

14. The model is also a "continuous time–continuous state" model. The model is a continuous time model because it is meaningful to speak of *any* value of the time variable t. Thus we can speak of $t = 1997.0123$, or $t = 1997.0124$, and so on. The model is a continuous state model because the random variable z can take on *any* value between $-\infty$ and $+\infty$ (although a value greater than $+5$ or less than -5 is highly unlikely), so the value of the firm can take on *any* positive value.

$$\mathrm{var}[\ln[W(t+\Delta t)] - \ln[W(t)]] = \mathrm{Ex}[\{\ln[W(t+\Delta t)] - \ln[W(t)]$$
$$- \mathrm{Ex}[\ln[W(t+\Delta t)] - \ln[W(t)]]\}^2]$$
$$= \mathrm{Ex}[\{\ln[W(t+\Delta t)] - \ln[W(t)] - \mu \cdot \Delta t\}^2]$$
$$= \mathrm{Ex}[\{\sigma \cdot \Delta t^{1/2} \cdot z\}^2]$$
$$= \sigma^2 \cdot \Delta t \cdot \mathrm{Ex}[z^2]$$

or since $\mathrm{Ex}[z^2] = 1$,

$$\mathrm{var}[\ln[W(t+\Delta t)] - \ln[W(t)]] = \sigma^2 \cdot \Delta t \tag{1.16}$$

Thus, also as stated, σ^2 is the variance per annum of the change in the log of the value of the firm.

Characteristics of a Lognormal Random Walk

It will be useful to examine briefly some characteristics of a lognormal random walk. Let θ denote the ratio of the value of the firm at time $t + \Delta t$ to its value at time t:

$$\theta = \frac{W(t+\Delta t)}{W(t)} \tag{1.17}$$

It follows that

$$\ln[\theta] = \ln[W(t+\Delta t)] - \ln[W(t)]$$

or from the specification of the change in the log of the value of the firm in equation (1.14),

$$\ln[\theta] = \mu \cdot \Delta t + \sigma \cdot \Delta t^{1/2} \cdot z \tag{1.18}$$

We specified in the text following equation (1.14) that z is a normally distributed random variable with a mean of zero and a variance of unity. Equation (1.18) implies that $\ln[\theta]$ is a normally distributed random variable with mean $\mu \cdot \Delta t$ and variance $\sigma^2 \cdot \Delta t$. It follows that the value ratio θ is a lognormal random variable[15] with the probability density function

$$f(\theta) = (2 \cdot \pi \cdot \sigma^2 \cdot \Delta t \cdot \theta^2)^{-1/2} \cdot \exp\left[\frac{-\frac{1}{2}(\ln[\theta] - \mu \cdot \Delta t)^2}{\sigma^2 \cdot \Delta t}\right] \tag{1.19}$$

Using the definition of θ in equation (1.17), we can express the value of the firm at time $t + \Delta t$ as a function of the value of the firm at time t:

$$W(t + \Delta t) = \theta \cdot W(t)$$

---

15. Lognormal random variables are described in Aitchson and Brown (1957).

This says that the value of the firm at time $t + \Delta t$ varies *proportionally* with the value of the firm at time t, where the factor of proportionality, θ, is a lognormal random variable. If the realized value of θ is 1.07, then $W(t + \Delta t)$ will be 7% larger than $W(t)$, regardless of the value of $W(t)$. If $W(t)$ was 100, then $W(t + \Delta t)$ will be 107. If the firm had grown more rapidly prior to time t so that $W(t)$ was 200, then $W(t + \Delta t)$ will be 214. In other words, the lognormal random walk model assumes that the economic forces operating between time t and time $t + \Delta t$ affect the value of the firm strictly in proportion to the value of the firm at time t.

The Expectation and Variance of θ

We observed at equation (1.19) that the value ratio θ is a lognormal random variable. It is of some interest to identify the mean and variance of θ.

From the probability density function in equation (1.19) it can be shown that the kth moment of θ about the origin is[16]

$$\text{Ex}[\theta^k] = \exp\left[k \cdot \mu \cdot \Delta t + \tfrac{1}{2}k^2 \cdot \sigma^2 \cdot \Delta t\right] \tag{1.20}$$

so the mean and variance of θ are[17]

$$\text{Ex}[\theta] = \exp\left[\mu \cdot \Delta t + \tfrac{1}{2}\sigma^2 \cdot \Delta t\right] \tag{1.21a}$$

$$\text{var}[\theta] = \exp[2 \cdot \mu \cdot \Delta t + \sigma^2 \cdot \Delta t] \cdot (\exp[\sigma^2 \cdot \Delta t] - 1) \tag{1.21b}$$

The mean and variance can be approximated (to first order in Δt) as

$$\text{Ex}[\theta] = 1 + \left(\mu + \tfrac{1}{2}\sigma^2\right) \cdot \Delta t \tag{1.22a}$$

$$\text{var}[\theta] = \sigma^2 \cdot \Delta t \tag{1.22b}$$

Equation (1.22a) implies that over a short interval of time, the expected value of the firm will grow at approximately the rate $\mu + \tfrac{1}{2}\sigma^2$ per annum. Equation (1.22b) implies that the standard deviation of the value ratio over an interval of time of length Δt is approximately proportional to the square root of Δt. The factor of proportionality is σ, the volatility of the log of the value of the firm.

An Example

It may be helpful to illustrate the foregoing ideas with a numerical example. Suppose that the parameters of the lognormal random walk are $\mu = 0.08$ and $\sigma = 0.20$. Using the approximation in equation (1.22a), the expected value of the firm will grow at an annualized rate of approxi-

16. Aitchison and Brown (1957, p. 8, eq. 2.6).

17. Equation (1.21a) is equation (1.20) for the case of $k = 1$. Equation (1.21b) follows because $\text{var}[\theta] = \text{Ex}[\{\theta - \text{Ex}[\theta]\}^2] = \text{Ex}[\theta^2] - \text{Ex}[\theta]^2$, where (from equation 1.20 for the case of $k = 2$) $\text{Ex}[\theta^2] = \exp[2 \cdot \mu \cdot \Delta t + 2 \cdot \sigma^2 \cdot \Delta t]$ and $\text{Ex}[\theta]$ is as given in equation (1.21a).

mately $\mu + \frac{1}{2}\sigma^2 = (0.08) + \frac{1}{2}(0.20)^2 = 0.10$, or 10% per annum. From equation (1.22b) the standard deviation of the value ratio over an interval of one year is approximately $\sigma = 0.20$. This implies that the standard deviation of the value of the firm after one year is approximately 20% of the value of the firm at the beginning of the year.

Now consider the probability distribution of θ after an interval of two years. From equation (1.18), the log of θ is normally distributed with mean $\mu \cdot \Delta t = (0.08) \cdot (2.0) = 0.16$, and variance $\sigma^2 \cdot \Delta t = (0.20)^2 \cdot (2.0) = 0.08$, implying a standard deviation for $\ln[\theta]$ of 0.2828 ($0.2828 = (0.08)^{1/2}$). The upper panel of figure 1.1 shows the probability density of $\ln[\theta]$. The lower panel shows the probability density of θ.

1.5 An Assumption on Corporate Governance

In some of the models described in this book, the managers of the firm will, from time to time, have occasion to choose among several alternative actions, such as calling or not calling debt for early redemption or paying interest on a PIK bond in cash or kind. We assume that *whenever a solvent firm has a choice of actions, its managers act in the best interest of shareholders and choose the action that maximizes the value of equity.*[18]

Mechanisms for Aligning Managerial Behavior with Shareholder Interests

There are several reasons for postulating an alignment of managerial behavior with shareholder interests.[19]

First, the income and wealth of senior corporate officers may be linked to the level of the company's stock price, giving those officers a personal financial incentive to maximize the value of equity. The linkage can take several forms:

1. The base salary and bonus compensation of the chief executive officer (CEO) and other senior officers may depend (implicitly or explicitly) on the price of the company's stock.[20]

18. Nimmer and Feinberg (1989) and Frost (1992) discuss the governance of *insolvent* firms. See also chapter 4 below.

19. Shleifer and Vishny (1997) survey the economics of corporate governance, focusing on the more general question of how suppliers of capital to the firm "assure themselves of getting a return on their investment."

20. Baker, Jensen, and Murphy (1988) present an overview of corporate compensation practices, and Tehranian and Waegelein (1985) describe the characteristics of bonus plans. Murphy (1985) reports that salary and bonus compensation of senior officers is positively correlated with stock prices, and Coughlan and Schmidt (1985) find that the rate of increase in CEO compensation is positively correlated with market-adjusted stock returns. Jensen and Murphy (1990a) provide estimates of the sensitivity of CEO compensation to change in the value of a firm's equity. Gilson and Vetsuypens (1993) report sharp reductions in compensation paid to senior managers when a firm encounters financial distress.

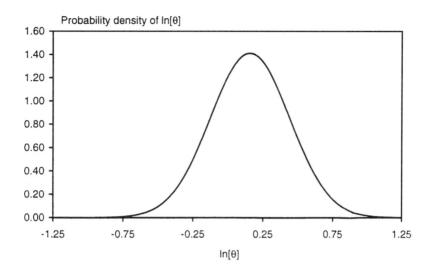

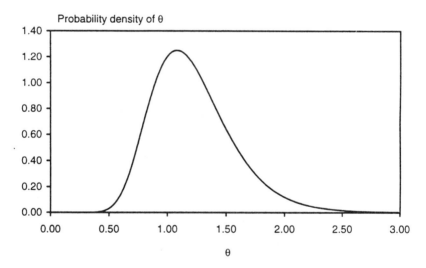

Figure 1.1
Probability density functions of $\ln[\theta]$ and θ when $\mu = 0.08$, $\sigma = 0.20$, and $\Delta t = 2.00$

2. The continued employment of the CEO and other senior officers may depend on the stock price.[21]

3. The CEO and other senior officers may own stock in the firm and may continue to hold incentivizing distributions of executive stock options received in the past.[22]

In addition a senior officer who is perceived to act in other than the best interest of shareholders could suffer a loss of reputation in the market for managerial services and a reduction in future earnings.[23]

The second reason for postulating an alignment of managerial behavior with shareholder interests is the right of shareholders to replace a board of directors that they believe is not acting in their best interests.[24] (Setting the compensation of senior corporate officers and deciding whether a senior officer should be replaced are among the most important duties of a board.[25] Boards also have general oversight and monitoring responsibilities and are empowered to approve or reject significant corporate actions proposed by senior officers.[26]) Stockholders may exercise this

21. Several studies find that the rate of departure of CEOs and other senior officers is inversely related to stock returns, including Coughlan and Schmidt (1985), Warner, Watts, and Wruck (1988) (effect apparent only at relatively extreme positive and negative returns), Weisbach (1988), and Jensen and Murphy (1990a). Gilson (1989, 1990) and Gilson and Vetsuypens (1993) find sharply higher departure rates at firms in financial distress.

22. Benston (1985) and Jensen and Murphy (1990a) emphasize the importance of managers' stock holdings for aligning managerial behavior with shareholder interests. Smith and Watts (1982), Brickley, Bhagat, and Lease (1985), and Clark (1986, pp. 200–19) describe several varieties of incentivizing compensation. Yermack (1995) examines the determinants of stock option awards to CEOs (see also Yermack 1997). Jensen and Meckling (1976, p. 353) and Smith and Watts (1982, pp. 147–48) observe that stock options offset the "debt-like" characteristics of a manager's wage contract. See also the papers in Carpenter and Yermack (1999).

23. Fama (1980) emphasizes the importance of the labor market for managerial services.

24. Clark (1986) discusses the duty of a director to act in the best interest of shareholders. A shareholder can file a shareholder's derivative suit against a director, seeking recovery of damages suffered by the corporation, if the shareholder believes the director violated his or her duties of care and loyalty and if the corporation declines to pursue the suit in its own name (Clark 1986, pp. 396–400 and ch. 15; Shleifer and Vishny 1997, p. 752).

25. Clark (1986, ch. 6) discusses the responsibility of a board to set the compensation of senior officers. Jensen and Murphy (1990a, b) suggest that shareholder value can be enhanced by strengthening the linkage between stock price performance and executive income and wealth. Baker, Jensen, and Murphy (1988) suggest that one reason why the link between CEO pay and performance is not stronger is because directors do not have sufficient incentive to fashion compensation contracts with stronger links. Fama (1980, p. 294) emphasizes the importance of the board's power to replace corporate officers.

26. Fama and Jensen (1983a) emphasize the importance of the ratification and monitoring, or "decision-control," functions of the board and distinguish those functions from the "decision-management" functions of senior officers: initiating and implementing corporate actions. Jensen (1993) suggests that internal corporate control systems, including especially boards of directors, failed to adequately promote efficient corporate decision-making in the 1970s and 1980s.

right themselves (as in a proxy contest), or (in response to a takeover bid) they may sell their stock to others who are seeking to exercise the right and assume control of the firm.[27]

The third and final reason for the alignment of managerial behavior with shareholder interests is the right (specified in the corporation's charter) of shareholders to vote directly on fundamental, or organic, corporate actions such as charter amendments, mergers, recapitalizations, and

27. Jensen and Ruback (1983, pp. 5–6) view the market for corporate control, including both proxy contests and takeover bids, "as a market in which alternative managerial teams compete for the right to manage corporate resources.... [This competition] limits divergence from shareholder wealth maximization by managers and provides the mechanism through which economies of scale or other synergies available from combining or reorganizing control and management of corporate resources are realized."

Proxy contests have been examined by Dodd and Warner (1983) (effect of proxy contests on stock prices), Pound (1988) (determinants of the probability of successfully challenging incumbent management in a proxy contest for control), and DeAngelo and DeAngelo (1989) (proxy contests are frequently followed by sale or liquidation of the company or replacement of a senior manager, and are an important device for disciplining management). Easterbrook and Fischel (1983) analyze the economic basis for stockholder voting rights, and Pound (1991) describes the evolution of the proxy process since the mid-1800s. Henriques (2000) describes corporate governance and proxy contests in the late 1940s and 1950s.

The conceptual foundations of takeover bids have been examined by Grossman and Hart (1980) (pointing out the free-rider problem that when the postacquisition value of a firm's shares is common knowledge, shareholders may decline to sell to a bidder offering less, and observing that the prospect of dilution of minority shareholders can facilitate value-enhancing takeovers), Shleifer and Vishny (1986) (extending the analysis to cases of asymmetric information and identifying takeover bids from large, albeit minority, shareholders as an alternative device to facilitate value-enhancing takeovers), Stulz (1988) (examining the effect of managerial stock ownership on the likelihood and premium price of a takeover bid), and Hirshleifer and Titman (1990) (analyzing bidder behavior when the response of small shareholders to a takeover bid is not perfectly predictable). The reaction of the equity value of target and bidder firms to takeover bids has been examined by Dodd and Ruback (1977), Kummer and Hoffmeister (1978), Bradley (1980), Bradley, Desai, and Kim (1983, 1988), and Mitchell and Lehn (1990). See also the literature reviews by Jensen and Ruback (1983) and Jarrell, Brickley, and Netter (1988). Ruback (1983a) examines whether the market for takeover transactions is competitive. Clinical articles by Ruback (1982, 1983b) and Lys and Vincent (1995) illustrate the complexity of takeover contests.

The relationship between voting rights and takeover bids is well illustrated by a series of studies of firms capitalized with two classes of common stock with differential voting rights, including Stevens (1938) (types of differential voting rights), Lease, McConnell, and Mikkelson (1983, 1984), and Levy (1983) (when the two classes have identical cash flow rights, stock with superior voting rights has, on average, a higher market price than stock with inferior voting rights), DeAngelo and DeAngelo (1985) (disproportionate managerial ownership of voting rights compared to cash flow rights), Partch (1987) and Jarrell and Poulsen (1988) (stock price impact of management proposals to create a second class of equity with inferior voting rights), Ruback (1988) (coercive nature of offer to exchange a new class of common stock with inferior voting rights and greater cash flow rights for existing stock), Gordon (1988) (distinguishing between dual class stock issued in an initial public offering versus a recapitalization), Grossman and Hart (1988) and Harris and Raviv (1988) (when differential voting rights may enhance the aggregate value of equity), and Megginson (1990), Bergstrom and Rydqvist (1992), Smith and Amoako-Adu (1995), and Zingales (1995) (incidence and magnitude of differentiated takeover bids for issuers of dual class stock and anticipatory pricing of dual class shares in secondary market trading before a takeover).

liquidations.[28] This right provides shareholders the opportunity to veto a fundamental action even when it is advocated by senior officers and approved by the board of directors, and thus reduces the likelihood that senior managers will initiate a fundamental action likely to impair shareholder value.

A Caveat

The assumption that managers always act to maximize the value of equity simplifies many of the analyses in this book, but it is not entirely accurate. Over the past two decades researchers have documented a variety of discretionary managerial acts that appear to be undertaken to advance the personal interests of managers and that, on average, impair the value of equity.[29] Prominent examples include retention of free cash flow and adoption of deterrents and defenses to hostile takeovers.[30] Additionally

28. Empirical studies of charter amendments have focused on takeover defenses such as supermajority provisions, elimination of cumulative voting for corporate directors, and staggered election of directors (DeAngelo and Rice 1983; Linn and McConnell 1983; Bhagat and Brickley 1984; Jarrell and Poulsen 1987; Pound 1987, 1989; Brickley, Lease, and Smith 1988; Bhagat and Jefferis 1991; Van Nuys 1993). The reaction of the equity value of target and bidder firms to merger proposals has been examined by Dodd (1980), Asquith (1983), and Asquith, Bruner, and Mullins (1983). Empirical studies of recapitalizations have examined proposals for dual class common stock recapitalizations (Partch 1987; Jarrell and Poulsen 1988). Voluntary liquidation has been examined by Titman (1984), Hite, Owers, and Rogers (1987), Kim and Schatzberg (1987), Ghosh, Owers, and Rogers (1991), Fleming and Moon (1995), and Mehran, Nogler, and Schwartz (1998). Other studies of actions requiring shareholder approval include Dodd and Leftwich (1980) (change in state of incorporation), Bhagat (1983) (elimination of preemptive stock purchase rights), and Brickley, Bhagat, and Lease (1985) (adoption of long-term management incentive plans). Examples of shareholder voting on fundamental corporate actions appear below in chapter 17 (recapitalization of Colt Industries) and chapter 18 (spin-off of Marriott International).

29. Jensen and Meckling (1976), drawing on the observation of Berle and Means (1932) that ownership (or risk-bearing) and control (or decision-making) are separate functions in the modern corporation, emphasize the divergence of the interests of managers and the interests of shareholders. See also Manne (1965), Williamson (1975), Fama and Jensen (1983a, b), Jensen and Smith (1985, pp. 98–111), Grundfest (1990), Roe (1990, 1993, 1994), Monks and Minow (1995), and Shleifer and Vishny (1997).

30. Jensen (1986, p. 323) defines the free cash flow of a firm as "cash flow in excess of that required to fund all projects that have positive net present values when discounted at the relevant cost of capital." Studies identifying uneconomic retention of free cash flow include McConnell and Muscarella (1985, pp. 418–19) (exploration and development of oil and gas fields during the period from 1975 to 1981, cited in Jensen 1986, pp. 326–28), Mitchell and Lehn (1990) (acquisitions by firms that subsequently became takeover targets), and Denis and Denis (1993) (capital investments by firms that were subsequently forced to undertake large defensive leveraged recapitalizations). See also the studies cited by Shleifer and Vishny (1997, pp. 746–47) of corporate acquisitions intended to enlarge and diversify the acquiring company. Uneconomic retention of free cash flow is discussed further in chapter 17 below.

Deterrents and defenses to hostile takeovers have been studied by Bradley and Wakeman (1983) (targeted share repurchases to terminate control contests), Dann and DeAngelo (1983) (targeted share repurchases and standstill agreements), Dann and DeAngelo (1988) (defensive changes in asset, capital, and ownership structures in response to takeover threats), Malatesta and Walking (1988), Ryngaert (1988), and Comment and Schwert (1995) (adoption of poison pill securities), and Kamma, Weintrop, and Weir (1988) (discriminatory

there is some evidence that the value of the firm depends on the owner-ship structure of the firm in ways consistent with the proposition that managers sometimes act to advance their own interests at the expense of shareholders.[31] The assumption that existing managerial incentives and con-trols serve to align the behavior of senior managers with shareholder inter-ests is an imperfect abstraction of a complex decision-making environment.

1.6   Assumptions on Taxes and Transactions Costs

For analytical and expositional simplicity, we ignore taxes and transac-tions costs, including liquidity costs, in our formal assessments, although

self-tender offers). None of these actions required shareholder approval. (Empirical studies of deterrent and defensive actions requiring shareholder approval are cited in note 28 above.) Walking and Long (1984) found that the probability of managerial resistance to a takeover bid is inversely related to the magnitude of the change in the managers' wealth conditional on the bid succeeding. Lambert and Larcker (1985) note that managerial resistance may be reduced with the adoption of "golden parachutes," or contingent compensation contracts providing for payments to senior managers following a change in control of the firm.

31. Jensen and Meckling (1976, p. 305, n. 1, and p. 343) show that when management has uncontestable control of a firm, the value of the firm increases with management's ownership share because of the increasing alignment of management and shareholder interests. Stulz (1988) shows that when this alignment is ignored and control is contestable, greater mana-gerial ownership can "entrench" an inefficient management and reduce the value of the firm. Morck, Shleifer, and Vishny (1988) suggest that the nature of the variation in the value of the firm with management's ownership share is an empirical issue. They report that ceteris par-ibus, the value of the firm typically increases with the equity ownership of senior management up to a 5% share, then decreases with management's share up to a 25% share, and then rises again as management's share increases beyond 25%. Wruck (1989) reports corroborating results derived from the effect of private sales of new equity on the aggregate value of equity. Using a different empirical specification, McConnell and Servaes (1990) find that the value of the firm is a concave function of management's equity ownership share. See also Bagani, Milonis, Saunders, and Travlos (1994) (operating risk and leverage is a concave function of management's equity ownership share when that share exceeds 5%, supporting hypothesis of conflict of interest between managers and nonmanagerial shareholders not completely miti-gated by structure of managerial compensation and market for corporate control).

Several authors have pointed out that the value of the firm may further depend on whether some significant fraction of equity ownership is concentrated in one or more large blocks, with the balance dispersed among numerous "smallholders." Shleifer and Vishny (1986) suggest that a blockholder can overcome free rider problems in monitoring management and facilitating value enhancing change, and Denis and Serrano (1996) report that the addition of unaffiliated blockholders during an unsuccessful attempt to acquire control of a company is associated with elevated rates of CEO turnover and asset restructuring. Barclay and Holderness (1989, 1991, 1992) observe that transactions in large blocks of stock are asso-ciated with unusual increases in stock prices and elevated rates of turnover of senior man-agement (and should therefore be considered change of control events similar to successful takeover bids and proxy contests) and that block transactions commonly occur at prices in excess of subsequent round-lot prices (indicating the existence of private benefits of control). See also Demsetz and Lehn (1985) (concentration of equity ownership is inversely related to firm size and directly related to the volatility of the operating environment), Holderness and Sheehan (1985) (consequences of block purchases by several well-known participants in the market for corporate control), and Mikkelson and Ruback (1985) (effect of block purchases on stock prices and events subsequent to purchase). Meeker and Joy (1980) and Holderness and Sheehan (1988) examine transactions in blocks of more than 50% of an issuer's stock.

we will point out where they can be expected to play an important role in more extensive analyses of corporate securities pricing.[32]

32. Long (1974) points out the significance of ignoring taxes and transactions costs. Taxes are typically incorporated into contingent value models used to address issues in corporate capital structure. See the articles cited in note 3 to this chapter.

Analysts have begun to pay close attention to the value of liquidity in the wake of a series of papers establishing a connection between liquidity and asset pricing. See, generally, Amihud and Mendelson (1991b). Amihud and Mendelson (1986) show that the return on common stock listed on the New York Stock Exchange is, inter alia, a convex function of the bid-ask spread on the stock. Silber (1991) observes that companies issue unregistered stock (that cannot be resold in open market transactions for two years and that is relatively illiquid during that interval) at an average discount of more than 30% relative to the price of registered, but otherwise identical, stock. See also Wruck (1989, pp. 16–18). Amihud, Mendelson, and Lauterbach (1997) show how liquidity (and securities prices) can be enhanced by improving the microstructure of a market. Amihud and Mendelson (1996) suggest that an issuer should have a property right to determine the market or markets in which its securities are traded, as a way to incentivize the innovation of liquidity-enhancing micro-structures. The effect of liquidity on the price of a security is also discussed in Zwick (1980), Sarig and Warga (1989), Amihud and Mendelson (1991a), Boudoukh and Whitelaw (1991, 1993), Warga (1992), Kamara (1994), Garbade (1996, ch. 7), Elton and Green (1998), Amihud, Garbade, and Kahan (1999, 2000), Bennett, Garbade, and Kambhu (2000), and Brenner, Eldor, and Hauser (2001).

I BASIC CONCEPTS

2   The Contingent Value of Debt and Equity

This chapter examines the contingent value of the securities issued by a firm capitalized with common stock and a single issue of zero-coupon debt.[1] The objective is to introduce, in a simple setting, the essential features of contingent value analysis. We begin by describing the institutional framework of the valuation problem, including our assumptions regarding the capital structure of the firm and the consequences of default and bankruptcy.

2.1   Capital Structure of the Firm

We assume the firm is capitalized with two classes of securities: a single issue of zero coupon debt and common stock. The debt matures at time T and promises to pay its face amount F at that time. (Example 2.1 describes the first zero-coupon corporate debt security.) The common stock cannot pay a dividend and cannot be repurchased by the firm until after the debt has been redeemed.[2]

We denote the aggregate value of the debt at time t as $V_1(t)$ and the aggregate value of equity as $V_2(t)$. (Throughout this book we denote a more senior security with a lower index number. Since debt is senior to equity, debt is indexed as the first security and equity is indexed as the second security in the present chapter.) The value of the firm is the sum of the contemporaneous values of the firm's securities:

$$W(t) = V_1(t) + V_2(t) \tag{2.1}$$

2.2   Default and Bankruptcy

At time T creditors have a claim on the firm for payment of the face amount of the debt. If the firm does not satisfy this contractual obligation, meaning that if it defaults on it's promise to pay, it goes into bankruptcy.

We assume that bankruptcy can take either of two forms. First, it can result in an instantaneous and costless *liquidation* of the assets of the firm (piecemeal, in bulk, or as a going concern) and distribution of the

1. Merton (1974) provided the first extensive analysis of this problem. Long (1974), Lee (1981), and Pitts and Selby (1983) comment on Merton's analysis. See also Merton (1977).

2. This assumption presumes a covenant in the bond indenture or loan agreement for the zero coupon debt intended to protect creditors by preventing a diversion of corporate wealth to stockholders. See Black and Scholes (1973, p. 651) and Black (1976, p. 7). Covenants prohibiting dividend payments and stock repurchases are not unknown, but they are far stronger than the usual dividend covenant, which is described in section 15.2.

Example 2.1   The First Zero-Coupon Corporate Note

In the spring of 1981, J.C. Penny Company, Inc., an apparel, home and automotive products retailer, issued the first zero-coupon corporate debt security. The noncallable note matured on May 1, 1989, and had a maturity value of \$200 million. It was offered to investors at an aggregate price of \$66,494,000 for delivery and settlement on May 1, 1981.

The offering yield, computed using the convention of semiannual compounding, is the value of R_m that satisfies the equation

$$66.494 = \frac{200.0}{(1 + \frac{1}{2}R_m)^{16}}$$

so that $R_m = 0.1425$, or or 14.25% per annum, compounded semiannually. Computed using the convention of continuous compounding, the offering yield is the value of R_m that satisfies the equation

$$66.494 = 200.0 \cdot e^{-R_m \cdot 8.0}$$

so that $R_m = 0.1377$, or 13.77% per annum, compounded continuously.

The J.C. Penny note is described in Jansson (1981). See also the related discussions in Silver (1981–82), Kalotay (1984), Miller (1986), and Varma and Chambers (1990).

---

proceeds according to the absolute priority rule.[3] Creditors receive all of the proceeds of the liquidation up to the amount of their claims. Stockholders, as residual claimants, receive the balance (if any) of the proceeds.

Alternatively (and for our purposes, equivalently), bankruptcy can result in an instantaneous and costless *recapitalization* of the firm. This involves canceling the old securities of the firm and distributing new securities of the recapitalized enterprise to the old claimants pursuant to the absolute priority rule.

The Contingent Value of the Debt and Equity at Time T

In view of our assumptions regarding default and bankruptcy, we can specify how the value of the firm will be apportioned between creditors and stockholders when the debt matures at time T.

If $W(T)$ exceeds F, the firm can redeem its debt as promised. Redemption can follow either of two channels. First, the firm can liquidate voluntarily and (ignoring transactions costs) generate cash proceeds of $W(T)$. Creditors would then receive the promised amount F and stockholders would receive the balance of the proceeds, or $W(T) - F$. Alternatively, the firm can finance redemption of the maturing debt by selling new securities worth F. Creditors would receive what they were promised, and

---

3. As noted in section 1.2, the absolute priority rule provides that senior claimants must be paid in full before junior claimants get anything.

the original equity would be worth the difference between the value of the firm and the value of the new securities, or $W(T) - F$.

If the value of the firm is less than F at time T, the firm will be unable to redeem its debt as promised. Liquidation would generate proceeds of $W(T)$—which is less than F by hypothesis—and the firm clearly cannot sell securities worth F if it has a value less than F. In this case the firm must default and file for bankruptcy. At the moment of default and bankruptcy,

1. the debt is worth the value of the firm (because, pursuant to the absolute priority rule, creditors will receive *all* of the proceeds of a bankruptcy liquidation or *all* of the securities issued in a recapitalization), and therefore

2. the stock is worthless.

The foregoing observations can be summarized in a table showing the value of the debt and equity at time T contingent on the contemporaneous value of the firm:

	$W(T) < F$	$F \le W(T)$
$V_1(T)$	$W(T)$	F
$V_2(T)$	0	$W(T) - F$

Figure 2.1 shows a graphical representation of the contingent value of the debt and equity at time T.[4]

The contingent value of the debt and equity at time T can also be represented algebraically as

$$V_1(T) = \begin{cases} W(T) & \text{if } W(T) < F \\ F & \text{if } F \le W(T) \end{cases} \tag{2.2a}$$

$$V_2(T) = \begin{cases} 0 & \text{if } W(T) < F \\ W(T) - F & \text{if } F \le W(T) \end{cases} \tag{2.2b}$$

or as

$$V_1(T) = \min[W(T), F] \tag{2.3a}$$

$$V_2(T) = \max[0, W(T) - F] \tag{2.3b}$$

---

4. Should the firm choose to default on repayment of its indebtedness at time T even though $W(T)$ is greater than F, our assumption of a bankruptcy process that is instantaneous and costless and that results in distributions in accord with the absolute priority rule means that creditors will nevertheless receive cash or securities worth F and that stockholders will nevertheless receive cash or securities worth $W(T) - F$. Thus neither creditors nor stockholders can either gain or lose from what is sometimes called "strategic default," or default in the absence of an actual inability to make a required payment.

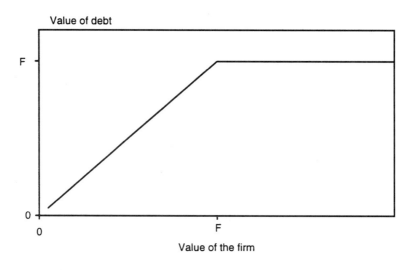

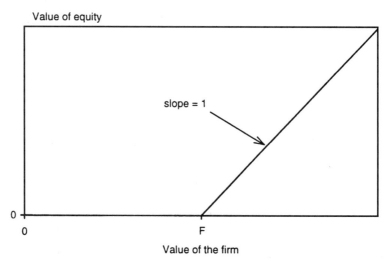

Figure 2.1
Contingent value of debt and equity at time T

Equity as a Call Option on the Firm

The form of the contingent value function in the lower panel of figure 2.1 suggests that equity can be viewed as a call option on the firm, where the option has a strike price of F and expires at time T.

The simplest way to appreciate the analogy between the corporation's stock and a call option on the firm is to suppose that at time T the shareholders consider subscribing an amount F for new shares of stock and that, if they buy the new stock, the firm uses the proceeds to redeem the maturing debt. Following redemption, the creditors have no remaining interest in the enterprise, and the stockholders have full and complete control of the firm. Stockholders may choose to exercise this call option, or choose to purchase new stock and cause the firm to redeem its debt, if the value of the firm, $W(T)$, exceeds the option strike price, F. They will certainly decline to exercise the option if $W(T)$ is less than F.

The foregoing mechanism for debt redemption does not require that stockholders own and run an unlevered enterprise following redemption. The stockholders could also

1. liquidate the firm voluntarily, receiving gross proceeds of $W(T)$ or (subtracting what they paid for the new stock issued to redeem the debt) net proceeds of $W(T) - F$, or

2. cause the firm to issue new debt or equity securities with a value of F, with the stipulation that the firm will immediately pay out the proceeds to the existing shareholders in the form of a cash dividend.[5]

Regardless of how the firm chooses to fund the redemption of the debt at time T, the choice can be deconstructed into a two-step process where the first step is the exercise of a call option on the firm by the existing shareholders. The call option and alternative 1 above is functionally equivalent to the firm liquidating an instant before time T and paying (from the proceeds of the liquidation) F to creditors and $W(T) - F$ to stockholders. The stockholders' call option and alternative 2 is functionally equivalent to financing the debt redemption with a sale of new securities an instant before time T. Thus whether the company redeems its debt is essentially a matter of whether its shareholders would rationally exercise a call option on the firm with strike price F and expiration date T.

---

5. Such a dividend would not violate the covenant (prohibiting dividend payments) in the indenture for the original debt (see note 2 above) because that debt has been retired and its covenants no longer bind the actions of the firm.

Who Wrote the Stockholders' Call Option?

Accepting the argument that stockholders have a call option on the firm, we might also inquire about the identity of the writer of the option.

Creditors will receive the full value of the firm (up to the amount F) if the stockholders fail to exercise their option to redeem the debt. On the other hand, the creditors must relinquish their interest in the firm (in exchange for the payment of F) if the stockholders choose to exercise their option. It follows that the creditors are in the economic position of being long the firm and short the call option held by the stockholders.

2.3   The Valuation Problem

We can now state the problem of primary interest in this chapter.

We assume that there exists a pair of contingent value functions, f_1 and f_2, with two arguments: time (t) and the value of the firm (W), such that the value of the ith security at time $t \leq T$ can be calculated as

$$V_i(t) = f_i(W(t), t), \qquad i = 1, 2 \tag{2.4}$$

The primary problem is identifying the forms of the contingent value functions, or identifying how the value of each class of the firm's securities depends on time and the value of the firm.

We have already solved this problem in the special case of $t = T$. From equations (2.3a, b) we have

$$f_1(W, T) = \min[W, F] \tag{2.5a}$$

$$f_2(W, T) = \max[0, W - F] \tag{2.5b}$$

We now want to extend these "terminal" contingent value functions backward in time, to times prior to the maturity of the debt.

2.4   Solving the Valuation Problem

The valuation problem asks for the form of the contingent value function f_i. We already know the form of f_i at time T (see equations 2.5a, b). In this section we describe an algorithm for computing the value of $f_i(W^*, t^*)$ for *any* positive value of W^* and for *any* value of t^* less than T. This is tantamount to completing the identification of the form of f_i.

The key to the valuation algorithm is approximating the continuous time–continuous state process describing the dynamic evolution of the value of the firm (see equation 1.14) with a simpler model. The first step is to recast time as a discrete variable.

Consider the interval between time t* and time T:

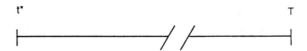

Divide the interval into K subintervals of length Δt = (T − t*)/K and define
t_k = t* + (k − 1) Δt for k = 1, 2, ..., K + 1:

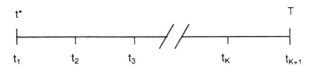

Figure 2.2
Dividing the interval between time t^* and time T into K subintervals

The Discretization of Time

We can make time a discrete variable within the interval between time t^* and time T by dividing the interval into K subintervals of equal length, where K is a positive integer.[6] Since the subintervals are of equal length, the length of each subinterval is Δt, where

$$\Delta t = \frac{T - t^*}{K} \tag{2.6}$$

Defining a sequence of $K + 1$ discrete points in time, we have

$$t_k = t^* + (k - 1) \cdot \Delta t, \qquad k = 1, 2, \ldots, K + 1 \tag{2.7}$$

Observe (see figure 2.2) that the first subinterval runs from t_1 to t_2, the second subinterval runs from t_2 to t_3, and so on, to the last subinterval running from t_K to t_{K+1}. Observe also that $t_1 = t^*$ and that $t_{K+1} = T$.

For the purpose of constructing a valuation algorithm, we assume that time evolves from time t^* to time T as a discrete (rather than continuous) variable and that, as illustrated in figure 2.3, it does not assume any value between t^* and T other than the values in the sequence $t_1, t_2, \ldots, t_{K+1}$.

6. The value of K must be large enough to satisfy the conditions described in appendix A. A larger value of K is "better" for the reason noted in the text at note 8 below.

If time is a continuous variable then, as t increases from t* to T, it takes on *every* value in the interval between t* and T:

However, if time is a discrete variable then, as t increases from t* to T, it takes on *only* the values in the sequence t_1, t_2, ..., t_{K+1}:

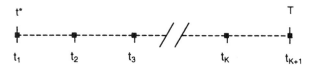

Figure 2.3
The distinction between time as a continuous variable and time as a discrete variable

A Discrete Time–Discrete State Approximation to the Evolution of the Value of the Firm

We specified at equation (1.14) that the natural logarithm of the value of the firm evolves through time as a Gaussian random walk. Given our discretization of time, this means that the log of the value of the firm at time t_{k+1} is related to the log of the value of the firm at time t_k as

$$\ln[W(t_{k+1})] = \ln[W(t_k)] + \mu \cdot \Delta t + \sigma \cdot \Delta t^{1/2} \cdot z_k, \qquad k = 1, 2, \ldots, K \tag{2.8}$$

where z_k is a normally distributed random variable with mean zero and a variance of unity and is statistically independent of z_j if $k \neq j$.

We now replace this continuous state model of the evolution (in discrete time) of the log of the value of the firm with a simpler discrete state model:

$$\ln[W(t_{k+1})] = \ln[W(t_k)] + \mu \cdot \Delta t + \sigma \cdot \Delta t^{1/2} \cdot e_k, \qquad k = 1, 2, \ldots, K \tag{2.9}$$

where e_k is a "binomial," or "two-state," random variable

$$e_k = \begin{cases} +1 & \text{with probability } \frac{1}{2} \\ -1 & \text{with probability } \frac{1}{2} \end{cases} \tag{2.10}$$

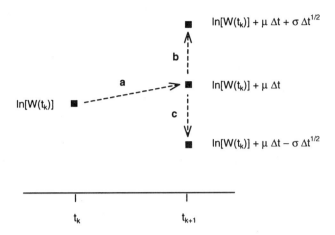

Path **a** shows a deterministic change of $\mu \, \Delta t$. Path **b** shows a jump of $+\, \sigma \, \Delta t^{1/2}$. Path **c** shows a jump of $-\, \sigma \, \Delta t^{1/2}$. There is a 50% probability of the jump along path **b** and a 50% probability of the jump along path **c**.

Figure 2.4
Change in the log of the value of the firm over the interval from time t_k to time t_{k+1}, as calculated in equation (2.11)

with e_k statistically independent of e_j if $k \neq j$. The mean and variance of e_k are zero and unity respectively, so e_k has the same mean and variance as z_k. The difference between e_k and z_k is that e_k cannot have any value other than -1 and $+1$, while z_k can take on any value between $-\infty$ and $+\infty$. The model of equation (2.9) is commonly called a "binomial random walk."[7]

We can combine equations (2.9) and (2.10) to express $\ln[W(t_{k+1})]$ as

$$\ln[W(t_{k+1})] = \ln[W(t_k)] + \mu \cdot \Delta t + \begin{cases} +\sigma \cdot \Delta t^{1/2} & \text{with probability } \frac{1}{2} \\ -\sigma \cdot \Delta t^{1/2} & \text{with probability } \frac{1}{2} \end{cases}$$

$$(2.11)$$

As shown in figure 2.4, the change in the log of the value of the firm over the interval from time t_k to time t_{k+1} can be interpreted as the sum of (1) a deterministic (or nonrandom) change of $\mu \cdot \Delta t$ and (2) a random jump of either $+\sigma \cdot \Delta t^{1/2}$ (with probability $\frac{1}{2}$) or $-\sigma \cdot \Delta t^{1/2}$ (with probability $\frac{1}{2}$).

7. Binomial random walks were introduced into the contingent claims literature by Sharpe (1978, pp. 366–71) and Cox, Ross, and Rubinstein (1979). See also Cox and Rubinstein (1985).

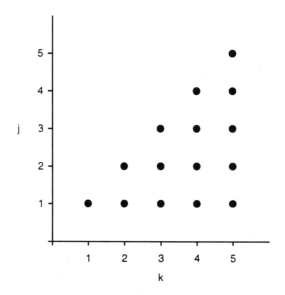

Figure 2.5
Elements of the $W_{j,k}$ array when $K = 4$

Convergence of the Binomial Random Walk to the Gaussian Random Walk as Δt Goes to Zero

It follows from the central limit theorem that the binomial random walk in equation (2.9) converges to the Gaussian random walk in equation (1.14) as Δt goes to zero.[8] The approximation of the continuous time Gaussian model with the discrete time binomial model may be made arbitrarily close by choosing a sufficiently small value for Δt, or by choosing a sufficiently large value for K in equation (2.6).

Some Notation

It will be helpful to introduce at this point a convenient way to represent the binomial evolution of the value of the firm.

Consider an array of values of the firm: $W_{j,k}$ for $j = 1, 2, \ldots, k$ and $k = 1, 2, \ldots, K+1$. (Figure 2.5 shows such an array for $K = 4$.) We define the natural logarithm of $W_{j,k}$ as

$$\ln[W_{j,k}] = \ln[W^*] + (k-1) \cdot \mu \cdot \Delta t + (2 \cdot j - k - 1) \cdot \sigma \cdot \Delta t^{1/2},$$

$$j = 1, 2, \ldots, k; \ k = 1, 2, \ldots, K+1 \quad (2.12)$$

8. Cox and Rubinstein (1985, pp. 196–204), using $q = \frac{1}{2}$, $\ln[u] = \mu \cdot \Delta t + \sigma \cdot \Delta t^{1/2}$, and $\ln[d] = \mu \cdot \Delta t - \sigma \cdot \Delta t^{1/2}$ in place of the choices at the top of their p. 200.

Three characteristics of the $W_{j,k}$ array are notable:

$$\ln[W_{1,1}] = \ln[W^*] \tag{2.13a}$$

$$\ln[W_{j+1,k+1}] = \ln[W_{j,k}] + \mu \cdot \Delta t + \sigma \cdot \Delta t^{1/2} \tag{2.13b}$$

$$\ln[W_{j,k+1}] = \ln[W_{j,k}] + \mu \cdot \Delta t - \sigma \cdot \Delta t^{1/2} \tag{2.13c}$$

Equation (2.13a) follows directly from equation (2.12) in the special case where $j = k = 1$. Equation (2.13b) follows because, from equation (2.12),

$$\ln[W_{j,k}] = \ln[W^*] + (k-1) \cdot \mu \cdot \Delta t + (2 \cdot j - k - 1) \cdot \sigma \cdot \Delta t^{1/2}$$

and

$$\ln[W_{j+1,k+1}] = \ln[W^*] + ((k+1) - 1) \cdot \mu \cdot \Delta t$$
$$+ (2 \cdot (j+1) - (k+1) - 1) \cdot \sigma \cdot \Delta t^{1/2}$$
$$= \ln[W^*] + k \cdot \mu \cdot \Delta t + (2 \cdot j - k) \cdot \sigma \cdot \Delta t^{1/2}$$

Therefore

$$\ln[W_{j+1,k+1}] - \ln[W_{j,k}] = \mu \cdot \Delta t + \sigma \cdot \Delta t^{1/2}$$

Equation (2.13c) follows similarly.

Taken together, equations (2.13a, b, c) imply that specifying that

the log of the value of the firm evolves over the interval from time t^* to time T as a binomial random walk, beginning at $\ln[W^*]$ at time t^*, with a change of either $\mu \cdot \Delta t + \sigma \cdot \Delta t^{1/2}$ (with probability $\frac{1}{2}$) or $\mu \cdot \Delta t - \sigma \cdot \Delta t^{1/2}$ (with probability $\frac{1}{2}$) over each subinterval of time of length $\Delta t = (T - t^*)/K$,

is equivalent to specifying that

the value of the firm evolves through the $W_{j,k}$ array over the interval from time t_1 to time t_{K+1}, beginning at $W_{1,1}$ at time t_1, such that if the value of the firm is $W_{j,k}$ at time t_k, then the value of the firm at time t_{k+1} will be either $W_{j+1,k+1}$ (with probability $\frac{1}{2}$) or $W_{j,k+1}$ (with probability $\frac{1}{2}$).

A binomial evolution of the value of the firm is illustrated in figure 2.6 for the case of $K = 4$.

Interpreting the Elements of the $W_{j,k}$ Array

The $W_{j,k}$ array lies at the heart of our algorithm for assessing the value of $f_i(W^*, t^*)$, and it is worth spending some time developing an intuitive appreciation for the structure of the array.

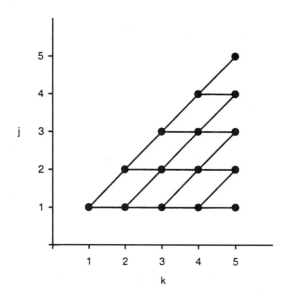

Figure 2.6
Evolutionary paths through the $W_{j,k}$ array when $K = 4$

We claim that the element $W_{j,k}$ can be interpreted as the value of the firm at time t_k following $j - 1$ random jumps of $+\sigma \cdot \Delta t^{1/2}$ in the log of the value of the firm and $k - j$ random jumps of $-\sigma \cdot \Delta t^{1/2}$. To see this, observe (from equation 2.7) that since $t_k = t^* + (k - 1) \cdot \Delta t$, time t_k is $k - 1$ subintervals of time (each of length Δt) after time t^*. At time t_k the log of the value of the firm must have experienced a cumulative deterministic change of $(k - 1) \cdot \mu \cdot \Delta t$, as well as a total of $k - 1$ random jumps of magnitude $\sigma \cdot \Delta t^{1/2}$ (see figure 2.4). If $j - 1$ of the jumps had a value of $+\sigma \cdot \Delta t^{1/2}$ and $k - j$ of the jumps had a value of $-\sigma \cdot \Delta t^{1/2}$, then the arithmetic sum of the jumps is $(j - 1) \cdot (+\sigma \cdot \Delta t^{1/2}) + (k - j) \cdot (-\sigma \cdot \Delta t^{1/2}) = (2 \cdot j - k - 1) \cdot \sigma \cdot \Delta t^{1/2}$. This gives an aggregate net change in the log of the value of the firm over the interval from time t^* to time t_k of $(k - 1) \cdot \mu \cdot \Delta t + (2 \cdot j - k - 1) \cdot \sigma \cdot \Delta t^{1/2}$. Since the log of the value of the firm at time t^* was $\ln[W^*]$, it follows that the log of the value of the firm at time t_k is $\ln[W^*] + (k - 1) \cdot \mu \cdot \Delta t + (2 \cdot j - k - 1) \cdot \sigma \cdot \Delta t^{1/2}$. This is exactly the value of $\ln[W_{j,k}]$ that appears in equation (2.12).

The foregoing interpretation of $W_{j,k}$ illustrates what the j and k subscripts are indexing:

· The subscript k indexes time: larger values of k are associated with later points in time.

· For a given value of k, j is an index of firm value such that larger values of j are associated with higher values of the firm. If $j = 1$, all of the preceding random jumps in the log of the value of the firm had the value $-\sigma \cdot \Delta t^{1/2}$ and the value of the firm is the lowest attainable at time t_k. If $j = k$, all of the jumps have the value $+\sigma \cdot \Delta t^{1/2}$ and the firm has the highest value attainable at time t_k.

An Example

It may be helpful to examine a numerical example of the construction and interpretation of the $W_{j,k}$ array. Suppose that the value of the firm is $W^* = 100.0$ at time $t^* = 1997.0$, meaning at the beginning of 1997, and that the zero-coupon debt issued by the firm matures in one year, at time $T = 1998.0$. Let $\mu = 0.08$, or 8% per annum, and $\sigma = 0.20$, or a volatility of 20% over one year. We will examine the construction of the $W_{j,k}$ array for the case where $K = 4$, so the interval between t^* and T is divided into four subintervals of length $\Delta t = 0.25$ years.

From the definition of the discrete time sequence $t_1, t_2, \ldots, t_{K+1}$ in equation (2.7), we have

$$t_1 = 1997.00 \tag{2.14a}$$

$$t_2 = 1997.25 \tag{2.14b}$$

$$t_3 = 1997.50 \tag{2.14c}$$

$$t_4 = 1997.75 \tag{2.14d}$$

$$t_5 = 1998.00 \tag{2.14e}$$

The $W_{j,k}$ array describes every value of the firm that can be realized at each of these five discrete points in time, assuming that the log of the value of the firm evolves according to the binomial random walk specified in equation (2.9).

The first element of the $W_{j,k}$ array, $W_{1,1}$, is the value of the firm at time $t_1 = 1997.0$. From equation (2.12) we have $W_{1,1} = W^*$. It follows that $W_{1,1} = 100.0$.

At time $t_2 = 1997.25$ the value of the firm can be either of two values: $W_{2,2}$ or $W_{1,2}$. Setting $j = 2$ and $k = 2$ in equation (2.12), we can compute

$$\ln[W_{2,2}] = \ln[W^*] + (k-1) \cdot \mu \cdot \Delta t + (2 \cdot j - k - 1) \cdot \sigma \cdot \Delta t^{1/2}$$

$$= \ln[100.0] + (1) \cdot (0.08) \cdot (0.25) + (1) \cdot (0.20) \cdot (0.25)^{1/2}$$

$$= 4.7252 \tag{2.15}$$

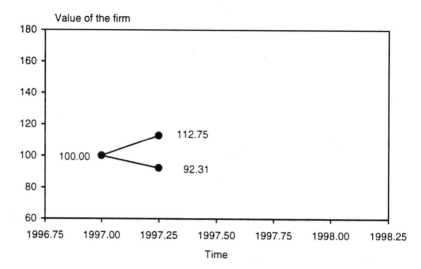

Figure 2.7
Evolution of the value of the firm from time $t_1 = 1997.00$ to time $t_2 = 1997.25$

so $W_{2,2} = 112.75$. $W_{2,2}$ is the value of the firm at time t_2 following a deterministic change of $\mu \cdot \Delta t = 0.02$ and a single random jump of $+\sigma \cdot \Delta t^{1/2} = 0.1$ in the log of the value of the firm.

Using equation (2.12) with $j = 1$ and $k = 2$, we can also compute

$$\ln[W_{1,2}] = \ln[W^*] + (k-1) \cdot \mu \cdot \Delta t + (2 \cdot j - k - 1) \cdot \sigma \cdot \Delta t^{1/2}$$

$$= \ln[100.0] + (1) \cdot (0.08) \cdot (0.25) + (-1) \cdot (0.20) \cdot (0.25)^{1/2}$$

$$= 4.5252 \tag{2.16}$$

so $W_{1,2} = 92.31$. $W_{1,2}$ is the value of the firm at time t_2 following a deterministic change of $\mu \cdot \Delta t = 0.02$ and a single random jump of $-\sigma \cdot \Delta t^{1/2} = -0.1$ in the log of the value of the firm.

Figure 2.7 shows the two possible ways the value of the firm can evolve over the subinterval from time t_1 to time t_2.

At time $t_3 = 1997.50$ the value of the firm can be any one of three values: $W_{3,3}$, $W_{2,3}$, or $W_{1,3}$. Using equation (2.12) with $j = 3$ and $k = 3$, we have

$$\ln[W_{3,3}] = \ln[W^*] + (k-1) \cdot \mu \cdot \Delta t + (2 \cdot j - k - 1) \cdot \sigma \cdot \Delta t^{1/2}$$

$$= \ln[100.0] + (2) \cdot (0.08) \cdot (0.25) + (2) \cdot (0.20) \cdot (0.25)^{1/2}$$

$$= 4.8452 \tag{2.17}$$

so $W_{3,3} = 127.12$. $W_{3,3}$ is the value of the firm at time t_3 following a

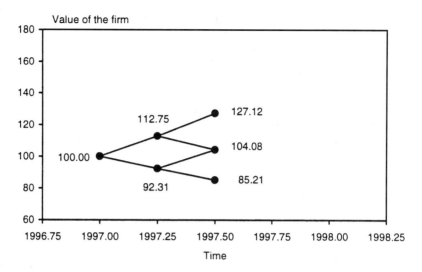

Figure 2.8
Evolution of the value of the firm from time $t_1 = 1997.00$ to time $t_3 - 1997.50$

deterministic change of $2 \cdot \mu \cdot \Delta t$ and two random jumps of $+\sigma \cdot \Delta t^{1/2}$ in the log of the value of the firm.

Using equation (2.12) with $j = 2$ and $k = 3$, we have

$$\ln[W_{2,3}] = \ln[W^*] + (k - 1) \cdot \mu \cdot \Delta t + (2 \cdot j - k - 1) \cdot \sigma \cdot \Delta t^{1/2}$$

$$= \ln[100.0] + (2) \cdot (0.08) \cdot (0.25) + (0) \cdot (0.20) \cdot (0.25)^{1/2}$$

$$= 4.6452 \tag{2.18}$$

so $W_{2,3} = 104.08$. $W_{2,3}$ is the value of the firm at time t_3 following a deterministic change of $2 \cdot \mu \cdot \Delta t$, a random jump of $-\sigma \cdot \Delta t^{1/2}$ and a random jump of $+\sigma \cdot \Delta t^{1/2}$ in the log of the value of the firm.

Finally, using equation (2.12) with $j = 1$ and $k = 3$, we have

$$\ln[W_{1,3}] = \ln[W^*] + (k - 1) \cdot \mu \cdot \Delta t + (2 \cdot j - k - 1) \cdot \sigma \cdot \Delta t^{1/2}$$

$$= \ln[100.0] + (2) \cdot (0.08) \cdot (0.25) + (-2) \cdot (0.20) \cdot (0.25)^{1/2}$$

$$= 4.4452 \tag{2.19}$$

so $W_{1,3} = 85.21$. $W_{1,3}$ is the value of the firm at time t_3 following a deterministic change of $2 \cdot \mu \cdot \Delta t$ and two random jumps of $-\sigma \cdot \Delta t^{1/2}$ in the log of the value of the firm.

Figure 2.8 shows how the value of the firm can evolve from time t_1 to time t_3. There are four possible trajectories for the value of the firm:

Trajectory A: $100.00 \Rightarrow 112.75 \Rightarrow 127.12$ $\tag{2.20a}$

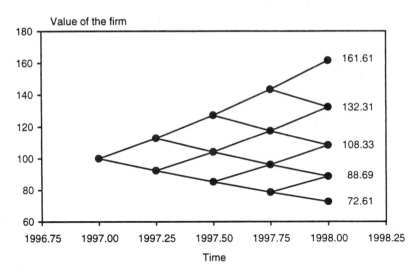

Figure 2.9
Evolution of the value of the firm from time $t_1 = 1997.00$ to time $t_5 = 1998.00$

Trajectory *B*:	$100.00 \Rightarrow 112.75 \Rightarrow 104.08$	(2.20b)

Trajectory *B*: $100.00 \Rightarrow 112.75 \Rightarrow 104.08$ (2.20b)

Trajectory *C*: $100.00 \Rightarrow 92.31 \Rightarrow 104.08$ (2.20c)

Trajectory *D*: $100.00 \Rightarrow 92.31 \Rightarrow 85.21$ (2.20d)

Trajectory *A* is the result of two consecutive random jumps of $+\sigma \cdot \Delta t^{1/2}$. Trajectory *B* occurs if there is a random jump of $+\sigma \cdot \Delta t^{1/2}$ during the subinterval between t_1 and t_2, followed by a jump of $-\sigma \cdot \Delta t^{1/2}$ during the subinterval between t_2 and t_3. Trajectory *C* occurs if the negative jump precedes the positive jump. Finally, trajectory *D* results from two consecutive random jumps of $-\sigma \cdot \Delta t^{1/2}$.

Figure 2.9 summarizes how the value of the firm can evolve from time $t_1 = 1997.0$ to time $t_5 = 1998.0$.

Some More Notation

Having introduced a convenient way to represent the binomial evolution of the value of the firm, we now specify a related notational scheme for the values of the firm's securities.

Let $V_{j,k,i}$ denote the value of the *i*th security at time t_k when the value of the firm is $W_{j,k}$:

$$V_{j,k,i} = f_i(W_{j,k}, t_k) \tag{2.21}$$

We want to compute the value of $f_i(W^*, t^*)$ or, equivalently, the value of $V_{1,1,i}$. ($V_{1,1,i} = f_i(W^*, t^*)$ because $V_{1,1,i} = f_i(W_{1,1}, t_1)$ (equation 2.21),

$W_{1,1} = W^*$ (equation 2.12), and $t_1 = t^*$ (equation 2.7). We will show how to compute *all* the $V_{j,k,i}$ terms using a recursion algorithm on k that begins at $k = K + 1$ and proceeds backward to $k = 1$.

Constructing the $V_{j,k,i}$ Terms for $k = K + 1$

The values of $V_{j,K+1,i}$ for $j = 1, 2, \ldots, K + 1$ follow from our specification of the consequences of default and bankruptcy at time T.

If the value of the firm at time $T = t_{K+1}$ is less than F, the firm will default and creditors will receive the full bankruptcy distribution of either cash (if bankruptcy results in liquidation) or securities (if bankruptcy results in a recapitalization). Creditors will be paid F if the value of the firm exceeds F. This implies that

$$V_{j,K+1,1} = \begin{cases} W_{j,K+1} & \text{if } W_{j,K+1} < F \\ F & \text{if } F \le W_{j,K+1} \end{cases} \tag{2.22}$$

Stockholders receive the residual value of the firm after the creditors have been paid, so:

$$V_{j,K+1,2} = \begin{cases} 0 & \text{if } W_{j,K+1} < F \\ W_{j,K+1} - F & \text{if } F \le W_{j,K+1} \end{cases} \tag{2.23}$$

Equations (2.22) and (2.23) are the discrete time–discrete state analogues of the terminal conditions in equations (2.2a, b) respectively.

An Example

The application of equations (2.22) and (2.23) can be illustrated with the numerical example discussed above at equations (2.14) to (2.20). Recall that the value of the firm at time $t^* = 1997.0$ is $W^* = 100.0$ and that the debt matures at time $T = 1998.0$. We assumed that $\mu = 0.08$ and $\sigma = 0.20$. Setting $K = 4$, we identified, in figure 2.9, the five possible values of the firm at the time the debt matures.

Assume now that the face amount of the zero coupon debt is $F = 100.0$. Table 2.1 shows the value of the debt and equity at time t_5 contingent on each of the five possible values of the firm. For example, $W_{3,5} = 108.33$, so from equation (2.22) the contingent value of the debt is $V_{3,5,1} = 100.0$, and from equation (2.23) the contingent value of equity is $V_{3,5,2} = 8.33$.

Calculating the $V_{j,k,i}$ Terms for $k < K + 1$

Consider now the problem of computing $V_{j,k,i}$ for some value of k less than $K + 1$, assuming that we know the values of $V_{j,k+1,i}$ for $j = 1, 2, \ldots, k + 1$. (This assumption is clearly justified if we are computing $V_{j,K,i}$

Table 2.1
Contingent value of debt and equity at time $t_5 = 1998.0$

j	$W_{j,5}$[a]	$V_{j,5,1}$[b]	$V_{j,5,2}$[c]
5	161.61	100.00	61.61
4	132.31	100.00	32.31
3	108.33	100.00	8.33
2	88.69	88.69	0.00
1	72.61	72.61	0.00

a. As shown in figure 2.9.
b. Computed with equation (2.22) using $F = 100.0$.
c. Computed with equation (2.23) using $F = 100.0$.

because we just showed how to construct the $V_{j,K+1,i}$ terms. We show below that we will always know the values of the $V_{j,k+1,i}$ terms when we begin to compute the $V_{j,k,i}$ terms for values of k less than K.)

$V_{j,k,i}$ is the value of the ith security at time t_k when the value of the firm is $W_{j,k}$ (see equation 2.21). As shown in figure 2.10, the value of the firm will evolve (over the subinterval from time t_k to time t_{k+1}) from $W_{j,k}$ to either

1. $W_{j+1,k+1}$, where the ith security will be worth $V_{j+1,k+1,i}$, or

2. $W_{j,k+1}$, where the ith security will be worth $V_{j,k+1,i}$.

A Portfolio Constructed at Time t_k

Suppose that the debt and equity of the firm are both publicly traded. Consider, at time t_k when the value of the firm is $W_{j,k}$, a portfolio consisting of (1) an investment of Q in U.S. Treasury securities and (2) a fraction h of all of the debt of the firm and the same fraction of all of the equity of the firm (or, equivalently, a fraction h of the firm as a whole), where h and Q are chosen to satisfy the equations

$$V_{j+1,k+1,i} = h \cdot W_{j+1,k+1} + Q \cdot e^{R_f \cdot \Delta t} \tag{2.24a}$$

$$V_{j,k+1,i} = h \cdot W_{j,k+1} + Q \cdot e^{R_f \cdot \Delta t} \tag{2.24b}$$

Note that h and Q are computable because, by hypothesis, we know the values of $V_{j+1,k+1,i}$ and $V_{j,k+1,i}$.[9] (We clearly know the values of R_f, Δt, $W_{j+1,k+1}$, and $W_{j,k+1}$.) Note also that if the value of Q that satisfies

9. The values of h and Q that satisfy equations (2.24a, b) are

$$h = \frac{V_{j+1,k+1,i} - V_{j,k+1,i}}{W_{j+1,k+1} - W_{j,k+1}}$$

$$Q = \frac{V_{j,k+1,i} \cdot W_{j+1,k+1} - V_{j+1,k+1,i} \cdot W_{j,k+1}}{W_{j+1,k+1} - W_{j,k+1}} \cdot e^{-R_f \cdot \Delta t}$$

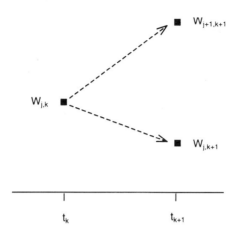

If the value of the firm evolves to $W_{j+1,k+1}$ at time t_{k+1}, the value of the ith security will be $V_{j+1,k+1,i}$. If the value of the firm evolves to $W_{j,k+1}$, the value of the ith security will be $V_{j,k+1,i}$.

Figure 2.10
One-step binomial random walk beginning at $W_{j,k}$ at time t_k

equations (2.24a, b) is negative, the portfolio will have a short position, rather than a long position, in Treasury securities.

The Value of the Portfolio at Time t_{k+1}

At time t_{k+1} the investment in Treasury securities will be worth $Q \cdot e^{R_f \cdot \Delta t}$. (This follows from the assumption in section 1.3 that the yield curve for U.S. Treasury debt is flat and stationary at the continuously compounded yield R_f per annum.) The fraction h of the firm as a whole will be worth $h \cdot W_{j+1,k+1}$ if the value of the firm evolves to $W_{j+1,k+1}$ and it will be worth $h \cdot W_{j,k+1}$ if the value of the firm evolves to $W_{j,k+1}$.

Thus the value of the portfolio will be $h \cdot W_{j+1,k+1} + Q \cdot e^{R_f \cdot \Delta t}$ if the value of the firm evolves to $W_{j+1,k+1}$ (and if the value of the ith security consequently evolves to $V_{j+1,k+1,i}$). The value of the portfolio will be $h \cdot W_{j,k+1} + Q \cdot e^{R_f \cdot \Delta t}$ if the value of the firm evolves to $W_{j,k+1}$ (and if the value of the ith security evolves to $V_{j,k+1,i}$).

It follows from equations (2.24a, b) that the value of the portfolio will be *identical* to the value of the ith security at time t_{k+1}, *regardless* of whether the value of the firm evolves to $W_{j,k+1}$ or to $W_{j+1,k+1}$.

An Arbitrage Argument

Consider now the relationship, at time t_k when the value of the firm is $W_{j,k}$, between the value of the ith security, $V_{j,k,i}$, and the value of the portfolio, $h \cdot W_{j,k} + Q$. There are three possibilities:

$$V_{j,k,i} < h \cdot W_{j,k} + Q \tag{2.25a}$$

$$V_{j,k,i} = h \cdot W_{j,k} + Q \tag{2.25b}$$

$$V_{j,k,i} > h \cdot W_{j,k} + Q \tag{2.25c}$$

If $V_{j,k,i}$ is less than $h \cdot W_{j,k} + Q$, a market participant can generate *riskless* income of $\theta \cdot [h \cdot W_{j,k} + Q - V_{j,k,i}]$ by purchasing a fraction θ (in a realistic case, θ will be a small positive number, e.g., 0.001 or 0.0001) of the ith security (at a cost of $\theta \cdot V_{j,k,i}$) and short-selling an identical fraction of the portfolio (generating proceeds of $\theta \cdot [h \cdot W_{j,k} + Q]$).[10] (This assumes that the market participant has full use of the proceeds of the short sale.) The income is riskless because, as noted above, the value of the portfolio at time t_{k+1} will be *identical* to the value of the ith security at time t_{k+1} *regardless* of whether the value of the firm evolves to $W_{j,k+1}$ or to $W_{j+1,k+1}$, so the long position in the ith security and the short position in the portfolio can be liquidated at time t_{k+1} at zero net cost with no uncertainty. Such riskless purchases and short sales will continue as long as $V_{j,k,i} < h \cdot W_{j,k} + Q$ and will drive up the value of the ith security and drive down the value of the portfolio until $V_{j,k,i} \geq h \cdot W_{j,k} + Q$.

Conversely, if $V_{j,k,i}$ exceeds $h \cdot W_{j,k} + Q$, a market participant can generate riskless income of $\theta \cdot [V_{j,k,i} - h \cdot W_{j,k} - Q]$ at time t_k by purchasing a fraction θ of the portfolio and short selling an identical fraction of the ith security. These arbitrage transactions will drive up the value of the portfolio and drive down the value of the ith security until $V_{j,k,i} \leq h \cdot W_{j,k} + Q$.

Since a market participant can generate riskless income if $V_{j,k,i}$ is less than $h \cdot W_{j,k} + Q$ or if $V_{j,k,i}$ exceeds $h \cdot W_{j,k} + Q$, it follows that, in equilibrium, the value of the ith security must be identical to the value of the portfolio:

$$V_{j,k,i} = h \cdot W_{j,k} + Q \tag{2.26}$$

Since we can solve equations (2.24a, b) for h and Q, we can use equation

---

10. If $i = 1$, this is identical to a net long position in a fraction $\theta \cdot (1 - h)$ of the firm's debt, a short position in a fraction $\theta \cdot h$ of the firm's equity, and (assuming that Q is positive) a short position in Treasury securities that have a market value of $\theta \cdot Q$. If $i = 2$, it is identical to a net long position in a fraction $\theta \cdot (1 - h)$ of the firm's equity, a short position in a fraction $\theta \cdot h$ of the firm's debt, and (assuming that Q is negative) a long position in Treasury securities with a market value of $\theta \cdot |Q|$.

(2.26) to compute the value of $V_{j,k,i}$.[11] Example 2.2 illustrates the application of equations (2.24a, b) and (2.26).

The Recursion Algorithm

We can now place the foregoing computational procedure in a recursive algorithm for calculating the value of $V_{1,1,i}$.

Since we know the values of $V_{j,K+1,i}$ for $j = 1, 2, \ldots, K+1$ (see equations 2.22 and 2.23), we can compute the values of $V_{j,K,i}$ for $j = 1, 2, \ldots, K$. Using the latter values, we can compute the values of $V_{j,K-1,i}$ for $j = 1, 2, \ldots, K-1$. This continues through the computation of $V_{1,1,i}$. Since $f_i(W^*, t^*) = V_{1,1,i}$, this completes the computation of $f_i(W^*, t^*)$ for the case where the value of the firm evolves according to the discrete time binomial process of equation (2.9).

Convergence of the Value of $V_{1,1,i}$ as Δt Goes to Zero

We noted above that the binomial random walk of equation (2.9) converges to the continuous time Gaussian random walk of equation (1.14) as K grows large and Δt goes to zero. Thus, as K grows large, the value of $V_{1,1,i}$ converges to the value of $f_i(W^*, t^*)$ for the case where the value of the firm evolves according to the continuous time Gaussian random walk.

---

11. Substituting the expressions for h and Q from note 9 into equation (2.26) and rearranging terms gives

$$V_{j,k,i} = \left[\left[\frac{W_{j,k} \cdot e^{R_f \cdot \Delta t} - W_{j,k+1}}{W_{j+1,k+1} - W_{j,k+1}} \right] \cdot V_{j+1,k+1,i} + \left[\frac{W_{j+1,k+1} - W_{j,k} \cdot e^{R_f \cdot \Delta t}}{W_{j+1,k+1} - W_{j,k+1}} \right] \cdot V_{j,k+1,i} \right] \cdot e^{-R_f \cdot \Delta t}$$

From equations (2.13b, c) we have $W_{j+1,k+1} = W_{j,k} \cdot \exp[\mu \cdot \Delta t + \sigma \cdot \Delta t^{1/2}]$ and $W_{j,k+1} = W_{j,k} \cdot \exp[\mu \cdot \Delta t - \sigma \cdot \Delta t^{1/2}]$. Thus we can express $V_{j,k,i}$ as

$$V_{j,k,i} = [\tilde{p} \cdot V_{j+1,k+1,i} + (1 - \tilde{p}) \cdot V_{j,k+1,i}] \cdot e^{-R_f \cdot \Delta t}$$

where

$$\tilde{p} = \frac{e^{(R_f - \mu) \cdot \Delta t} - e^{-\sigma \cdot \Delta t^{1/2}}}{e^{\sigma \cdot \Delta t^{1/2}} - e^{-\sigma \cdot \Delta t^{1/2}}}$$

The scalar $\tilde{p}$ is the "risk neutral" probability that the value of the firm evolves from $W_{j,k}$ at time t_k to $W_{j+1,k+1}$ at time t_{k+1}. (The risk neutral probability that the value of the firm evolves to $W_{j,k+1}$ is $1 - \tilde{p}$.) The expression for $V_{j,k,i}$ can be interpreted as the expectation (at time t_k when the value of the firm is $W_{j,k}$) of the value of the ith security at time t_{k+1} (where the expectation is assessed using the risk neutral probabilities of $\tilde{p}$ and $1 - \tilde{p}$ rather than the objective probabilities of $\frac{1}{2}$ and $\frac{1}{2}$), discounted back to time t_k at the Treasury yield R_f. Note that the objective probabilities would be equal to the risk neutral probabilities if market participants were indifferent to risk (Cox, Ross, and Rubinstein 1979, p. 235, Cox and Rubinstein 1985, p. 174). Risk neutral pricing was introduced into the contingent claims literature by Cox and Ross (1976). See also Harrison and Kreps (1979).

Example 2.2   Contingent Value of the Debt and Equity at Time $t_4 = 1997.75$ When the Value of the Firm Is $W_{2,4} = 96.08$

This example continues the numerical example discussed in the text at equations (2.14) to (2.20) and in table 2.1.

Suppose that at time $t_4 = 1997.75$ the value of the firm is $W_{2,4} = 96.08$. As shown in figure 2.9, the value of the firm can evolve to $W_{2,5} = 88.69$ or to $W_{3,5} = 108.33$ at time $t_5 = 1998.00$.

Table 2.1 shows that if the value of the firm evolves to 88.69, the value of the debt will be $V_{2,5,1} = 88.69$ and the equity will be worthless. If the value of the firm evolves to 108.33, the value of the debt will be $V_{3,5,1} = 100.00$ and the value of the equity will be $V_{3,5,2} = 8.33$.

We want to compute, with equations (2.24a, b) and (2.26), the contingent value of the debt and equity at time t_4 when the value of the firm is $W_{2,4}$. We assume that the yield on U.S. Treasury debt is $R_f = 0.10$, or 10% per annum, compounded continuously.

Consider first the matter of assessing the contingent value of the debt, $V_{2,4,1}$. From equation (2.26), we want to compute

$$V_{2,4,1} = h \cdot W_{2,4} + Q$$

where, from equations (2.24a, b), h and Q satisfy the equations

$$V_{3,5,1} = h \cdot W_{3,5} + Q \cdot e^{R_f \cdot \Delta t}$$

$$V_{2,5,1} = h \cdot W_{2,5} + Q \cdot e^{R_f \cdot \Delta t}$$

or

$$100.0 = h \cdot 108.33 + Q \cdot e^{(0.10) \cdot (0.25)}$$

$$88.69 = h \cdot 88.69 + Q \cdot e^{(0.10) \cdot (0.25)}$$

So

$$h = 0.5759$$

$$Q = 36.68$$

This gives

$$V_{2,4,1} = h \cdot W_{2,4} + Q$$

$$= 0.5759 \cdot 96.08 + 36.68$$

$$= 92.01$$

Consider next the matter of assessing the contingent value of the equity, $V_{2,4,2}$. From equation (2.26), we want to compute

$$V_{2,4,2} = h \cdot W_{2,4} + Q$$

where, from equations (2.24a, b), h and Q satisfy the equations

$$V_{3,5,2} = h \cdot W_{3,5} + Q \cdot e^{R_f \cdot \Delta t}$$

$$V_{2,5,2} = h \cdot W_{2,5} + Q \cdot e^{R_f \cdot \Delta t}$$

or

$$8.33 = h \cdot 108.33 + Q \cdot e^{(0.10) \cdot (0.25)}$$

$$0.00 = h \cdot 88.69 + Q \cdot e^{(0.10) \cdot (0.25)}$$

Example 2.2 (continued)

So

$h = 0.4241$

$Q = -36.68$

This gives

$$V_{2,4,2} = h \cdot W_{2,4} + Q$$

$$= 0.4241 \cdot 96.08 - 36.68$$

$$= 4.07$$

2.5   Summary and Comments

It may be helpful to summarize the key assumptions of the contingent value problem and to point out where the assumptions appeared in our solution to the problem.

First, we assumed that the natural logarithm of the value of the firm evolves as a Gaussian random walk in continuous time, and we approximated that process with a discrete time binomial random walk.

Second, we established the contingent value of the debt and equity on the maturity date of the debt from our assumptions regarding default and bankruptcy. It should be clear that the contingent values of the firm's securities would be different if the absolute priority rule is not observed, for example, if stockholders receive something from a bankruptcy proceeding even though creditors are not paid in full.

Third, we established the contingent value of the debt and equity prior to the maturity of the debt with a recursion algorithm. The essential feature of the algorithm was replicating the two possible values of a corporate security at the end of a subinterval of time with a portfolio of Treasury debt and the firm as a whole (see equations 2.24a, b). We then argued that the value of the security at the beginning of the subinterval must be identical to the value of the replicating portfolio at the beginning of the subinterval (see equation 2.26).

Three Features of the Contingent Value Functions

Three important features of the contingent value functions are not particularly obvious from the development of the algorithm in section 2.4.

Replication and the Problem of Privately Held Securities

The notion that we can replicate a corporate security with a portfolio of Treasury debt and the firm as a whole requires that we can actually buy or sell positions in the firm as a whole. This in turn requires that we can buy or sell *each* of the securities issued by the firm—so that we can buy (or sell) 1% of the firm by buying (or selling) 1% of each security in the firm's capital structure. The algorithm described in the preceding section cannot be used to construct contingent value functions for the debt and equity of the firm when either of the firm's securities are privately held, because in that case the replicating transactions cannot be executed.

The Adding-up Constraint

We defined, in equation (2.1), the value of the firm as the sum of the values of the securities capitalizing the firm: $W(t) = V_1(t) + V_2(t)$. Replacing $V_1(t)$ and $V_2(t)$ with the equivalent expressions from the right-hand side of equation (2.4) gives $W(t) = f_1(W(t), t) + f_2(W(t), t)$. Since $W(t)$ is arbitrary, the contingent value functions must satisfy the "adding-up" constraint:

$$W = f_1(W, t) + f_2(W, t) \tag{2.27}$$

for all positive values of W and for all values of t less than or equal to T. Appendix B demonstrates that the algorithm leads to contingent value functions that satisfy equation (2.27).

The Irrelevance of μ for the Contingent Value of a Security

The value of the ith security at time t when the value of the firm is W clearly depends on the variables t and W. At least intuitively, it appears that the value of the security should also depend on the parameters F, T, R_f, μ, and σ. (The value of the debt and equity should clearly depend on the face amount and maturity date of the debt. R_f appears in the arbitrage pricing procedure; see equations 2.24a, b. μ and σ affect the structure of the $W_{j,k}$ array; see equation 2.12.)

Debt and equity values do indeed depend on F, T, σ, and R_f. However, they do *not* depend on μ. Appendix C demonstrates this important feature.

2.6   Some Examples

At this point it will be useful to examine some numerical examples of our contingent value problem. We assume the U.S. Treasury yield curve is flat and stationary at $R_f = 0.10$ (or 10% per annum) and that the volatility of the value of the firm is $\sigma = 0.20$ (or a volatility of 20% over one year).

Setting μ Equal to the Risk Neutral Drift Rate $R_f - \frac{1}{2}\sigma^2$

We noted in the preceding section that the contingent value of a corporate security is invariant with respect to the drift rate μ. This implies, inter alia, that the contingent value of the company's debt and equity does not depend on the probability that the firm will default. (The probability of default is the probability that the value of the firm will be less than F at time T. This probability clearly depends on μ. The implication that the contingent value of the debt and equity does not depend on μ may not hold if bankruptcy is costly. See sections 4.6 and 5.1.)

However, it is useful, as an expository matter, to interpret the characteristics of contingent value functions in terms of the likelihood of default. We will adopt the convention of setting μ equal to the "risk neutral" drift rate $R_f - \frac{1}{2}\sigma^2$. Appendix D discusses the basis for describing $R_f - \frac{1}{2}\sigma^2$ as a risk neutral drift rate. References to the likelihood of default are calibrated to this risk neutral process. In the following examples, where $R_f = 0.10$ and $\sigma = 0.20$, we set $\mu = 0.08$, or 8% per annum.

Example A

The first example assumes the face amount of the zero-coupon debt is $F = 164.872$ and that we are valuing the debt five years prior to maturity, so $T - t^* = 5.0$ years. Ignoring the risk of default, the debt has a default free value of 100.0 ($F \cdot \exp[-R_f \cdot (T - t^*)] = 100.0$ when $F = 164.872$, $R_f = 0.10$ and $T - t^* = 5.0$).

The Contingent Value of Debt

The top panel of figure 2.11 shows the contingent value of the debt.

When the value of the firm is less than about 50, the value of the debt is essentially identical to the value of the firm. This reflects (1) the virtual certainty (assuming the risk neutral drift rate) of default and bankruptcy in five years and (2) the seniority of the debt relative to equity. Since creditors are virtually certain to receive the full value of the firm at time T, the value of the debt is equal to the value of the firm at time t^*.

It is not difficult to show that the debt must be worth less than the value of the firm when the value of the firm is not so low as to make default and bankruptcy a virtual certainty, such as when the value of the firm is 75 or 100 or more. Consider two portfolios, labeled A and B. Portfolio A consists of 1% of each of the securities of the firm, or 1% of the firm as a whole, and portfolio B consists of 1% of the firm's zero-coupon debt. Portfolio A dominates portfolio B in the sense that when the debt matures at time T, portfolio A will be more valuable than portfolio B if the firm avoids default and will be no less valuable if the firm defaults. Thus prior to time T the value of portfolio B must be less than the value of portfolio A.

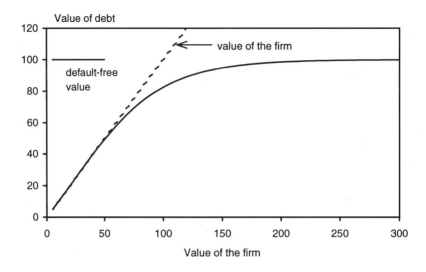

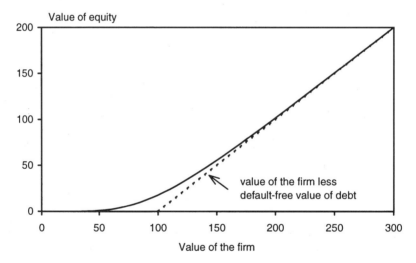

Figure 2.11
Contingent value of debt and equity five years before the debt matures

When the value of the firm is more than about 250, the value of the debt is essentially identical to its default free value of 100. This reflects the virtual certainty (assuming the risk neutral drift rate) that the firm will avoid default and that creditors will be paid the full amount of their claims.

The corporate debt must be worth less than default-proof debt promising to pay 164.872 in five years when the value of the firm is not so high as to virtually preclude default and bankruptcy, such as when the value of the firm is 175 or 150 or less. To see this, consider two portfolios, labeled B and C. As above, portfolio B consists of 1% of the firm's debt. Portfolio C consists of zero-coupon Treasury debt with the same face value. Portfolio C dominates portfolio B in the sense that portfolio B will never pay more than portfolio C and will pay less if the company defaults at time T. Thus, prior to time T, the value of portfolio B must be less than the value of portfolio C.

The Contingent Value of Equity

The bottom panel of figure 2.11 shows the contingent value of the company's stock. The stock is virtually worthless when the value of the firm is less than 50 and default and bankruptcy are virtually certain. At the other extreme, if the value of the firm exceeds 250, there is almost no chance that creditors will not be paid in full at time T. In this case the value of the stock is equal to the value of the firm less the default-free value of the debt.

Cross Valuation and Hedging

Figure 2.12 shows the value of the debt as a function of the value of the stock.[12] The figure illustrates two of the uses of contingent value functions. First, the figure shows how the debt can be cross-valued from the stock. Second, since the value of the debt and equity vary together, we can hedge the credit risk on a position in the debt by short-selling the stock.[13]

The slope of the cross-value function in figure 2.12 is a direct measure of the appropriate hedge ratio. If the slope of the curve is 0.75 at some value of equity, then a change of 1.0 in the value of the stock is associated with a change of 0.75 in the value of the debt. We could hedge the credit risk on all of the company's debt by short-selling 75% of the company's

---

12. Figure 2.12 is a graph of pairs of points of the form (x, y), where $x = f_2(W, t)$ and $y = f_1(W, t)$ for $t = T - 5.0$ and for values of W ranging between 0 and 300.

13. For an example of the covariation of the prices of corporate debt and equity see "Rite Aid, Paring Back, Explores a Sale of All or Most of 1,000 West Coast Stores," *Wall Street Journal*, November 12, 1999, p. A3 (reporting a 31% decline in the price of Rite Aid stock and a decline of "about one-third" in the price of one of its publicly traded bonds).

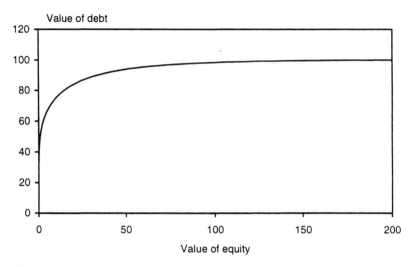

Figure 2.12
Value of debt five years before maturity as a function of the value of equity

equity. More realistically, we could hedge the credit risk on a position in 1.00% of the company's debt by short-selling 0.75% of the company's equity.

Example B

The second example extends the first example by examining the variation of contingent debt and equity values as a function of the term to maturity of the debt. We continue to assume that the face amount of the debt is $F = 164.872$.

Figure 2.13 shows the contingent value of the debt and equity when the debt has 7.5, 5.0, and 2.5 years remaining to maturity, and when it is maturing. Holding the value of the firm constant, we observe that the contingent value of equity falls through time and that the contingent value of the debt rises. This is consistent with the declining time value of the stockholders' call option on the firm as the option approaches expiration, namely as the debt approaches maturity.

Figure 2.14 illustrates the changing relationship between debt and equity values as the debt approaches maturity.

Example C

The third example is similar to example A, except that we here consider the effect of varying the volatility of the value of the firm from $\sigma = 0.20$ to $\sigma = 0.10$ and to $\sigma = 0.30$. The debt remains as five-year zero-coupon debt with a face amount of 164.872.

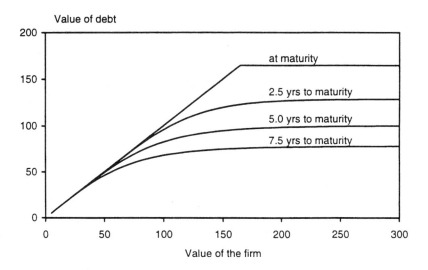

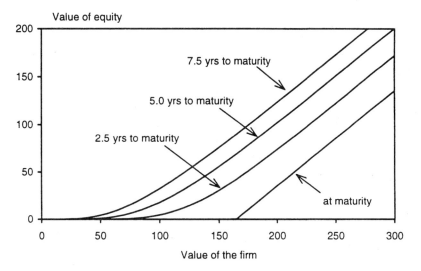

Figure 2.13
Contingent value of debt and equity at various dates prior to the maturity of the debt

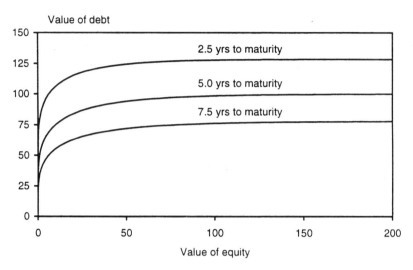

Figure 2.14
Value of debt as a function of the value of equity at various dates prior to the maturity of the debt

Figure 2.15 shows that ceteris paribus, increasing the volatility of the value of the firm reduces the contingent value of the firm's debt and enhances the contingent value of equity. This accords with the intuitive notion that greater uncertainty about the prospective value of the enterprise should enhance the present value of equity. This is because (at the maturity of the debt) equity captures all of the value of the firm in excess of the face amount of the firm's debt and bears none of the costs of a shortfall. Conversely, greater uncertainty reduces the value of the debt because the debt bears all of the consequences of a shortfall in the value of the firm below the face amount of the debt and captures none of the benefits of an excess.[14]

14. The articles cited in note 2 above observe that stockholders can expropriate wealth from creditors by causing the firm to pay out substantial dividends and that bond indentures and loan agreements commonly include covenants limiting the payment of dividends to protect the interests of creditors. Galai and Masulis (1976, pp. 62–64), Jensen and Meckling (1976, pp. 335–36), and Smith and Warner (1979, pp. 118–19) observe that stockholders can also expropriate wealth from creditors by altering the operating characteristics of the enterprise and increasing the volatility of the value of the firm. Smith and Warner (1979, pp. 125–29, 138, and 140–42) point out a variety of contractual provisions that protect creditors from this second type of expropriation. Green (1984) describes how the anticipation by creditors of "asset substitution" by shareholders can lead to inefficient investment decisions. We suppressed the possibility of such asset substitution when we assumed in equation (1.14) that the volatility parameter σ is fixed.

Jensen and Meckling (1976, p. 353) observe that managerial wage contracts have some of the characteristics of debt, so a manager might appear to have little incentive to undertake (on behalf of shareholders) any asset substitution, but they also note that this disincentive may be overcome by granting stock options to the manager. Agrawal and Mandelker (1987) report a direct relationship between increases in corporate asset volatilities following mergers, acquisitions and divestitures and the positions of senior managers in stock and stock options.

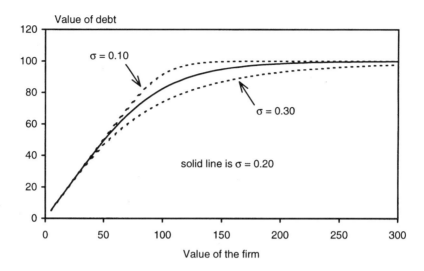

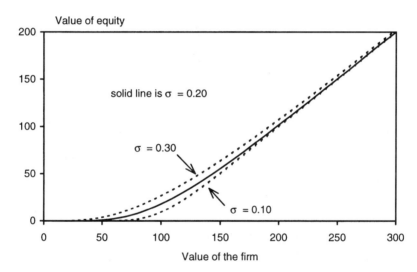

Figure 2.15
Contingent value of debt and equity five years before the debt matures for various volatilities
of the value of the firm

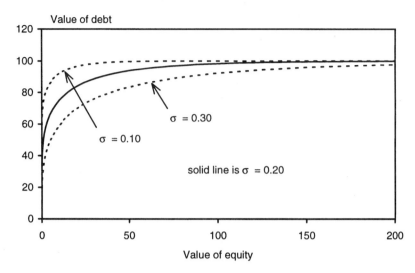

Figure 2.15
Value of debt as a function of the value of equity for various volatilities of the value of the firm

Cross Valuation and Hedging

Figure 2.16 shows that the volatility of the value of the firm also affects the implicit relationship between debt and equity values. For equity of a given market value, the imputed value of the debt will be lower the greater the volatility.

There are two reasons for this phenomenon. First, the value of the debt is directly related to the value of the firm and the value of the firm associated with the observed equity value will be lower the greater the volatility (see the lower panel of figure 2.15). Second, the value of the debt is inversely related to volatility even if we hold the value of the firm constant (see the upper panel of figure 2.15).

The variation of the implicit relationship between the value of debt and equity shown in figure 2.16 means that we cannot accurately cross-value or hedge one class of the corporation's securities with the other class of securities if we do not know the volatility of the value of the firm.

Example D

Our last example shows that ceteris paribus, time to maturity affects the contingent value of debt and equity like volatility: a longer time to maturity (like a higher volatility) creates greater uncertainty in the value of the firm at the maturity date of the debt and leads to higher equity values and lower debt values prior to maturity.[15]

15. See also the related analysis in Ho and Singer (1982, pp. 378–86).

To see this, consider three firms, each capitalized with equity and a single class of zero-coupon debt. The face amounts and times to maturity of the debt are

Firm A: 113.315 payable in 1.25 years

Firm B: 164.872 payable in 5.00 years

Firm C: 308.022 payable in 11.25 years

In each case the debt has a default-free value of 100.0 computed at a Treasury yield of 10% per annum $(F \cdot \exp[-R_f \cdot (T - t^*)] = 100.0$ when $R_f = 0.10$ and, as with firm A, $F = 113.315$ and $T - t^* = 1.25$ or, as with firm B, $F = 164.872$ and $T - t^* = 5.0$ or, as with firm C, $F = 308.022$ and $T - t^* = 11.25$).

Figure 2.17 shows how the value of the debt and equity of each firm varies with the value of the firm. Observe that the contingent value of equity is greater the longer the time to maturity of the firm's debt even when we hold constant the default-free value of the debt. This illustrates the value to stockholders of the greater uncertainty of the maturity value of the firm associated with longer maturity debt.

Comparing figures 2.15 and 2.17 suggests that longer debt maturity affects securities prices in about the same way as greater volatility of enterprise value. This is consistent with the observation that variance of future value can be expressed as the product of (1) time and (2) variance of value per unit time.[16] Increasing either time to maturity or variance per unit time increases variance of enterprise value at maturity and hence increases equity values—and reduces debt values—prior to maturity.

2.7   A Concluding Remark

Nothing in the model described in this chapter depends on whether the firm is managed for the benefit of stockholders or for the benefit of creditors, because nothing in the model requires managerial discretion. At time t the value of the firm stands at $W(t)$ and evolves randomly (like a child's windup toy) until the maturity of the debt at time T. In chapters 6, 8, and 13 we will examine corporate capital structures that require management decisions and we will then invoke the assumption, from section 1.5, that managers act in the best interest of shareholders. The issue of managerial discretion will become much more important in part IV, where we examine discretionary distributions to shareholders.

16. See, for example, equations (1.21b) and (1.22b), showing how the variance of the value ratio θ depends on the time interval Δt and the variance per annum σ^2.

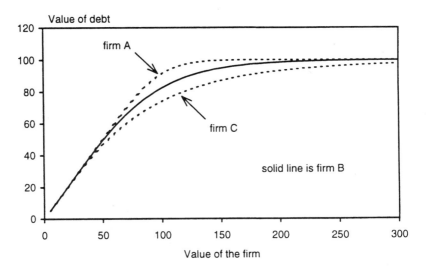

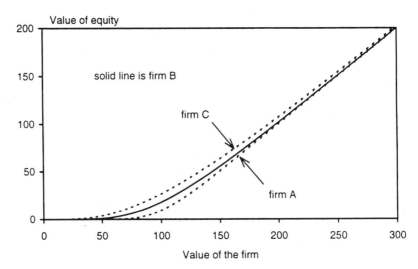

Figure 2.17
Contingent value of debt and equity for three firms capitalized with debt with a default-free
value of 100.0

Appendix A

This appendix describes an important technical condition on the maximum size of Δt and the minimum size of K in the discrete time binomial random walk specified in section 2.4.

Suppose that at some time t_k the value of the firm is $W_{j,k}$. From equations (2.13b, c) the value of the firm at time t_{k+1} will be either $W_{j+1,k+1}$ or $W_{j,k+1}$, where

$$W_{j+1,k+1} = W_{j,k} \cdot e^{\mu \cdot \Delta t + \sigma \cdot \Delta t^{1/2}} \tag{A2.1a}$$

$$W_{j,k+1} = W_{j,k} \cdot e^{\mu \cdot \Delta t - \sigma \cdot \Delta t^{1/2}} \tag{A2.1b}$$

It is clearly the case that $W_{j,k+1} < W_{j+1,k+1}$. However, we must also have

$$W_{j,k+1} < W_{j,k} \cdot e^{R_f \cdot \Delta t} < W_{j+1,k+1} \tag{A2.2}$$

That is, it must not be the case that the value of the firm will, with certainty, appreciate more slowly than the rate R_f, meaning that we cannot have $W_{j+1,k+1} < W_{j,k} \cdot e^{R_f \cdot \Delta t}$, because U.S. Treasury debt would then dominate an investment in the firm as a whole. Similarly it must not be the case that the value of the firm will, with certainty, appreciate faster than the rate R_f, meaning that we can not have $W_{j,k} \cdot e^{R_f \cdot \Delta t} < W_{j,k+1}$, because an investment in the firm as a whole would then dominate Treasury debt.

The inequalities in equation (A2.2) are equivalent to

$$\frac{W_{j,k+1}}{W_{j,k}} < e^{R_f \cdot \Delta t} < \frac{W_{j+1,k+1}}{W_{j,k}}$$

So, from equations (A2.1a, b),

$$e^{\mu \cdot \Delta t - \sigma \cdot \Delta t^{1/2}} < e^{R_f \cdot \Delta t} < e^{\mu \cdot \Delta t + \sigma \cdot \Delta t^{1/2}}$$

or

$$-\sigma \cdot \Delta t^{-1/2} < R_f - \mu < \sigma \cdot \Delta t^{-1/2} \tag{A2.3}$$

The inequalities in equation (A2.3) can be satisfied with a sufficiently small value of Δt, regardless of the values of σ, R_f, and μ. From equation (2.6) this is equivalent to choosing a value of K large enough to satisfy the inequalities

$$\frac{-\sigma \cdot K^{1/2}}{(T - t^*)^{1/2}} < R_f - \mu < \frac{\sigma \cdot K^{1/2}}{(T - t^*)^{1/2}} \tag{A2.4}$$

Appendix B

This appendix demonstrates that the algorithm for computing $f_i(W^*, t^*)$ described in section 2.4 leads to contingent security values that satisfy the adding-up constraint

$$W^* = f_1(W^*, t^*) + f_2(W^*, t^*) \tag{A2.5}$$

Since, in the notation of the algorithm, $W^* = W_{1,1}$ (see equation 2.13a) and $f_i(W^*, t^*) = V_{1,1,i}$ (see text following equation 2.21), we have to show that

$$W_{1,1} = V_{1,1,1} + V_{1,1,2} \tag{A2.6}$$

Equation (A2.6) follows as a special case of the more general result that

$$W_{j,k} = V_{j,k,1} + V_{j,k,2} \tag{A2.7}$$

for any $k \in \{1, 2, \ldots, K+1\}$ and for any $j \in \{1, 2, \ldots, k\}$.

Equation (A2.7) is clearly true for $k = K+1$ and for any $j \in \{1, 2, \ldots, K+1\}$ by the terminal conditions of equations (2.22) and (2.23). Proof of the equation for values of k smaller than $K+1$ follows from an induction argument.

Suppose that equation (A2.7) is true for $k+1$ and for any $j \in \{1, 2, \ldots, k+1\}$. We want to show it is true for k and for any $j \in \{1, 2, \ldots, k\}$. Define Φ as

$$\Phi = V_{j,k,1} + V_{j,k,2} \tag{A2.8}$$

From equation (2.26) we have

$$\Phi = (h_1 + h_2) \cdot W_{j,k} + Q_1 + Q_2 \tag{A2.9}$$

where h_i and Q_i are the values of h and Q that satisfy equations (2.24a, b) for the ith security. Hence they are computed as

$$h_i = \frac{V_{j+1,k+1,i} - V_{j,k+1,i}}{W_{j+1,k+1} - W_{j,k+1}} \tag{A2.10a}$$

$$Q_i = [V_{j+1,k+1,i} - h_i \cdot W_{j+1,k+1}] \cdot e^{-R_f \cdot \Delta t} \tag{A2.10b}$$

Since, by the induction argument, $V_{j,k+1,1} + V_{j,k+1,2} = W_{j,k+1}$ for any $j \in \{1, 2, \ldots, k+1\}$, equation (A2.10a) implies that

$$h_1 + h_2 = 1 \tag{A2.11}$$

It follows from equation (A2.10b) that

$$Q_1 + Q_2 = 0 \tag{A2.12}$$

Substituting these expressions into equation (A2.9) gives $\Phi = W_{j,k}$. By definition of Φ, we have

$$V_{j,k,1} + V_{j,k,2} = W_{j,k} \tag{A2.13}$$

This demonstrates equation (A2.7) and hence the special case of equation (A2.6).

Appendix C

This appendix demonstrates that the contingent value functions are invariant with respect to the drift rate μ in the specification of the stochastic evolution of the log of the value of the firm at equation (1.14).[17]

Consider the following discrete time model of the evolution of the log of the value of the firm:

$$\ln[W(t_{k+1})] = \ln[W(t_k)] + \mu \cdot \Delta t + \sigma \cdot \Delta t^{1/2} \cdot e_k, \qquad k = 1, 2, \ldots, K \tag{A2.14}$$

where e_k is a binomial random variable:

$$e_k = \begin{cases} +1 & \text{with probability } p \\ -1 & \text{with probability } 1 - p \end{cases} \tag{A2.15}$$

The mean and second moment of e_k are

$$\text{Ex}[e_k] = p \cdot (+1) + (1 - p) \cdot (-1)$$
$$= 2 \cdot p - 1 \tag{A2.16a}$$
$$\text{Ex}[e_k^2] = p \cdot (+1)^2 + (1 - p) \cdot (-1)^2$$
$$= 1 \tag{A2.16b}$$

This model generalizes the model at equations (2.9) and (2.10) by allowing the probability that $e_k = +1$ to be an arbitrary number (p) between zero and unity.

The $W_{j,k}$ array defined in equation (2.12) can be used with any binomial process that has the characteristic that the change in the log of the value of the firm between time t_k and time t_{k+1} is either $\mu \cdot \Delta t + \sigma \cdot \Delta t^{1/2}$ or $\mu \cdot \Delta t - \sigma \cdot \Delta t^{1/2}$. It follows that specifying that

---

17. See also Cox and Ross (1976) and Harrison and Kreps (1979).

the log of the value of the firm evolves over the interval from time t^* to time T as a binomial random walk, beginning at $\ln[W^*]$ at time t^*, with a change of either $\mu \cdot \Delta t + \sigma \cdot \Delta t^{1/2}$ (with probability p) or $\mu \cdot \Delta t - \sigma \cdot \Delta t^{1/2}$ (with probability $1 - p$) over each subinterval of time of length $\Delta t = (T - t^*)/K$,

is equivalent to specifying that

the value of the firm evolves through the $W_{j,k}$ array over the interval from time t_1 to time t_{K+1}, beginning at $W_{1,1}$ at time t_1, such that if the value of the firm is $W_{j,k}$ at time t_k, then the value of the firm at time t_{k+1} will be either $W_{j+1,k+1}$ (with probability p) or $W_{j,k+1}$ (with probability $1 - p$).

More specifically, the value of the firm here evolves in the same way as in section 2.4, except that the probabilities of evolving from $W_{j,k}$ to $W_{j+1,k+1}$ and $W_{j,k+1}$ are p and $1 - p$, respectively, rather than $\frac{1}{2}$ and $\frac{1}{2}$.

Consider now the problem of computing the value of the ith security at time t^* when the value of the firm is W^* (or, in the notation introduced at equation 2.21, the problem of computing $V_{1,1,i}$) and when the value of the firm evolves as in equations (A2.14) and (A2.15). A review of the algorithm for computing $V_{1,1,i}$ (described in the text at equations 2.22 through 2.26) shows that the value of $V_{1,1,i}$ does not depend on the *probabilities* of evolving from $W_{j,k}$ to $W_{j+1,k+1}$ or $W_{j,k+1}$. Thus the value of the ith security at time t^* when the value of the firm is W^* is invariant with respect to the value of p in the model of equations (A2.14) and (A2.15).

Now consider the consequences of assigning a value to p according to the rule

$$p = \frac{1}{2} + \frac{1}{2} \cdot \left(\frac{v - \mu}{\sigma}\right) \cdot \Delta t^{1/2} \qquad (A2.17)$$

where v is an arbitrary number and, as in equation (2.6), $\Delta t = (T - t^*)/K$.[18] Observe that p converges to $\frac{1}{2}$ as Δt goes to zero, regardless of the value of v.

We can compute, from the binomial model in equations (A2.14) and (A2.15), the expected value of the change in the log of the value of the firm over the interval from time t_k to time t_{k+1} as

18. The scalar quantity p is a probability and must lie in the interval between zero and unity, so (from equation A2.17) we require that $-1 < [(v - \mu)/\sigma] \cdot \Delta t^{1/2} < +1$. These inequalities can be satisfied for any value of v by making K in equation (2.6) large enough and Δt small enough.

$$\mathrm{Ex}[\ln[W(t_{k+1})] - \ln[W(t_k)]] = \mathrm{Ex}[\mu \cdot \Delta t + \sigma \cdot \Delta t^{1/2} \cdot e_k]$$

$$= \mathrm{Ex}[\mu \cdot \Delta t] + \mathrm{Ex}[\sigma \cdot \Delta t^{1/2} \cdot e_k]$$

$$= \mu \cdot \Delta t + \sigma \cdot \Delta t^{1/2} \cdot \mathrm{Ex}[e_k]$$

or since $\mathrm{Ex}[e_k] = 2 \cdot p - 1$ (see equation A2.16a),

$$\mathrm{Ex}[\ln[W(t_{k+1})] - \ln[W(t_k)]] = \mu \cdot \Delta t + \sigma \cdot \Delta t^{1/2} \cdot (2 \cdot p - 1)$$

Replacing p with the specification on the right-hand side of equation (A2.17) gives

$$\mathrm{Ex}[\ln[W(t_{k+1})] - \ln[W(t_k)]] = v \cdot \Delta t \qquad (A2.18)$$

Equation (A2.18) shows that the expected change in the log of the value of the firm is v per annum when the transition probability p is as in equation (A2.17).

We can also compute the variance of the change in the log of the value of the firm over the same interval:

$$\mathrm{var}[\ln[W(t_{k+1})] - \ln[W(t_k)]]$$

$$= \mathrm{Ex}[\{\ln[W(t_{k+1})] - \ln[W(t_k)] - \mathrm{Ex}[\ln[W(t_{k+1})] - \ln[W(t_k)]]\}^2]$$

$$= \mathrm{Ex}[\{\ln[W(t_{k+1})] - \ln[W(t_k)] - v \cdot \Delta t\}^2]$$

$$= \mathrm{Ex}[\{(\mu - v) \cdot \Delta t + \sigma \cdot \Delta t^{1/2} \cdot e_k\}^2]$$

$$= \mathrm{Ex}[(\mu - v)^2 \cdot \Delta t^2 + 2 \cdot (\mu - v) \cdot \Delta t \cdot \sigma \cdot \Delta t^{1/2} \cdot e_k + \sigma^2 \cdot \Delta t \cdot e_k^2]$$

$$= (\mu - v)^2 \cdot \Delta t^2 + 2 \cdot (\mu - v) \cdot \Delta t \cdot \sigma \cdot \Delta t^{1/2} \cdot \mathrm{Ex}[e_k] + \sigma^2 \cdot \Delta t \cdot \mathrm{Ex}[e_k^2]$$

or since $\mathrm{Ex}[e_k] = 2 \cdot p - 1$ and $\mathrm{Ex}[e_k^2] = 1$ (see equation A2.16b),

$$\mathrm{var}[\ln[W(t_{k+1})] - \ln[W(t_k)]]$$

$$= (\mu - v)^2 \cdot \Delta t^2 + 2 \cdot (\mu - v) \cdot \Delta t \cdot \sigma \cdot \Delta t^{1/2} \cdot (2 \cdot p - 1) + \sigma^2 \cdot \Delta t$$

Replacing p with the specification on the right-hand side of equation (A2.17) gives

$$\mathrm{var}[\ln[W(t_{k+1})] - \ln[W(t_k)]]$$

$$= (\mu - v)^2 \cdot \Delta t^2 + 2 \cdot (\mu - v) \cdot \Delta t \cdot \sigma \cdot \Delta t^{1/2} \cdot \left[\frac{v - \mu}{\sigma}\right] \cdot \Delta t^{1/2} + \sigma^2 \cdot \Delta t$$

or

$$\mathrm{var}[\ln[W(t_{k+1})] - \ln[W(t_k)]] = \sigma^2 \cdot \Delta t - (\mu - v)^2 \cdot \Delta t^2 \qquad (A2.19)$$

Equation (A2.19) shows that the variance of the change in the log of the value of the firm is $\sigma^2 - (\mu - \nu)^2 \cdot \Delta t$ per annum when the transition probability p is as in equation (A2.17). Note that this variance rate converges to σ^2 as Δt goes to zero.

It follows from the central limit theorem that as Δt becomes small, that is, as K in equation (2.6) becomes large, the binomial random walk specified in equations (A2.14), (A2.15), and (A2.17) converges to a Gaussian random walk with expected change ν per annum (see equation A2.18) and variance σ^2 per annum (see equation A2.19), or to a continuous time stochastic process of the form

$$\ln[W(t + \Delta t)] - \ln[W(t)] = \nu \cdot \Delta t + \sigma \cdot \Delta t^{1/2} \cdot z \tag{A2.20}$$

where z is a normally distributed random variable with mean zero and a variance of unity.

We have now shown that

1. we can assign values to the transition probability p such that the discrete time binomial random walk in equations (A2.14) and (A2.15) converges to a continuous time Gaussian random walk with an arbitrarily specified drift rate ν and that

2. the contingent value of the ith security does not depend on the values assigned to p.

Thus the contingent value of the ith security is invariant with respect to the specified drift rate.

Appendix D

This appendix discusses why, at the beginning of section 2.6, we characterized the drift rate $R_f - \frac{1}{2}\sigma^2$ as a risk neutral drift rate.

From equation (1.17) we can express the value of the firm at time $t + \Delta t$ as a function of the value of the firm at time t:

$$W(t + \Delta t) = \theta \cdot W(t) \tag{A2.21}$$

where θ is a lognormal random variable with the probability density function shown in equation (1.19). Since the distribution of θ does not depend on $W(t)$, the expectation of the value of the firm at time $t + \Delta t$, conditional on the value of the firm at time t, is

$$\mathrm{Ex}[W(t + \Delta t) \mid W(t)] = \mathrm{Ex}[\theta \cdot W(t) \mid W(t)]$$

$$= W(t) \cdot \mathrm{Ex}[\theta]$$

or since $\mathrm{Ex}[\theta] = \exp[\mu \cdot \Delta t + \frac{1}{2}\sigma^2 \cdot \Delta t]$ (see equation 1.21a),

$$\text{Ex}[W(t+\Delta t) \mid W(t)] = W(t) \cdot \exp[\mu \cdot \Delta t + \tfrac{1}{2}\sigma^2 \cdot \Delta t]$$

If we set the drift rate μ equal to $R_{\text{f}} - \tfrac{1}{2}\sigma^2$, the conditional expectation of $W(t+\Delta t)$ becomes

$$\text{Ex}[W(t+\Delta t) \mid W(t)] = W(t) \cdot \exp[R_{\text{f}} \cdot \Delta t]$$

or equivalently,

$$W(t) = \text{Ex}[W(t+\Delta t) \mid W(t)] \cdot \exp[-R_{\text{f}} \cdot \Delta t] \tag{A2.22}$$

Equation (A2.22) says that the value of the firm at time t is equal to the *expected* value of the firm at some future time $t+\Delta t$, discounted back to time t at the yield on (riskless) U.S. Treasury debt. This valuation is appropriate if market participants are indifferent to risk,[19] so the drift rate $R_{\text{f}} - \tfrac{1}{2}\sigma^2$ is called a risk neutral drift rate.

An Alternative Characterization Using Risk Neutral Probabilities

We indicated in note 11 to this chapter that the price of a contingent claim can be computed using risk neutral transition probabilities in lieu of objective probabilities in a binomial random walk approximation to the Gaussian model of equation (1.14). These probabilities can also be used to justify the identification of $R_{\text{f}} - \tfrac{1}{2}\sigma^2$ as a risk neutral drift rate.

Recall from the binomial model that if the value of the firm at time t_k is $W_{j,k}$, then the value of the firm at time t_{k+1} will be either $W_{j+1,k+1}$ or $W_{j,k+1}$. Let $\tilde{p}$ denote the probability that the value of the firm evolves from $W_{j,k}$ to $W_{j+1,k+1}$ when market participants are indifferent to risk. The expectation (at time t_k when the value of the firm is $W_{j,k}$) of the value of the firm at time t_{k+1} is then $\tilde{p} \cdot W_{j+1,k+1} + (1 - \tilde{p}) \cdot W_{j,k+1}$. Since, when market participants are indifferent to risk, the value of the firm at time t_k must be equal to the expectation of the value of the firm at time t_{k+1}, discounted back to time t_k at the Treasury yield R_{f}, we must have

$$W_{j,k} = [\tilde{p} \cdot W_{j+1,k+1} + (1 - \tilde{p}) \cdot W_{j,k+1}] \cdot e^{-R_{\text{f}} \cdot \Delta t} \tag{A2.23}$$

and the risk neutral probability $\tilde{p}$ must be

$$\tilde{p} = \frac{W_{j,k} \cdot e^{R_{\text{f}} \cdot \Delta t} - W_{j,k+1}}{W_{j+1,k+1} - W_{j,k+1}} \tag{A2.24}$$

or since $W_{j+1,k+1} = W_{j,k} \cdot \exp[\mu \cdot \Delta t + \sigma \cdot \Delta t^{1/2}]$ and $W_{j,k+1} = W_{j,k} \cdot \exp[\mu \cdot \Delta t - \sigma \cdot \Delta t^{1/2}]$,

19. Cox and Ross (1976, pp. 153–54), Cox, Ross, and Rubinstein (1979, p. 235), and Cox and Rubinstein (1985, p. 174).

$$\tilde{p} = \frac{e^{(R_f - \mu) \cdot \Delta t} - e^{-\sigma \cdot \Delta t^{1/2}}}{e^{\sigma \cdot \Delta t^{1/2}} - e^{-\sigma \cdot \Delta t^{1/2}}} \tag{A2.25}$$

The drift rate, or expected change per annum, of the log of the value of the firm, computed with the risk neutral probabilities $\tilde{p}$ and $1 - \tilde{p}$, is

$$\frac{\tilde{p} \cdot (\ln[W_{j+1,k+1}] - \ln[W_{j,k}]) + (1 - \tilde{p}) \cdot (\ln[W_{j,k+1}] - \ln[W_{j,k}])}{\Delta t}$$

$$= \frac{\tilde{p} \cdot (\mu \cdot \Delta t + \sigma \cdot \Delta t^{1/2}) + (1 - \tilde{p}) \cdot (\mu \cdot \Delta t - \sigma \cdot \Delta t^{1/2})}{\Delta t}$$

$$= \frac{\mu \cdot \Delta t + (2 \cdot \tilde{p} - 1) \cdot \sigma \cdot \Delta t^{1/2}}{\Delta t}$$

It can be shown that to a first-order approximation in Δt, $(2 \cdot \tilde{p} - 1) \cdot \sigma \cdot \Delta t^{1/2} = (R_f - \mu - \frac{1}{2}\sigma^2) \cdot \Delta t$, so the drift rate (computed with the risk neutral probabilities) converges to $R_f - \frac{1}{2}\sigma^2$ as Δt goes to zero. This justifies the identification of $R_f - \frac{1}{2}\sigma^2$ as a risk neutral drift rate.

3 Senior and Subordinated Debt

Corporations sometimes issue debt of different priorities, designating some of their debt as "senior" and other debt as "subordinated." All of a corporation's debt is comparable in the sense that the issuer is obligated to make all of its contractually promised payments to creditors: failure to make any promised payment is an event of default. However, if a company is unable to make a promised payment, and consequently files for bankruptcy, senior creditors stand in front of subordinated creditors as well as shareholders when the proceeds of liquidation (or the securities of a recapitalization) are distributed. This priority in bankruptcy makes senior debt more valuable than otherwise comparable subordinated debt prior to bankruptcy.[1] This chapter describes how seniority and subordination can be incorporated into a contingent value model.[2]

3.1 Framework of the Analysis

We begin by describing the institutional setting of the valuation problem, including our assumptions regarding the capital structure of the firm and the consequences of default and bankruptcy.

Corporate Capital Structure

We assume that the firm is capitalized with three classes of securities: a senior issue of zero-coupon debt, a subordinated issue of zero-coupon debt, and common stock. The senior debt matures at time T and promises to pay its aggregate face amount F_1 at that time. The subordinated debt also matures at time T and promises to pay face amount F_2.[3] The common stock cannot pay a dividend and cannot be repurchased by the firm until the firm has redeemed all of its debt.

We denote the value of the senior debt at time t as $V_1(t)$, the value of the subordinated debt as $V_2(t)$, and the value of equity as $V_3(t)$.[4] The value of the firm is the sum of the values of the firm's securities: $W(t) = V_1(t) + V_2(t) + V_3(t)$.

---

1. Roberts and Viscione (1984) examine the empirical characteristics of the market value of senior debt relative to subordinated debt.

2. Black and Cox (1976) provided the first extensive analysis of the problem of valuing debt of different priorities.

3. Chapter 11 examines the problem of valuing senior and subordinated debt that matures at different times.

4. The index numbers for the securities follow the convention (see section 2.1) of denoting a more senior security with a lower index number.

Default and Bankruptcy

At time T creditors have a claim on the firm for payment of the total face amount of the debt: $F_1 + F_2$. The firm goes into bankruptcy if it defaults on this contractual obligation.

We assume that bankruptcy results in an instantaneous and costless liquidation of the assets of the firm (piecemeal, in bulk, or as a going concern) and distribution of the proceeds according to the absolute priority rule.[5] Senior creditors receive all of the proceeds of the liquidation up to the amount F_1. Remaining proceeds are distributed to subordinated creditors up to the amount F_2. Stockholders are residual claimants and receive the balance (if any) of the proceeds of the liquidation.

The Contingent Value of the Debt and Equity at Time T

In view of our assumptions regarding default and bankruptcy, we can specify how the value of the firm will be apportioned among senior creditors, junior creditors and stockholders when the debt matures at time T.

If the value of the firm exceeds $F_1 + F_2$, the firm can redeem its debt as promised. Redemption can follow voluntary liquidation of the firm and distribution of the amount F_1 to senior creditors, F_2 to subordinated creditors, and the balance of the proceeds, $W(T) - F_1 - F_2$, to stockholders. Alternatively, the firm can issue new securities (worth a total of $F_1 + F_2$) to finance the redemption, leaving the original shareholders holding equity worth $W(T) - F_1 - F_2$.

If the value of the firm at time T is less than $F_1 + F_2$, the firm will be unable to redeem its debt as promised and its stock will be worthless. The value of the senior debt and the value of the subordinated debt will depend on whether $W(T)$ is less or greater than F_1. If $W(T)$ is less than F_1, senior creditors receive all of the proceeds of the bankruptcy liquidation and junior creditors get nothing. If $W(T)$ is greater than F_1, senior creditors will be paid in full and junior creditors will receive the balance of the proceeds of the liquidation: $W(T) - F_1$.

The foregoing observations on the contingent value of the company's debt and equity at time T can be summarized in tabular form as

---

5. The analysis would be identical if we assumed the bankrupt firm is instantaneously and costlessly recapitalized and that the new securities issued by the recapitalized enterprise are distributed to the old claimants according to the absolute priority rule.

	$W(T) < F_1$	$F_1 \leq W(T) < F_1 + F_2$	$F_1 + F_2 \leq W(T)$
$V_1(T)$	$W(T)$	F_1	F_1
$V_2(T)$	0	$W(T) - F_1$	F_2
$V_3(T)$	0	0	$W(T) - F_1 - F_2$

Figure 3.1 shows a graphical representation of the contingent security values. The contingent value of the debt and equity at time T can be represented algebraically as

$$V_1(T) = \begin{cases} W(T) & \text{if } W(T) < F_1 \\ F_1 & \text{if } F_1 \leq W(T) \end{cases} \tag{3.1a}$$

$$V_2(T) = \begin{cases} 0 & \text{if } W(T) < F_1 \\ W(T) - F_1 & \text{if } F_1 \leq W(T) < F_1 + F_2 \\ F_2 & \text{if } F_1 + F_2 \leq W(T) \end{cases} \tag{3.1b}$$

$$V_3(T) = \begin{cases} 0 & \text{if } W(T) < F_1 + F_2 \\ W(T) - F_1 - F_2 & \text{if } F_1 + F_2 \leq W(T) \end{cases} \tag{3.1c}$$

or as

$$V_1(T) = \min[W(T), F_1] \tag{3.2a}$$

$$V_2(T) = \min[\max[0, W(T) - F_1], F_2] \tag{3.2b}$$

$$V_3(T) = \max[0, W(T) - F_1 - F_2] \tag{3.2c}$$

The Option Positions of Stockholders, Junior Creditors, and Senior Creditors

When we examined (in the preceding chapter) the debt and equity of a firm capitalized with common stock and a single issue of zero-coupon debt, we observed that stockholders have a call option on the firm with an exercise price equal to the face amount of the debt and an expiration date equal to the maturity date of the debt, and that creditors are in the economic position of being long the firm and short the call option held by stockholders. It is instructive to examine the option positions of security holders in the more complicated case of a firm capitalized with common stock and *two* classes of zero-coupon debt, one senior to the other.

The lower panel of figure 3.1 suggests that stockholders have a call option on the firm that expires at time T with an exercise price equal to the total contractual obligation to creditors, or $F_1 + F_2$. The upper panel of the same figure suggests that senior creditors are in the economic

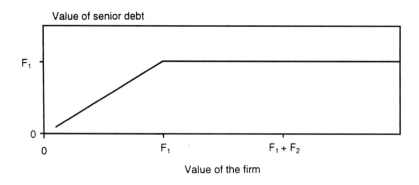

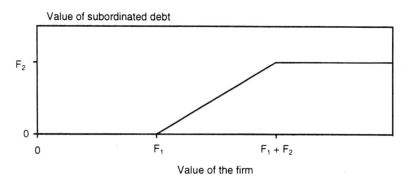

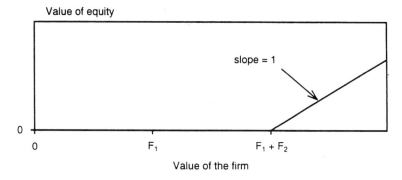

Figure 3.1
Contingent value of senior debt, subordinated debt, and equity at time T

position of being long the firm and short a call option on the firm with exercise price F_1 expiring at time T.

The puzzling feature of these characterizations is that stockholders are long an option with a strike price of $F_1 + F_2$, while senior creditors are short an option with a strike price of F_1, so the stockholders are long a different option than the option written by senior creditors. This raises two questions: Who holds the option written by the senior creditors? And who wrote the option held by the stockholders?

The answer to both questions is the subordinated creditors. Those creditors are long a call option on the firm with an exercise price of F_1 because they can acquire control of the firm by paying senior creditors the full amount (F_1) of their claims. However, the subordinated creditors are also short a call option on the firm with an exercise price of $F_1 + F_2$ because stockholders can acquire control of the firm from the subordinated creditors by paying $F_1 + F_2$ to those creditors. If the stockholders choose to exercise their option, subordinated creditors will be left with the difference between what they were paid by the stockholders, $F_1 + F_2$, and what they paid to senior creditors (F_1), or F_2—which is exactly the face amount of the debt held by the junior creditors.[6]

3.2   The Valuation Problem

We assume that there exists a set of three functions, f_1, f_2, and f_3, with two arguments: time and the value of the firm, such that the value of the ith security at time t can be calculated as

$$V_i(t) = f_i(W(t), t), \qquad i = 1, 2, 3 \tag{3.3}$$

The valuation problem is to identify the forms of these contingent value functions.

3.3   Solving the Valuation Problem

We already know the forms of the contingent value functions at time T from equations (3.2a, b, c):

$$f_1(W, T) = \min[W, F_1] \tag{3.4a}$$

$$f_2(W, T) = \min[\max[0, W - F_1], F_2] \tag{3.4b}$$

---

6. The subordinated creditors are long a "bull spread," or long a call option with a lower strike price and short a call option on the same underlying asset with a higher strike price.

$$f_3(W, T) = \max[0, W - F_1 - F_2] \tag{3.4c}$$

This section describes an algorithm for computing, for any positive value of W^*, the value of $f_i(W^*, t^*)$ for any value of t^* less than T. This is tantamount to completing the identification of the form of f_i.

As in section 2.4 we approximate the dynamic evolution of the value of the firm with a binomial random walk in discrete time. Dividing the interval between t^* and T into K subintervals of length Δt ($\Delta t = (T - t^*)/K$) and defining a sequence of $K + 1$ discrete points in time:

$$t_k = t^* + (k - 1) \cdot \Delta t, \qquad k = 1, 2, \ldots, K + 1 \tag{3.5}$$

we construct an array $W_{j,k}$ for $j = 1, 2, \ldots, k$ and $k = 1, 2, \ldots, K + 1$, where the natural logarithm of $W_{j,k}$ is defined as

$$\ln[W_{j,k}] = \ln[W^*] + (k - 1) \cdot \mu \cdot \Delta t + (2 \cdot j - k - 1) \cdot \sigma \cdot \Delta t^{1/2},$$

$$j = 1, 2, \ldots, k; \ k = 1, 2, \ldots, K + 1 \tag{3.6}$$

The value of the firm is $W_{1,1} = W^*$ at time $t_1 = t^*$ and subsequently evolves through the $W_{j,k}$ array. If the value of the firm is $W_{j,k}$ at time t_k, then the value of the firm at time t_{k+1} will be either $W_{j+1,k+1}$ or $W_{j,k+1}$.

Let $V_{j,k,i}$ denote the value of the ith security at time t_k when the value of the firm is $W_{j,k}$:

$$V_{j,k,i} = f_i(W_{j,k}, t_k) \tag{3.7}$$

We compute the $V_{j,k,i}$ terms using a recursion algorithm on k, beginning at $k = K + 1$ and proceeding backwards to $k = 1$.

Constructing the $V_{j,k,i}$ Terms for $k = K + 1$

The values of $V_{j,K+1,i}$ for $j = 1, 2, \ldots, K + 1$ follow from our discussion of the consequences of default and bankruptcy at time T.

If the value of the firm at time $T = t_{K+1}$ is less than F_1, the firm will default and senior creditors will receive the full bankruptcy distribution. If the value of the firm at time t_{K+1} exceeds F_1, senior creditors will be paid F_1. This implies that

$$V_{j,K+1,1} = \begin{cases} W_{j,K+1} & \text{if } W_{j,K+1} < F_1 \\ F_1 & \text{if } F_1 \le W_{j,K+1} \end{cases} \tag{3.8}$$

If the value of the firm is less than F_1 at time t_{K+1}, the firm will default and subordinated creditors will receive nothing. If the value of the firm exceeds F_1 but is less than $F_1 + F_2$, the firm will default and subordinated creditors will receive whatever remains after the senior creditors have been paid in full. If the value of the firm exceeds $F_1 + F_2$, subordinated creditors will be paid in full. Thus we also have

$$V_{j,K+1,2} = \begin{cases} 0 & \text{if } W_{j,K+1} < F_1 \\ W_{j,K+1} - F_1 & \text{if } F_1 \le W_{j,K+1} < F_1 + F_2 \\ F_2 & \text{if } F_1 + F_2 \le W_{j,K+1} \end{cases} \qquad (3.9)$$

Stockholders are residual claimants, so

$$V_{j,K+1,3} = \begin{cases} 0 & \text{if } W_{j,K+1} < F_1 + F_2 \\ W_{j,K+1} - F_1 - F_2 & \text{if } F_1 + F_2 \le W_{j,K+1} \end{cases} \qquad (3.10)$$

Equations (3.8), (3.9), and (3.10) are the discrete time—discrete state analogues of the terminal conditions in equations (3.1a, b, c).

Calculating the $V_{j,k,i}$ Terms for $k < K + 1$

Consider now the problem of computing $V_{j,k,i}$ for some value of k less than $K + 1$, assuming that we know the values of $V_{j,k+1,i}$ for $j = 1, 2, \ldots,$ $k + 1$.

$V_{j,k,i}$ is the value of the ith security at time t_k when the value of the firm is $W_{j,k}$ (see equation 3.7). Over the subinterval from t_k to t_{k+1} the value of the firm will evolve to either

1. $W_{j+1,k+1}$, where the ith security will be worth $V_{j+1,k+1,i}$, or
2. $W_{j,k+1}$, where the ith security will be worth $V_{j,k+1,i}$.

Assuming that the markets do not allow opportunities for riskless arbitrage profits, we have[7]

$$V_{j,k,i} = h \cdot W_{j,k} + Q \qquad (3.11)$$

where h and Q satisfy the equations

$$V_{j+1,k+1,i} = h \cdot W_{j+1,k+1} + Q \cdot e^{R_f \cdot \Delta t} \qquad (3.12a)$$

$$V_{j,k+1,i} = h \cdot W_{j,k+1} + Q \cdot e^{R_f \cdot \Delta t} \qquad (3.12b)$$

The foregoing algorithm can be applied recursively, beginning at $k = K$ and continuing through the computation of $V_{1,1,i}$. Since $V_{1,1,i} = f_i(W_{1,1}, t_1) = f_i(W^*, t^*)$, this completes the computation of $f_i(W^*, t^*)$

---

7. See the discussion at equations (2.24a, b) to (2.26) in chapter 2. The validity of equation (3.11) hinges on the assumption that we can replicate a corporate security with a portfolio of Treasury debt and the firm as a whole, and hence on the assumption that each of the three securities that capitalize the firm is publicly traded.

for the case where the value of the firm evolves according to the discrete time binomial process.[8]

Convergence of the Value of $V_{1,1,i}$ as Δt Goes to Zero

As the value of K defined in the text preceding equation (3.5) grows large and Δt goes to zero, the discrete time binomial random walk converges to the continuous time Gaussian process of equation (1.14) and the value of $V_{1,1,i}$ converges to the value of $f_i(W^*, t^*)$ for the case where the value of the firm evolves according to that Gaussian process.

Comment

The only time the seniority or subordination of a security appears in the foregoing algorithm is in the specification of the terminal conditions, where we identify the priority of senior creditors over subordinated creditors, as well as the priority of both classes of creditors over stockholders. The terminal conditions—and hence contingent security values prior to time T—will be different if senior creditors do not have absolute priority over subordinated creditors, such as if subordinated creditors receive something even when senior creditors are not paid in full.

3.4   Some Examples

At this point it will be helpful to examine some examples of the problem of valuing senior and subordinated debt. We assume the U.S. Treasury yield curve is flat and stationary at $R_f = 0.10$ (or 10% per annum) and that the volatility of the value of the firm is $\sigma = 0.20$ (or a volatility of 20% over one year).[9]

Example A

The first example assumes that the face amount of each class of zero-coupon debt is 82.436 (so that $F_1 = F_2 = 82.436$) and that we are valuing the debt five years prior to maturity (so $T - t^* = 5.0$ years). Ignoring the risk of default, each class of debt has a default free value of 50.0 (50.0 =

---

8. It is not difficult to show, by an argument virtually identical to appendix B to chapter 2, that the algorithm leads to contingent security values that satisfy the adding-up constraint $W = f_1(W, t) + f_2(W, t) + f_3(W, t)$ for all positive values of W and for all times t prior to T. The only significant change is to observe that equation (A2.7), generalized to the three security case of $W_{j,k} = V_{j,k,1} + V_{j,k,2} + V_{j,k,3}$, is true for $k = K + 1$ and $j \in \{1, 2, \ldots, K+1\}$ by the terminal conditions of equations (3.8), (3.9), and (3.10).

9. The contingent values of the corporation's securities are independent of the drift rate μ for the reason identified in appendix C to chapter 2.

82.436 discounted for five years at the 10% per annum yield on Treasury debt).

Consequences of Seniority and Subordination

Figure 3.2 shows with solid lines the contingent value of the senior debt (upper panel) and subordinated debt (lower panel). The broken lines show how the obligations would be valued if they had the same priority in bankruptcy, that is, if each ranked pari passu with respect to the other.[10] The lower priority of the subordinated debt *in the event of bankruptcy* reduces the contingent value of that debt *prior* to bankruptcy and enhances the contingent value of the senior debt. Seniority and subordination is, therefore, a bankruptcy concept that affects debt values well before the debt matures.

The Contingent Value of the Senior Debt

The contingent value of the senior debt is similar to the contingent value of the debt in example A of section 2.6. (Compare the upper panel of figure 3.2 with the upper panel of figure 2.11.). When the value of the firm is less than 25, the value of the senior debt is comparable to the value of the firm. In this case default is virtually certain (assuming the rate neutral drift rate), and subordinated creditors and stockholders are unlikely to receive anything following bankruptcy. Clearly, owning the senior debt is economically equivalent to owning the firm. At the other extreme, when the value of the firm exceeds 125, the senior creditors are virtually certain to receive F_1 regardless of whether or not the firm defaults. Here the value of the senior debt is comparable to the default-free value of that debt. Between these two extremes the value of the senior debt increases at a decreasing rate and the contingent value function is concave to the horizontal axis.

The Contingent Value of the Subordinated Debt

The contingent value of the subordinated debt in the lower panel of figure 3.2 is distinctly different from the contingent value of the senior debt.

---

10. If the two obligations rank pari passu with respect to each other, creditors share the proceeds of any bankruptcy liquidation in proportion to their claims. The terminal conditions in equations (3.8) and (3.9) become

$$V_{j,K+1,i} = \begin{cases} \dfrac{F_i}{F_1 + F_2} \cdot W_{j,K+1} & \text{if } W_{j,K+1} < F_1 + F_2 \\ F_i & \text{if } F_1 + F_2 \le W_{j,K+1} \end{cases}$$

for $i = 1$ and 2.

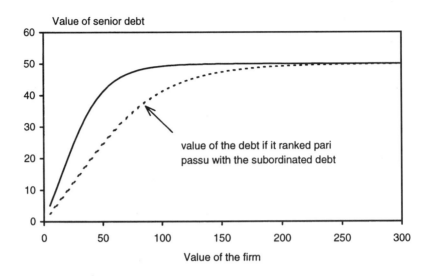

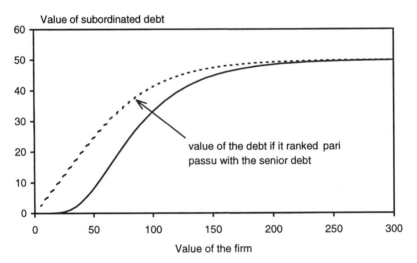

Figure 3.2
Contingent value of senior and subordinated debt five years before the debt matures

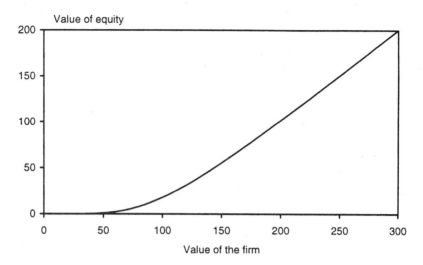

Figure 3.3
Contingent value of equity five years before the debt matures

When the value of the firm is below 25, the value of the subordinated debt is negligible and insensitive to changes in the value of the firm. This reflects the virtual certainty of default and the remote prospect that subordinated creditors will receive any of the proceeds of liquidation following bankruptcy.

As the value of the firm begins to rise above 25, default initially remains a virtual certainty, but it becomes increasingly likely that the subordinated creditors will receive some of the proceeds of the bankruptcy liquidation. As a result the value of the subordinated debt starts to rise. The value of that debt rises at an increasing rate, and the contingent value function becomes convex to the horizontal axis.

However, the value of the subordinated debt can never exceed its default-free value of 50.0 because the subordinated debt can never be more valuable than zero-coupon Treasury debt that promises to pay 82.436 in five years. After the value of the firm grows beyond about 70, the rate of increase of the value of the subordinated debt slows, and the contingent value function becomes concave to the horizontal axis.

The Contingent Value of Equity

Figure 3.3 shows the contingent value of equity. A comparison of the data used to graph figure 3.3 with the data used to graph the lower panel of figure 2.11 shows that the contingent value of equity does not depend on whether the firm is capitalized with (1) a single issue of zero coupon debt that promises to pay 164.872 in five years, or (2) a pair of issues of zero-

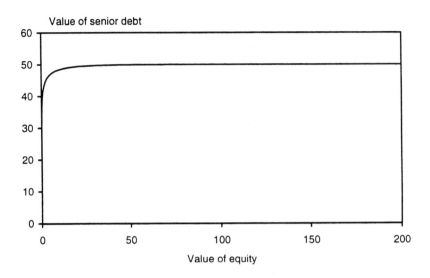

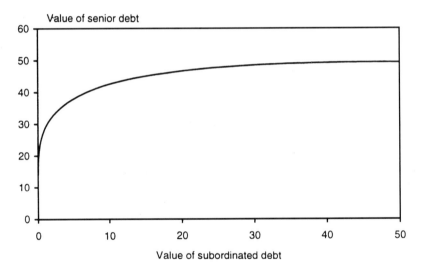

Figure 3.4
Value of senior debt five years before maturity as a function of the value of equity and as a
function of the value of subordinated debt

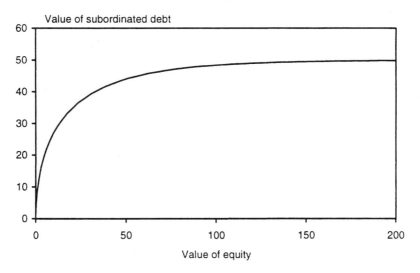

Figure 3.5
Value of subordinated debt five years before maturity as a function of the value of equity

coupon debt, one senior to the other and each promising to pay 82.436 in five years. More generally, the contingent value of equity is invariant with respect to the relative priorities of more senior claims.[11]

Cross Valuation and Hedging

The upper panel of figure 3.4 shows the value of the senior debt as a function of the value of equity. The presence of subordinated debt in the capital structure of the firm means that a negligible equity value is associated with a wide range of values for the senior debt, or that the cross-value function is very nearly vertical at equity values close to zero. This makes it difficult to impute the value of the senior debt from observed equity values when the senior debt bears material credit risk, as well as practically impossible to hedge the credit risk on the senior debt by selling the stock short.

The lower panel of figure 3.4 shows the value of the senior debt as a function of the value of the subordinated debt. The more moderate slope of the cross-value schedule suggests that we can cross-value and hedge the senior debt with the subordinated debt.

Finally, figure 3.5 shows the value of the subordinated debt as a function of the value of equity. Equity can be used to cross-value and hedge

11. Similarly, the contingent value of the senior debt is invariant with respect to the relative priorities of more junior claims.

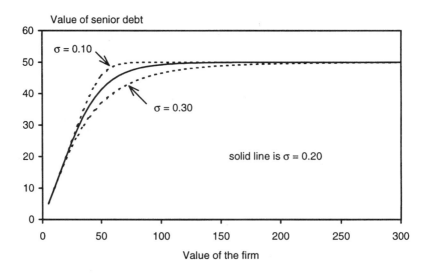

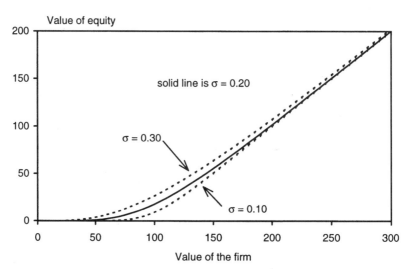

Figure 3.6
Contingent value of senior debt and equity for various volatilities of the value of the firm

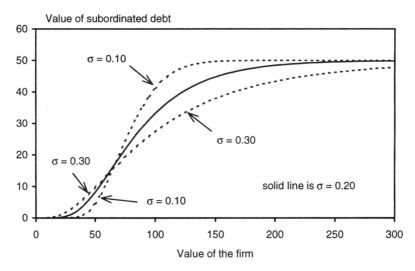

Figure 3.7
Contingent value of subordinated debt for various volatilities of the value of the firm

subordinated debt even if it cannot be used to cross-value and hedge senior debt.

Example B

The second example is similar to example A except that we here consider the effect of varying the volatility of the value of the firm. The debt remains as before: a senior issue that promises to pay 82.436 in five years and a subordinated issue that also promises to pay 82.436 in five years.

The two panels in figure 3.6 show that ceteris paribus, the contingent value of the senior debt is inversely related to the volatility of the value of the firm and that the contingent value of equity is directly related to volatility. These results parallel the results from example C in section 2.6.

Since subordinated debt lies between equity and senior debt in terms of priority, one might conjecture that the relationship between the contingent value of the subordinated debt and the volatility of the value of the firm should lie between the relationships illustrated in figure 3.6: perhaps a moderate to negligible positive or negative function of volatility. However, figure 3.7 shows that the contingent value of the subordinated debt is *not* monotonically related to the volatility of the value of the firm. If the value of the firm is above 70, the contingent value of the subordinated debt falls when volatility rises. However, at lower values of the firm the contingent value of the subordinated debt is *directly* related to volatility.

A little reflection reveals why the effect of volatility on the contingent value of the subordinated debt changes sign as the value of the firm rises.

When the value of the firm is low, subordinated creditors benefit from greater uncertainty about the value of the firm at time T because the subordinated debt captures all of the benefits of any excess in the value of the firm above F_1 (up to the limit of $F_1 + F_2$) and bears none of the costs of a shortfall below F_1. However, as the value of the firm increases, the likelihood that $W(T)$ will be less than F_1 declines and ultimately falls below the rising probability that $W(T)$ will exceed $F_1 + F_2$. Greater volatility then begins to reduce the contingent value of the subordinated debt because that debt then bears the burden of any shortfall of $W(T)$ below $F_1 + F_2$ (down to the limit of F_1) and receives none of the benefits of an excess of $W(T)$ over $F_1 + F_2$.[12]

12. Another way to characterize the effect of volatility on the contingent value of the subordinated debt is to observe that (a) greater volatility *enhances* the value of the subordinated debt when the value of that debt is a *convex* function of the value of the firm, at values of the firm below 70, and that (b) greater volatility *reduces* the value of the subordinated debt when the value of that debt is a *concave* function of the value of the firm, at values of the firm above 70.

4 Institutional and Empirical Characteristics of Bankruptcy

The analyses in chapters 2 and 3 illustrate the importance of bankruptcy for the contingent value of corporate securities.[1] In both chapters we assumed that bankruptcy is instantaneous, costless, and results in distributions (of cash or securities) in accord with the absolute priority rule. It is important to examine the validity of these assumptions, because the market prices of corporate securities may differ from model values if the assumptions are violated in practice.

This chapter describes the institutional and empirical characteristics of corporate bankruptcy in the United States.[2] We begin in section 4.1 with a brief exposition of the economic justification for bankruptcy. The following four sections review some important practical aspects of American bankruptcy procedure, and section 4.6 summarizes the empirical characteristics of large corporate bankruptcies. An appendix discusses the related topic of private recapitalizations.

4.1 The Economic Justification for Bankruptcy

Bankruptcy has been described[3] as "a collective forum for sorting out the rights of the various claimants against the assets of a debtor where there are not enough assets to go around." Understanding the justification for such a forum will provide a conceptual framework for examining American bankruptcy procedure.

Consider a firm capitalized with common stock and various classes of debt, including trade credit, commercial paper, bank debt, privately placed debt, and publicly traded bonds. Except for short maturity items like trade credit and commercial paper, the debt of the firm contains covenants, or promises; their breach gives creditors the right to accelerate the maturities of their loans. ("Acceleration" means that the principal amount of a loan becomes immediately due and payable, reflecting the decision of creditors to exercise their right to demand the return of their

---

1. The importance of bankruptcy is particularly evident in the case (examined in example A in section 3.4) of a firm capitalized with senior and subordinated zero-coupon bonds maturing on the same future date and promising to pay the same face amount, where the two bonds have different values only because they have different priorities in bankruptcy.

2. The chapter draws extensively from Epstein, Nickles, and White (1993) and has benefited from survey articles by John and John (1992) and John (1993). See also Wruck (1990). Foreign bankruptcy codes are described in Franks and Torous (1992), Kaiser (1996), and Franks, Nyborg, and Torous (1996). Bebchuk and Guzman (1999) discuss transnational bankruptcies.

3. Epstein, Nickles, and White (1993, p. 2), citing Radin (1940).

money when the firm is not behaving as it promised when the money was originally contributed.[4])

Acceleration of maturity following breach of a covenant will usually trigger acceleration of other indebtedness of the firm. These secondary accelerations occur because loan agreements and bond indentures frequently also contain "cross-acceleration" clauses. The clauses ensure that some creditors are not left behind when other creditors are accelerating, or liable to accelerate, their loans.[5]

In the absence of any bankruptcy process and assuming, as is almost always the case, that the firm cannot satisfy the cascading demands of its creditors for repayment, individual creditors, acting under state debt collection law, will seek judgment liens to recover on their claims with the proceeds from judicially mandated sales—commonly called foreclosure sales—of the firm's assets.[6] Their actions can quickly lead to the dismemberment and piecemeal liquidation of the enterprise. Creditors who act promptly may recover on substantially all of their claims; slower creditors will be left with unsatisfied claims and no recourse.

The Social Costs of Relying Exclusively on State Debt Collection Law and an Alternative Legal Structure

There are two widely recognized social costs associated with leaving the creditors of an insolvent enterprise relying exclusively on state debt collection law.[7]

First, piecemeal liquidation imposes a net loss on society if a company has greater value as a going concern. Sale of the company as a going concern, rather than piece by piece, would raise enough money to pay

---

4. For example, the firm may have promised to pay interest periodically, to reduce the principal amount of its indebtedness according to some sinking fund schedule, and to maintain the aggregate value of its assets above some specified level. The significance of a breach of a promise to pay interest and to repay principal is obvious. Black and Cox (1976, p. 357) observe that a covenant to maintain the value of assets above a specified level protects creditors at times when the managers of the firm have a substantial incentive to take actions favorable to stockholders and adverse to the interests of creditors. Such actions include, for example, increasing the volatility of the aggregate value of the firm when the value of the firm has declined and its stock has *de minimis* value. (See example C in section 2.6.)

5. Wruck (1991, p. 87) describes how the decision of one group of bondholders to accelerate the maturity of their bonds triggered acceleration of all of the debt of Revco D. S., Inc. in 1988.

6. Baird and Jackson (1990, pp. 4–10) and LoPucki (1982, pp. 316–19).

7. See LoPucki (1982), Jackson (1986, pp. 7–19) and White (1989, 1994).

everything that individual creditors can recover by their own efforts and still leave something for other unsatisfied claimants.[8]

Second, since creditors who act quickly are likely to recover on a larger fraction of their claims, individual creditors will devote valuable resources to a race that has no social benefit. (White 1989, p. 130, characterizes the race as "costly and unproductive.") The race determines *which* creditors get paid but has little bearing on how much creditors are paid *in aggregate*. The resources devoted to the race include the costs of monitoring the performance of firms close to insolvency (so a creditor can assess when the race is likely to begin), as well as the costs of seeking to encumber (as quickly as possible) the assets of an insolvent firm.

The social costs of relying exclusively on state debt collection law suggests that any alternative or supplementary insolvency procedure should have two characteristics. First, it should reduce or eliminate the incentive for creditors to devote valuable resources to a race for recovery on their individual claims, without thereby reducing what the creditors recover in aggregate. Second, it should maintain an insolvent company as a going concern when piecemeal liquidation would lead to a loss of value. A legal structure with these characteristics is commonly called a "bankruptcy" process. The key attribute of a bankruptcy process is the substitution of *collective* remedies for *individual* remedies when a debtor with multiple creditors becomes insolvent.

4.2 An Overview of Bankruptcy

All bankruptcies filed in the United States since October 1, 1979, are governed by the provisions of the federal Bankruptcy Reform Act of 1978, commonly known as "the Code" (to distinguish it from the previously effective provisions of the Bankruptcy Act of 1898, commonly known as "the Act"). This section sketches the broad provisions of the Code in cases of corporate bankruptcy.

Bankruptcy petitions, or requests to initiate a bankruptcy process, are almost always filed by debtors and when so filed are called "voluntary"

---

8. Railroads have provided the classic example of this phenomenon for 150 years. See Baird and Jackson (1990, pp. 959–66) and *Macon & Western Railroad Co. v. Parker*, 9 Ga. 377 (1851) (discussed in Coogan 1982, pp. 304 and 307). In an era of low leverage, default is typically associated with companies in contracting industries with little or no excess of going concern value over piecemeal liquidation value, where dismemberment is likely to be a socially efficient resolution of insolvency. Jensen (1989, 1991) suggested that the high leverage associated with LBOs and leveraged recapitalizations in the 1980s meant that firms with a substantial excess of going concern value over piecemeal liquidation value would be more likely to default on their debt than was previously the case, making the potential loss of the excess more important than previously.

petitions.[9] A bankruptcy petition is filed in a federal judicial district and the resulting case is supervised by a federal bankruptcy judge and/or district court judge.[10]

The Code has two principle provisions for corporate bankruptcy:

• Chapter 7—which generally provides for liquidation of the assets of the debtor and distribution of the proceeds to creditors (and possibly stockholders), and

• Chapter 11—which generally provides for maintenance of the debtor as a going concern, recapitalization of the debtor, and distribution of the securities of the recapitalized company to creditors (and possibly stockholders).

Large corporations almost always choose to file for reorganization under Chapter 11. Small companies more commonly file for liquidation under Chapter 7. Midsize companies frequently file for reorganization, but many end up in liquidation.[11]

The Framework of a Chapter 7 Case

One of the most important features of Chapter 7 is its provisions for satisfying claims on a bankrupt debtor.

Upon initiation of a Chapter 7 case, the supervising court appoints a trustee to collect and sell the assets of the debtor and to distribute the proceeds to creditors and other claimants. The most senior claimants are secured creditors, or creditors who have a direct security interest in specified property of the debtor. A secured creditor will receive his or her collateral property if (1) the market value of the property does not exceed the creditor's claim and if (2) separation of the property from the balance of the debtor's assets does not reduce the value of the other assets. In other cases the collateral property is sold by the trustee and the secured

9. The Code also provides for "involuntary" petitions filed by creditors against a debtor, but such petitions are rare. White (1994, p. E7-4) suggests that creditors "can do better for themselves by bargaining individually with the firm's managers for better treatment of their claims in return for not initiating bankruptcy." LoPucki (1982, p. 369) observes that "the economic interests of the diligent individual creditor currently are served best by ... state remedies...." See also LoPucki (1982, pp. 352–59). Baird (1991) discusses some of the public policy issues associated with designating who can initiate a bankruptcy case.

10. Large corporations have substantial discretion about the choice of a district in which to file. Weiss (1990) and LoPucki and Whitford (1991a) have examined the factors that can affect their choice. See also Betker (1995a).

11. The economic incentive of a firm to choose between filing for liquidation in Chapter 7 and reorganization in Chapter 11 has been addressed by White (1983, 1989, 1994) and Gertner and Scharfstein (1991).

creditor receives a cash payment equal to the lesser of (1) the creditor's claim and (2) the proceeds from the sale of the property (if the property was sold as an individual item) or the appraised value of the property (if the property was bundled together with other assets of the debtor). Any residual proceeds from the sale of the property remain with the trustee for distribution to other claimants. If the claim of a secured creditor exceeds the value of the property or cash payment he or she receives, the excess is treated as an unsecured claim on the debtor.

The next most senior claims are administrative expenses—defined as the actual, necessary costs of preserving the debtor's assets, including wages, salaries, and commissions for services rendered after filing for bankruptcy. The high priority accorded administrative expenses ensures that the trustee and his or her agents will be paid for their efforts. Administrative expenses are followed by "priority" claims specified in the Code, including taxes and employee wages earned but not paid prior to filing for bankruptcy.

Any remaining funds are divided among the unsecured creditors and stockholders according to the absolute priority rule. Senior creditors are paid first, followed by subordinated creditors (respecting any priorities among different categories of subordinated creditors). If there are insufficient funds to pay the claims of a particular class in full, the available funds are distributed to class members in proportion to their claims. (This accords with the notion of bankruptcy as a *collective* remedy for insolvency.) Any residual balance that remains after all of the creditors have been paid goes to the shareholders in proportion to their stock holdings.

The Framework of a Chapter 11 Case

There are two major components to a Chapter 11 case: (1) developing a plan of reorganization and (2) operating the debtor between filing for bankruptcy and emergence from bankruptcy pursuant to a judicially confirmed plan of reorganization.

Operating in Chapter 11

In many Chapter 11 cases the debtor is managed by substantially the same board of directors, chief executive officer, and other senior officials who managed the company prior to filing (although there is frequently a change in the identities of some of the managers).[12] This is characterized

---

12. Continuity and replacement of the senior management of a company in Chapter 11 has been examined by LoPucki and Whitford (1993a, b) and Gilson (1989, 1990).

by saying that the debtor is in possession of its own affairs and by labeling the debtor a "debtor in possession," or "DIP."[13]

Developing a Plan of Reorganization

The responsibility for developing a plan of reorganization lies initially with the DIP. The Code gives a DIP the exclusive right to propose a plan for 120 days after filing and allows the supervising court to extend this so-called exclusivity period at its discretion.

Creditor and Stockholder Committees

Upon initiation of a Chapter 11 case, the supervising court appoints a committee to represent the interests of unsecured creditors during the reorganization. The appointees are usually the holders of the seven largest unsecured claims.

Depending on the complexity of a particular case, the court may authorize separate committees to represent different classes of unsecured creditors, such as trade creditors, bank creditors, holders of publicly traded debt, and/or creditors who are also competitors.[14] The court may also authorize a committee to represent the interests of stockholders if it appears that stockholders may receive something of value at the conclusion of the bankruptcy and that their interests may not be represented diligently by the officers and directors of the company.

Creditor and stockholder committees are important participants in a Chapter 11 reorganization. They are empowered to negotiate with the DIP in the course of developing a plan of reorganization, they can make recommendations to their constituencies concerning acceptance or rejection of a proposed plan, and they can investigate the affairs of the debtor. Most important, their representatives can demand to be heard in any judicial proceeding connected with the case. A committee can retain (at the debtor's expense) accountants, attorneys, and other advisors to assist it in carrying out its functions.

The Stay

Regardless of whether a petition for bankruptcy is filed under Chapter 7 or Chapter 11, the first and automatic consequence of filing is "the stay."

13. Nimmer and Feinberg (1989) and Frost (1992) describe the corporate governance of a debtor-in-possession and contrast it with the governance of a solvent firm.

14. A separate committee for unsecured debenture holders was authorized in the McLean Industries bankruptcy (Epstein, Nickles, and White 1993, p. 742), and a separate committee for creditors who were also competitors was authorized in the Texaco bankruptcy (Epstein, Nickles, and White 1993, p. 753). See also the variety of committees noted in Blain and Erne (1984, pp. 498–99).

Immediately upon filing, all payments to prepetition creditors, all fore-closure sales, and all other collection efforts must cease. This requirement applies to *all* parties in *every* bankruptcy *automatically* upon filing.

The stay, a crucial and prominent feature of bankruptcy, serves two important public policy objectives. First, it largely eliminates the incentive for creditors to continue to devote resources to a race for recovery on their individual claims. No creditor can improve his or her position after a filing for bankruptcy has invoked the stay.[15] Second, in a Chapter 11 case the stay blocks the piecemeal liquidation of the debtor that would other-wise occur under state debt collection law and provides time for the DIP to prepare a plan of reorganization. In a Chapter 7 case the stay provides time to identify, collect, and sell the assets of the debtor in an orderly manner.

Preferences and Avoidance

Taken by itself, the stay distinguishes between prepetition and post-petition payments to prepetition creditors. (The former are acceptable; the latter are prohibited.) This might be sufficient if bankruptcy always came as a surprise to market participants. In fact bankruptcy rarely comes with no warning. Provision for the stay, without more, would thus create the moral hazard that creditors might begin to move to protect their interests in *anticipation* of filing by a debtor, and thus precipitate the creditors' race that bankruptcy seeks to avoid.

The Code reduces the incentive for a prepetition race by providing that "preferences" (broadly, transfers of a debtor's property on the eve of bankruptcy to satisfy old debts) can be "avoided," or reversed, by a trustee or DIP. The Code defines a preference as any transfer of any interest of the debtor in property, to or for the benefit of a creditor, made within 90 days before the filing for bankruptcy (or within one year if the creditor is an insider) that enables the creditor to receive more than he or she would receive in a Chapter 7 liquidation.[16]

---

15. Texaco filed for bankruptcy in 1987 in order to continue its litigation with Pennzoil while forestalling the possibility that Pennzoil's unsecured claim for $10.5 billion might be elevated to a secured claim (Mnookin and Wilson 1989, pp. 324–29).

16. Epstein, Nickles, and White (1993, pp. 278–79). Nance (1984, pp. 167n. 6, 175 and 195n. 1) describes the anxiety of commercial bank and insurance company creditors that Braniff International might file for bankruptcy during the 90 days following collateralization of previously unsecured loans with aircraft owned by the financially distressed airline. See, similarly, the description in LoPucki (1982, pp. 337–38) of the collateralization of bank debt a year before the bankruptcy of W.T. Grant. White (1983, 1989, 1994) discusses the effi-ciency losses that may occur when a creditor can be induced to convert a maturing unsecured loan into a secured loan with a longer maturity.

Special Treatment of Property Collateralizing a Secured Loan

The stay can be lifted, as it applies to property collateralizing a secured loan, if it serves no public policy objective, or if

1. sale of the property will not generate proceeds in excess of what is due the secured creditors, *and* if

2. the property does not enhance the recovery of other creditors in a Chapter 7 case and is not necessary to an effective reorganization of the debtor in a Chapter 11 case.

The stay can also be lifted if the value of the collateral property is subject to fluctuation and if the secured creditors cannot be protected against the risk of loss. (Protection is usually accomplished with an equity cushion favoring the secured creditors and by insuring against loss due to fire, flood, etc.)

4.3   Reorganizing in Chapter 11

Chapter 11 advances the public policy objective that a company should continue operating if its value as a going concern exceeds what can be recovered through piecemeal liquidation. Thus, developing a plan of reorganization is one of the two major components of a Chapter 11 case.

Reorganization is primarily a matter of recapitalizing the debtor and distributing the securities of the recapitalized company to the creditors (and possibly the shareholders) of the bankrupt enterprise. This section outlines the principle features of reorganizing in Chapter 11. (The following section outlines the basic features of the other major component of a Chapter 11 case: operating in Chapter 11.)

The Plan

Chapter 11 provides a DIP with the exclusive right to propose a plan of reorganization for 120 days following filing for bankruptcy, and provides further that no other person can propose a plan for an additional 60 days if the DIP proposes a plan within 120 days. These exclusivity periods are commonly extended at the request of a DIP.

A conventional plan of reorganization includes the following:

• A description of the proposed business activities and capital structure of the reorganized company.

• Designation of "classes" of substantially similar creditor claims and equity interests.

• An explanation of what each class would receive in the proposed reorganization.

The classes created by the plan need not be coterminous with the classes used to establish payment priorities in a Chapter 7 liquidation. Unsecured trade creditors, unsecured bank creditors, and holders of senior unsecured debentures may be placed in different classes even if they would be treated identically in Chapter 7.[17] Secured creditors are always placed in distinct classes.[18]

The specifics of a plan of reorganization emerge from private and sometimes lengthy negotiations between the DIP and the creditor and stockholder committees. The negotiations commonly result in a mutually agreeable plan.[19] Less frequently the negotiations may lead a DIP to propose a plan known to be objectionable to some creditors and/or stockholders.

In either case the DIP brings a disclosure document describing the plan before the supervising court for a hearing on whether the document contains information sufficient to enable creditors and stockholders to make an informed judgment about whether to accept the plan. The court may approve the document, or it may request revisions and additional information. Following court approval, the document is distributed to creditors and stockholders for a vote on the plan.

Voting on a Plan

Voting on a plan of reorganization is stratified by the classes specified in the plan. A creditor class accepts the plan if more than one-half of the voting members of the class holding more than two-thirds of the aggregate voting claims of the class vote for approval. A stockholder class accepts the plan if more than two-thirds of the voting shares favor approval. The absence of a requirement for unanimous approval ensures that a recalcitrant minority can not block adoption of a plan that commands widespread support among other class members.

17. Broude (1984, pp. 443–44).

18. If the claim of a secured creditor exceeds the value of the property securing the claim, the excess is allocated to a class of unsecured claims (but see Klee 1979, pp. 152–53, and Broude 1984, pp. 445–48). Thus a secured creditor may be a member of two classes and have a distinct claim within each of the classes. This parallels the treatment of the excess claim of a secured creditor in Chapter 7.

19. LoPucki and Whitford (1990, p. 138) report that plans of reorganization that are ultimately confirmed are unanimously supported by all committees, including the equity committee if one was appointed, in more than 90% of the Chapter 11 cases that they examined.

A class is not permitted to vote on a plan, and is deemed to accept the plan, if the plan leaves the claims of the class "unimpaired."[20] A claim is left unimpaired if the plan provides for cash payment of the claim or if it cures any default in the claim and reinstates the original maturity date of the claim.[21] Conversely, a class is not permitted to vote on a plan, and is deemed to reject the plan, if the plan does not provide for the distribution of anything of value to the members of the class, that is, if it "freezes out" the class.[22]

Confirmation of a Plan Accepted by All Impaired Classes

If a plan is accepted by all of the classes impaired under the plan, the supervising court can confirm the plan if it determines that the plan is

1. "feasible" and

2. in the "best interests" of each *individual* dissenting creditor and stockholder.

The "feasibility" test requires that the court determine that the recapitalized debtor will be economically viable and that confirmation of the plan is not likely to be followed by another bankruptcy.[23] The "best interests" test requires that the court determine that each dissenting creditor and stockholder will receive greater value under the plan than he or she would receive in a Chapter 7 liquidation.

Since a class is deemed to reject a plan if it is frozen out, a plan cannot be accepted by all of the classes that are impaired under the plan if it freezes out *any* class. Thus a consensual plan of reorganization requires, inter alia, that every class, including stockholders, receive something of value.[24]

20. An unimpaired class can not reject a plan by actual vote. It is "conclusively deemed" to accept the plan and not merely "presumed" to accept the plan (where the presumption might be reversed by an actual vote); see Booth (1986, p. 84).

21. This "de-acceleration" allows a debtor to retain the benefits of a bond with a low coupon rate.

22. LoPucki and Whitford (1990, p. 130n. 14) and Klee (1979, p. 136n. 7).

23. Roe (1983, pp. 535–36). Hotchkiss (1995) reports that about 40% of a sample of firms reorganized under Chapter 11 experienced operating losses in the two years following emergence from bankruptcy and that over 16% of the firms in the sample filed for bankruptcy a second time. She concludes that there are biases in Chapter 11 favoring continued operation of unprofitable firms, and she attributes the biases to the frequency with which prepetition management retains postpetition control of a debtor.

24. LoPucki and Whitford (1990, p. 140) report that almost 60% of the plans of reorganization that are ultimately confirmed are accepted by all impaired classes. Broude (1984) describes the incentives for a consensual plan of reorganization. See also White (1989, pp. 139–40).

Confirmation of a Plan Accepted by at Least One Impaired Class

If a plan is not accepted by all of the classes impaired under the plan (either because one or more classes voted to reject the plan or because the plan would freeze out one or more classes), but if it is accepted by at least one impaired class, the supervising court can confirm the plan if it determines that the plan is

1. feasible,

2. in the best interests of each individual dissenting creditor and stockholder, and

3. "fair and equitable" to the members of each *class* that rejected the plan.

A plan is "fair and equitable" to an impaired class of unsecured creditors or stockholders if the plan does not violate the absolute priority rule *with respect to that class*. This means that either (1) the members of the class receive property with a value equal to their claims or (2) no member of any more senior class receives property with a value in excess of his or her claim and every member of every more junior class is frozen out.[25]

The process of assessing whether a plan is fair and equitable to the members of a dissenting class is known as a "cramdown hearing." A plan that is rejected by an impaired class but nevertheless confirmed by the court is said to be "crammed down" on the members of the dissenting class.[26]

Contested cramdown hearings are commonly considered to be expensive, time-consuming, and risky.[27] The DIP must establish, to the satis-

---

25. Klee (1979, pp. 143–44), Gerber (1987, p. 316n. 84), and Epstein, Nickles, and White (1993, pp. 764–65). Since common stock is a residual claim for purposes of the absolute priority rule, there is no class more junior than the class of common shareholders. Thus the operative aspect of the absolute priority rule with respect to shareholders is that no member of any other (necessarily more senior) class receives property with a value in excess of his or her claim. (Klee 1979, p. 146).

26. See, for example, the cramdown on junior creditors of a plan of reorganization for E-II Holdings, Inc. described in "Icahn May Face Uphill Battle in Winning Support for His Sweetened Bid for E-II," *Wall Street Journal*, May 10, 1993, p. B6B (describing a reorganization plan that would give senior creditors a package of cash, debt, and equity valued at about 100% of their claims, and that would give junior creditors a package of debt and equity valued at about 70% of their claims), "E-II Holding's Plan for Reorganization Is Focus of Hearings," *Wall Street Journal*, May 24, 1993, p. A4 (reporting commencement of a cramdown hearing), and "Icahn Loses Bid for E-II in Blow to Investment Style," *Wall Street Journal*, May 26, 1993, p. C1 (reporting court approval of a modified plan of reorganization and cramdown of the plan on dissenting junior creditors).

27. Broude (1984), Booth (1986), LoPucki and Whitford (1990, p. 130), and Epstein, Nickles, and White (1993, p. 754).

faction of the court, that each dissenting class will receive property with a value equal to the aggregate claims of the class, or that every more senior class will receive property with a value not in excess of the claims of the respective class. In most cases this involves establishing the aggregate value of the reorganized enterprise and the values of the securities to be issued by that enterprise—a matter of assumptions, forecasts, and analyses that are open to challenge by a dissenting class.[28]

Rejection of a Plan

If a plan is not accepted by *any* impaired class, or if it can not be crammed down on a dissenting class because it violates the absolute priority rule with respect to that class, the plan cannot be confirmed by the supervising court, and the process of developing a plan of reorganization starts all over again. If, over the course of time, it becomes apparent that the business affairs of the debtor cannot be reorganized pursuant to Chapter 11, the case will usually be converted to a Chapter 7 liquidation.[29]

The Absolute Priority Rule in Chapter 11

We observed in section 4.2 that Chapter 7 requires that the proceeds from sale of a debtor's unencumbered assets be distributed to unsecured credi-

---

28. Some of the junior creditors in the E-II Holdings bankruptcy (see note 26 above) objected to a proposed plan of reorganization because, in their view, it undervalued the equity of the recapitalized enterprise (see "Icahn May Face Uphill Battle in Winning Support for His Sweetened Bid for E-II," *Wall Street Journal*, May 10, 1993, p. B6B). Since senior creditors were to receive about one-third of the equity of the reorganized firm as part of a package valued—in aggregate—at about 100% of their claims, any undervaluation of the new equity would result in the senior creditors receiving property with a value in excess of their claims. The new equity was subsequently revalued from $14.55 to $20.25 per share, some of the new equity was reallocated from senior creditors to junior creditors, and the plan was crammed down on the junior creditors (see "Icahn's $1.18 Billion Cash Bid for E-II Is His Latest Effort to Block Rival Black," *Wall Street Journal*, May 17, 1993, p. B6, "E-II Holdings' Plan for Reorganization Is Focus of Hearings," *Wall Street Journal*, May 24, 1993, p. A4, and "Icahn Loses Bid for E-II in Blow to Investment Style," *Wall Street Journal*, May 26, 1993, p. C1). See also the contested valuations in *In re* Pullman Construction Industries, Inc., 107 B.R. 909, 918–33 (Bankr. N.D. Ill. 1990).

29. Alternatively, the parties may agree to a Chapter 11 plan of reorganization that provides for liquidation of the debtor's assets and distribution of the proceeds to creditors (Anderson and Wright 1982). Hotchkiss (1994) examines the factors influencing the disposition of cases originally filed as reorganizations in Chapter 11. See also Wruck (1990, pp. 425–27), Morse and Shaw (1988), and Weiss (1990).

Weiss and Wruck (1998) observe that the emphasis in Chapter 11 on avoiding inefficient liquidation of a bankrupt enterprise can prove costly when the firm is not economically viable and liquidation is the most efficient option. They point out that this can lead to "asset stripping," or the sale of assets to finance continuing operating losses (rather than to satisfy creditor claims) during the interval of attempted reorganization.

tors and stockholders according to the absolute priority rule (the "APR"). Chapter 11 *does not* require observance of the APR.[30]

In particular, a creditor class can waive its right to a reorganization that observes the APR by a vote of one-half of the voting class members and holders of two-thirds of the value of the voting class claims.[31] An individual creditor can demand observance of the APR only in the more limited sense that he or she can demand at least as much in a Chapter 11 reorganization as would be paid in a Chapter 7 liquidation. (This is the "best interests" test described above.)

4.4   Operating in Chapter 11

Chapter 11 provides for operation of a debtor corporation between filing for and emergence from bankruptcy. The operating provisions of Chapter 11 are crucial to maintenance of the debtor as a going concern during the frequently lengthy process of negotiating a plan of reorganization. We remarked in section 4.2 that in many Chapter 11 cases the debtor is managed by substantially the same board of directors, chief executive officer, and other senior officials who managed the company prior to filing. However, Chapter 11 limits the independence of the managers and provides for scrutiny of their actions by the supervising court and by creditor and stockholder committees.[32]

Chapter 11 provides that actions of a debtor during bankruptcy—including sales and leases of assets and postpetition borrowings—that are outside the "ordinary course of business" cannot be undertaken without giving notice of the proposed action, a court hearing and court approval.

---

30. The absence of a general requirement for observing the absolute priority rule was an express policy decision of Congress at the time it enacted the Code: Congress sought to eliminate the requirement for judicial valuation of a reorganized company when the reorganization is consensual (Broude 1984, pp. 441–43; LoPucki and Whitford 1990, pp. 131–33; Frost 1992, pp. 96–97). Coogan (1982) and Gerber (1987) examine the common and different features of corporate reorganization under Chapter 11 of the Code and Chapters X and XI of the Act.

31. Klee (1979, p. 141n. 67). For example, suppose that a debtor has stockholders and two classes of creditors, where the senior creditors and the subordinated creditors have claims of $100 million each. Suppose also that the plan of reorganization proposes to distribute $80 million of securities in the recapitalized company to the senior creditors and $30 million to the subordinated creditors. If the senior creditors vote to accept the plan, the plan can be crammed down on the subordinated creditors and stockholders because it does not violate the APR with respect to those two classes. The violation of the APR with respect to the senior creditors is irrelevant because those creditors voted to accept the plan.

32. Nimmer and Feinberg (1989) and Frost (1992) discuss the corporate governance of a company reorganizing in Chapter 11 and compare it to the governance of a solvent firm.

(Actions in the ordinary course of business can be taken without notice, hearing and approval. For simplicity of exposition we will label these actions as "extraordinary" and "ordinary," respectively.) This raises two questions: What distinguishes an extraordinary action from an ordinary action, and what standard should a court use in deciding whether to approve an extraordinary action?[33]

Most commentary on the difference between ordinary and extraordinary actions seeks to identify a threshold beyond which an action should be considered extraordinary. Any action that materially alters the position of creditors and/or that materially affects how the debtor can be reorganized would certainly be extraordinary and appropriate for judicial review. Additionally any "large" transaction (a criterion calibrated to the size of the debtor) would probably be extraordinary.

Despite efforts to distinguish extraordinary actions from ordinary actions, many corporate acts fall in the penumbra between the categories. The absence of a bright line separating the categories means that creditors and stockholders seeking leverage in the negotiations over a plan of reorganization can harass a DIP with complaints that it has taken an extraordinary action without the requisite notice, hearing, and approval.[34]

Given that a contemplated act is extraordinary and requires notice, hearing, and approval, the next issue is the standard a court should use in deciding whether to approve the act. Most courts have concluded that an extraordinary action must be in the "best interests" of creditors, or that there must be a valid "business justification" for the act.[35] One court opined that even if an extraordinary act has a valid business justification, it should be disallowed if it deprives creditors or stockholders of rights or benefits otherwise provided by Chapter 11.[36]

These standards are no more specific than the distinction between ordinary and extraordinary actions. Whether a DIP should be allowed to take an extraordinary action therefore has to be assessed on a case by case basis.

---

33. Outside of bankruptcy, a senior corporate officer generally can not undertake an extraordinary action without the approval of the board of directors of the company. This can also lead to questions about the nature of a particular action and the standards that a board should use in approving an extraordinary action. See Clark (1986, pp. 113–40).

34. On the other hand, a DIP management closely allied with a particular class of creditors or stockholders might well be tempted to take actions detrimental to the interests of other classes. It seems unlikely that a DIP could be allowed to operate without judicial supervision (Gertner and Scharfstein 1991, p. 1210). Outside of bankruptcy, creditors limit the actions of firms with covenants in their bond indentures and loan agreements (Smith and Warner 1979). This form of control is ineffective in bankruptcy.

35. Epstein, Nickles, and White (1993, pp. 177–78).

36. Epstein, Nickles, and White (1993, pp. 185–86).

4.5   Bargaining in Chapter 11

After providing for administrative expenses and priority claims, Chapter 7 specifies that the proceeds from liquidating a debtor's unencumbered assets should be distributed to unsecured creditors and stockholders according to the absolute priority rule. The outcome of a Chapter 11 case is not similarly predictable because Chapter 11 provides for—and encourages—creditors, stockholders, and managers to bargain over a plan of reorganization, and because the scope for bargaining is extensive.[37]

Senior Management of the DIP

The debtor's senior management plays a pivotal role in the negotiations leading to a plan of reorganization because only the DIP can bring a plan before the supervising court during the exclusivity period.

The exclusive right of a DIP to propose a plan of reorganization is important because it allows the senior managers of the DIP to control the details of the recapitalization and because it allows the managers to specify how creditors will be divided into classes for purposes of voting. A small group of recalcitrant creditors might, for example, be lumped into a larger group of more amenable creditors to suppress the access of the recalcitrant creditors to a cramdown hearing. Alternatively, a group of recalcitrant creditors might be placed in a class of their own and the plan structured to leave their claims unimpaired—thereby suppressing their right to vote on the plan.[38]

There are two fairly common possibilities concerning the interests of the senior management of a DIP. First, the managers may be among the largest holders of the debtor's common stock. We would then expect them to advance the interests of stockholders generally.

Alternatively, the senior managers may be relatively independent professionals with no substantial equity investment in the debtor. They would be interested primarily in their compensation, in maintaining their reputations, and perhaps also in continued employment with the debtor after it emerges from bankruptcy. Their actions can be expected to advance the interests of whatever group actually controls the debtor and/or whatever

---

37. LoPucki and Whitford (1990, pp. 132–33). Broude (1984) describes the incentives for a consensual plan of reorganization. One of the principle draftsmen of the Code observed that "the complexity of cram down should encourage the debtor to bargain with creditors to gain acceptance of a plan" and that "[i]n the majority of cases in which a plan is confirmed, all classes of claims and interests will accept the plan ..." (Klee 1979, pp. 171 and 136).

38. White (1994, p. E7-17) comments that "one explanation given for Pennzoil's willingness to accept a $3 billion settlement for its $10.5 billion damage claim against Texaco was its fear that Texaco would [be able to place Pennzoil in a separate class and] to pay Pennzoil less than its other unsecured creditors." See also Mnookin and Wilson (1989, p. 328).

group appears likely to receive the common stock of the recapitalized enterprise.[39]

Creditors and Creditor Committees

Creditors, acting individually and through committees, have an obvious interest in maximizing the value of the property they receive. In addition senior creditors—who are most likely to be paid in full (in cash or securities) regardless of the details of a reorganization—have an interest in emerging from bankruptcy as quickly as possible. Junior creditors who stand to receive little or nothing frequently want to delay emergence because they may benefit if the value of the enterprise rises before the terms of a recapitalization are finalized but will not suffer if the value of the enterprise falls.

Creditors and creditor committees derive negotiating power from their ability to block, delay, or render more costly actions that others might favor. For example, junior creditors can block distribution of the disclosure document describing an objectionable plan of reorganization (and thereby delay a vote on the plan) if they can convince the supervising court that, irrespective of the merits of the plan, the document does not adequately describe the plan. If the disclosure document is approved by the court and the plan appears likely to be approved by senior creditors, junior creditors can delay confirmation of the plan, pending a cramdown hearing, by voting as a class to reject the plan. They can subsequently block confirmation of the plan if its proponents cannot demonstrate that the plan does not violate the absolute priority rule with respect to the junior creditors.[40]

---

39. LoPucki and Whitford (1993a, p. 673) observe that most analysts assume that managers of companies in Chapter 11 always—or at least commonly—act in the best interests of shareholders. (See, e.g., the works cited in their note 8, including Bebchuk 1988, p. 799, and Franks and Torous 1989, p. 748.) They present empirical evidence supporting the proposition that managers are more commonly aligned with creditors in cases where (a) the debtor's assets are worth less than its liabilities *and* (b) no manager owns a control block of stock. Managers are usually aligned with stockholders when the debtor is solvent *or* when a manager owns a control block of stock. See also Gilson (1989, 1990), Betker (1995a), and LoPucki and Whitford (1990, p. 134n. 26, pp. 146–51 and p. 190n. 170). Gilson and Vetsuypens (1993) report that senior managers sometimes receive personal financial incentives to bring a firm out of bankruptcy more rapidly or to otherwise enhance creditor recoveries.

The right of shareholders to replace directors (and, ultimately, senior corporate officers) that they believe are not acting in their best interests is an important device for aligning managerial behavior with the interests of the shareholders of a solvent corporation. See text at notes 24–27 to Chapter 1. This right is attenuated, but not eliminated, when a company is reorganizing in Chapter 11 (Gerber 1987; Nimmer and Feinberg 1989, pp. 60–64; Fortgang and Mayer 1990, pp. 64–75; Chou 1991). See, for example, *In re* Johns-Manville Corp., 52 B.R. 879 (Bankr. S.D.N.Y. 1985), *affirmed* 60 B.R. 842 (S.D.N.Y. 1986), *reversed* 801 F. 2nd 60 (2nd Cir. 1986), *on remand* 66 B.R. 517 (Bankr. S.D.N.Y. 1986).

40. LoPucki and Whitford (1990, pp. 163–64) report that subordinated creditors frequently raise issues about (a) ambiguities in subordination clauses and (b) transactions between parents and subsidiaries that were fraudulent as to particular debenture issues, in order to elevate their status or to obtain bargaining leverage.

It has been widely noted that the ability of junior creditors to block or delay a plan of reorganization, together with the inherent conflict between senior creditors and junior creditors over the speed of emergence from bankruptcy, can lead to a bargain whereby senior creditors give up some of the value that they might otherwise receive to junior creditors in order to get the support of the latter for quicker emergence.[41]

Secured Creditors

Secured creditors have a special negotiating advantage in cases where they have a security interest in property crucial to the debtor's reorganization and can reasonably assert that their claims are not adequately protected against a decline in the value of the property. They can then threaten to petition the court for relief from the stay and immediate transfer of the property. In extreme cases this can give secured creditors effective control over a reorganization.[42]

Stockholders and Stockholder Committees

In many Chapter 11 cases any distribution to stockholders is essentially a payment from creditors in return for their cooperation in reorganizing the company more promptly. Stockholders, like junior creditors, derive negotiating power from their ability to block, delay, or render more costly actions that others might favor.[43]

Stockholders have an additional bargaining advantage in cases where the debtor's senior managers are themselves large shareholders. The stock-

---

41. Baird and Jackson (1988, pp. 780 and 788) and LoPucki and Whitford (1990, p. 133). An investment manager described the financier Leon Black, who played an important role in several large bankruptcy reorganizations in the early and mid-1990s, as "understanding the time value of money. When he makes a lot of money in a quick period of time, he's willing to let someone else make a little too, to get the deal done." In one reorganization, Black "cut a deal with the most junior levels of subordinated debt that gave them disproportionately more than they were entitled to. In exchange, those creditors voted to accept the plan." "Icahn Loses Bid for E-II in Blow to Investment Style," *Wall Street Journal*, May 26, 1993, p. C1. See also the discussion of the Evans Products bankruptcy in Weiss (1990, p. 296), LoPucki and Whitford (1990, pp. 144–45) and LoPucki and Whitford (1991a, p. 36n. 85).

42. LoPucki and Whitford (1993a, pp. 702–703).

43. LoPucki and Whitford (1990, pp. 158–60) emphasize the importance of stockholders obtaining official representation through a judicially recognized equity committee. See, for example, the actions of the equity committee in *In re* Heck's, 112 B.R. 775 (Bankr. S.D.W.Va. 1990). The Heck's court observed that "the litigation commenced by the Equity Committee ... [was] solely for the purpose of extorting a settlement or extorting a compromise for equity interest holders above and beyond that to which they were entitled ..." (at p. 803), that many pleadings were "... purely for reasons of harassment, delay and intimidation ..." (at p. 804) and that "... lead counsel of the Equity Committee launched a barrage of meritless demands and threats ... that were intended to coerce other creditors in the case and put in jeopardy the ability of the DIP to provide recovery for anyone. Their actions were improper in the representation of equity interests and damaged the DIP by creating substantial administrative expense, delay and confusion ..." (at p. 808).

holders can then delay even the submission of a plan of reorganization to the supervising court, and they can affect directly the terms of a
recapitalization.[44]

Summary

The outcome of a Chapter 11 case is not readily predictable solely on the
basis of the aggregate value and capital structure of the debtor at the time
of filing for bankruptcy. "Who gets what" also depends on the incentives
and abilities of creditors, stockholders, and managers to block or delay an
objectionable outcome in the hope of obtaining a more favorable result
later. Since the costs of delay may be of small account to those who would
be eliminated in a recapitalization, stockholders benefit most (and senior
unsecured creditors benefit least) from bargaining in Chapter 11.[45]

44. This negotiating advantage can be eliminated by terminating exclusivity and allowing
submission of a plan of reorganization from a creditor committee (Nimmer and Feinberg
1989, pp. 64–70). However, it appears that bankruptcy courts are frequently reluctant to
broaden the negotiating context of a Chapter 11 case and that they more commonly terminate or threaten to terminate exclusivity to "motivate" a seemingly obdurate DIP management. See, for example, the termination of exclusivity in the Public Service Co. of New
Hampshire bankruptcy (Epstein, Nickles, and White 1993, p. 817) and the threat to terminate exclusivity in the Texaco bankruptcy (LoPucki and Whitford 1990, p. 157; Mnookin
and Wilson 1989, p. 308); see also Epstein, Nickles, and White (1993, p. 818n. 9). Rosen and
Rodriguez (1982) observe that a creditor committee may face substantial practical problems
in developing a plan of reorganization and will frequently be limited to threatening to convert the case to a Chapter 7 liquidation.

45. White (1994, pp. E7-26–E7-29) summarizes several proposals for bankruptcy reform,
most of which emphasize greater reliance on market processes and stricter adherence to the
absolute priority rule, that have appeared since 1978. Roe (1983) suggests that a reorganized
firm should be capitalized entirely with common stock and that 10% of the stock should be
sold in a public offering to establish the value of the firm and to provide a basis for distributing the balance of the stock to the original claimants pursuant to the APR. Baird (1986)
urges greater reliance on liquidating sale of a firm as a going concern and distribution of the
proceeds pursuant to the APR. (But see Easterbook 1990, who points out the absence of any
demand by creditors that Chapter 11 facilitate such sales and notes that private debt
restructurings rarely resort to such sales.) Bebchuk (1988) suggests that the holders of the
securities of a firm in Chapter 11 should be granted "distribution rights" to the securities of
the recapitalized enterprise, where the terms of the rights follow from the priorities and
amounts of the original claims so that rational exercise results in a distribution of the securities of the recapitalized enterprise pursuant to the APR. LoPucki and Whitford (1990,
pp. 186–90 and 1991b) recommend "preemptive cram down" of equity (and, in some cases,
junior creditors) at an early stage in a Chapter 11 case when the interests and claims of the
target classes are clearly without value, with the effect of extinguishing the legal rights of the
target classes, limiting their bargaining leverage, simplifying bargaining among the remaining claimants, and limiting consensual deviations from the APR. Two additional proposals
emphasize the importance of facilitating replacement of the senior managers of a financially
distressed firm as well as adherence to the absolute priority rule. Aghion, Hart, and Moore
(1992) suggest that a reorganized firm should be capitalized entirely with common stock (as
in Roe 1983), that the holders of the old securities of the firm should be granted distribution
rights to the stock (as in Bebchuk 1988), and that (following exercise of the distribution
rights) the holders of the new stock should vote on competing proposals to purchase the
stock for cash or securities. Bradley and Rosenzweig (1992) propose that the common stock
and the most junior class of debt of a firm should be canceled promptly following default on

4.6 Empirical Characteristics of Large Corporate Reorganizations

The contingent value models presented in chapters 2 and 3 assume that bankruptcy is instantaneous, costless, and results in distributions (of cash or securities) pursuant to the absolute priority rule. This section summarizes a series of empirical studies that suggest that all three assumptions are erroneous in the case of Chapter 11 reorganizations of large corporations with publicly traded securities.[46]

Time in Bankruptcy

Six studies have examined the length of the interval between filing for bankruptcy and confirmation of a plan of reorganization. Table 4.1 summarizes the results.

With one exception, the results indicate that the average duration of bankruptcy is somewhat over two years. Observed durations range from essentially zero (Franks and Torous 1989 report one case that lasted only 37 days) to more than seven years. The single exceptional study is Warner's (1977a) examination of railroads that filed for and emerged from bankruptcy between 1930 and 1955. Railroads had unusually complex capital structures and their bankruptcies were subject to close supervision by courts and regulatory agencies.

The authors of the studies identified in table 4.1 conjectured that bankruptcy is a lengthy process, in part because a confirmed plan of reorganization is the end result of a multilateral bargaining process within which the parties derive negotiating advantage from their ability to block or delay actions that others might favor. It takes time for the parties to explore the bargaining strengths and weaknesses of their adversaries, and it takes time for a DIP to develop a plan of reorganization that can command unanimous class consents or that can be crammed down on dissenting classes.

---

any obligation and that new common stock should be issued to the former creditors. The new shareholders must either make the required payments or face similar displacement by the next most junior class of creditors. (LoPucki 1992 and Warren 1992 critique the empirical and analytical foundations of the Bradley and Rosenzweig proposal.) Bhattacharyya and Singh (1999) point out that claimants with different seniorities, such as creditors and shareholders, have preferences for different auction mechanisms based on the dispersion of prospective outcomes and the convexity or concavity of their claims. These differences make the right to choose the method of auctioning corporate assets a valuable right whose allocation can engender conflict among the claimants to a bankrupt enterprise.

46. Brennan (1995, p. 15) has remarked that "No subject of study better exemplifies the developments that have taken place in the field of corporate finance than that of bankruptcy. Twenty-five years ago bankruptcy was a neglected topic in the theory of corporate finance, being taken as virtually synonymous with liquidation,... the absolute priority rule being implicitly assumed to hold, and the details of the legal code neglected."

Table 4.1
Studies of the duration of bankruptcy

| | Duration (years) | | |
	Average	Range	Sample
Warner (1977a)	12.2	3.9 to 22.9	20 railroads with annual revenues over $1 million that filed for reorganization after 1929 and emerged from bankruptcy before 1956.
Franks and Torous (1989)	3.7	0.1 to 13.3	30 large firms that defaulted on bonds between 1970 and 1984 and that filed for reorganization under Chapter X of the Act or Chapter 11 of the Code and subsequently emerged from bankruptcy.
Weiss (1990)	2.5	0.7 to 8.3	37 large firms that filed for reorganization or liquidation under the Code and that emerged from bankruptcy or were liquidated before June 1989.
Eberhart, Moore, and Roenfeldt (1990)	2.1	0.8 to 6.2	29 large firms that filed for reorganization under the Code and that emerged from bankruptcy before Mar 1989.
Eberhart and Sweeney (1992)	2.1	0.3 to 6.3	74 large firms that filed for reorganization under the Code and that emerged from bankruptcy before Jan 1991.
Altman and Eberhart (1994)	2.0	Not reported	91 firms that filed for reorganization under the Code and that emerged from bankruptcy or were liquidated or acquired before Aug 1992.

Costs of Bankruptcy

Three studies have examined the direct costs of bankruptcy, namely the costs of lawyers, accountants, investment bankers, and other advisors. Warner (1977b) found that the direct costs of bankruptcy for a sample of eleven large railroad bankruptcies averaged 5.3% and ranged between 1.7% and 9.1% of the aggregate value of the debtor's securities at the time of filing. For a sample of seven industrial firms and twelve retailers, Altman (1984) identified direct costs that averaged 6.0% of the debtor's value at the time of filing and ranged from less than 1.0% to more than 20.0%. Weiss (1990) examined the direct costs of bankruptcy for a sample of 31 large companies that filed for bankruptcy under the Code and emerged from bankruptcy or were liquidated before June 1989. The costs averaged 3.1% and ranged between 1.0% and 6.6% of the debtor's value at the end of the fiscal year preceding filing.

In addition to payments to lawyers and others, bankruptcy also burdens a debtor with a variety of indirect costs, including

1. lower product sale prices (frequently needed to retain customers who would otherwise do business with competitors out of concern that the debtor may ultimately cease operating),[47]

2. higher factor purchase prices (including especially the cost of post-petition credit and conventional and managerial[48] labor services), and

3. foregone investments and strategic opportunities resulting from diversion of senior management attention and/or limitation of the extraordinary business activities of a DIP.

Only one author has examined empirically the indirect costs of bankruptcy. Altman (1984) concludes that indirect costs may, on average, be twice as large as the direct costs and can be substantially greater in individual cases.[49] Two studies of the indirect costs of litigation support the proposition that indirect costs of bankruptcy can exceed direct costs by a substantial margin.[50]

Violation of the Absolute Priority Rule

Six studies have examined whether bankruptcy recapitalizations violate the absolute priority rule.

Franks and Torous (1989) examined a sample of 27 large firms that defaulted on publicly traded debt between 1970 and 1984, filed for reorganization under the Bankruptcy Act of 1898 or under Chapter 11 of the Code, and subsequently emerged from bankruptcy. Of the recapitalizations 78% (21 out of 27) exhibited a violation of the APR. Most (18) of the violations occurred because stockholders were not frozen out, even though unsecured creditors received less than the full amount of their claims. Weiss (1990) reports substantially similar results for a sample of 35 large firms that filed for reorganization under the Code and emerged from bankruptcy or were liquidated before June 1989.

Eberhart, Moore, and Roenfeldt (1990) examined a sample of 30 large firms that filed for reorganization under the Code and emerged from

---

47. See Jensen and Meckling (1976, pp. 341–42) and Titman (1984, pp. 138–39) (customer demand for durable goods depends on manufacturer's ability to provide parts and service in the future and hence on probability that manufacturer will remain in business).

48. Gilson and Vetsuypens (1993, p. 426) report that an outside CEO of a financially distressed firm earns, on average, 36% more than the CEO he or she replaced.

49. Haugen and Senbet (1988, pp. 31–32) and Wruck (1990, p. 438) comment on Altman's methodology.

50. Engelmann and Cornell (1988) and Cutler and Summers (1988). See similarly Mnookin and Wilson (1989) and LoPucki and Whitford (1993a, p. 753).

bankruptcy before March 1989. They defined the "relative deviation" from the APR in a recapitalization as

$$
\delta = \frac{\min\left[\left\{ \begin{array}{c} \text{Value of creditor} \\ \text{deficiences} \end{array} \right\}, \left\{ \begin{array}{c} \text{Value of distributions to} \\ \text{common shareholders} \end{array} \right\} \right]}{\text{Total value of all distributions}}
\tag{4.1}
$$

The value of δ is zero if creditors are paid in full *or* if stockholders are frozen out, that is, if the absolute priority of creditors over stockholders is maintained. A positive value of δ reflects a transfer of value from creditors to stockholders in violation of the APR. The authors found that δ averaged 7.6% over all 30 cases in their sample and 9.9% over the 23 cases where it was positive, and that it ranged as high as 36%. They also found that the speed of emergence from bankruptcy was directly related to the magnitude of δ. This is consistent with the proposition that creditors sometimes "purchase" the cooperation of shareholders in hastening emergence.

LoPucki and Whitford (1990) examined a sample of 41 firms with assets of more than $100 million that filed for reorganization under the Code and emerged from bankruptcy before April 1988. Thirty of the recapitalizations resulted in distributions with a total value less than the aggregate claims of creditors. Stockholders received something of value in 21 (70%) of the 30 cases. On average over all 30 cases, stockholders received 5.6% of the total value of all distributions. For the 21 cases where they were not frozen out, stockholders received an average of 8.1% of the total value of all distributions.

The other 11 recapitalizations examined by LoPucki and Whitford involved distributions with a total value in excess of the aggregate claims of creditors. Stockholders received something in every one of the 11 cases but unsecured creditors did not fully recover on their claims in six of the cases. Their payments in those six cases averaged 90.7% of their claims and ranged between 85.6% and 96.8%.

Eberhart and Sweeney (1992) reported (in their table I) what bondholders actually received and what they would have received under the absolute priority rule for a sample of 40 publicly traded bonds issued by 13 large companies that filed for reorganization under the Code and emerged from bankruptcy prior to 1991. The difference in value averaged only $7 per $1,000 principal value of bonds but ranged between −$450 and +$577. This is consistent with the proposition that violation of the APR can benefit a creditor (as when the cooperation of junior creditors is "purchased" by more senior creditors) and may sometimes appear to harm a creditor (as when senior creditors choose to purchase the cooper-

Table 4.2
Distribution of δ

δ (%)	Number of firms
0	21
0–1	20
1–2	7
2–3	9
3–4	2
4–5	3
5–10	7
10–15	3
15–20	0
20–25	2
25–30	1

Source: From Betker (1995a, table 2).

ation of junior creditors, or when junior creditors choose to purchase the cooperation of shareholders).

The Cross-sectional Characteristics of Departures from Absolute Priority

Each of the foregoing studies hypothesized that a recapitalization is more likely to favor shareholders if they have a strong negotiating position. Betker (1995a) tested this hypothesis with data from a sample of 75 firms that filed for reorganization under Chapter 11 and emerged from bankruptcy before 1991. He began by defining δ as in equation (4.1). Table 4.2 shows that δ was zero in 21 cases and less than 1% in another 20 cases, but that it had a highly skewed distribution and exceeded 25% in one case.

Betker found that δ was smaller the deeper the debtor's insolvency—as measured by the ratio of creditor claims to the aggregate value of all securities distributed in a recapitalization. This is consistent with a proposition set forth by Franks and Torous (1989) that—assuming the management of a DIP represents the interests of shareholders—Chapter 11 puts shareholders in a bargaining position comparable to that of an option holder.[51]

---

51. Exclusivity gives the DIP the exclusive right to bring the debtor out of Chapter 11. Stockholders cannot benefit from exercising this right unilaterally if the firm is insolvent because unilateral exercise requires observance of the absolute priority rule; that is, creditors can block any nonconsensual plan of reorganization that does not respect the rule. However, creditors have an incentive to bargain with the DIP to "purchase" the right (by agreeing to a consensual plan of reorganization and a deviation from absolute priority in favor of shareholders) to terminate the accrual of bankruptcy costs. The value to stockholders of the exclusive right to bring the firm out of bankruptcy, relative to the value of the firm, varies directly with the value of the firm; that is, the value of the right is (like the value of a call option) a convex function of the value of the firm, so creditors have to give up relatively less value to stockholders the deeper the firm's insolvency.

Betker also found that δ was influenced by factors indicative of the strength of management representation of shareholder interests and the legal position and bargaining skills of creditors. In particular, δ was smaller,

- the smaller the fraction of common stock owned by the CEO at the time of filing in cases where the CEO was not replaced prior to emergence from bankruptcy—a result consistent with the proposition that shareholders do relatively better when the CEO has a greater personal financial interest in their welfare and was not selected to represent the interests of creditors (as may be the case with a replacement CEO),

- in cases where CEO compensation rose and the price of the debtor's stock declined during bankruptcy—a phenomenon indicative of creditor influence over the actions of the firm,[52]

- if exclusivity was terminated during bankruptcy, and

- the greater the fraction of creditor claims held by banks and secured creditors—reflecting the superior bargaining skill of bank creditors as well as the special treatment of secured creditors under the Code.[53]

Whether Violations of the Absolute Priority Rule Come as a Surprise to Market Participants

It can be argued that reorganization in Chapter 11 is unfair to unsecured creditors, and delivers windfall gains to stockholders, because bankruptcy reorganizations violate the absolute priority rule with such regularity. Creditors purportedly lend money at relatively low rates of interest because they believe they will be paid ahead of stockholders. It is unfair to deprive them of their seniority, and to elevate the standing of stockholders, when the business affairs of the debtor turn sour.[54]

This argument would have merit if a creditor believed (at the time he or she lent money or purchased debt securities) that the APR would be observed in any future recapitalization of the debtor. (Why a creditor

---

52. When CEO compensation rises and the price of the debtor's stock falls during bankruptcy, we can reasonably conjecture that the CEO's compensation was not set by the agents of shareholders.

53. This is consistent with the observation of Marsh (1985, p. 263) that the senior managers of International Harvester understood that if they elevated the firm's bank creditors to the status of secured creditors (to avoid an imminent default) shareholders "would have far less clout" if the firm was later forced to file for bankruptcy.

54. Jensen (1991) advances the different complaint that erosion of the distinction between unsecured debt and equity can lead to increased agency costs as a result of a loss of efficiencies in risk bearing, monitoring, and corporate control associated with the prioritization of claims.

would have such a belief in view of the regularity with which the APR is violated is not obvious.) It has little or no merit if the creditor is lending money with the understanding that any future recapitalization is likely to violate the APR, since the creditor can then negotiate a higher rate of interest. More generally, it has no merit if corporate debt prices are determined in an efficient market.

Assessing the efficiency of the corporate bond market with respect to violations of the absolute priority rule is not a trivial exercise, since violations necessarily follow in the wake of financial distress. It may be difficult to identify fluctuations in securities prices associated with changing assessments of the likelihood and significance of a violation of the APR when the prices of the securities are declining rapidly.[55] Several studies have, however, examined the narrower question of the efficiency of the markets for securities issued by firms that are *already* in bankruptcy.

Warner (1977a) examined the behavior during bankruptcy of railroad bond prices between 1930 and 1955. On average, and after adjusting for differences in systematic risk, a portfolio of defaulted railroad bonds *outperformed* a portfolio of common stock issued by nondefaulting railroads.[56] Warner's results do not support the hypothesis that holders of defaulted railroad bonds suffered unanticipated losses during bankruptcy due to prospective violations of the absolute priority rule.

Eberhart and Sweeney (1992) examined the behavior during bankruptcy of corporate bond prices between 1980 and 1990. They were generally unable to reject the hypothesis that the price of a bond at the time of the issuer's filing for bankruptcy is an informationally efficient estimate of subsequent bond prices, including the price at the time of emergence from bankruptcy. Similar results were reported by Altman and Eberhart (1994).

Morse and Shaw (1988) and Eberhart, Moore, and Roenfeldt (1990) examined the efficiency of the markets for the common stock of companies in bankruptcy. Neither study found any evidence of inefficiency. The latter authors found evidence that stock prices at the time of filing for bankruptcy are positively correlated with subsequent distributions to shareholders in violation of the absolute priority rule, as well as with subsequent distributions in accord with the rule.

---

55. See, however, Baldwin and Mason (1983), who conclude that market participants anticipated (in the late 1970s and early 1980s) that Massey Ferguson's debt and equity would be restructured in violation of the absolute priority rule.

56. The superior performance occurred primarily during a few exceptional months in 1940, 1941, and 1942, when the U.S. Supreme Court announced decisions favorable to bondholders in a series of railroad recapitalization cases (Warner 1977a, pp. 267–72).

Summary

The foregoing studies suggest four important characteristics of recapitalizations in Chapter 11:

1. The recapitalizations are neither quick nor costless.

2. The recapitalizations commonly result in smaller distributions to senior unsecured creditors and larger distributions to shareholders compared to what would be distributed pursuant to the absolute priority rule. Junior creditors sometimes receive more and sometimes less than what they would receive under the rule.

3. The extent to which a recapitalization favors shareholders depends on the depth of the firm's insolvency, the strength of management representation of shareholder interests, and the legal position and bargaining skill of creditors.

4. Violation of the absolute priority rule does not come as a surprise to market participants. Senior debt is not priced on the assumption that it will be paid in full before subordinated creditors and stockholders get anything, and common stock is not priced as a residual claim.

The first characteristic implies that the administrative, supervisory and bargaining costs of the bankruptcy process dissipate some nontrivial fraction of the value of a bankrupt enterprise. The last characteristic implies that on average, we will overstate the contingent value of debt, and understate the contingent value of equity, if we fail to incorporate the prospect for violations of the absolute priority rule following default and bankruptcy into the specification of terminal contingent value functions.

Appendix: Private Recapitalizations

In discussing the economic justification for bankruptcy in section 4.1, we assumed that creditors accelerate the maturities of their loans following breach of a loan covenant, whereupon the firm, unable to satisfy the demands of its creditors, files for bankruptcy.[57] Empirical evidence (summarized in section 4.6) suggests that reorganizing in Chapter 11 is costly and impairs the value of the firm. It is therefore not surprising that the managers of a firm on the verge of default may try to avoid the dis-

---

57. In practice, a firm may anticipate both the breach of a covenant and the acceleration of its debt and choose to file for bankruptcy before the breach occurs.

sipative costs of bankruptcy by meeting with its creditors and share-holders and negotiating a *private* recapitalization.[58]

Private recapitalization has the same objective as Chapter 11: rearrang-ing the capital structure of a financially distressed firm while maintaining its value as a going concern. However, the two modes of recapitalization are not dichotomous substitutes for each other. Empirical evidence shows that almost all firms attempt to recapitalize privately before filing for Chapter 11 and that they reorganize in Chapter 11 only if the attempt at private recapitalization fails.[59]

Negotiating a Private Recapitalization

The most important characteristic of negotiating a private recapitaliza-tion is the prospect of Chapter 11 if the negotiations fail. This prospect means that no party is likely to accept less than what can be obtained from recapitalizing in Chapter 11 and that the essential matter being negotiated is the allocation of the savings derived from staying out of Chapter 11. This savings can be substantial—creating a strong incentive to reach agreement but also possibly making agreement more difficult in the absence of any benchmark standard for allocating the savings among creditors and shareholders.[60]

Scope of Negotiations

Negotiations aimed at recapitalizing a large company outside of Chapter 11 are more flexible than negotiations in Chapter 11 because not every

58. Asquith, Gertner, and Scharfstein (1994) describe some of the wide variety of ways in which the capital structure of a firm can be restructured privately. There is no hard empirical evidence supporting the proposition that firms try to recapitalize privately to avoid the dis-sipative costs of Chapter 11, but the proposition is cited in virtually every comparison of private recapitalizations with reorganizations in Chapter 11. See Haugen and Senbet (1978, 1988), Roe (1987, pp. 235–36), Kashner (1988, p. 123), Jensen (1989, p. 43), Gilson, John, and Lang (1990, p. 319), Gilson (1991, p. 63), Jensen (1991, pp. 24–25), and Asquith, Gert-ner and Scharfstein (1994, p. 652). Gilson (1989, pp. 247–48) observes that senior managers have a personal incentive to try to restructure outside of Chapter 11 because executive turn-over is lower for firms that recapitalize privately than for firms that reorganize in Chapter 11.

59. Gilson, John, and Lang (1990) examined a sample of 169 large firms that experienced severe financial distress sometime in the interval between 1978 and 1987. Only 13 of the firms filed for Chapter 11 without first attempting a private recapitalization. Gilson (1991) dis-cusses the comparative advantages of recapitalizing privately and in Chapter 11.

60. Roe (1987, p. 238). For some firms reorganization in bankruptcy may not be practical (see Baldwin and Mason 1983, pp. 512–13, on Massey Ferguson's financial distress in 1980 and Moritz and Seaman 1981, pp. 279–80, 286, and 337; Reich and Donahue 1985, pp. 103, 106, 120–121, 131, and 135 on Chrysler Corporation's distress in 1979 and 1980), and liquidation may be the only alternative to a private recapitalization. In these cases where the costs of default and bankruptcy include loss of the excess of the going concern value over the liquidation value, the incentive for negotiating a private recapitalization can be quite significant.

creditor has to be represented. Some secured claims may be left undisturbed because they are oversecured and the claims of trade creditors may be satisfied in full because they are immaterial. Similarly the negotiations might exclude publicly traded debt if it appears, for reasons noted below, that consensual restructuring of that debt will be difficult.[61]

The Free-Rider Problem

Individual creditors are generally free to decline to participate in a private recapitalization. In fact each creditor usually has a substantial individual incentive to retain his or her original claim and to let others pay the price (in terms of reduced principal and interest payments and more distant redemption dates) of keeping the debtor out of Chapter 11. This leads to a free-rider problem: if too many creditors opt out of a proposed recapitalization, there may not be enough consenting creditors to make the recapitalization viable.[62] An important element of negotiating a private recapitalization is convincing enough creditors that the recapitalization will fail without their participation.[63]

Restructuring Syndicated Bank Loans

Special creditor consent problems arise in the context of negotiating a private recapitalization with a syndicate of bank lenders. Bank syndicate agreements commonly provide that their core terms, including terms relating to interest and principal payments, cannot be altered without the *unanimous* consent of all of the participating banks.[64] This can lead to a

---

61. Outside of Chapter 11, nothing compels the managers of a financially distressed firm to negotiate with all of the firm's creditors in a collective proceeding. In some cases it may be in the best interests of shareholders for the managers to negotiate with a subset of the creditors. Any resulting private (and limited) debt restructuring may lead to economically inefficient actions (e.g., continuing to operate a firm that would have a higher value in liquidation, or investing in a project with a negative net present value) and impose costs on other creditors. See Bulow and Shoven (1978), Ang and Chua (1980), White (1980, 1983, 1989, 1994), LoPucki (1982, pp. 337–38), and Gertner and Scharfstein (1991).

62. Chapter 11 has two important provisions for binding dissenting creditors to a plan of reorganization. First, an *individual* dissenting creditor can be bound to a plan upon a favorable vote by the other creditors in his or her class. Second, a *class* of dissenting creditors can be bound to a plan if the supervising court finds that the plan does not violate the absolute priority rule with respect to the class.

63. See, for example, the description of the negotiations in the first half of 1980 leading to the restructuring of the bank debt of Chrysler Corporation in Moritz and Seaman (1981, pp. 297–317) and Reich and Donahue (1985, pp. 167–94), and the description of the negotiations between December 1980 and December 1981 leading to the restructuring of the bank debt of International Harvester Company in Marsh (1985, pp. 242–65). Free-rider problems can also be controlled by negotiating a plan of reorganization outside of Chapter 11 and then filing for Chapter 11 in order to use its provisions for binding dissenting creditors to the plan. This is called a "pre-packaged" bankruptcy. See McConnell and Servaes (1991), Betker (1995b), and Tashjian, Lease, and McConnell (1996).

64. Roe (1987, p. 274n. 130).

"holdout" problem if a syndicate member demands to be cashed out of its loan or otherwise granted preferential treatment in return for not vetoing a restructuring favored by other syndicate members.[65]

Although a putative holdout is sometimes able to obtain special treatment, it more commonly agrees to whatever terms are acceptable to the preponderance of syndicate members. Failure to agree to terms viewed as reasonable by most other banks runs the risk that the holdout will acquire a reputation for making unreasonable demands, and the risk that it will not be invited to participate in future syndicates.[66]

Restructuring Publicly Traded Debt

Special creditor consent problems also arise in the context of negotiating a private recapitalization with holders of publicly traded debt. Section 316(b) of the Trust Indenture Act of 1939 prohibits modification of the principal amount, interest rate, or maturity date of publicly traded debt except upon approval of all of the holders of the debt. This leads to a more severe holdout problem than in the context of restructuring a syndicated bank loan. This is partly because there are usually more holders of the publicly traded debt, each with the power to veto a restructuring, and partly because the benefits of holding out are not balanced by any costs from acquiring a reputation for unreasonable behavior: there is no mechanism for precluding a person or institution from acquiring publicly traded securities. As a practical matter, it is usually impossible to renegotiate the core terms of publicly traded corporate debt.[67]

A distressed company capitalized with substantial amounts of publicly traded debt will typically offer to *exchange* equity (or new debt with reduced interest or principal payments) for its old debt. (Gertner and Scharfstein 1991, p. 1199n. 14, cite the example of AP Industries, who in 1990 offered to exchange $50 in cash, one share of common stock, and $340.91 face amount of zero-coupon senior subordinated notes maturing in 1997 for each $1,000 principal value of its outstanding $12\frac{30}{8}$% sub-

---

65. See Marsh (1985, p. 265) for an example.

66. See Reich and Donahue (1985, p. 189) ("continued resistance [to agreeing to a renegotiated loan to a distressed borrower] could gain [a bank] a reputation as a 'bad actor,' which would likely keep it out of future syndicated credits") and Marsh (1985, pp. 263–65) (describing a holdout bank that ultimately agreed to a renegotiated loan because holding out "might strain its business relationships with major money-center banks" and quoting an executive vice-president of the putative holdout as saying that "Banks of our size ... work cooperatively in too many transactions to have [a reputation for holding out] hanging over your head."). See also Roe (1987, pp. 274–75n. 130).

67. Asquith, Gertner, and Scharfstein (1994, p. 641). Amihud, Garbade, and Kahan (1999, 2000) propose an institutional innovation for incorporating some of the valuable aspects of bank debt, including nonopportunistic renegotiation, into publicly traded debt.

ordinated debentures maturing in 2001.) To minimize the incidence of free-riding, the company will specify that consummation of the exchange offer is contingent upon acceptance of the offer by holders of 85% or 90% of the old debt and that it plans to file for Chapter 11 if the exchange offer fails.[68]

Disclosure of Information

Private recapitalizations are not subject to judicial supervision and are not encumbered with statutorily mandated disclosures and plan filings. Creditor committees organized outside of Chapter 11 do not have a statutory right to investigate the business affairs of a debtor.

This means that creditors negotiating a private recapitalization may have less and less reliable information about the debtor's prospects than they would have in Chapter 11. Phrased another way, there may be more significant information asymmetries in private recapitalizations than in Chapter 11 reorganizations. Game-theoretic analyses suggest that such asymmetries may lead less well-informed participants to prefer a more costly, judicially supervised, reorganization.[69]

Empirical Characteristics of Private Recapitalizations

Two empirical characteristics of private recapitalizations are of special interest. First, since most financially distressed firms attempt to recapitalize privately but only about half succeed,[70] it is of some interest to identify the factors that influence the likelihood of success. Second, it is important to identify whether private recapitalizations result in distributions to creditors and shareholders substantially different from what those parties would have received under Chapter 11.

Factors Affecting the Likelihood That an Attempt at Private Recapitalization Will Succeed

Gilson, John, and Lang (1990, p. 338) report that an attempt at recapitalizing privately is more likely to succeed the greater the ratio of bank debt to total debt[71] and the greater the ratio of the firm's market value to replacement cost. They conjecture that bank creditors are more knowledgeable than, for example, bondholders and trade creditors—and hence

---

68. Roe (1987, pp. 236–37) and Bab (1991, p. 850).

69. Giammarino (1989) and Baird and Picker (1991, p. 335).

70. Of the 156 firms that tried to recapitalize privately examined by Gilson, John, and Lang (1990), 80 succeeded; 76 failed and filed for reorganization in Chapter 11.

71. See, however, the contrary results of Asquith, Gertner, and Scharfstein (1994, pp. 653–54).

less likely to reject the terms of a proposed recapitalization because of information asymmetries—and that free-riders and holdouts are less common among banks than among other creditors. The authors also conjecture that firms with a higher ratio of market value to replacement cost are more likely to recapitalize privately because such firms have relatively more intangible assets that can be dissipated in a Chapter 11 reorganization.

Characteristics of Successful Private Recapitalizations

Franks and Torous (1994) report two significant characteristics of the distributions to creditors and shareholders that result from successful attempts at private recapitalization.

First, private recapitalizations commonly violate the absolute priority rule. On average, stockholders capture 9.5% of the aggregate value of the securities being restructured in excess of what they would have received pursuant to the APR. The excess comes largely at the expense of bank creditors and holders of senior public debt. This is consistent with the proposition that stockholders will not accept less in a private recapitalization than what they can get in Chapter 11, and with the observation that Chapter 11 reorganizations commonly favor shareholders.

Second, holding constant the depth of a firm's insolvency, there is some evidence that stockholders do *relatively* better in private recapitalizations than in Chapter 11. This may be the result of more aggressive management representation of shareholder interests, or it may reflect the ability of managers to extract value from the greater information asymmetries inherent in voluntary recapitalizations. However, this does not mean that creditors would do better in absolute terms in Chapter 11. Rather, it may reflect the ability of stockholders to capture a disproportionate share of the bankruptcy costs saved by recapitalizing privately.

Bankruptcy Costs and Violations of the Absolute Priority Rule

Data from large corporate bankruptcies (summarized in section 4.6) suggest that Chapter 11 recapitalizations dissipate a nontrivial fraction of enterprise value and commonly violate the absolute priority rule. In view of the likely significance of these characteristics for pricing corporate securities, it is important to consider whether we can relax the assumptions (made in chapters 2 and 3) that bankruptcy is costless and results in distributions of cash or securities in accord with the rule.

5.1   Bankruptcy Costs

This section examines whether we can incorporate bankruptcy costs into the specification of a contingent value model. For expositional simplicity, we address the issue in the context of the model presented in chapter 2, where the firm is capitalized with common stock and a single issue of zero-coupon debt that promises to pay F when it matures at time T. We begin by describing an analytical framework that incorporates bankruptcy costs.

An Analytical Framework

Let $\tilde{W}(t)$ denote the value the firm would have at time t if it were capitalized entirely with common stock. We will call $\tilde{W}(t)$ the value of the *unlevered* firm and we will be careful to distinguish between $\tilde{W}(t)$ and the value of the *levered* firm, denoted $W(t)$ and defined—in equation (2.1)—as the aggregate value of the debt and equity of the levered firm: $W(t) = V_1(t) + V_2(t)$. It is reasonable to suppose that the prospect of incurring bankruptcy costs reduces the value of the levered firm below the value of the unlevered firm.[1]

We assume that the natural logarithm of the value of the unlevered firm evolves as a Gaussian random walk with drift μ and variance σ^2 per annum.[2] The change in the log of the value of the unlevered firm over an

1. See Anderson and Sundaresan (1996, p. 43) ("the value of the levered firm ... is the [value of the firm were it to be financed entirely by equity] less the expected bankruptcy costs") and Mella-Barral and Perraudin (1997, caption to figure 1) (difference between value of unlevered firm and value of levered firm reflects "assumptions of both direct and indirect bankruptcy costs").

2. Contingent value models of corporate securities prices in the presence of bankruptcy costs commonly assume that the value of the unlevered firm evolves as a primitive stochastic process. See, for example, Brennan and Schwartz (1978, p. 106), Wiggins (1990, p. 378), Kane, Marcus, and McDonald (1984, p. 843) (state variable A, the market value of the assets of the unlevered firm, follows a Gaussian diffusion process), Fischer, Heinkel, and Zechner (1989, pp. 21–22), Leland (1994, p. 1217) (state variable V, the asset value of the firm, follows a Gaussian diffusion process), Leland and Toft (1996, p. 989), Anderson and Sundaresan (1996, p. 42) who state that variable V_t, which "may be interpreted as the ... value of the firm were it to be financed entirely with equity," follows a binomial process, and Leland (1998, p. 1216).

interval of time Δt may be written as

$$\ln[\tilde{W}(t + \Delta t)] - \ln[\tilde{W}(t)] = \mu \cdot \Delta t + \sigma \cdot \Delta t^{1/2} \cdot z \qquad (5.1)$$

where z is a normally distributed random variable with mean zero and a variance of unity.

We further assume that the firm redeems its debt as promised if $\tilde{W}(T)$ is greater than F, in which case creditors receive F and stockholders receive $\tilde{W}(T) - F$. If $\tilde{W}(T)$ is less than F the company defaults, goes into bankruptcy, and incurs bankruptcy costs equal to $(1 - \lambda) \cdot \tilde{W}(T)$, where λ is a fixed and known quantity. (The studies summarized in section 4.6 suggest that bankruptcy dissipates between 5% and 20% of the value of an enterprise, so $1 - \lambda$ is between 0.05 and 0.20.) The balance of the value of the firm, $\lambda \cdot \tilde{W}(T)$, is distributed (to creditors and stockholders) according to the absolute priority rule, with creditors receiving $\lambda \cdot \tilde{W}(T)$ and shareholders receiving nothing. (We ignore here the prospect of violations of the absolute priority rule in order to focus on the issue of bankruptcy costs.)

Finally, we assume there exists a pair of contingent value functions, $\tilde{f}_1$ and $\tilde{f}_2$, such that the value of the ith security at time t can be computed as

$$V_i(t) = \tilde{f}_i(\tilde{W}(t), t), \qquad i = 1, 2 \qquad (5.2)$$

The $\tilde{f}_i$ functions are *not* the contingent value functions of equation (2.4); we are here expressing the value of the ith security as a function of the value of the *unlevered* firm, rather than as a function of the value of the *levered* firm.[3]

From our assumptions regarding default and bankruptcy, the contingent value functions at time T have the form

$$\tilde{f}_1(\tilde{W}, T) = \begin{cases} \lambda \cdot \tilde{W} & \text{if } \tilde{W} < F \\ F & \text{if } F \le \tilde{W} \end{cases} \qquad (5.3a)$$

$$\tilde{f}_2(\tilde{W}, T) = \begin{cases} 0 & \text{if } \tilde{W} < F \\ \tilde{W} - F & \text{if } F \le \tilde{W} \end{cases} \qquad (5.3b)$$

Figure 5.1 illustrates these terminal contingent value functions.

---

3. However, we can identify the contingent value functions of equation (2.4) if we can identify the forms of the $\tilde{f}_i$ contingent value functions. Let W be an arbitrary value of the levered firm, and let $\tilde{W}_w$ denote the value of the unlevered firm that is consistent with W at time t and therefore satisfies the equation $W = \tilde{f}_1(\tilde{W}_w, t) + \tilde{f}_2(\tilde{W}_w, t)$. We can then define the value of the ith security at time t as a function of the value W of the *levered* firm as $f_i(W, t) = \tilde{f}_i(\tilde{W}_w, t)$.

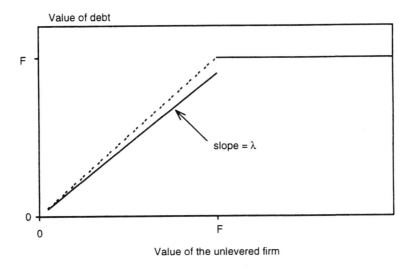

Value of debt

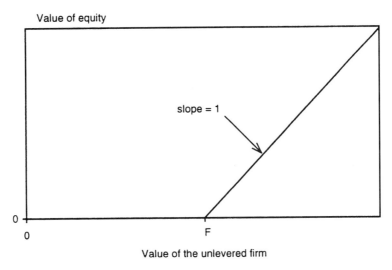

Value of equity

Figure 5.1
Value of debt and equity at time T as a function of the value of the unlevered firm, with bankruptcy costs

Identifying the $\tilde{f}_i$ Contingent Value Functions

Identifying the function $\tilde{f}_i$ is a matter of computing the value of $\tilde{f}_i(\tilde{W}^*, t^*)$ for any positive value of $\tilde{W}^*$ and for any value of t^* less than T.[4] This computation would appear to be only a minor variant of the computation described in section 2.4. Let us therefore consider whether we can use the arbitrage pricing algorithm described in that section to compute the value of $\tilde{f}_i(\tilde{W}^*, t^*)$.

As in section 2.4 we approximate the dynamic evolution of the value of the unlevered firm with a binomial random walk in discrete time. Dividing the interval between t^* and T into K subintervals of length $\Delta t = (T - t^*)/K$ and defining a sequence of $K + 1$ discrete points in time:

$$t_k = t^* + (k - 1) \cdot \Delta t, \qquad k = 1, 2, \ldots, K + 1 \tag{5.4}$$

we construct an array $\tilde{W}_{j,k}$ by defining the natural logarithm of $\tilde{W}_{j,k}$ as

$$\ln[\tilde{W}_{j,k}] = \ln[\tilde{W}^*] + (k - 1) \cdot \mu \cdot \Delta t + (2 \cdot j - k - 1) \cdot \sigma \cdot \Delta t^{1/2},$$
$$j = 1, 2, \ldots, k; k = 1, 2, \ldots, K + 1 \tag{5.5}$$

The value of the unlevered firm is $\tilde{W}_{1,1} = \tilde{W}^*$ at time $t_1 = t^*$ and subsequently evolves through the $\tilde{W}_{j,k}$ array. If the value of the unlevered firm is $\tilde{W}_{j,k}$ at time t_k, then the value of the unlevered firm at time t_{k+1} will be either $\tilde{W}_{j+1,k+1}$ or $\tilde{W}_{j,k+1}$.

Let $V_{j,k,i}$ denote the value of the ith security at time t_k when the value of the unlevered firm is $\tilde{W}_{j,k}$:

$$V_{j,k,i} = \tilde{f}_i(\tilde{W}_{j,k}, t_k) \tag{5.6}$$

We seek to compute the $V_{j,k,i}$ terms with a recursion algorithm on k, beginning at $k = K + 1$ and proceeding backward to $k = 1$.

Constructing the $V_{j,K+1,i}$ Terms

The values of $V_{j,K+1,i}$ for $j = 1, 2, \ldots, K + 1$ follow from our specification of the consequences of default and bankruptcy at time T.

If the value of the unlevered firm at time $T = t_{K+1}$ is less than F, the firm will default and creditors will receive whatever remains after bankruptcy costs. Creditors will be paid in full if the value of the unlevered firm exceeds F. Thus

$$V_{j,K+1,1} = \begin{cases} \lambda \cdot \tilde{W}_{j,K+1} & \text{if } \tilde{W}_{j,K+1} < F \\ F & \text{if } F \leq \tilde{W}_{j,K+1} \end{cases} \tag{5.7}$$

---

4. We can compute $\tilde{f}_i(\tilde{W}^*, T)$ using the terminal conditions in equations (5.3a, b).

Stockholders are residual claimants, so

$$V_{j,K+1,2} = \begin{cases} 0 & \text{if } \tilde{W}_{j,K+1} < F \\ \tilde{W}_{j,K+1} - F & \text{if } F \le \tilde{W}_{j,K+1} \end{cases} \tag{5.8}$$

A Problem with Calculating $V_{j,K,i}$ for a Special Value of j

At this point in the development of the computational algorithm in section 2.4 we described a recursive procedure for computing $V_{j,k,i}$ for values of k less than or equal to K.[5] A comparable procedure *cannot* be used to solve the present problem.

Suppose that the value of the unlevered firm at time t_K is $\tilde{W}_{\phi,K}$, where ϕ is an integer between 1 and K. Over the subinterval from t_K to t_{K+1} the value of the unlevered firm will evolve from $\tilde{W}_{\phi,K}$ to either

1. $\tilde{W}_{\phi+1,K+1}$, where the ith security will be worth the known quantity $V_{\phi+1,K+1,i}$, or

2. $\tilde{W}_{\phi,K+1}$, where the ith security will be worth the known quantity $V_{\phi,K+1,i}$.

Identify the value of ϕ such that $\tilde{W}_{\phi,K+1} < F \le \tilde{W}_{\phi+1,K+1}$. The firm redeems its debt as promised if the value of the unlevered firm evolves to $\tilde{W}_{\phi+1,K+1}$, and the firm defaults and files for bankruptcy if the value of the unlevered firm evolves to $\tilde{W}_{\phi,K+1}$. When the value of the unlevered firm is $\tilde{W}_{\phi,K}$ at time t_K, both bankruptcy and the avoidance of bankruptcy at time t_{K+1} are possible *but neither is certain*.[6]

Now consider constructing at time t_K a portfolio consisting of (1) an investment of Q in U.S. Treasury securities and (2) a fraction h of all of the debt of the firm and the same fraction of all of the equity of the firm (or, equivalently, a fraction h of the *levered* firm), where h and Q are chosen to satisfy the equations

$$V_{\phi+1,K+1,i} = h \cdot \tilde{W}_{\phi+1,K+1} + Q \cdot e^{R_f \cdot \Delta t} \tag{5.9a}$$

$$V_{\phi,K+1,i} = h \cdot \lambda \cdot \tilde{W}_{\phi,K+1} + Q \cdot e^{R_f \cdot \Delta t} \tag{5.9b}$$

There are two possibilities for the value of the portfolio at time t_{K+1}:

5. See text at equations (2.24a, b), (2.25a, b, c) and (2.26).

6. Such a value of ϕ will not exist if $F \le \tilde{W}_{1,K+1}$ (in which case the firm will never default on its debt because the value of the unlevered firm at time T will exceed the face amount of the debt regardless of the evolution of the value of the unlevered firm through the $\tilde{W}_{j,k}$ array) or if $\tilde{W}_{K+1,K+1} < F$ (in which case the firm will, with certainty, default on its debt at time T). These cases are artifacts of the discrete time binomial approximation of the continuous time Gaussian process in equation (5.1) and can be eliminated by choosing a sufficiently large value of K, that is, by choosing a sufficiently fine partitioning of the interval between t^* and T.

· If the value of the unlevered firm evolves to $\tilde{W}_{\phi+1,K+1}$ and the firm redeems its debt as promised, the firm will not incur any bankruptcy costs and the value of the levered firm will be identical to the value of the unlevered firm.[7] The fraction h of the levered firm will be worth $h \cdot \tilde{W}_{\phi+1,K+1}$, and the value of the replicating portfolio will be $h \cdot \tilde{W}_{\phi+1,K+1} + Q \cdot e^{R_f \cdot \Delta t}$. Equation (5.9a) shows that this is exactly the contemporaneous value of the ith security.

· Alternatively, if the value of the unlevered firm evolves to $\tilde{W}_{\phi,K+1}$ and the firm defaults and files for bankruptcy, the firm will incur bankruptcy costs of $(1 - \lambda) \cdot \tilde{W}_{\phi,K+1}$, and the value of the levered firm will be $\lambda \cdot \tilde{W}_{\phi,K+1}$.[8] The fraction h of the levered firm will be worth $h \cdot \lambda \cdot \tilde{W}_{\phi,K+1}$, and the value of the replicating portfolio will be $h \cdot \lambda \cdot \tilde{W}_{\phi,K+1} + Q \cdot e^{R_f \cdot \Delta t}$. Equation (5.9b) shows that this is, again, exactly the contemporaneous value of the ith security.

It follows that the portfolio constructed at time t_K replicates the value of the ith security at time t_{K+1}.

Assuming that the markets do not allow opportunities for riskless arbitrage profits, the value $(V_{\phi,K,i})$ of the ith security at time t_K when the value of the unlevered firm is $\tilde{W}_{\phi,K}$ must be the cost of constructing the replicating portfolio, or Q plus the fraction h of the value of the *levered* firm. Unfortunately, this does not lead to a value for $V_{\phi,K,i}$ because we cannot identify (with an arbitrage pricing argument) the value of the levered firm at time t_K when the value of the *unlevered* firm is $\tilde{W}_{\phi,K}$. When bankruptcy is a possible (but not certain) prospect, we cannot price the individual securities that capitalize the levered firm unless we know how the market prices the levered firm as a whole.[9]

Since we cannot calculate $V_{\phi,K,i}$, we cannot calculate the value of $V_{j,K,i}$ for all values of j in the interval from 1 to K. This means that we cannot

---

7. The value of the levered firm will be the sum of the value of its debt (F) and equity $(\tilde{W}_{\phi+1,K+1} - F)$, and hence will be exactly $\tilde{W}_{\phi+1,K+1}$.

8. The value of the levered firm will be the value of its debt, $\lambda \cdot \tilde{W}_{\phi,K+1}$, because its equity is worthless.

9. Since $V_{\phi,K,1} + V_{\phi,K,2}$ is the value of the levered firm at time t_K when the value of the unlevered firm is $\tilde{W}_{\phi,K}$, it might seem feasible to write

$$V_{\phi,K,1} = h_1 \cdot (V_{\phi,K,1} + V_{\phi,K,2}) + Q_1$$

$$V_{\phi,K,2} = h_2 \cdot (V_{\phi,K,1} + V_{\phi,K,2}) + Q_2$$

(where h_1 and Q_1 are the values of h and Q that satisfy equations (5.9a, b) when $i = 1$, and similarly with h_2 and Q_2) and then to solve these two equations for the unknown values of $V_{\phi,K,1}$ and $V_{\phi,K,2}$. However, it can be shown that $h_1 + h_2 = 1$ and that $Q_1 + Q_2 = 0$, so the equations are not linearly independent: *any* values of $V_{\phi,K,1}$ and $V_{\phi,K,2}$ that satisfy the first equation will also satisfy the second equation.

construct a recursive algorithm for computing all of the $V_{j,k,i}$ terms, and hence that we cannot identify the $\tilde{f}_i$ contingent value function.

Remark

If we can construct, at time t_k when the value of the unlevered firm is $\tilde{W}_{j,k}$, a portfolio consisting of (1) an investment of Q in U.S. Treasury securities and (2) a fraction h of the value of the *unlevered* firm, where Q and h satisfy the equations

$$V_{j+1,k+1,i} = h \cdot \tilde{W}_{j+1,k+1} + Q \cdot e^{R_f \cdot \Delta t} \tag{5.10a}$$

$$V_{j,k+1,i} = h \cdot \tilde{W}_{j,k+1} + Q \cdot e^{R_f \cdot \Delta t} \tag{5.10b}$$

then we can compute the value of the ith security at time t_k as

$$V_{j,k,i} = h \cdot \tilde{W}_{j,k} + Q \tag{5.11}$$

and we can identify the $\tilde{f}_i$ contingent value function.

We can construct a position in the value of the unlevered firm if fluctuations in that value can be replicated with a portfolio of traded claims[10] so that the value of the unlevered firm is (effectively) the price of a publicly traded claim. In particular, there may exist a "credit derivative" that promises to pay to a holder an amount equal to the costs (to the firm) of default and bankruptcy.[11] This way the value of the unlevered firm can be replicated with the credit derivative and the debt and equity of the levered firm. Although these possibilities are important conceptually, the credit derivatives market does not now appear to offer claims that pay out as a function of the direct and indirect costs of bankruptcy (indeed, the indirect costs of bankruptcy are notoriously difficult to identify; see Altman 1984; Haugen and Senbet 1988, pp. 31–32; Wruck 1990, p. 438) and the practical ability of market participants to otherwise replicate fluctuations in the value of the unlevered firm is unclear.

5.2   Violations of the Absolute Priority Rule

This section examines whether we can incorporate the prospect for violations of the absolute priority rule into the specification of a contingent value model. For expository convenience we will continue to use the

---

10. As assumed in, for example, Leland (1998). See also Brennan and Schwartz (1978), who assume more simply that there exists an identical unlevered firm whose equity is publicly traded.

11. Credit derivatives are described in Whittaker and Kumar (1996), Iacono (1997), Caouette, Altman, and Narayan (1998, ch. 20), Das (1998), Tavakoli (1998), and Francis, Frost, and Whittaker (1999).

model presented in chapter 2, where the firm is capitalized with common stock and a single issue of zero-coupon debt that promises to pay F at time T. We ignore bankruptcy costs in order to focus on violations of the rule.

To relax the assumption that bankruptcy results in distributions of cash or securities in accord with the absolute priority rule, we have to specify terminal contingent value functions that reflect the empirical observation that stockholders derive value from the bankruptcy process in excess of their entitlements under the rule. One simple possibility is to replace the terminal conditions shown in equations (2.5a, b) and figure 2.1 with those shown in figure 5.2. The terminal conditions in figure 5.2 assume that the firm will default and file for bankruptcy if the value of the firm is less than F and that bankruptcy results in a distribution to shareholders even though creditors are not paid in full. (Following Betker 1995a, the bankruptcy distribution to shareholders is a convex function of the value of the firm: shareholders receive proportionately less the deeper the insolvency of the firm.) If the value of the firm exceeds F, the firm redeems its debt as promised.[12]

The terminal contingent value functions in figure 5.2 are subject to two criticisms. First, they ignore the prospect of *strategic* default, or default in the absence of an actual inability to make a required payment, when the value of the firm exceeds F. The incentive for strategic default arises because stockholders may benefit if the firm defaults and negotiates with creditors in bankruptcy, instead of redeeming its debt as promised, when the value of the firm exceeds F by a small margin. As illustrated in figure 5.3, this criticism can be addressed by relaxing the assumption that the

---

12. Alternatively, we could postulate terminal contingent value functions that violate the absolute priority rule as a consequence of a private recapitalization. We noted in the appendix to chapter 4 that the creditors and stockholders of a firm on the verge of default have an incentive to negotiate a consensual recapitalization to avoid incurring the dissipative costs of bankruptcy. If, as in section 5.1, the costs of bankruptcy are equal to a fraction $1 - \lambda$ of the value of the firm, and if market participants are confident that the claimants will agree to a costless private recapitalization that allocates a fraction α of the cost savings to creditors and $1 - \alpha$ to stockholders (where α is between zero and unity), the terminal contingent value functions for the debt and equity in equation (2.5a, b) become

$$f_1(W, T) = \begin{cases} \lambda \cdot W + \alpha \cdot (1 - \lambda) \cdot W & \text{if } W < F \\ F & \text{if } F \leq W \end{cases}$$

$$f_2(W, T) = \begin{cases} (1 - \alpha) \cdot (1 - \lambda) \cdot W & \text{if } W < F \\ W - F & \text{if } F \leq W \end{cases}$$

These terminal contingent value functions do not satisfy the absolute priority rule: if W is less than F the common stock has a positive value even though the value of the debt is less than the face amount of the debt. This breach of the rule stems from the ability of stockholders to capture some of the bankruptcy costs saved by recapitalizing privately. It should be noted that nothing guarantees that the creditors and stockholders will be able to agree to such a private recapitalization (see note 70 in Chapter 4).

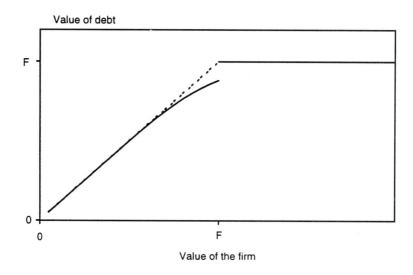

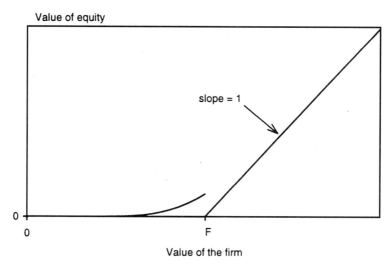

Figure 5.2
Contingent value of debt and equity at time T

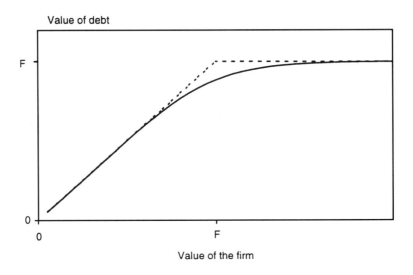

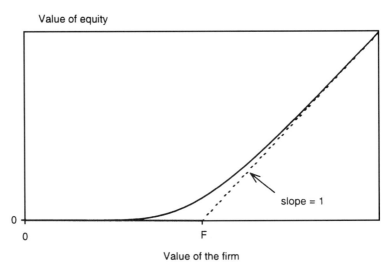

Figure 5.3
Contingent value of debt and equity at time T, allowing for strategic default

firm will redeem its debt as promised if the value of the firm exceeds F and by extending the representation of the violation of the absolute priority rule to values of the firm in excess of F.[13]

The second criticism stems from the empirical observation that departures from the absolute priority rule are not invariant with respect to the strength of management's representation of shareholder interests and with respect to the legal position and bargaining skill of creditors. Following the results reported in Betker (1995a) and summarized in section 4.6, the contingent value of equity at time T should be lower, and the contingent value of debt should be higher, if the CEO at the time of filing for bankruptcy does not own a substantial block of common stock, if the CEO is likely to be replaced, if the bankruptcy court is likely to terminate exclusivity, or if a significant fraction of the firm's debt is owned by secured or bank creditors.

It may be possible to incorporate the effect of factors like the strength of management representation of shareholder interests by adding an ancillary variable, here denoted θ, to the terminal contingent value functions. The value of θ would reflect the characteristics identified by Betker as affecting the terms of a recapitalization. The contingent value of the ith security at time T when the value of the firm is W could then be represented as $f_i(W, T, \theta)$. As illustrated in figure 5.4, different values of θ would be associated with different locations of the terminal contingent value functions.

---

13. Anderson and Sundaresan (1996) point out that the prospect of capturing for shareholders some of the savings derived from staying out of bankruptcy (see the preceding note) can give the managers of the firm an incentive to offer to redeem the firm's debt for less than F even when the value of the firm exceeds F at time T (see, especially, the discussion in their section 2.1). Such opportunistic, or strategic, debt service changes the terminal contingent value functions in the preceding note to

$$f_1(W, T) = \begin{cases} \lambda \cdot W + \alpha \cdot (1 - \lambda) \cdot W & \text{if } W < (\alpha + \lambda - \alpha \cdot \lambda)^{-1} \cdot F \\ F & \text{if } (\alpha + \lambda - \alpha \cdot \lambda)^{-1} \cdot F \leq W \end{cases}$$

$$f_2(W, T) = \begin{cases} (1 - \alpha) \cdot (1 - \lambda) \cdot W & \text{if } W < (\alpha + \lambda - \alpha \cdot \lambda)^{-1} \cdot F \\ W - F & \text{if } (\alpha + \lambda - \alpha \cdot \lambda)^{-1} \cdot F \leq W \end{cases}$$

where $(\alpha + \lambda - \alpha \cdot \lambda)^{-1} \cdot F$ is the threshold value of W that satisfies the equation $(1 - \alpha) \cdot (1 - \lambda) \cdot W = W - F$. (Observe that $f_2(W, T)$ exceeds $W - F$ when W lies in the interval between $W - F$ and $(\alpha + \lambda - \alpha \cdot \lambda)^{-1} \cdot F$.) Anderson and Sundaresan examine the special case of $\alpha = 0$, where managers have a "first-mover" advantage and can make a take-it-or-leave-it offer to creditors. If $\alpha = 1$, that is, if creditors have a first-mover advantage, the terminal contingent value functions collapse to $f_1(W, T) = \min[W, F]$ and $f_2(W, T) = \max[0, W - F]$. Mella-Barral and Perraudin (1997) and Mella-Barral (1999) offer related analyses of strategic debt service for coupon-bearing perpetual debt. An incentive for strategic default did not appear in chapter 2 because we assumed in that chapter that bankruptcy is costless and always results in distributions in accord with the absolute priority rule.

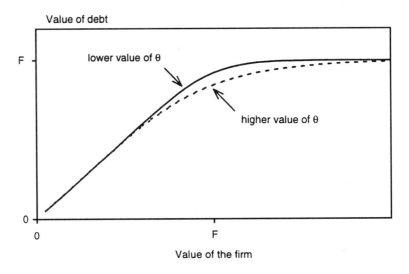

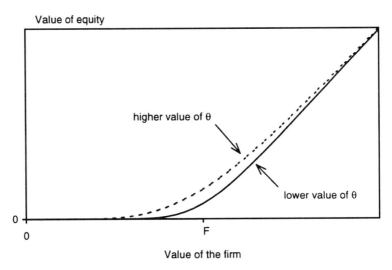

Figure 5.4
Consequence of different values of θ for the contingent value of debt and equity at time T, where a higher value of θ is associated with, for example, stronger management representation of shareholder interests

Unfortunately, introducing such an ancillary variable creates a problem in assessing the contingent values of the corporation's securities prior to the maturity of the debt. It is unlikely that the value of θ (and hence the locations of the terminal contingent value functions) will be known with certainty prior to time T. However, interpreting θ as a random variable introduces a novel source of uncertainty, and hence risk, into the contingent valuation of the corporation's securities. Unlike the risk of fluctuations in the value of the firm, this new risk may not be replicable with traded claims. If we cannot replicate (with traded claims) fluctuations in the values of the firm's securities associated with revisions in the market's assessment of the prospective value of θ, we cannot appeal to an arbitrage pricing argument to identify the contingent value of the firm's debt and equity prior to the maturity of the debt as we did in section 2.4.[14]

5.3   Summary

The studies summarized in section 4.6 suggest that bankruptcy is not costless and that recapitalizations in Chapter 11 frequently violate the absolute priority rule. However, it does not appear to be possible to incorporate either bankruptcy costs or prospective violations of the absolute priority rule into the specification of a conventional contingent value model. The principle impediment to a more realistic representation of bankruptcy costs and violations of the APR is the appearance of uncertainties that affect securities prices but that, as a practical matter, may not be replicable with traded claims. These are, respectively, the risk that a firm might or might not incur bankruptcy costs (and uncertainty about the magnitude of those costs) and uncertainty about the strength of management representation of shareholder interests and the legal position and bargaining skill of creditors.

14. Uncertain bankruptcy costs will similarly impair the contingent pricing of corporate securities.

II SECURITIES WITH CALL AND CONVERSION OPTIONS

6 Callable Debt

Contingent value analysis views common stock as a call option on the firm, where the dates and amounts of payments promised to creditors define the terms of the option.[1] However, stockholders (acting through the management of a company) frequently have options other than simply making, or not making, promised payments. Most prominently, they may be able to "call" debt for early redemption. This chapter shows how an issuer's option to redeem debt before its stated maturity date can be incorporated into a contingent value model.[2]

6.1 Framework of the Analysis

We begin by stating our assumptions on the capital structure of the firm and the consequences of default and bankruptcy.

Corporate Capital Structure

We assume the firm is capitalized with two classes of securities: a single issue of zero-coupon callable debt and common stock that cannot pay a dividend and cannot be repurchased by the firm until the debt has been redeemed.

The debt matures at time T and promises to pay its face amount F at that time. At any time t prior to maturity, the company can call the debt for early redemption by paying creditors the contractually specified amount $C(t)$. (Example 6.1 describes a callable zero-coupon note issued

1. The concept of common stock as a call option was discussed in sections 2.2 and 3.1 and is discussed further in section 12.1.

2. Companies commonly call their debt following an improvement in creditworthiness or a decline in the general level of interest rates. We will not be able to examine calls in the latter category because we assumed (in section 1.3) that the Treasury yield curve is flat and stationary through time. Acharya and Carpenter (1999) examine the pricing of callable corporate debt when the yield curve for default-proof debt evolves as in the model of Cox, Ingersoll, and Ross (1985).

Symmetry suggests that creditors could have the option to "put" debt back to the issuer following a deterioration in the creditworthiness of the issuer or an increase in the general level of interest rates. Unconditionally putable debt is rare in American capital markets (but see the putable debt described in example 8.1). However, many bonds issued in the second half of the 1980s and subsequently carried "contingent" put options (commonly called "poison puts") providing that a holder can demand early redemption following specified control, capital structure, and/or credit events. See Lehn and Poulsen (1991) (describing poison puts as a contractual device to protect creditors from losses associated with leveraged buyouts and related events), Crabbe (1991) (estimating the market value of poison puts), Kahan and Klausner (1993) (assessing whether poison puts might have been designed primarily to protect managers), and Cook and Easterwood (1994) (announcement of new debt with poison put option associated with an abnormal decrease in the price of the issuer's equity (consistent with management entrenchment hypothesis) and an abnormal increase in the price of the issuer's outstanding debt (consistent with creditor protection hypothesis)).

by the Student Loan Marketing Association in August 1984.[3]) Following our assumption on corporate governance (see section 1.5), the firm will call the debt whenever immediate redemption is in the best interests of shareholders. We ignore any requirement for a notice period and assume that call and redemption occur instantaneously.[4]

We denote the value of the callable debt at time t as $V_1(t)$ and the value of equity as $V_2(t)$. The value of the firm is the sum of the values of the firm's securities: $W(t) = V_1(t) + V_2(t)$.

Default and Bankruptcy

If the debt has not been redeemed prior to time T, creditors have a claim for the face amount of the debt. If the firm does not pay this contractually specified sum, the firm defaults and goes into bankruptcy.

For simplicity (and despite the observations in section 4.6 regarding the duration, cost and distributional characteristics of bankruptcy) we assume that bankruptcy results in an instantaneous and costless liquidation of the assets of the firm and distribution of the proceeds according to the absolute priority rule. Creditors are paid the entire proceeds of liquidation up to the amount of their claims and stockholders receive any residual bal-

---

3. The 30-year notes in example 6.1 cannot, under any circumstances, be called for early redemption during the first 25 years of their life, but are unconditionally callable thereafter. Some callable debt with partial call protection provides that the issuer has a contingent call option during the call protection period, giving it the right to call the debt under specified circumstances. The most common contingent option provides that the issuer can redeem its debt if the proceeds of redemption are not derived from the sale of new indebtedness yielding less than the yield on the original debt at the time it was issued (Thatcher 1985; Allen, Lamy, and Thompson 1987). This protects the creditor from the risk that his investment will, inexorably, be refunded with new, lower yielding, debt following a decline in the general level of interest rates or an improvement in the creditworthiness of the issuer, but gives the issuer the right to redeem the debt with proceeds from a sale of assets or new equity securities. Laber (1990) discusses a second case: when a firm is required to allocate a specified fraction of revenues to a "maintenance and replacement fund," it may have the option of using balances in the fund to finance early redemption of debt pursuant to a special call provision in lieu of maintaining and replacing physical plant. In some cases creditors have disputed whether the contingency allowing exercise of a contingent call option has been satisfied; see *Franklin Life Insurance Co. v. Commonwealth Edison*, 451 F. Supp. 602 (S.D.Ill. 1978) and *Morgan Stanley & Co. v. Archer Daniels Midland Co.*, 570 F. Supp. 1529 (S.D.N.Y. 1983). In other cases, in a transaction known as a "simultaneous tender and call" (or "Stac"), an issuer has sought to avoid complying with a contingency requirement by offering to repurchase debt at a price slightly above the current exercise price specified in a contingent call option, while simultaneously threatening to satisfy the contingency requirement and exercise the option at the lower option price. See "May Stores, Morgan Stanley Settle Suit Filed by Bondholders over Refinancing," *Wall Street Journal*, August 22, 1994, p. A2, and "James River, Merrill Are Sued on Refinancing," *Wall Street Journal*, September 2, 1994, p. A5A.

4. If a notice period of τ years is required (where τ is typically on the order of 30 days or 0.0822 years $(0.0822 = 30/365)$), then debt called for redemption at time t will be redeemed at time $t + \tau$ upon payment of $C(t + \tau)$. Equivalently we could define the discounted call price $C_d(t) = C(t + \tau) \cdot \exp[-R_f \cdot \tau]$, and say that the debt is callable with no notice upon payment of $C_d(t)$ at time t.

Example 6.1   A Callable Zero-Coupon Note

In August, 1984, the Student Loan Marketing Association ("Sallie Mae"), a corporation chartered by Congress in 1972 to provide liquidity for lenders participating in the Federal Guaranteed Student Loan Program, sold callable zero-coupon notes maturing on May 15, 2014, with a face value of $2 billion.

The notes were not callable prior to May 15, 2009. On and after that date, they were callable pursuant to the contractually specified schedule:

Interval	Call value (% of redemption value)
May 15, 2009–May 14, 2010	100.50
May 15, 2010–May 14, 2011	100.40
May 15, 2011–May 14, 2012	100.30
May 15, 2012–May 14, 2013	100.20
May 15, 2013–May 14, 2014	100.10

where the redemption value of the notes is computed as the present value of the $2 billion face amount of the notes, discounted back to the redemption date using an interest rate of 11.50% per annum, compounded semiannually. Thus the redemption value on a date n semiannual periods from maturity would be computed as

$$\text{Redemption value} = \frac{\$2 \text{ billion}}{(1 + \frac{1}{2} \cdot 0.1150)^n}$$

For example, the redemption value of the notes on November 15, 2011 ($n = 5$ semiannual periods before maturity) would be computed as

$$\text{Redemption value} = \frac{\$2 \text{ billion}}{(1 + \frac{1}{2} \cdot 0.1150)^5} = \$1.512 \text{ billion}$$

The call value of the notes for redemption on November 15, 2011, would be 100.30% of the $1.512 billion redemption value, or $1.517 billion.

---

ance. This leads to terminal contingent value conditions identical to those stated at equations (2.2a, b).[5]

6.2   The Valuation Problem

We assume there exists a pair of functions, f_1 and f_2, with two arguments: time and the value of the firm, such that the value of the ith security at time t can be calculated as

$$V_i(t) = f_i(W(t), t), \qquad i = 1, 2 \tag{6.1}$$

---

5. Whatever else may be the case, the option to call debt for early redemption is not a matter of terminal conditions. This contrasts with the analysis in chapter 3, where the distinction between senior and subordinated debt was *only* a matter of the terminal conditions for the respective securities.

The valuation problem is identifying the forms of these contingent value functions.

6.3   Solving the Valuation Problem

We already know the forms of the contingent value functions at time T: $f_1(W, T) = \min[W, F]$ and $f_2(W, T) = \max[0, W - F]$. An algorithm for assessing the value of $f_i(W^*, t^*)$ for any value of t^* less than T can be constructed as in section 2.4, except that here we have to take account of the issuer's option to call the debt for early redemption.

As in section 2.4 we approximate the dynamic evolution of the value of the firm with a binomial random walk in discrete time. Dividing the interval between t^* and T into K subintervals of length Δt and defining a sequence of $K + 1$ discrete points in time,

$$t_k = t^* + (k - 1) \cdot \Delta t, \qquad k = 1, 2, \ldots, K + 1 \tag{6.2}$$

we construct an array $W_{j,k}$, where the natural logarithm of $W_{j,k}$ is defined as

$$\ln[W_{j,k}] = \ln[W^*] + (k - 1) \cdot \mu \cdot \Delta t + (2 \cdot j - k - 1) \cdot \sigma \cdot \Delta t^{1/2},$$
$$j = 1, 2, \ldots, k; \; k = 1, 2, \ldots, K + 1 \tag{6.3}$$

The value of the firm is $W_{1,1} = W^*$ at time $t_1 = t^*$ and subsequently evolves through the array. If the value of the firm is $W_{j,k}$ at time t_k, then the value of the firm at time t_{k+1} will be either $W_{j+1,k+1}$ or $W_{j,k+1}$.

Let $V_{j,k,i}$ denote the value of the ith security at time t_k when the value of the firm is $W_{j,k}$:

$$V_{j,k,i} = f_i(W_{j,k}, t_k) \tag{6.4}$$

We compute the $V_{j,k,i}$ terms using a recursion algorithm on k, beginning at $k = K + 1$ and proceeding backward to $k = 1$.

The values of $V_{j,K+1,i}$ for $j = 1, 2, \ldots, K + 1$ follow from our specification of the consequences of default and bankruptcy at time $t_{K+1} = T$ exactly as in equations (2.22) and (2.23).

Calculating the $V_{j,k,i}$ Terms for $k < K + 1$

Consider the problem of computing $V_{j,k,i}$ for some value of k less than $K + 1$, assuming that we know $V_{j,k+1,i}$ for $j = 1, 2, \ldots, k + 1$.

$V_{j,k,i}$ is the value of the ith security at time t_k when the value of the firm is $W_{j,k}$ (see equation 6.4). Either of two events can happen at time t_k when the value of the firm is $W_{j,k}$:

· The firm can call its debt for early redemption by paying the contractually specified amount $C(t_k)$ to its creditors.

· The firm can abstain from calling the debt and leave the debt with creditors until time t_{k+1}.

Which event actually occurs depends on which maximizes the value of the company's stock.

If the firm calls the debt for early redemption, the debt will be worth the call value $C(t_k)$. Ignoring transactions costs associated with financing the redemption, the stock will be worth the balance of the value of the firm, or $W_{j,k} - C(t_k)$.[6]

Alternatively, the firm can maintain the status quo by not calling the debt. Let $V_{j,k,i}^{sq}$ denote the value of the ith security conditional on this event. The value of $V_{j,k,i}^{sq}$ can be computed with an arbitrage pricing argument.

If the firm chooses to maintain the status quo, the value of the firm will evolve over the subinterval from t_k to t_{k+1} to either

1. $W_{j+1,k+1}$, where the ith security will be worth $V_{j+1,k+1,i}$, or

2. $W_{j,k+1}$, where the ith security will be worth $V_{j,k+1,i}$.

Assuming that the markets do not allow opportunities for riskless arbitrage profits, we have[7]

$$V_{j,k,i}^{sq} = h \cdot W_{j,k} + Q \tag{6.5}$$

where h and Q satisfy the equations

$$V_{j+1,k+1,i} = h \cdot W_{j+1,k+1} + Q \cdot e^{R_f \cdot \Delta t} \tag{6.6a}$$

$$V_{j,k+1,i} = h \cdot W_{j,k+1} + Q \cdot e^{R_f \cdot \Delta t} \tag{6.6b}$$

The corporation will act to maximize the value of equity, calling the debt if the value of equity following early redemption, $W_{j,k} - C(t_k)$, exceeds the value of equity in the absence of early redemption, $V_{j,k,2}^{sq}$, and leaving the debt outstanding if the inequality runs in the opposite direction. Thus the value of equity at time t_k when the value of the firm is $W_{j,k}$ is

$$V_{j,k,2} = \max[W_{j,k} - C(t_k), V_{j,k,2}^{sq}] \tag{6.7}$$

---

6. Mauer (1993) examines the effect of transactions costs associated with financing an early redemption of debt on the exercise of an early redemption option and the pricing of callable debt. His analysis is limited to default-proof debt and, for reasons similar to the difficulty of incorporating bankruptcy costs into a contingent valuation model (see section 5.1), does not extend readily to corporate debt.

7. See the discussion in the text at equations (2.24a, b) to (2.26).

Equivalently the corporation will act to *minimize* the value of the *debt* (because the value of the firm is equal to the sum of the value of the debt and equity): calling the debt if $C(t_k)$ is less than $V^{sq}_{j,k,1}$, and conversely. Thus the value of the debt at time t_k when the value of the firm is $W_{j,k}$ is

$$V_{j,k,1} = \min[C(t_k), V^{sq}_{j,k,1}] \tag{6.8}$$

The foregoing algorithm can be applied recursively, beginning at $k = K$ and continuing through computation of $V_{1,1,i}$. Since $V_{1,1,i} = f_i(W_{1,1}, t_1) = f_i(W^*, t^*)$, this completes the computation of $f_i(W^*, t^*)$ for the case where the value of the firm evolves according to the discrete time binomial process. As Δt goes to zero, the binomial process converges to the continuous time Gaussian process of equation (1.14) and the value of $V_{1,1,i}$ converges to the value of $f_i(W^*, t^*)$ for the case where the value of the firm evolves according to the Gaussian process.

Comments

It may be helpful to compare the foregoing contingent value model with the model of equity and noncallable debt presented in chapter 2.

Both models assume that the natural logarithm of the value of the firm evolves in continuous time as a Gaussian random walk, and both models approximate that process with a discrete time binomial random walk. The two models also establish the contingent value of the debt and equity on the maturity date of the debt from identical assumptions regarding default and bankruptcy.

The difference between the models lies in the valuation of the debt and equity prior to the maturity of the debt. The model in chapter 2 uses a recursive arbitrage pricing algorithm. The model in this chapter employs the same algorithm but supplements it with a specific examination—*at each point in time and at every value of the firm*—of whether the firm should exercise its option for early redemption.

An Alternative Assumption on Managerial Behavior

We assumed that managers act to maximize shareholder value. This assumption is conventional. It is based on important institutional characteristics of corporate governance, but it is not inexorable.

Suppose, for example, that the firm is controlled by (or managed on behalf of) a coalition of claimants that owns a fraction x_1 of the debt and a fraction x_2 of the equity. If the debt is called at time t_k when the value of the firm is $W_{j,k}$, the value of the coalition's holdings will be $x_1 \cdot C(t_k) + x_2 \cdot [W_{j,k} - C(t_k)]$. If the debt is not called, the value of the coalition's holdings will be $x_1 \cdot V^{sq}_{j,k,1} + x_2 \cdot V^{sq}_{j,k,2}$. Thus the debt will be called if

$$x_1 \cdot C(t_k) + x_2 \cdot [W_{j,k} - C(t_k)] > x_1 \cdot V^{\mathrm{sq}}_{j,k,1} + x_2 \cdot V^{\mathrm{sq}}_{j,k,2} \tag{6.9}$$

Since $V^{\mathrm{sq}}_{j,k,1} + V^{\mathrm{sq}}_{j,k,2} = W_{j,k}$,[8] equation (6.9) is equivalent to

$$x_1 \cdot C(t_k) + x_2 \cdot [W_{j,k} - C(t_k)] > x_1 \cdot V^{\mathrm{sq}}_{j,k,1} + x_2 \cdot [W_{j,k} - V^{\mathrm{sq}}_{j,k,1}]$$

or

$$(x_1 - x_2) \cdot C(t_k) > (x_1 - x_2) \cdot V^{\mathrm{sq}}_{j,k,1} \tag{6.10}$$

If the coalition owns a larger fraction of debt than equity, that is, if $x_1 > x_2$, the debt will be called when $C(t_k) > V^{\mathrm{sq}}_{j,k,1}$. This is in the best interests of the coalition (and in the best interests of the firm's creditors as a class), but it is *contrary* to the best interests of shareholders as a class.[9]

6.4   Some Examples

At this point it may be helpful to examine some examples of valuing the securities of a firm capitalized with zero-coupon callable debt and common stock. We assume that the U.S. Treasury yield curve is flat and stationary at $R_f = 0.10$ (or 10% per annum) and that the volatility of the value of the firm is $\sigma = 0.20$ (or a volatility of 20% over one year).

We also assume that the face amount of the zero-coupon debt is $F = 164.872$ and that we are valuing the debt five years prior to maturity. Ignoring the risk of default and the issuer's option for early redemption, the debt has a "contingency-free" value of 100.0.[10]

---

8. The proof of this assertion follows from an analysis similar to the analysis in appendix B to chapter 2.

9. Vu (1986) examined the possibility that a firm might call its debt for early redemption in order to transfer wealth from stockholders to creditors. He concludes that the magnitude of any such wealth transfer is small. However, there are some cases of managers acting in the best interests of creditors. See, for example, the fact situation in *Farmers' Loan & Trust Company v. New York & Northern Railway*, 150 N.Y. 410 (1896), where, as described by Berle and Means (1932, p. 240), a controlling shareholder owned a majority of mortgage bonds issued by the railroad, caused the railroad to default on its debt, and foreclosed on the collateral property. Jensen and Meckling (1976, p. 339n. 49) also note, in a different context, the possibility that creditors may sometimes be in a position to exploit stockholders.

10. In chapters 2 and 3 we spoke of the "default-free" value of debt when we wanted to refer to the value of debt assuming that it is redeemed at face value at maturity, because default was the only alternative to redemption at maturity. In the present case the debt may not be redeemed at maturity either because the issuer defaults or because the issuer redeemed the debt early. Thus we now have to speak more generally of the "contingency-free" value of the debt when we want to refer to the value of the debt assuming that it is redeemed at face value at maturity, where the excluded contingencies include early redemption as well as default at maturity.

Example A

The first example assumes the debt is callable pursuant to a schedule of call values that rise to F at time T:

$$C(t) = F \cdot e^{-\rho \cdot (T-t)}, \qquad t < T \tag{6.11}$$

We use $\rho = 0.12$, or 12% per annum, so the debt is callable at a yield 200 basis points over the yield on Treasury debt. The call value of the debt five years before maturity is 90.484 (90.484 = 164.872 discounted for five years at 12% per annum, compounded continuously).

The upper panel of figure 6.1 shows, with a solid line, the contingent value of the callable debt. The dashed line shows what the debt would be worth in the absence of the call provision.[11] The difference between the dashed and solid lines reflects the reduction in contingent value attributable to the issuer's call option. The lower panel of figure 6.1 shows how the company's option to redeem its debt prior to time T enhances the contingent value of equity.

Observe in the upper panel of figure 6.1 that when the value of the firm exceeds 155 the value of the callable debt is identical to the debt's call value. (This is the segment of the contingent value function marked A–A.) This reflects the consequence of a decision to call the debt for immediate redemption if the value of the firm exceeds 155 five years before the debt matures.[12] If the value of the firm is less than 155, immediate redemption is not in the best interest of shareholders and the value of the debt is less than the debt's call value.

Cross Valuation

Figure 6.2 shows how the option of the firm to call its debt for early redemption affects the implicit relationship between debt and equity values. For equity of a given market value, the imputed value of the debt will be lower if the debt is callable. There are two reasons for this shift in the cross value function. First, the value of the debt is directly related to the value of the firm and the value of the firm associated with a given equity value will be lower if the debt is callable (see the lower panel of figure 6.1).

---

11. The dashed line is identical to the solid line in the upper panel of figure 2.11. Noncallable debt can be represented as a special case of callable debt by setting the call value of the debt to an arbitrarily high level, or by specifying $C(t) = \infty$ for all values of t.

12. The contemporaneous call decision of the firm can be identified at the last stage of the valuation algorithm described in section 6.3, when $j = 1$ and $k = 1$. The discussion leading up to equation (6.8) implies that the firm will call the debt at time t_1 when the value of the firm is $W_{1,1}$ if $C(t_1)$ is less than $V_{1,1,1}^{sq}$ and that it will defer calling the debt if the inequality runs in the opposite direction.

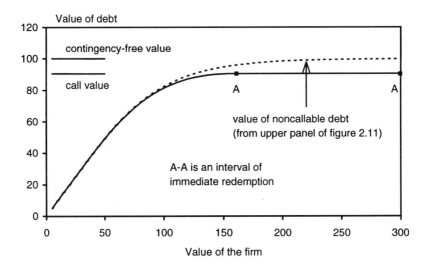

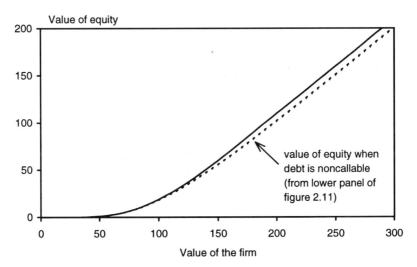

Figure 6.1
Contingent value of callable debt and equity five years before the debt matures

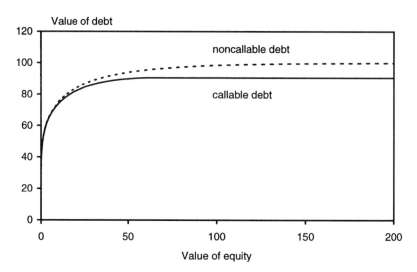

Figure 6.2
Value of debt five years before maturity as a function of the value of equity

Second, the value of the debt is lower if the debt is callable even if we hold the value of the firm constant (see the upper panel of figure 6.1).

The difference between the cross-value functions in figure 6.2 carries an important warning for relative value analyses of corporate securities. Suppose that we want to impute the value of a corporate bond from the value of the company's stock but fail to account for the fact that the bond is callable. The cross-value functions in figure 6.2 imply that the market value of the bond would appear to be low compared to the model value of the bond, given the observed market value of equity, because the market will value the bond on the solid line cross-value function and we would value the bond on the higher dashed line function. The bond appears to be cheap (relative to equity) because we failed to include in our model an option controlled by a management that acts in the best interests of shareholders. This illustrates the important principle that contingent corporate security values can be misleading if they fail to include the values of options embedded in the securities.

Example B

The second example is identical to example A, except that we here assume $\rho = 0.11$, or 11% per annum, so the debt is callable at a yield 100 basis points over the yield on Treasury debt. It follows that at every point in time prior to time T, the call value of the debt is greater in this example than in the preceding example, where the debt was callable at a yield spread of 200 basis points over Treasury yields. For example, if at time t the debt matures in five years, then $C(t) = 95.123$ when $\rho = 0.11$ compared to $C(t) = 90.484$ when $\rho = 0.12$.

The upper panel of figure 6.3 shows that ceteris paribus, a higher schedule of call values enhances the contingent value of callable debt. The lower panel of the figure shows that a higher schedule of call values reduces the contingent value of equity. This is consistent with the notion that the value of a call option is an inverse function of the option's strike price.

Inspection of the data used to construct the graphs in the upper panel of figure 6.3 shows that the threshold value of the firm above which the debt will be called is greater the higher the schedule of call values. When $\rho = 0.12$, the debt will be called five years before maturity if the value of the firm exceeds 155, but if $\rho = 0.11$ the debt will not be called unless the value of the firm exceeds 195.

If we reduce the value of ρ down to the level of Treasury yields, namely to $\rho = R_f = 0.10$, we will find that the debt is *never* called prior to maturity, regardless of the value of the firm. This accords with the intuitive notion that it is contrary to the best interests of the shareholders of a limited liability corporation for the firm to redeem its debt at a price equal to the price of comparable Treasury debt. Such a redemption would enhance the position of creditors (they could, at no cost to themselves, replace their risky corporate debt with default-free Treasury debt that promises to pay the same amount on the same future date) and thus impair the position of stockholders.

Example C

The last example assumes that the debt is protected from call until three years prior to maturity:

$$C(t) = \begin{cases} F \cdot e^{-\rho \cdot (T-t)} & T - 3 \le t < T \\ \infty & t < T - 3 \end{cases} \tag{6.12}$$

As in example A, we assume that $\rho = 0.12$.

As shown by the solid line in the upper panel of figure 6.4, the contingent value of the debt five years before maturity (when the debt is still protected from immediate call) is intermediate between the contingent value of noncallable debt and the contingent value of debt that is immediately callable. The contingent value function for the call protected debt will move closer to the upper dashed line in the upper panel of figure 6.4 the longer the remaining interval of call protection, and closer to the lower dashed line the shorter the interval.

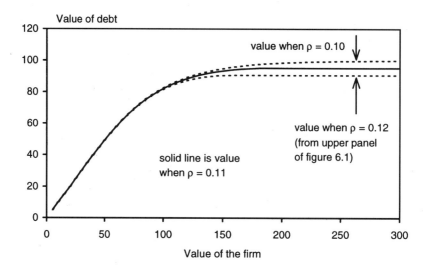

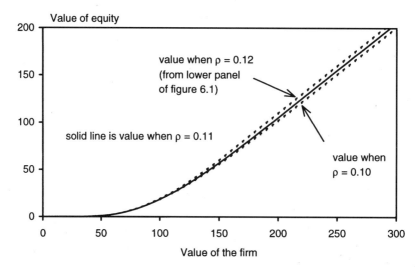

Figure 6.3
Contingent value of callable debt and equity five years before the debt matures for various values of ρ

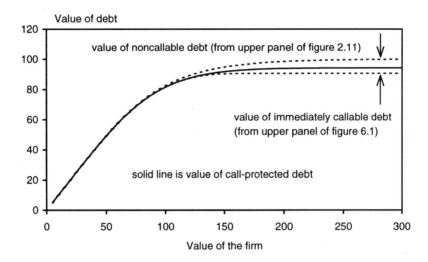

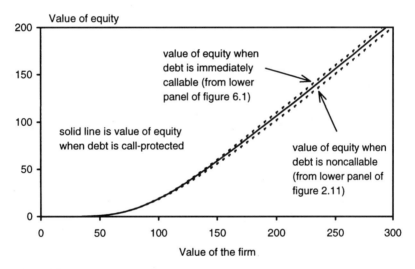

Figure 6.4
Contingent value of callable debt and equity five years before the debt matures when call protection has not yet lapsed

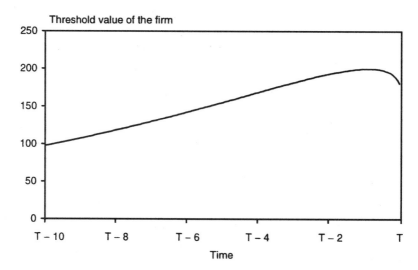

Figure 6.5
Threshold value of the firm above which the firm will call its debt for early redemption

Comment

Example A demonstrated that the firm will call its debt for early redemption five years before maturity pursuant to the call schedule in equation (6.11) if the value of the firm exceeds 155. Thus 155 is a "threshold" value of the firm above which the firm will immediately call its debt. Similar threshold values of the firm exist at other maturities, and it is instructive to examine their characteristics.

Consider, as in example A, a firm capitalized with debt with face amount $F = 164.872$ callable pursuant to the schedule of call values in equation (6.11) with $\rho = 0.12$. Let $W_c(t)$ denote the threshold value of the firm at time t such that the firm will immediately call the debt at time t if $W(t)$ exceeds $W_c(t)$.

Figure 6.5 shows the behavior of $W_c(t)$ as a function of time. The threshold value of the firm generally rises over time because the call value of the debt increases as the debt approaches maturity. $W_c(t)$ falls back toward the face amount of the debt when the debt approaches maturity because the time value of the issuer's call option declines to zero.

The idea of the $W_c(t)$ boundary suggests an important characteristic of the temporal evolution of the value of a firm capitalized with callable debt and equity. Suppose that the value of the firm is 50.0 ten years before the debt matures, so that $W(t) = 50.0$ when $t = T - 10$. The value of the firm will evolve over the next ten years according to the stochastic process in equation (1.14). Some trajectories, such as trajectory A in the upper panel of figure 6.6, result in default and bankruptcy at time T. Other tra-

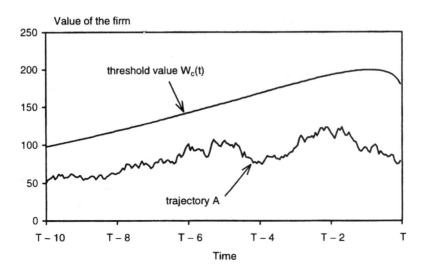

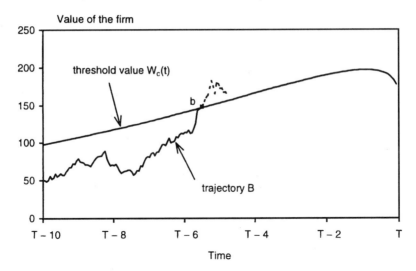

Figure 6.6
Two alternative trajectories of the value of the firm, starting at $W(t) = 50$ at time $t = T - 10$

jectories, such as trajectory *B* in the lower panel of the same figure, are characterized by a rising value and improving creditworthiness of the firm, such that the value of the firm hits the $W_c(t)$ boundary before the debt matures. In these cases the debt will be called for early redemption.

Early redemption should occur *promptly* at point *b* on trajectory *B*, and we should not observe the value of the firm evolving beyond point b in the absence of a call for early redemption.[13] Moreover the decision of the firm to call its debt should not come as a surprise (or convey any new information) to market participants, since the location of the $W_c(t)$ boundary is readily identifiable.

13. Point *b* lies immediately above the $W_c(t)$ boundary on trajectory *B*.

7 Early Redemption of Callable Debt

Contingent value analysis of callable debt requires identification of the circumstances that lead to exercise of the issuer's option for early redemption. We assumed in chapter 6 that a corporation will call its debt if the call maximizes the value of equity. It should be clear that the contingent value of the debt would change if we made a different assumption regarding exercise of the redemption option.[1] This suggests that the validity of a contingent value model for callable debt can be examined in terms of its assumptions regarding early redemption.

The first section of this chapter reviews empirical evidence bearing on the question of whether the model presented in chapter 6 describes accurately the early redemption of corporate debt.[2] It appears that corporations sometimes call debt in circumstances where the model would identify exercise of the option as contrary to the best interests of shareholders, and that they sometimes fail to call debt in circumstances where the model would identify immediate call as consistent with the best interests of shareholders. Section 7.2 comments on the significance of this evidence for contingent value models of callable debt.

7.1 Empirical Characteristics of Early Redemption

The analysis in chapter 6 assumed that a company will call debt for early redemption if call maximizes the value of equity. In the case of a firm capitalized with only a single callable bond and equity, this is equivalent to assuming that the firm will call the bond if call minimizes the value of the bond, or if and only if the value of the bond if it is not called exceeds the bond's call value.[3] It follows that as shown in equation (6.8), the market price of the bond will be the lesser of (1) the bond's call value and (2) the value of the bond if it is not called.

This characterization of the option to call a bond for early redemption has three testable implications:

1. A company will not call a bond for early redemption if the market price of the bond is below the bond's call price.

---

1. See, for example, the discussion in the text at equations (6.9) and (6.10). The effect of assumptions regarding exercise of a contingent claim on the value of the claim have been explored most extensively in the literature on valuation of employee and executive stock options. See Lambert, Larcker, and Verrecchia (1991), Jennergren and Naslund (1993), Huddart (1994), Kulatilaka and Marcus (1994), Cuny and Jorion (1995), Rubinstein (1995), and Carpenter (1998).

2. See similarly the empirical evidence presented by Huddart and Lang (1996) on exercise of employee stock options.

3. Jones, Mason, and Rosenfeld (1984, pp. 614–15) and Longstaff and Tuckman (1994) point out that calling to minimize the value of a bond is not equivalent to calling to maximize the value of equity if there is more than one bond in the capital structure of the firm.

2. Call will occur simultaneously with the market price of the bond rising to the call price.

3. The market price of the bond will never exceed the bond's call price.[4]

Vu (1986) tested the validity of these implications with a sample of 133 publicly traded bonds called for early redemption between October 1962 and April 1978.[5] He found some evidence of "unexpectedly late" redemption (when the market price of the bond has been at or above the bond's call price for a significant interval of time prior to redemption) and more compelling evidence of "unexpectedly early" redemption (when the market price of the bond is below the bond's call price at the time of call).

Unexpectedly Late Redemption

Vu was able to identify market prices prior to and at the time of call for a subsample of 102 bonds. He observed that 41 bonds from his subsample were called at least two months *after* the market price of the bond first exceeded the bond's call price. In 85% of the 41 cases, the market price exceeded the call price in at least four of the first twelve months following the first instance of market price in excess of call price. In 63% of the 41 cases, the market price exceeded the call price in at least four *consecutive* months out of the first twelve months following the first instance of market price in excess of call price. And in 22% of the 41 cases, the market price exceeded 101% of the call price in at least four consecutive months out of the first twelve months following the first instance of market price in excess of call price. However, there was only a single case where the market price exceeded 102% of the call price in at least four consecutive months out of the first twelve months following the first instance of market price in excess of call price.

These results refute the proposition that a company will call a bond simultaneously with the market price of the bond rising to the bond's call price, as well as the proposition that the market price of a callable bond can never exceed the contemporaneous call price of the bond. However, while it appears that a company may not call a bond as soon as the market price of the bond exceeds the bond's call price, it does not appear that the market price exceeds the call price by more than a modest amount for any significant interval. Thus a contingent value model of callable debt

---

4. The last two implications may not hold if there is more than one bond in the capital structure of the firm (Jones, Mason, and Rosenfeld 1984, pp. 614–15; Longstaff and Tuckman 1994).

5. See also King and Mauer (2000).

may value the debt reasonably accurately, even if it does not identify the timing of the exercise of the issuer's call option with great precision.[6]

Unexpectedly Early Redemption

From the subsample of 102 bonds for which he could determine market prices at the time of call, Vu also concluded as follows:

1. 75% of the bonds had market prices *lower* than their call prices at the time of call. The mean discount of market price from call price was 4.7% of the call price.

2. 15% of the bonds had market prices at more than a 10% discount to their call prices at the time of call.

These results refute the proposition that a firm will not call debt for early redemption if the market price of the debt is less than the debt's call price. In fact, and contrary to the assumption of the model in chapter 6, a firm may call a bond for early redemption even though the market price of the bond is well below its call price.

Why a Company May Choose to Redeem Debt Earlier Than Expected

We can imagine several reasons why a company may not call a bond for early redemption, even though the market price of the bond exceeds the bond's call price: interest rates could have declined sharply and unexpectedly and the company is not prepared to finance immediate redemption of the debt, management may be distracted by litigation or by negotiations for a merger or acquisition, early redemption of senior debt may benefit junior creditors rather than shareholders, or the excess of the market price over the call price may be smaller than the transactions costs associated with calling and refinancing the debt.[7] Vu's other finding, that companies sometimes call debt for early redemption even though the market price of the debt is substantially below the call price, is not so easily explained.

6. King and Mauer (2000) report that the average difference between the market price and the call price at the time of a bond call, as well as the length of the interval between the first instance of market price in excess of call price and the announcement of call, increased after 1985, and they examine the determinants of the price premiums and call delays.

7. Debt has been called during a call protection period pursuant to a contingent call option (see note 3 in chapter 6) under circumstances where market participants did not realize that the issuer could satisfy the contingency requirement and exercise the option, and hence where they were pricing the debt in excess of its contingent call price. See *Franklin Life Insurance Co. v. Commonwealth Edison*, 451 F. Supp. 602 (S.D.Ill. 1978) (callable preferred stock trading at $119.6875 per share called for redemption at a price of $110 per share) and *Morgan Stanley & Co. v. Archer Daniels Midland Co.*, 570 F. Supp. 1529 (S.D.N.Y. 1983) (callable debentures trading at 120% of principal called at a price of 113.95% of principal).

Vu conjectured that firms sometimes call debt to eliminate restrictive covenants.[8] To test this hypothesis, he divided his subsample of 102 bonds into two categories: bonds issued by industrial companies (55 bonds) and bonds issued by public utilities (47 bonds). Nineteen of the 55 industrial bonds represented the issuer's only public debt. Eighteen of the remaining 36 industrial bonds had covenants that were more restrictive than the covenants on bonds of the same issuer that remained outstanding. For these 18 bonds, redemption clearly relaxed restrictions on the activities of the issuer. Vu reported that for the 18 bonds, the mean discount of market price from call price at the time of call was 8.1% of the call price. Vu did not report the mean discount for the 18 bond calls that did not relax restrictions on the issuer, or for the 19 bond calls that eliminated the issuer's only public debt. However, the 8.1% average discount on the restriction relaxing calls exceeded the average discount of 4.7% on the full subsample of 102 bond calls.

Vu concluded that a significant fraction of unexpectedly early redemptions of industrial bonds are motivated by the issuer's desire to undertake an action prohibited by covenant. The value to stockholders of eliminating a covenant restriction accounts for the willingness of the issuer to pay a call price materially in excess of the market price of the bond.[9]

Additional Evidence on Early Redemption to Eliminate Restrictive Covenants

A subsequent study by Asquith and Wizman (1990) provides additional evidence in support of the proposition that firms sometimes call debt for early redemption to eliminate restrictive covenants.[10]

Asquith and Wizman identified a sample of 149 publicly traded bonds issued by firms subsequently involved in a leveraged buyout (LBO) between 1980 and 1988.[11] They were able to obtain prospectuses for 118

---

8. This basis for exercising an option for early redemption was noted earlier by Smith and Warner (1979, pp. 142–43). See, for example, the decision of Marriott Corporation (described in note 54 in chapter 18) to call its Series F Senior Notes for early redemption to eliminate the need to comply with a negative pledge clause in the indenture for the notes, and the decision of Silgan Corporation (described in note 12 in chapter 16) to call an issue of senior subordinated notes to eliminate a restrictive dividend covenant. See also "Market Place: Owners of Preferred Stock Find a Prize in the Fine Print in a Merger," *New York Times*, March 29, 1996, p. D8 (redemption, at a price of $110 per share, of preferred stock when it was trading at $66 per share to eliminate a coalition of preferred shareholders threatening to vote against and thereby block a value-enhancing merger of the issuer).

9. From the sample of 47 public utility bonds described in the preceding paragraph, Vu was able to identify only 5 cases where a bond call resulted in redemption of debt that had stronger covenants than the issuer's remaining public debt. He concluded that calls of public utility debt were not usually motivated by a desire to undertake a prohibited action.

10. See also the related study by Cook, Easterwood, and Martin (1992).

11. The structure, origin and evolution of leveraged buyouts is described by Burrough and Helyar (1990, pp. 128–53), Blair (1993), Baker and Smith (1998), and McCauley, Ruud, and Iacono (1999, pp. 13–61).

of the bonds. On the basis of the information contained in the prospectuses, they classified each bond into one of three categories:

• A bond was said to have *strong* covenant protection if the indenture for the bond included a net worth restriction on the surviving firm in a merger, or if the indenture limited total funded debt. They noted that an LBO will often result in a violation of such restrictions, so a bond with strong covenant protection is likely to be redeemed before, or concurrently with, a leveraged buyout of the issuer. Their sample included 14 bonds with strong covenant protection.

• A bond was said to have *weak* covenant protection if it did not have strong covenant protection and if the indenture for the bond included a limitation on senior funded debt or a limitation on payments of dividends to stockholders. They noted that an LBO may or may not result in a violation of such restrictions, depending on the details of the buyout. Their sample included 36 bonds with weak covenant protection.

• A bond was said to have *no* covenant protection if it did not have either strong or weak covenant protection. Their sample included 68 bonds with no covenant protection.

Asquith and Wizman observed that 36% of the bonds with strong covenant protection (5 of the 14 bonds) and 33% of the bonds with weak protection (12 of the 36 bonds) were called for early redemption before or concurrently with completion of a leveraged buyout of the issuer.[12] Only 7% of the bonds with no covenant protection (or 5 of the 68 bonds) were called. The authors concluded that firms commonly call bonds for early redemption to eliminate restrictive covenants that would otherwise impede a planned buyout.[13]

Asquith and Wizman also observed that early redemption of debt issued by firms involved in an LBO works to the advantage of the bondholders. The authors obtained market price data on 138 of the 149 bonds in their sample. On average, over an interval beginning two months before the announcement of an ultimately successful LBO and ending two months after completion of the buyout, the values of bonds called for early redemption appreciated 5.8% above where they would have been had they behaved like a broad market index of bond prices over the same interval.[14] In contrast, the values of bonds left outstanding after comple-

12. Asquith and Wizman (1990, table 3). Some bonds were redeemed by open market or privately negotiated purchases rather than by exercise of a call option.

13. The indentures for 2 of the 5 bonds that were called for early redemption even though they were said to have no covenant protection had provisions restricting the issuance of new *secured* debt that would have been violated if the bonds had not been redeemed. These two bonds also support the conclusion stated in the text.

14. Asquith and Wizman (1990, table 4).

tion of an LBO depreciated, on average, 5.9% below where they would have been. These results are consistent with Vu's conjecture that an issuer calling a bond to eliminate a restrictive covenant may call the bond even if the market price of the bond is materially below the call price, and hence even if call results in an unanticipated gain for bondholders.

7.2   Implications

The empirical results reported by Vu (1986) and Asquith and Wizman (1990) support the proposition that a company may call debt to eliminate a restrictive covenant even when the market price of the debt is materially below the call price. This implies that the model described in chapter 6 does not identify correctly all of the circumstances that lead to exercise of an issuer's early redemption option. More important, it implies that ceteris paribus, the market price of callable debt is likely to differ from the value derived from the model.

Altering the specification of the model to reflect more accurately the realities of the marketplace may be difficult. The prospect that debt may be called for early redemption to eliminate a restrictive covenant is a discrete "event risk" distinctly different from the prospect that debt may be called as a result of the continuous temporal evolution of the aggregate value of the firm. A call for redemption to relax a restrictive covenant depends on factors other than the value of the firm, and may result in a discontinuous change in the value of the debt being called.

Any valuation of the prospect of a call for early redemption to eliminate a restrictive covenant will depend on the likelihood that such a call will occur. However, it is difficult to imagine how we might assess the probability that a firm will want to eliminate a restrictive covenant. A wide variety of circumstances can trigger such a call, including the identification of an investment project with a substantial net present value, the appearance of an opportunity for a beneficial merger or divestiture, or—as in the study of Asquith and Wizman—the desire to undertake a leveraged buyout of existing stockholders.[15] Even if we can assess the probability of each possible triggering circumstance, we would still have to address the problem of identifying how the market prices the uncertainty, or risk, that a particular circumstance will materialize.

15. A comparison with the literature on exercise of executive and employee stock options (see note 2 above) is illuminating. That literature has emphasized exercise to maximize the holder's utility (by reducing risk or facilitating diversification; see Huddart 1994 and Kulatilaka and Marcus 1994) and exercise to avoid option termination concurrently with termination of employment (see Jennergren and Naslund 1993; Cuny and Jorion 1995; Carpenter 1998).

8 Convertible Debt

Corporate debt is said to be "convertible" if a holder has the right to exchange the debt for a specified quantity of the issuer's common stock. Convertible debt is almost always callable at the option of the issuer.[1] The dual options of call and conversion mean that an issuer's call for early redemption will not necessarily result in cash redemption, but may instead lead creditors to convert their debt to equity. This chapter shows how call and conversion options can be incorporated into a contingent value model.[2]

8.1 Framework of the Analysis

As in earlier chapters we begin by describing the institutional setting of the valuation problem, including our assumptions regarding the capital structure of the firm and the consequences of default and bankruptcy.

Corporate Capital Structure

We assume the firm is capitalized with two classes of securities: a single issue of zero-coupon callable convertible debt and common stock.

The debt matures at time T and promises to pay its face amount F at that time. At any time t not later than its maturity date, the debt can be converted into a contractually specified fraction $\gamma(t)$ of the common stock of the firm, where $0 \leq \gamma(t) < 1$. If there are $N_s(t)$ shares of stock outstanding at time t, creditors will receive $N_c(t)$ shares upon conversion, where $N_c(t)$ satisfies the equation

$$\gamma(t) = \frac{N_c(t)}{N_c(t) + N_s(t)} \tag{8.1}$$

$\gamma(t)$ is called the "dilution factor" of the convertible debt.[3] Following conversion of the debt the firm will be capitalized entirely with common stock.[4]

At any time t prior to maturity, the company can call the debt for early redemption by offering to pay creditors the contractually specified amount $C(t)$. Following exercise of the company's call option, creditors

1. There are exceptions. In late 1999 Clear Channel Communications, Inc. sold $900 million of noncallable 1.5% Senior Convertible Notes maturing on December 1, 2002.

2. Ingersoll (1977a) and Brennan and Schwartz (1977, 1980) provided the first extensive analyses of the contingent value of convertible debt. See also McConnell and Schwartz (1986).

3. The terminology and notation follows Ingersoll (1977a).

4. For analytical simplicity we assume that creditors act as a cohesive group and that they convert all of their debt if they convert any debt. Emanuel (1983) and Constantinides (1984) examine the effects of permitting partial conversions and uncoordinated conversions.

Example 8.1   A Callable Convertible Zero-Coupon Note

In June 1991, Marriott Corporation, a lodging, food service, and facilities management company, issued a callable convertible zero-coupon note maturing on June 12,
2006, with a face value of $675 million.

The notes were convertible, at the option of a holder and at the rate of 13.277
shares of stock per $1,000 face amount of notes, into a total of 8.96 million shares of
Marriott common stock, or into about 8.6% of the stock of the company following
conversion.

The notes were also callable at any time (except as noted below) at the option of
the issuer at a redemption price computed as the present value of the $675 million
face amount of the notes, discounted back to the redemption date using an interest
rate of 8.25% per annum, compounded semiannually. Thus the redemption price of
the notes on June 12, 2000 (6 years, or 12 semiannual periods, before maturity) would
be computed as

$$\text{Redemption price} = \frac{\$675 \text{ million}}{(1 + \frac{1}{2} \cdot 0.0825)^{12}} = \$415.57 \text{ million}$$

The option to call the notes for early redemption before June 12, 1993, was not
unrestricted. The notes were not callable during the first two years after issuance unless the market price of Marriott common stock exceeded $33.60 per share for at least
20 business days during an interval of 30 consecutive business days ending not more
than 5 business days prior to the date of notice of early redemption. (Marriott common stock closed at a price of $22.50 per share on May 31, 1991.) This type of call
protection on a convertible security, which lapses when the price of the issuer's stock
rises to a specified level rather than with the passage of time, is sometimes called
"soft" call protection. Marriott's option to redeem the notes during the first two years
of their life can also be described as a "knock-in," or barrier, option that is not active
before the stock price reaches $33.60 per share.

Finally, the Marriott notes were redeemable at the option of a *holder* (i.e.,
"putable") at the redemption price on June 12, 1996, and June 12, 2001. However,
Marriott had the right to pay the exercise price of the holders' put option in cash or in
common stock of equal value.

---

can accept cash redemption or they can convert their debt to equity pursuant to the conversion privilege described above. We ignore any requirement for a notice period and assume that call and (if desired) conversion
occur instantaneously. An appendix examines the consequences of a notice
period. Example 8.1 describes a callable convertible zero-coupon note
issued by Marriott Corporation in June 1991.

The common stock cannot pay a dividend and cannot be repurchased
by the firm until the debt has been converted or redeemed. We denote the
value of the convertible debt at time t as $V_1(t)$ and the value of the stock
as $V_2(t)$. The value of the firm is the sum of the values of the firm's
securities: $W(t) = V_1(t) + V_2(t)$.

Default and Bankruptcy

If the debt has not been converted or redeemed prior to time T, and if
it is not converted at time T, creditors have a claim on the firm for the

face amount of the debt. If the company does not pay this contractually specified sum, the firm defaults and goes into bankruptcy. We assume that bankruptcy results in an instantaneous and costless liquidation of the assets of the firm and distribution of the proceeds according to the absolute priority rule.

The Contingent Value of the Debt and Equity at Time T

Our assumptions regarding (1) default and bankruptcy and (2) the creditors' conversion option determine how the value of the firm will be apportioned between creditors and stockholders when the debt matures at time T. If the value of the firm is less than F, the debt is worth the value of the firm (because the firm can not avoid default and its creditors will receive all of the proceeds of the ensuing liquidation) and the stock is worthless. If the value of the firm exceeds F, the creditors will be paid F—unless they choose to convert their debt into a fraction $\gamma(T)$ of the stock of the firm. They will choose the latter course if the value of the stock received upon conversion, $\gamma(T) \cdot W(T)$, is greater than F, or if $W(T)$ is greater than $\gamma(T)^{-1} \cdot F$. Thus we have

$$V_1(T) = \begin{cases} W(T) & \text{if } W(T) < F \\ F & \text{if } F \leq W(T) < \gamma(T)^{-1} \cdot F \\ \gamma(T) \cdot W(T) & \text{if } \gamma(T)^{-1} \cdot F \leq W(T) \end{cases} \qquad (8.2a)$$

When the value of the firm exceeds F, the stock will be worth $W(T) - F$ if creditors do not convert, and it will be worth $(1 - \gamma(T)) \cdot W(T)$ if they do convert, so

$$V_2(T) = \begin{cases} 0 & \text{if } W(T) < F \\ W(T) - F & \text{if } F \leq W(T) < \gamma(T)^{-1} \cdot F \\ (1 - \gamma(T)) \cdot W(T) & \text{if } \gamma(T)^{-1} \cdot F \leq W(T) \end{cases} \qquad (8.2b)$$

Equations (8.2a, b) can be expressed more compactly as

$$V_1(T) = \max[\min[W(T), F], \gamma(T) \cdot W(T)] \qquad (8.3a)$$

$$V_2(T) = \min[\max[0, W(T) - F], (1 - \gamma(T)) \cdot W(T)] \qquad (8.3b)$$

or in tabular form as

	$W(T) < F$	$F \leq W(T) < \gamma(T)^{-1} \cdot F$	$\gamma(T)^{-1} \cdot F \leq W(T)$
$V_1(T)$	$W(T)$	F	$\gamma(T) \cdot W(T)$
$V_2(T)$	0	$W(T) - F$	$(1 - \gamma(T)) \cdot W(T)$

Figure 8.1 illustrates the contingent value of the debt and equity at time T.

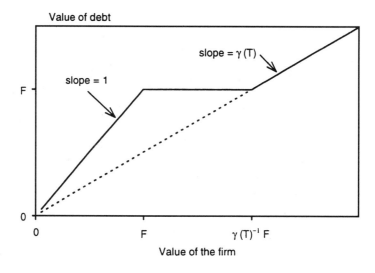

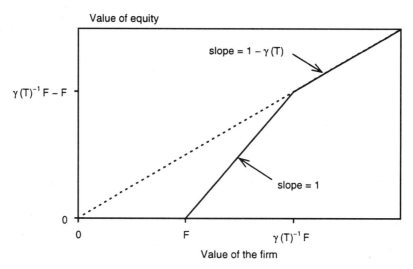

Figure 8.1
Contingent value of convertible debt and equity at time T

The Option Positions of Stockholders and Creditors

When we examined (in chapter 2) the debt and equity of a firm capitalized with common stock and nonconvertible zero-coupon debt, we observed that stockholders have a call option on the firm (with an exercise price equal to the face amount of the debt and an expiration date equal to the maturity date of the debt) and that creditors are in the economic position of being long the firm and short the call option held by stockholders. It is instructive to examine the option positions of stockholders and creditors in the more complicated case where the debt is convertible.

The upper panel of figure 8.1 and equation (8.2a) suggest that the holders of convertible debt are in the economic position of being

1. long the firm,

2. short a call option on the firm with an exercise price of F and an expiration date of T, and

3. long a call option on a fraction $\gamma(T)$ of the firm with an exercise price of F and the same expiration date.

The short option position (item 1 above) reflects the right of stockholders to eliminate the creditors' interest in the firm by paying creditors the face amount of the zero-coupon debt. The long option position (item 3) reflects the superceding right of the creditors to retain an interest in a fraction $\gamma(T)$ of the firm by repaying F to the stockholders or, equivalently and more concretely, by converting their debt immediately before it matures. Since the stockholders are the only other holders of the corporation's securities, the stockholders must hold the option written by the creditors, and they must be the writers of the option held by the creditors.

This characterization of the option positions of creditors and stockholders is illuminating, but it is not entirely accurate. The characterization ignores the company's option to call the debt *prior* to maturity, as well as the creditors' option to convert the debt *prior* to maturity. The options for redemption and conversion prior to maturity must not be ignored when we assess the contingent values of the securities prior to time T.

8.2   The Valuation Problem

We assume there exists a pair of contingent value functions, f_1 and f_2, with two arguments: time and the value of the firm, such that the value of the ith security at time t can be calculated as

$$V_i(t) = f_i(W(t), t), \qquad i = 1, 2 \tag{8.4}$$

The valuation problem is identifying the forms of these contingent value functions.

8.3   Solving the Valuation Problem

We have already solved the valuation problem in the special case of $t = T$. From equations (8.3a, b) we have

$$f_1(W, T) = \max[\min[W, F], \gamma(T) \cdot W] \tag{8.5a}$$

$$f_2(W, T) = \min[\max[0, W - F], (1 - \gamma(T)) \cdot W] \tag{8.5b}$$

We now want to extend these terminal contingent value functions backwards it time, to times prior to the maturity date of the debt.

Suppose that we want to compute $f_i(W^*, t^*)$: the value of the ith security at time t^* when the contemporaneous value of the firm is W^*, for a value of t^* less than T. An algorithm for computing $f_i(W^*, t^*)$ can be constructed along the same lines as the algorithm in section 6.3, except that we now have to account for the creditors' conversion option as well as the issuer's call option.

We approximate the dynamic evolution of the value of the firm with a binomial random walk in discrete time. Dividing the interval between t^* and T into K subintervals of length Δt and defining a sequence of $K + 1$ discrete points in time,

$$t_k = t^* + (k - 1) \cdot \Delta t, \qquad k = 1, 2, \ldots, K + 1 \tag{8.6}$$

we construct an array $W_{j,k}$ for $j = 1, 2, \ldots, k$ and $k = 1, 2, \ldots, K + 1$, where the natural logarithm of $W_{j,k}$ is defined as

$$\ln[W_{j,k}] = \ln[W^*] + (k - 1) \cdot \mu \cdot \Delta t + (2 \cdot j - k - 1) \cdot \sigma \cdot \Delta t^{1/2},$$

$$j = 1, 2, \ldots, k; \ k = 1, 2, \ldots, K + 1 \tag{8.7}$$

The value of the firm is $W_{1,1} = W^*$ at time $t_1 = t^*$, and it subsequently evolves as a binomial process through the $W_{j,k}$ array.

Let $V_{j,k,i}$ denote the value of the ith security at time t_k when the value of the firm is $W_{j,k}$, so that $V_{j,k,i} = f_i(W_{j,k}, t_k)$. We compute the $V_{j,k,i}$ values using a recursion algorithm on k, beginning at $k = K + 1$ and proceeding backward to $k = 1$.

Constructing the $V_{j,k,i}$ Terms for $k = K + 1$

The values of $V_{j,K+1,i}$ for $j = 1, 2, \ldots, K + 1$ follow from our specification of the consequences of default and bankruptcy at time T, as well as the creditors' option to convert their debt at maturity.

If the value of the firm at time $T = t_{K+1}$ is less than F, the firm defaults and creditors get the full proceeds of liquidation. If the value of the firm exceeds F, creditors will be paid F—unless they convert their debt into a fraction $\gamma(t_{K+1})$ of the common stock of the firm. They will choose the latter course if the value of the firm exceeds $\gamma(t_{K+1})^{-1} \cdot F$. Thus we have

$$
V_{j,K+1,1} = \begin{cases} W_{j,K+1} & \text{if } W_{j,K+1} < F \\ F & \text{if } F \le W_{j,K+1} < \gamma(t_{K+1})^{-1} \cdot F \\ \gamma(t_{K+1}) \cdot W_{j,K+1} & \text{if } \gamma(t_{K+1})^{-1} \cdot F \le W_{j,K+1} \end{cases} \tag{8.8}
$$

Stockholders either receive the residual value of the firm after the creditors have been paid the amount F or, if the creditors convert, they own a fraction $1 - \gamma(t_{K+1})$ of the unlevered firm. Therefore

$$
V_{j,K+1,2} = \begin{cases} 0 & \text{if } W_{j,K+1} < F \\ W_{j,K+1} - F & \text{if } F \le W_{j,K+1} < \gamma(t_{K+1})^{-1} \cdot F \\ (1 - \gamma(t_{K+1})) \cdot W_{j,K+1} & \text{if } \gamma(t_{K+1})^{-1} \cdot F \le W_{j,K+1} \end{cases}
$$

$$(8.9)$$

Equations (8.8) and (8.9) are the discrete time–discrete state analogues of the terminal conditions in equations (8.2a, b).

Calculating the $V_{j,k,i}$ Terms for $k < K + 1$

Consider now the problem of computing $V_{j,k,i}$ for some value of $k < K + 1$, assuming that we know $V_{j,k+1,i}$ for $j = 1, 2, \ldots, k + 1$. $V_{j,k,i}$ is the value of the ith security at time t_k when the value of the firm is $W_{j,k}$. Any one of four events can happen at time t_k when the value of the firm is $W_{j,k}$:

1. The firm can call its debt for early redemption by offering to pay $C(t_k)$, and creditors can accept the cash payment.

2. The firm can call its debt for early redemption and creditors can convert the debt to equity rather than accept the cash. (This is commonly called "forced conversion," because creditors would not usually choose to convert the debt in the absence of the issuer's call for early redemption.)

3. Creditors can convert their debt to equity in the absence of any action by the firm to call the debt for early redemption. (This is commonly called "voluntary conversion.")

4. The firm can abstain from calling the debt and creditors can abstain from converting the debt, thereby maintaining the status quo until time t_{k+1}.

Table 8.1
Value of the convertible debt and equity at time t_k when the value of the firm is $W_{j,k}$, conditional on the actions of creditors and the firm

	If the firm calls the debt	If the firm does not call the debt
If creditors convert	Debt: $\gamma(t_k) \cdot W_{j,k}$	Debt: $\gamma(t_k) \cdot W_{j,k}$
	Equity: $(1 - \gamma(t_k)) \cdot W_{j,k}$	Equity: $(1 - \gamma(t_k)) \cdot W_{j,k}$
If creditors do not convert	Debt: $C(t_k)$	Debt: $V_{j,k,1}^{sq}$
	Equity: $W_{j,k} - C(t_k)$	Equity: $V_{j,k,2}^{sq}$

Note: $V_{j,k,1}^{sq}$ and $V_{j,k,2}^{sq}$ are computed as described in the text at equations (8.10) and (8.11a, b).

Which event occurs depends on the value of the debt and the value of equity conditional on (1) whether or not the firm calls the debt and (2) whether or not creditors convert the debt.

Table 8.1 summarizes the value of the debt and equity conditional on the actions of creditors and the firm. If creditors convert the debt to equity, the debt will be worth $\gamma(t_k) \cdot W_{j,k}$ and the original shareholders' stock will be worth $(1 - \gamma(t_k)) \cdot W_{j,k}$. This follows because upon conversion, the firm will be capitalized entirely with common stock, the former creditors will hold a fraction $\gamma(t_k)$ of the stock, and the original shareholders will hold the balance of the stock.

If the firm calls the debt for early redemption and creditors accept the cash payment, the debt will be worth the call value $C(t_k)$ and (ignoring transactions costs associated with financing the redemption) the stock will be worth the balance of the value of the firm, or $W_{j,k} - C(t_k)$.

The last possibility is that the firm and the creditors elect to maintain the status quo. Let $V_{j,k,i}^{sq}$ denote the value of the ith security conditional on this event. Since the value of the firm will evolve over the subinterval from t_k to t_{k+1} to either

1. $W_{j+1,k+1}$, where the ith security will be worth $V_{j+1,k+1,i}$, or
2. $W_{j,k+1}$, where the ith security will be worth $V_{j,k+1,i}$,

we have (assuming the markets do not allow opportunities for riskless arbitrage profits)

$$V_{j,k,i}^{sq} = h \cdot W_{j,k} + Q \tag{8.10}$$

where h and Q satisfy the equations

$$V_{j+1,k+1,i} = h \cdot W_{j+1,k+1} + Q \cdot e^{R_f \cdot \Delta t} \tag{8.11a}$$

$$V_{j,k+1,i} = h \cdot W_{j,k+1} + Q \cdot e^{R_f \cdot \Delta t} \tag{8.11b}$$

A Decision Tree for the Firm and Its Creditors

Having established the values of the debt and equity *conditional* on the actions of the firm and its creditors, we now have to identify whether the firm calls the debt and whether creditors convert the debt. We identify the actions of the respective parties by working backwards through a decision tree. As shown in figure 8.2, the firm must first decide whether to call its debt and creditors must then decide whether to convert the debt.[5] We assume that creditors act to maximize the value of the debt and that the firm acts to maximize the value of equity.

Whether Creditors Convert Following a Call for Early Redemption

Suppose first that the firm calls its debt for early redemption. Creditors then face the subtree shown in figure 8.3 and must choose between cash redemption (where the debt will be worth $C(t_k)$) and conversion (where the debt will be worth $\gamma(t_k) \cdot W_{j,k}$). The creditors will accept cash redemption if $C(t_k)$ is greater than $\gamma(t_k) \cdot W_{j,k}$, in which case the debt will be worth $C(t_k)$. If $C(t_k)$ is less than $\gamma(t_k) \cdot W_{j,k}$, they will choose to convert and the debt will be worth $\gamma(t_k) \cdot W_{j,k}$. Thus, *if* the firm *does* call it's debt, the debt will be worth

$$\max[\gamma(t_k) \cdot W_{j,k}, C(t_k)] \tag{8.12a}$$

Since the value of the stock is equal to the value of the firm less the value of the debt, the stock will be worth

$$W_{j,k} - \max[\gamma(t_k) \cdot W_{j,k}, C(t_k)] = \min[(1 - \gamma(t_k)) \cdot W_{j,k}, W_{j,k} - C(t_k)] \tag{8.12b}$$

Whether Creditors Convert in the Absence of a Call for Early Redemption

Suppose, alternatively, that the firm abstains from calling it's debt. Creditors then face the subtree shown in figure 8.4 and must choose between voluntary conversion (where the debt will be worth $\gamma(t_k) \cdot W_{j,k}$) and maintenance of the status quo (where the debt will be worth $V_{j,k,1}^{sq}$). If $\gamma(t_k) \cdot W_{j,k} > V_{j,k,1}^{sq}$, creditors will choose to convert and the debt will be worth $\gamma(t_k) \cdot W_{j,k}$. If the inequality runs in the opposite direction, they will choose to maintain the status quo, and the debt will be worth $V_{j,k,1}^{sq}$. Thus, *if* the firm *does not* call it's debt, the debt will be worth

$$\max[\gamma(t_k) \cdot W_{j,k}, V_{j,k,1}^{sq}] \tag{8.13a}$$

---

5. The sequence of decisions reflects the terms of all convertible bond indentures that creditors have the right to convert *following* announcement of a call for early redemption. Dunn and Eades (1989) emphasize the importance of an issuer anticipating its creditors' conversion decision when deciding whether to call its debt.

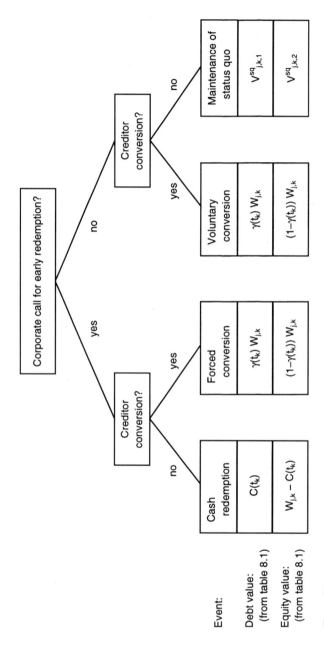

Figure 8.2
Decision tree for the corporation and for creditors at time t_k when the value of the firm is $W_{j,k}$

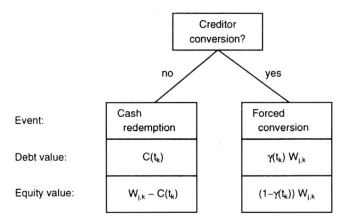

Figure 8.3
Decision sub-tree for creditors at time t_k when the value of the firm is $W_{j,k}$, given that the firm has called the debt for early redemption

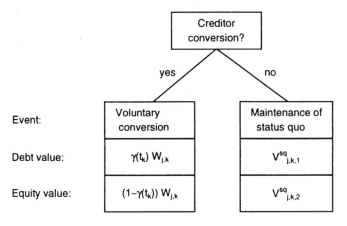

Figure 8.4
Decision sub-tree for creditors at time t_k when the value of the firm is $W_{j,k}$, given that the firm has abstained from calling the debt for early redemption

and the stock will be worth[6]

$$W_{j,k} - \max[\gamma(t_k) \cdot W_{j,k}, V^{\text{sq}}_{j,k,1}] = \min[(1 - \gamma(t_k)) \cdot W_{j,k}, V^{\text{sq}}_{j,k,2}] \qquad (8.13b)$$

Whether the Company Calls the Debt for Early Redemption

Having identified the creditors' conversion decision *conditional* on the redemption decision of the firm, we can now examine the decision of the firm to call its debt. The firm faces the subtree shown in figure 8.5

6. Equation (8.13b) makes use of the fact that $V^{\text{sq}}_{j,k,1} + V^{\text{sq}}_{j,k,2} = W_{j,k}$. The proof of this assertion follows from an analysis similar to the analysis in appendix B to chapter 2.

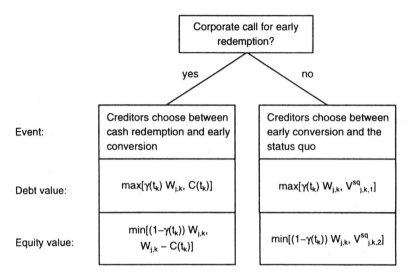

Figure 8.5
Decision sub-tree for the corporation at time t_k when the value of the firm is $W_{j,k}$, given the creditors' prospective decisions

and must choose between calling the debt (where, from equation 8.12b, the stock will be worth $\min[(1 - \gamma(t_k)) \cdot W_{j,k}, W_{j,k} - C(t_k)]$) and not calling the debt (where, from equation 8.13b, the stock will be worth $\min[(1 - \gamma(t_k)) \cdot W_{j,k}, V^{sq}_{j,k,2}]$).

Since the corporation acts to maximize the value of equity, the firm will call the debt if the quantity in equation (8.12b) is greater than the quantity in equation (8.13b). In this case the stock will be worth $\min[(1 - \gamma(t_k)) \cdot W_{j,k}, W_{j,k} - C(t_k)]$. If the inequality runs in the other direction, it will abstain from calling the debt and the stock will be worth $\min[(1 - \gamma(t_k)) \cdot W_{j,k}, V^{sq}_{j,k,2}]$. It follows that the value of the stock is the larger of the quantities shown in equations (8.12b) and (8.13b):

$$V_{j,k,2} = \max[\min[(1 - \gamma(t_k)) \cdot W_{j,k}, W_{j,k} - C(t_k)],$$
$$\min[(1 - \gamma(t_k)) \cdot W_{j,k}, V^{sq}_{j,k,2}]] \tag{8.14a}$$

Since the value of the debt is equal to the value of the firm less the value of the stock, the debt will be worth[7]

$$V_{j,k,1} = \min[\max[\gamma(t_k) \cdot W_{j,k}, C(t_k)], \max[\gamma(t_k) \cdot W_{j,k}, V^{sq}_{j,k,1}]] \tag{8.14b}$$

---

7. The value of the debt at time t_k when the value of the firm is $W_{j,k}$ can also be identified by observing that in acting to maximize the value of equity, the firm necessarily acts to minimize the value of the debt. (This follows because the sum of the value of the debt and equity is the specified value of the firm.) Thus the value of the debt will be the smaller of the quantities appearing in equations (8.12a) and (8.13a).

The foregoing algorithm can be applied recursively, beginning at $k = K$ and continuing through computation of $V_{1,1,i}$. Since $V_{1,1,i} = f_i(W_{1,1}, t_1) = f_i(W^*, t^*)$, this completes the computation of $f_i(W^*, t^*)$ for the case where the value of the firm evolves according to the discrete time binomial process. As the value of Δt goes to zero, the binomial process converges to the continuous time Gaussian process of equation (1.14), and the value of $V_{1,1,i}$ converges to the value of $f_i(W^*, t^*)$ for the case where the value of the firm evolves according to the Gaussian process.

8.4 Some Examples

Contingent valuation of convertible debt is complicated, and it may be helpful to examine some numerical examples. We assume that the U.S. Treasury yield curve is flat and stationary at $R_f = 0.10$ (or 10% per annum) and that the volatility of the value of the firm is $\sigma = 0.20$ (or a volatility of 20% over one year).

We also assume that the face amount of the debt is $F = 164.872$ and that we are valuing the debt five years prior to maturity. Ignoring the risk of default and the options for call and conversion, the debt has a contingency-free value of 100.0.

Example A

The first example assumes that the debt is noncallable but convertible throughout its life with a dilution factor of 0.35, so $\gamma(t) = 0.35$ for all values of $t \leq T$.[8]

The upper panel of figure 8.6 shows (with a solid line) the contingent value of the convertible debt. A dashed line shows what the debt would be worth in the absence of a conversion option. The difference between the solid and dashed lines reflects the enhanced value of the debt stemming from the creditors' conversion option. The lower panel shows how the conversion option reduces the contingent value of the firm's equity.

The conversion value of the debt (shown in the upper panel of figure 8.6) is 35% of the value of the firm. When the value of the firm is more than about 800, the value of the debt is essentially identical to the conversion value. This reflects the virtual certainty—assuming the risk neutral drift rate—that the debt will be converted, so the debt is tantamount to a 35% interest in the firm.

---

8. There is no economic difference between saying the debt is noncallable and saying it is callable only at a price so high that call is prohibitively expensive. We represent the absence of a call option by setting $C(t) = \infty$.

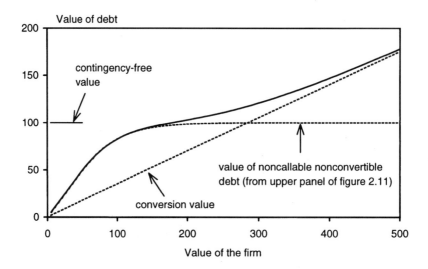

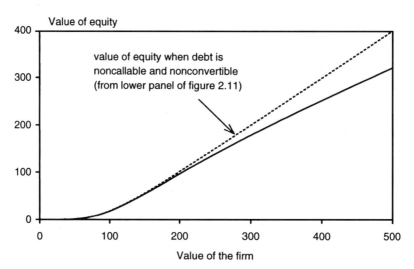

Figure 8.6
Contingent value of noncallable convertible debt and equity five years before the debt matures

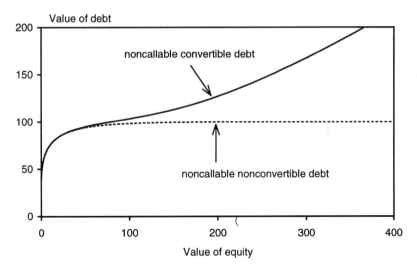

Figure 8.7
Value of debt five years before maturity as a function of the value of equity

It is not difficult to show that the debt must be worth more than its conversion value when the value of the firm is not so high as to make conversion a virtual certainty. Consider two portfolios, labeled *A* and *B*. Portfolio *A* consists of the convertible debt and portfolio *B* consists of 35% of all of the debt and 35% of all of the equity of the firm (or 35% of the firm as a whole). Portfolio *A* will be more valuable than portfolio *B* when the debt matures if conversion is uneconomical, and it will be no less valuable if conversion at maturity is more rewarding. Thus the current value of portfolio *A* must exceed the current value of portfolio *B* when the value of the firm is not so high as to virtually guarantee conversion.

The upper panel of figure 8.6 shows that as the value of the firm declines below 200, the value of the convertible debt converges to the value of comparable nonconvertible debt. This reflects the diminishing likelihood—assuming the risk neutral drift rate—that creditors will exercise their conversion option.

Cross Valuation

Figure 8.7 illustrates how the conversion option affects the implicit relationship between debt and equity values: the imputed value of the debt derived from an observed value of equity will be greater if the debt is convertible.

Figure 8.7 also shows that the convertible debt will look expensive relative to equity if we fail to recognize the debt's conversion option. At any given equity value the market will value the debt on the solid line but (if we ignore the conversion option) we would incorrectly value the debt on the lower dashed line. This is another example of the notion, introduced in example A in section 6.4, that a security may appear to be mispriced if we fail to recognize an option embedded in the security.

Example B

The second example assumes that the debt is convertible throughout its life with a dilution factor of 0.35 (i.e., $\gamma(t) = 0.35$ for all values of $t \le T$) and that it is callable pursuant to a schedule of call values that rise to F at time T:

$$C(t) = F \cdot e^{-\rho \cdot (T-t)}, \qquad t < T \tag{8.15}$$

We assume initially that $\rho = R_f$ (so the debt is callable at the price of a zero-coupon Treasury bond promising to pay F at time T). We examine the effect of other values of ρ below.

The upper panel of figure 8.8 shows (with a solid line) the contingent value of the debt. When the conversion value of the debt exceeds the call value, the contingent value of the debt is identical to the conversion value. (This is the segment of the contingent value function marked A–A.) This reflects the consequence of (1) a decision by the firm to call the debt immediately if the conversion value of the debt exceeds the contemporaneous call value and (2) a decision by creditors to convert the debt to equity to capture the higher conversion value.[9]

When the conversion value of the debt is less than the contemporaneous call value (so the firm can not force conversion by calling the debt for early redemption), the contingent value of the debt is also less than the call value (implying that the firm has no incentive to call the debt for cash redemption) and it is greater than the conversion value (implying creditors have no incentive to convert voluntarily). More generally, if the firm can not force conversion of its debt by exercising its call option, then neither it nor its creditors have an incentive to disturb the status quo. We do not observe either early cash redemption or voluntary conversion in this example.[10]

---

9. The call decision of the firm and the conversion decision of creditors can be identified at the last stage of the algorithm described in section 8.3, when $j = 1$ and $k = 1$. The discussion leading up to equations (8.14a, b) implies that the firm will call the debt for redemption at time $t^* = t_1$ when the value of the firm is $W^* = W_{1,1}$ if $\min[(1 - \gamma(t^*)) \cdot W^*, W^* - C(t^*)] > \min[(1 - \gamma(t^*)) \cdot W^*, V_{1,1,2}^{sq}]$. If the firm calls the debt, creditors will be forced to convert if $\gamma(t^*) \cdot W^* > C(t^*)$. If the firm does not call the debt, creditors will convert voluntarily if $\gamma(t^*) \cdot W^* > V_{1,1,1}^{sq}$.

10. Ingersoll (1977a) shows that creditors will not convert voluntarily into a non-dividend-paying stock except immediately prior to an adverse change in the dilution factor, and that they may not convert even then.

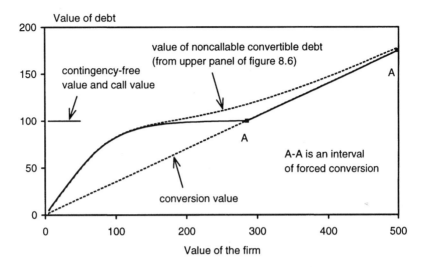

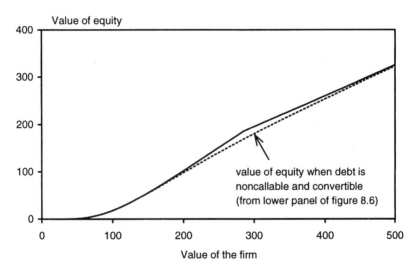

Figure 8.8
Contingent value of callable convertible debt and equity five years before the debt matures

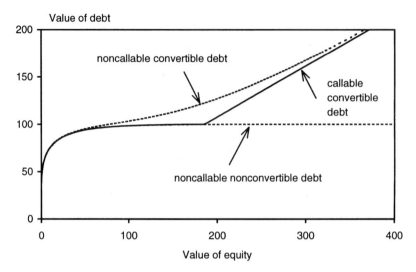

Figure 8.9
Value of debt five years before maturity as a function of the value of equity

Cross Valuation

Figure 8.9 shows how the dual options of call and conversion affect the implicit relationship between debt and equity values. If we fail to include the issuer's call option (but do include the creditors' conversion option) in assessing relative values, we would conclude that the debt is cheap relative to equity. This spurious result is attributable to ignoring the call option that managers exercise in the best interest of shareholders.

Example C

The next example is similar to example B, except that we here assume the debt is not callable earlier than three years prior to maturity:

$$C(t) = \begin{cases} F \cdot e^{-\rho \cdot (T-t)} & T - 3 \le t < T \\ \infty & t < T - 3 \end{cases} \qquad (8.16)$$

We continue to assume that $\rho = R_f$.

As shown by the solid line in the upper panel of figure 8.10, the contingent value of the debt five years before maturity (when the debt is still protected from immediate call) is intermediate between the behavior illustrated in figure 8.6 (when the debt is never callable) and the behavior in figure 8.8 (when the debt is immediately callable). The contingent value function for the call protected debt will move closer to the function in figure 8.6 the longer the remaining interval of call protection, and closer to the function in figure 8.8 the shorter the interval.

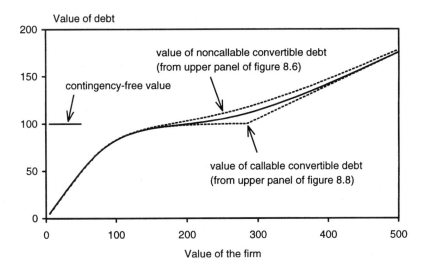

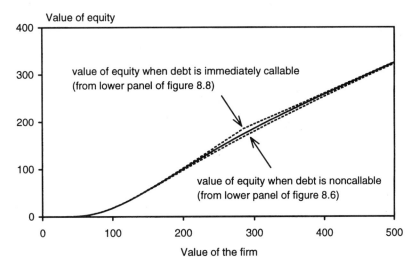

Figure 8.10
Contingent value of callable convertible debt and equity five years before the debt matures
when call protection has not yet lapsed

Example D

The fourth example is also similar to example B, except that we consider here the effect of values of ρ different from R_f.

The upper panel of figure 8.11 shows (with a solid line) the effect of lowering the value of ρ below the yield on Treasury debt, to $\rho = 0.08$, or 8% per annum. As in figure 8.8 the debt is called immediately if its conversion value exceeds its call value (thereby forcing conversion to equity) and is otherwise left outstanding.

The solid line in the lower panel of figure 8.11 shows that the situation is quite different if the value of ρ is raised above the yield on Treasury debt, to $\rho = 0.12$, or 12% per annum. The section of the contingent value function marked B–B indicates a range of values of the firm where management will call the debt for early redemption even though creditors have no incentive to convert the debt to equity. This demonstrates that a firm may redeem convertible debt for cash if it can call the debt at a price lower than the price of comparable of Treasury debt. The firm will not opt for early *cash* redemption if (as in figure 8.8 and the upper panel of figure 8.11) the cost of redemption equals or exceeds the price of comparable Treasury debt.[11]

Example E

The last example is similar to example A (the debt is noncallable, promises to pay 164.872 in five years, and is convertible into common stock with a dilution factor of 0.35), except that we here consider the effect of changing the volatility of the value of the firm from $\sigma = 0.20$ to $\sigma = 0.10$ and to $\sigma = 0.30$.

As shown in the upper panel of figure 8.12, the contingent value of the debt is inversely related to the volatility of the value of the firm when the value of the firm is around 100 and conversion is unlikely (assuming the risk neutral drift rate). This result parallels the result from example C in section 2.6 regarding the relationship between volatility and the contingent value of nonconvertible debt.

However, at values of the firm above about 200, where default is unlikely and conversion is a distinct possibility, greater volatility enhances the value of the convertible debt.[12] This follows because shortfalls of

11. As we noted in example C in section 6.4, it is not in the best interests of the shareholders of a limited liability corporation for the firm to redeem its debt for cash at a price equal to the price of comparable Treasury debt.

12. Conversely, greater volatility reduces the value of equity. Several authors have observed that this limits the incentive for "asset substitution." (Asset substitution was described in note 14 in chapter 2.) See Jensen and Meckling (1976, pp. 353–54), Smith and Warner (1979, p. 141), Green (1984), and Jensen and Smith (1985, pp. 117–18).

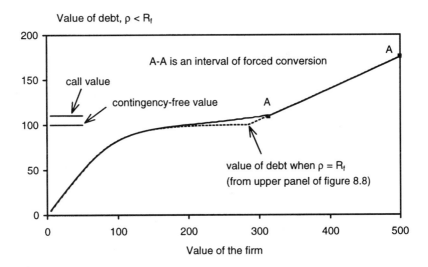

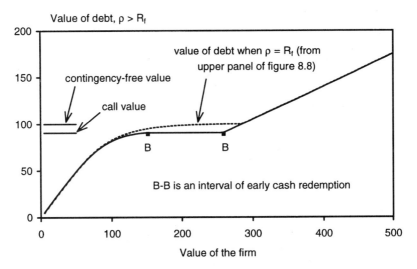

Figure 8.11
Contingent value of callable convertible debt five years before the debt matures for ρ less than R_f and for ρ greater than R_f

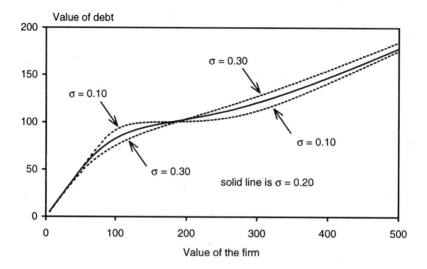

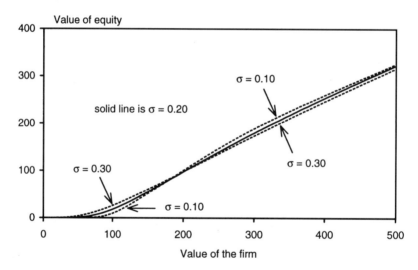

Figure 8.12
Contingent value of noncallable convertible debt and equity five years before the debt matures for various volatilities of the value of the firm

$W(T)$ below $\gamma^{-1}(T) \cdot F = 471.063$ (down to the limit of $F = 164.872$) do not reduce the payoff value of the debt, while an excess of $W(T)$ above $\gamma^{-1}(T) \cdot F$ increases the debt's payoff value.

We can characterize the effect of the volatility of the value of the firm on the contingent value of the convertible debt by observing that greater volatility reduces the value of convertible debt when the value of the debt is a concave function of the value of the firm, and enhances the value of convertible debt when the value of the debt is a convex function of the value of the firm.[13]

Appendix: Consequences of a Notice Period

This appendix examines the problem of valuing convertible debt when a notice period is required for early redemption. Except for the notice requirement, the framework of the analysis is identical to that specified in section 8.1.

The corporate capital structure described in section 8.1 provides that a company can call its debt for early redemption and that creditors can then decide whether to accept cash or convert to equity. We assumed that call and (if desired) conversion occur instantaneously. However, this assumption is inconsistent with an important characteristic of convertible debt: indentures for convertible bonds commonly specify that an issuer must provide notice (usually 30 days) of early redemption.[14] This gives creditors an opportunity to learn of the issuer's intent to redeem, and gives them time to decide whether to accept cash or stock.[15]

Recognition of a notice requirement introduces two novel features into the specification of a valuation model for convertible debt. First, it delays the distribution of cash or stock to some time after the announcement of redemption. More important, it allows creditors to postpone their decision whether to accept cash or stock, and thereby creates a valuable option.

13. This characterization parallels the characterization, in note 11 in chapter 3, of the effect of the volatility of the value of the firm on the contingent value of subordinated debt.

14. See, for example, section 11.5 in American Bar Foundation (1971, p. 500) and Section 3.03 of "Model Simplified Indenture," *Business Lawyer* 38: 741, 754 (1983).

15. Prior to the federal requirement that essentially all bonds must be registered (rather than bearer) securities, it was not uncommon for a holder of bearer convertible bonds to miss a published notice of early redemption and to complain when his or her request for conversion after the redemption date was denied. See *Gampel v. Burlington Industries*, 43 Misc. 2d 846, 252 N.Y.S. 2d 500 (1954), *Kaplan v. Vornado* 341 F. Supp. 212 (N.D. Ill. 1971), *Abramson v. Burroughs Corp.*, Fed. Sec. L. Rep. ¶93,456 (S.D.N.Y. 1972), *Terrell v. Lomas & Nettleton Financial Corp.*, 496 S.W. 2d 669 (1973), and *Van Gemert v. Boeing Co.*, 520 F. 2d 1373 (2d Cir. 1975), 553 F. 2d 812 (2d. Cir. 1977). See also Lampkin (1969) and Miller (1971).

To see the significance of the latter feature, consider two alternative versions of a requirement for an interval of τ years between an announcement of redemption and the actual distribution of cash or stock:[16]

Version 1: At any time $t < T - \tau$ (where T is the maturity date of the debt), the company can announce that it will redeem its debt at time $t + \tau$ for an aggregate cash payment of $C(t + \tau)$. Creditors can decide at any time s in the interval between t and $t + \tau$ whether to accept the cash to be paid at $t + \tau$ or whether to convert into a fraction $\gamma(s)$ of the common stock of the firm.

Version 2: At any time $t < T - \tau$, the company can announce that it will redeem its debt at time $t + \tau$ for an aggregate cash payment of $C(t + \tau)$. Creditors must decide *immediately*, at time t, whether to accept the cash to be paid at $t + \tau$ or whether to convert into a fraction $\gamma(s^*(t))$ of the common stock of the firm, where $s^*(t)$ is the value of s in the interval from t to $t + \tau$ where the dilution factor $\gamma(s)$ attains its highest value.[17] (If a creditor must decide at time t *whether* she will convert her debt to equity sometime during the interval between t and $t + \tau$, and if she decides that she *will* convert her debt, then she will clearly elect to convert at time $s^*(t)$.)

If version 2 applies and the issuer calls the debt at time t, creditors must choose immediately between receiving stock with a contemporaneous market value of $\gamma(s^*(t)) \cdot W(t)$ or cash with a present value of $C(t + \tau) \cdot e^{-R_f \cdot \tau}$.[18] It follows (from the assumption that creditors act to maximize the value of their debt) that conditional on a call announced at time t, the value of the convertible debt at time t will be

$$\max[\gamma(s^*(t)) \cdot W(t), C(t + \tau) \cdot e^{-R_f \cdot \tau}] \tag{A8.1}$$

This version of a delay between an announcement of redemption and the distribution of cash or stock can be accommodated within the model of section 8.1 if the call value at time t is interpreted as $C(t + \tau) \cdot e^{-R_f \cdot \tau}$ and if the dilution factor at time t is interpreted as $\gamma(s^*(t))$. Thus a requirement for a notice period that does not also allow delay of a creditor's decision to take cash or stock does not alter the contingent value problem in any material way.[19]

16. If the notice period is 30 days, τ will be 0.0822 years (0.0822 years = 30 days/365 days per year).

17. That is, $\gamma(s^*(t)) \geq \gamma(s)$ for all $s \in [t, t + \tau]$.

18. We ignore here the relatively minor risk that the firm will default on early redemption of the debt.

19. See similarly note 4 in chapter 6.

However, if version 1 applies, a redemption announcement at time t is tantamount to an immediate *exchange* of the convertible debt for a *new* security—which we will call a "redemption option"—that provides creditors with a choice (that can be made at any time s between t and $t + \tau$) between two alternatives

1. accept a cash payment of $C(t + \tau)$ at time $t + \tau$, or

2. convert into a fraction $\gamma(s)$ of the common stock of the firm.

If τ is nonnegligible, the value of this redemption option may be materially greater than the value shown in equation (A8.1). This can be expected to alter both the contingent value of the debt and the circumstances under which a company will choose to call its debt.

Valuing the Redemption Option

We begin the analysis of the consequences of a notice requirement by examining (at time t when the value of the firm is W) the value of the redemption option created by a contemporaneous announcement of the firm's decision to redeem the debt at time $t + \tau$.

The redemption option is essentially a "mini" convertible bond. The mini-bond is noncallable, promises to pay $C(t + \tau)$ at time $t + \tau$, and is convertible at any time s between t and $t + \tau$ into a fraction $\gamma(s)$ of the common stock of the company.

Following the analysis in section 8.3, there will exist a contingent value function, here denoted g_1, with two arguments: time and the value of the firm, such that the value of the redemption option, that is, the value of the mini convertible bond, at time t when the value of the firm is W can be calculated as $g_1(W, t)$. Computing the value of $g_1(W, t)$ for given values of W and t follows the form of the algorithm described in section 8.3.

An Example

Consider, as in example B of section 8.4, debt with a face value of $F = 164.872$ payable at time T that can be converted at any time $t \le T$ into a fraction $\gamma(t) = 0.35$ of the common stock of the issuer and that can be redeemed at any time $t < T$ upon payment of $C(t) = F \cdot e^{-\rho \cdot (T-t)}$. Assume, as in that example, that $R_f = 0.10$, $\sigma = 0.20$, and $\rho = 0.10$.

Figure 8.13 shows (with a solid line) the value of the debt five years before maturity, at time $t = T - 5.0$, *conditional* on announcement of a decision by the firm to redeem the debt in 30 days, or at time $t + \tau$ where $\tau = 0.0822$ years (0.0822 years = 30 days/365 days per year). That is, figure 8.13 shows the contingent value at time t of the redemption option created by a contemporaneous announcement of the firm's intent to redeem.

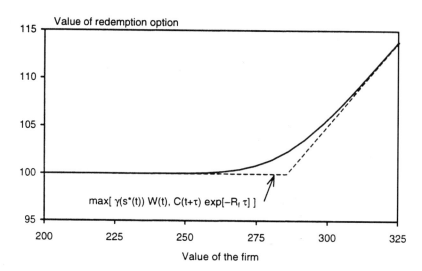

Figure 8.13
Contingent value, five years before maturity of debt, of redemption option following contemporaneous announcement of redemption in 30 days

The dashed line in figure 8.13 shows what the debt would be worth if creditors had to decide at time t whether to accept stock or cash at time $t + \tau$. The contingent value of the redemption option lies above the dashed line when the redemption option is at-the-money and there is material uncertainty over whether creditors will choose to exercise the option.

The Contingent Value of Debt and Equity When Notice Is Required for Early Redemption

We consider next how a notice requirement affects the algorithm described in section 8.3 for computing the value of convertible debt and equity at time t^* when the value of the firm is W^*, or for computing $f_i(W^*, t^*)$ for $i = 1$ and 2.

The preliminary steps of the algorithm are unchanged. We divide the interval between t^* and T into K subintervals and define a sequence $\{t_1, t_2, \ldots, t_{K+1}\}$ of $K + 1$ discrete points in time (equation 8.6), we specify an array $W_{j,k}$ of possible values of the firm (equation 8.7), and we denote the value of the ith security at time t_k when the value of the firm is $W_{j,k}$ as $V_{j,k,i}$. The values of $V_{j,K+1,i}$ for $j = 1, 2, \ldots, K + 1$ follow from the consequences of default and bankruptcy and from the creditors' option to convert their debt to equity at maturity. These values are not affected by the details of *early* redemption and are computed as in equations (8.8) and (8.9).

Consider now the problem of computing $V_{j,k,i}$ for $k < K+1$. Any one of three events can happen at time t_k when the value of the firm is $W_{j,k}$ and the firm must provide notice of early redemption of its debt:

1. The firm can announce that it plans to redeem its debt at time $t_k + \tau$. In this case the debt will have a value of $g_1(W_{j,k}, t_k)$ and equity will have a value of $W_{j,k} - g_1(W_{j,k}, t_k)$.

2. Creditors can convert their debt to equity in the absence of any action by the firm to call the debt for early redemption. In this case the debt will have a value of $\gamma(t_k) \cdot W_{j,k}$ and equity will have a value of $(1 - \gamma(t_k)) \cdot W_{j,k}$.

3. The firm can abstain from calling its debt and creditors can abstain from converting the debt. In this case the debt will have a value of $V^{sq}_{j,k,1}$ and equity will have a value of $V^{sq}_{j,k,2}$, where $V^{sq}_{j,k,i}$ is computed by the arbitrage pricing scheme of equations (8.10) and (8.11a, b).

Assuming that creditors act to maximize the value of their debt and that the firm acts to maximize the value of equity, we have[20]

$$V_{j,k,1} = \min[g_1(W_{j,k}, t_k), \max[\gamma(t_k) \cdot W_{j,k}, V^{sq}_{j,k,1}]] \qquad \text{(A8.2a)}$$

$$V_{j,k,2} = \max[W_{j,k} - g_1(W_{j,k}, t_k), \min[(1 - \gamma(t_k)) \cdot W_{j,k}, V^{sq}_{j,k,2}]] \qquad \text{(A8.2b)}$$

This procedure can be applied repeatedly, leading to the computation of $V_{1,1,i}$ or, equivalently, to the computation of $f_i(W^*, t^*)$.

Comment

There are two important differences between valuing convertible debt in the presence of a notice requirement and valuation in the absence of a notice requirement.

When notice is required, we can no longer express (as in equation 8.12a) the value of the debt conditional on a call for redemption as the greater of the converted value of the debt and the call value of the debt. Instead, the value of the debt conditional on a call for redemption is the value of the redemption option created by the redemption announcement.

Second, the decision of the firm to call its debt for early redemption depends on the value of the redemption option compared to the value the debt would have if creditors are allowed to choose between voluntary conversion and maintenance of the status quo. Since the value of the

20. The firm cannot announce at time t_k that it plans to redeem its debt at time $t_k + \tau$ if $t_k + \tau$ is greater than or equal to the maturity date of the debt. Creditors can, however, choose voluntarily to convert their debt into equity. Thus, if $t_k \geq T - \tau$, equations (A8.2a, b) simplify to $V_{j,k,1} = \max[\gamma(t_k) \cdot W_{j,k}, V^{sq}_{j,k,1}]$ and $V_{j,k,2} = \min[(1 - \gamma(t_k)) \cdot W_{j,k}, V^{sq}_{j,k,2}]$, respectively.

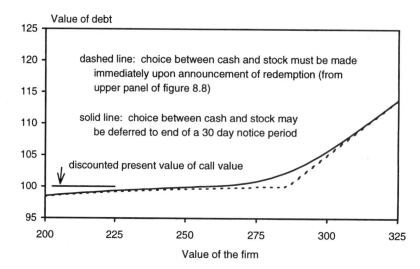

Figure 8.14
Contingent value of callable convertible debt five years before the debt matures

redemption option depends on the length of the notice period, the corporation's call decision, and the value of the convertible debt, will not be invariant with respect to the notice requirement.

An Example

Consider again debt with a face value of $F = 164.872$ payable at time T that can be converted at any time $t \leq T$ into a fraction $\gamma(t) = 0.35$ of the common stock of the firm and that can be redeemed, following 30 days notice, at any time $t < T$ upon payment of $C(t) = F \cdot e^{-\rho \cdot (T-t)}$. Assume again the parameter values $R_f = 0.10$, $\sigma = 0.20$ and $\rho = 0.10$.

Figure 8.14 shows (with a solid line) the contingent value of the debt five years before maturity. The dashed line shows what the debt would be worth if creditors had to choose between cash and stock immediately upon announcement of early redemption of the debt. The difference between the solid line and the dashed line reflects the value of the option to wait until the end of the notice period before choosing between cash and stock. In contrast to the case where call and (if desired) conversion occur instantaneously (see example B in section 8.4), the contingent value of the debt can exceed the discounted present value of the call value of the debt, even if the latter value exceeds the conversion value of the debt, and the contingent value of the debt can exceed the conversion value of the debt, even if the conversion value exceeds the discounted present value of the call value of the debt.

Comment

Ingersoll (1977b, p. 469) pointed out that a company will call its convertible debt for early redemption at somewhat lower values of the firm if it has to wait for a notice period to elapse before effecting redemption. This implies that the debt will always be called for early redemption *before* the conversion value of the debt has increased above the debt's call value. Whether a call for early redemption will actually force conversion of the debt depends on whether the conversion value of the debt exceeds the debt's call value at the *end* of the notice period. At the time the company calls the debt it is therefore uncertain whether it will have to disburse cash or stock at the end of the notice period. This uncertainty is immaterial in the absence of transactions costs, but it can affect the company's call decision if the firm does not have liquid assets or if it can not borrow funds or sell new securities on short notice. Chapter 9 examines this important aspect of a corporation's decision to call convertible debt.

Contingent valuation of callable convertible debt depends, in part, on assumptions about the circumstances that will lead the issuer to call the debt, as well as the circumstances that will lead a creditor to convert her debt.[1] This suggests that we can assess the validity of a convertible debt valuation model by examining the validity of its assumptions regarding exercise of the embedded call and conversion options.

This chapter describes the empirical characteristics of calls of convertible debt intended to force creditors to convert their debt to equity. It appears that issuers almost never announce conversion forcing calls as quickly as the model in chapter 8 predicts. The delay can be explained by the failure of the model to reflect accurately the consequences of a "failed forced conversion" (a call for early redemption that results in cash redemption even though it was intended to force conversion), or by the failure of the model to reflect the economic significance of after-tax corporate cash flows. The concluding section comments on the significance of these results for contingent value models of convertible debt. An appendix provides an example of a failed forced conversion.

9.1 Delays in Calling Convertible Debt for Early Redemption

Consider a convertible bond that a rational bondholder would not convert voluntarily.[2] It follows from the analyses at equations (8.12a, b) to (8.14a, b) that

1. the issuer should call the bond to force conversion as soon as the conversion value of the bond rises to the bond's call value,[3] and that

2. we should not observe an uncalled convertible bond with a conversion value in excess of its call value.[4]

---

1. See, for example, the analysis in section 8.3. As noted in note 1 in chapter 7, the effect of assumptions regarding exercise of a contingent claim on the value of the claim have been explored most extensively in the literature on valuation of employee and executive stock options.

2. Outside of unusual situations (like a proxy contest), voluntary conversion is unlikely if (a) the interest payments on a convertible bond equal or exceed the dividends paid on the stock that would be obtained in conversion and (b) any prospective change in the terms of conversion will not be adverse to the interests of bondholders.

3. This result may not hold if the managers of the firm believe that even if bondholders have an economic incentive to convert voluntarily they will not do so because of transactions costs or ignorance (Dunn and Eades 1989). For example, a firm may abstain from calling its convertible debt when the conversion value of the debt exceeds the call value if the dilution factor is scheduled to decline significantly in the near future and the firm's managers anticipate that a material fraction of bondholders will not convert voluntarily before the date of the decline.

4. We could observe a convertible bond with a conversion value in excess of its call value if the bond has been called for early redemption but the notice period has not yet expired. See the appendix to chapter 8.

Ingersoll (1977b) provided the first empirical evidence on the characteristics of conversion-forcing calls of convertible debt. For a sample of 179 convertible bonds called for early redemption between 1968 and 1975, he found a mean ratio of conversion value to call value at the time of call of 1.835 and a median ratio of 1.439. These ratios were so much larger than the hypothesized ratio of unity that Ingersoll concluded that companies commonly wait "too long" to call their convertible debt.

9.2   Why a Company Might Delay Calling Convertible Debt

Following publication of Ingersoll's surprising empirical results, Jaffee and Shliefer (1990) suggested that analyses of convertible bond calls—like those presented in Ingersoll (1977a), Brennan and Schwartz (1977, 1980), and chapter 8 in this book—are incomplete. In particular, Jaffee and Shliefer argued that the analyses fail to account for all of the consequences of the notice period between announcement of a call for early redemption and actual redemption.

Our analysis in the appendix to chapter 8 considered explicitly the existence of a notice period and demonstrated that a company that calls its debt cannot be certain whether the call will result in conversion or cash redemption. The outcome depends on whether the conversion value of the bond is greater or less than the bond's call value at the *end* of the notice period. We suppressed the practical significance of this uncertainty by assuming that the company can liquidate assets to fund bondholder demands for cash redemption as readily and inexpensively as it can issue new shares of common stock to satisfy bondholder demands for conversion.

Jaffee and Shliefer observed that the transactions costs of liquidating *physical* assets *quickly* are usually substantial. In the absence of a contingency plan to satisfy bondholder demands for cash redemption, a decline in the price of the firm's stock during the notice period can precipitate a financial crisis, that is, a need to liquidate physical assets quickly to satisfy a current liability. On the other hand, contingency arrangements appear to be quite expensive, including

1. accumulating an anticipatory hoard of liquid financial assets,

2. arranging for a contingent bank loan or bond sale, and

3. purchasing a put option for the common stock that would be issued upon conversion of the debt (with a strike price equal to the call value of the debt being called, i.e., an at-the-money put option).[5]

5. In the event bondholders choose cash redemption in lieu of conversion, the issuer can exercise the put option—thereby obtaining the cash needed to finance the redemption and issuing to the option writer the stock that it would have issued to bondholders had they elected to convert their bonds.

Jaffee and Shliefer conjectured that in the interest of maximizing shareholder value—without exposing the firm to excessive risk or incurring the expense of a contingency plan that may never be put into effect—companies commonly choose to wait to call their convertible debt until the conversion value exceeds the call value by a substantial margin, that is, until the bondholders' conversion option is deep-in-the-money. (The most commonly cited threshold is a conversion value equal to 120% of call value.[6]) In this case the risk of a failed forced conversion is small[7] and can be eliminated completely by purchasing a relatively inexpensive deep-out-of-the-money put option.[8]

At about the same time that Jaffee and Shliefer were developing their analysis of the implications of the risk of a failed forced conversion, Asquith and Mullins (1991) developed an alternative explanation for why a company might not call convertible debt even when the conversion value exceeds the call value. They observed that calling a bond and forcing conversion will reduce the issuer's after-tax cash flow if the annual dividends to be paid on the stock issued in conversion exceed the annual after-tax interest expenses of the convertible bond. It may be to the shareholders' advantage for the company to allow the convertible debt to remain outstanding, even if conversion value exceeds call value, if the company has attractive investment opportunities and if the cost of external financing exceeds the cost of internally generated funds.[9]

6. The 120% threshold was identified by Asquith and Mullins (1991, p. 1277) as the percentage given by managers in a survey conducted by Brigham (1966) and as the threshold most often mentioned by investment bankers.

7. Jaffee and Shleifer (1990, p. S108n. 1) identify only two instances of a failed forced conversion: an Echelin bond in 1973 and the example described in the appendix to this chapter. Singh, Cowan, and Nayar (1991, pp. 182–83) also note the failed forced conversion of the Echelin bond.

8. Singh, Cowan, and Nayar (1991) describe the use and pricing of out-of-the-money put options to eliminate the risk of a failed forced conversion.

9. Several additional explanations for why a company might abstain from calling convertible debt even when the conversion value of the debt exceeds the call value have appeared in the literature. Harris and Raviv (1985) proposed an explanation based on information asymmetries and signaling theory. Consistent with empirical evidence reported by Mikkelson (1981) (see also Singh, Cowan, and Nayar 1991), their model predicts that the price of a company's common stock should fall following announcement of a conversion forcing call of its debt. Subsequent studies by Mazzeo and Moore (1992) and Byrd and Moore (1996) attributed price declines following call announcements to transient liquidity effects (associated with anticipations of sales of stock by bondholders forced to convert but unable or unwilling to hold stock) that are reversed by the end of the notice period. See also Ofer and Natarajan (1987) (reporting a significant decline in the earnings growth rate of a firm following call of its convertible debt that is consistent with the model of Harris and Raviv), Cowan, Nayar, and Singh (1990) (pointing out a selection bias in the analysis of Ofer and Natarajan), and Campbell, Ederington, and Vankudre (1991) (showing that, as a result of the selection bais, the decline in the earnings growth rate following call of convertible debt is due to unusually strong earnings growth *prior* to call rather than unusually weak earnings growth *following* call). Additionally, as discussed in note 3 above, Dunn and Eades (1989)

9.3   Empirical Evidence

Asquith and Mullins (1991) and Asquith (1995) examined the empirical significance for convertible bond calls of (1) the risk of a failed forced conversion and (2) after-tax cash flows.

The Cross-sectional Study of Asquith and Mullins

Asquith and Mullins (1991) examined 208 convertible bonds outstanding at the end of January 1984, each of which had a contemporaneous conversion value in excess of its principal value and was either immediately callable at principal value or would become callable at principal value following the lapse of call protection. They found that

1. 30 bonds were still in their call protection periods,

2. 66 of the remaining 178 bonds had a conversion value less than 120% of their call value and thus did not have deep-in-the-money conversion options, and

3. 90 of the remaining 112 bonds had after-tax interest payments lower than the dividends that would have been paid on the common stock into which the bonds were convertible.

This left 22 "anomalous" bonds that apparently should have been called to force conversion. With respect to the anomalous bonds, Asquith and Mullins further found that

1. four bonds were in the process of being called,

2. ten bonds were called later in 1984,

3. four bonds had conversion values only slightly greater than 120% of call value,

4. two bonds were issued by companies that subsequently (within six calendar quarters) increased the dividend on their common stock to a level that created an after-tax cash flow advantage to leaving the bonds outstanding, and

5. one bond was retired during 1984 in the course of an acquisition of the issuer.

---

suggested that the managers of a firm may defer calling convertible debt when conversion value exceeds call value to take advantage of anticipated failures of bondholders to convert voluntarily when voluntary conversion would be in the best interests of the bondholders but contrary to the interests of stockholders. Finally, Stulz (1988) suggested that managers might delay forcing conversion if conversion would dilute their equity ownership share, thereby reducing the premium that an outside bidder might offer in a takeover contest and reducing the current market value of the firm.

This left only a single "truly anomalous" convertible bond out of the original sample of 208 bonds.

The authors concluded that the combination of a call threshold defined as conversion value in excess of 120% of call value and after-tax cash flow considerations explain why a bond may not be called to force conversion even when its conversion value exceeds its call value.

The Longitudinal Study of Asquith

A subsequent study by Asquith (1995) examined the behavior of 199 convertible bonds issued between January 1, 1980, and December 31, 1982, from the date of issue to the end of 1993. For 47 bonds, conversion value never exceeded call value during the sample interval, so there was no reason to expect the issuers to call the bonds to force conversion. (Asquith observes that 8 of the 47 bonds were called anyway. This shows that a company may call convertible debt for reasons other than to force conversion of the debt. See similarly the discussion of the lower panel of figure 8.11 in example D in section 8.4.)

Of the remaining 152 bonds, 116 bonds had after-tax interest expenses that exceeded (throughout the sample interval) the dividends that would have been paid on the common stock into which the bonds were convertible. Forcing conversion of these bonds would have been advantageous to the issuers in terms of increasing after-tax cash flow. Eighty-six of the 116 bonds were called. The mean number of trading days for which conversion value exceeded 120% of call value prior to the announcement of call was 37.8 days (median of 17.5 days). Twenty-seven bonds of the 30 remaining bonds were issued by firms that were acquired or that were restructured in bankruptcy during the sample interval. The final three bonds remained outstanding through the end of the sample interval. Conversion value never exceeded 120% of call value during the sample interval for two of the bonds, and exceeded 120% of call value for the third bond on only a single day. Asquith concluded that if there is a cash flow advantage to forcing conversion of a convertible bond, the issuer will call the bond reasonably promptly after the conversion value of the bond exceeds 120% of the bond's call value.

Asquith also pointed out that the high average ratio of conversion value to call value at the time of call reported by Ingersoll (1977b) can be explained by three factors:

1. A bond cannot be called during its call protection period, regardless of its conversion value,[10] so a bond with a high conversion value that is

---

10. See, however, the discussion of "soft" call protection in example 8.1.

called promptly at the end of its call protection period will necessarily exhibit a high ratio of conversion value to call value at the time of call.

2. A bond may not be called if there is an after-tax cash flow disadvantage to forcing conversion.

3. The price of a company's common stock may rise so quickly that conversion value is well in excess of call value at the time of call, even if the bond is called reasonably promptly after the bond's conversion value first exceeds 120% of its call value.

After accounting for these three factors, the premium of conversion value over call value at the time of call averages about 26% of call value.[11] This is not much greater than the 20% premium commonly used to identify deep-in-the-money conversion options.

9.4 Implications

The work of Jaffee and Shleifer (1990), Asquith and Mullins (1991), and Asquith (1995) suggests why corporations do not call convertible debt as soon as conversion value exceeds call value. Unfortunately, we do not know how to incorporate either cash flow considerations or the risk of a failed forced conversion into a contingent value model.

Fluctuations in corporate cash flows cannot be replicated with portfolios of traded securities. It is difficult to see how we might undertake the contingent valuation of convertible debt when the occurrence of an important event (call of the debt for early redemption) depends on a variable whose fluctuations cannot be replicated with traded claims.

Additionally the consequences of a failed forced conversion are difficult to express analytically in a contingent value model. The consequences may be small if the issuer has ample liquid assets or a substantial unused line of credit, but they may be overwhelming for a firm with significant intangible or firm-specific assets. This serves to identify additional variables, including asset structure and the ready availability of additional credit, whose fluctuations can not be replicated with traded claims.

Appendix: An Example of a Failed Forced Conversion

At various times in the early 1980s, International Business Machines Corporation bought a total of 22.6 million shares of Intel Corporation common stock at a cost of about $642.7 million to bolster the balance

---

11. See table III in Asquith (1995).

sheet of the financially ailing computer chip manufacturer.[12] By the end of 1985, demand for Intel's new 80386 chip was surging, the company's financial health was improving rapidly, and IBM began to think about liquidating its investment.

In February 1986 IBM issued (in the Eurobond market) $300 million principal value of $6\frac{30}{8}\%$ callable exchangeable subordinated debentures due in February 1996. The debentures were exchangeable for Intel common stock at a price of $38.50 per share, so each $1,000 principal value debenture was exchangeable for 25.97 shares of Intel (25.97 shares = $1,000/ $38.50 per share) and the entire issue was exchangeable for 7.8 million shares of Intel (7.8 million shares = $300 million/$38.50 per share).[13] Adding the exchange option to the subordinated debt allowed IBM to sell the debt with a lower coupon rate. This type of exchangeable debt financing is not uncommon for firms with large equity investments (in other firms) that have ceased to have strategic significance.

Following the sale of the debentures, IBM sold (in June 1987) 8.9 million shares of Intel back to the issuer in a private transaction at a price of $40.62 per share, and then sold (in August 1987) another 5.9 million shares in a secondary market transaction at a price of $52.50 per share. Following these sales, IBM retained only the 7.8 million shares of Intel needed to cover the exchange option on its $6\frac{30}{8}\%$ debentures.

On Friday, September 25, 1987, IBM announced that it was exercising its option to call the debentures for early redemption and that it would redeem the debentures on Tuesday, November 10, 1987, at the contractually specified call price of $1,094.09 per $1,000 principal value debenture. Intel common stock closed at $57.75 per share on the day of the announcement, so each debenture was then exchangeable for stock worth $1,500 ($1,500 = 25.97 shares per debenture, times $57.75 per share.) The exchange value of the debentures stood at a 37% premium to the call value of the debentures ($1,500 = 137% of $1,094.09), and the option to exchange the debentures was deep in the money.[14]

12. This appendix is based on "IBM Cuts Intel Stake Further to 7.1% and Takes Profit Totaling $80 Million," *Wall Street Journal*, August 31, 1987, p. 4, "IBM Letting Intel Loose with Stock Sale, Analysts Say the Move Signals Renewed Confidence in Chip Maker," *Los Angeles Times*, August 31, 1987, part IV, p. 1, "IBM Is Planning to Shed the Rest of Its Intel Stake," *Wall Street Journal*, September 28, 1987, p. 25, and "IBM Sells Rest of Intel Stake," *Wall Street Journal*, December 11, 1987, p. 10.

13. A bond is said to be "exchangeable," rather than "convertible," when—as in the present example—the stock obtained upon conveyance of the bond back to the issuer is not the stock of the issuer. The model described in chapter 8 is not appropriate for valuing exchangeable debt, but the idea of a forced exchange parallels the concept of a forced conversion.

14. The 37% premium of the exchange value over the call value at the time of the call was larger than the 20% or 25% premium usually observed when a bond is called to force conversion. A "soft" call protection provision in the indenture for the $6\frac{30}{8}\%$ debentures prohibited a call for early redemption so soon after issue unless Intel common stock traded at a price in excess of 130% of the $38.50 exchange price, or in excess of $50.05 per share, for at least 30 consecutive trading days.

The stock market declined sharply on Monday, October 19, 1987. The S&P 500 index dropped 20.4% (from 282.70 on Friday, October 16, to 224.99 on October 19) and Intel common stock dropped 19.2% (from $52.00 per share on the preceding Friday to $42.00 on October 19). By Monday, November 9, 1987, the stock had declined further, to a price of $33.19 per share,[15] and the exchange option on IBM's $6\frac{30}{8}$% debentures expired out of the money. As a result holders of only $180 million principal value of the debentures choose to exchange their debentures for Intel common stock (they received 4.7 million shares: 4.7 million shares = $180 million principal value of debentures, times 25.97 shares of Intel per $1,000 principal value debenture).[16] Holders of the remaining $120 million principal value of debentures accepted an aggregate cash redemption payment of $131.3 million ($131.3 million = $120 million principal value of debentures, times the call price of $1,094.09 per $1,000 principal value debenture).[17]

The market break in October 1987, and the subsequent further decline in the price of Intel stock, meant that IBM was unable to force the exchange of all of its debentures and that it had to finance an unexpected $131.3 million cash redemption payment on three weeks notice. Such an event could create a financial crisis for a smaller, less well capitalized, company.

15. On Thursday, October 29, 1987, Intel's stock split 3-for-2. This resulted in an adjustment of the exchange price of the $6\frac{30}{8}$% debentures to $25.66 per share ($25.66 = two-thirds of $38.50), so that each $1,000 principal value debenture became exchangeable for 38.96 shares of Intel common stock (38.96 = $1,000/$25.66 per share). For expositional clarity, references in the text to the price of Intel stock and to the terms of exchange for the $6\frac{30}{8}$% debentures after October 28, 1987, are on a pre-split basis.

16. It is reasonable to inquire why the holders of the $180 million principal value of debentures did not accept cash redemption and then use the cash to buy Intel stock at a price below $42.12 per share. There are two possibilities. First, exchange of the $6\frac{30}{8}$% debentures was not a taxable event, while cash redemption would expose a bondholder to capital gains taxes, so exchange may have been less costly on an after-tax basis. Second, the market price of Intel was quite volatile in early November 1987. A holder of a large quantity of bonds may not have been confident that he could acquire, with secondary market purchases, a correspondingly large stock position at a price lower than $42.12 per share less the capital gains tax due upon cash redemption of the bonds.

17. IBM subsequently sold the unexchanged balance of 3.1 million shares of Intel in secondary market transactions in early December 1987, when Intel was trading at a price of about $36 a share (on a pre-split basis; see note 15).

10 Warrants

This chapter extends contingent value analysis to firms capitalized with warrants as well as with debt and equity.[1] A warrant is a call option on the stock of the company that issued the warrant. A holder exercises his option by paying a specified sum of money to the issuer and receives in return a specified quantity of stock.[2]

10.1 Framework of the Analysis

We begin our analysis by describing the capital structure of the firm and the consequences of default and bankruptcy.

Corporate Capital Structure

We assume the firm is capitalized with three classes of securities: a single issue of zero coupon debt, common stock, and warrants.

The debt matures at time T and promises to pay its face amount F at maturity. It cannot be called for early redemption, and it cannot be converted into stock. The stock cannot pay a dividend and cannot be repurchased by the firm until the debt has been redeemed.

The warrants expire when the debt matures. At that time—but not earlier—the holders of the warrants have the right to purchase the con-

---

1. Schwartz (1977) and Galai and Schneller (1978) provided the first extensive analyses of warrants as contingent claims.

2. Employee and executive stock options (EESOs) are close cousins to warrants. The holder of an EESO usually forfeits her option upon termination of employment with the issuer. To enforce this forfeiture provision, the option is inalienable. This can lead to exercise of an EESO (to avoid forfeiture) in circumstances where a holder of a warrant with the same strike price and expiration date would not choose to exercise. (See the discussion of "stopping states" in Carpenter 1998.) Additionally EESOs commonly can not be exercised during a "vesting period" of (typically) one to three years and may not be exercisable subsequently during "blackout" periods specified by the issuer (usually preceding public disclosure of quarterly and annual financial statements). Jennergren and Naslund (1993), Cuny and Jorion (1995), and Carpenter (1998) emphasize the significance of early option exercise to avoid forfeiture. Valuation and exercise of EESOs is also discussed in Lambert, Larcker, and Verrechia (1991), Huddart (1994), Kulatilaka and Marcus (1994), Rubinstein (1995), and Hudart and Lang (1996).

Although uncommon, warrants are sometimes *redeemable* (or callable) at the option of the issuer. In May 1998, Ontro, Inc., a development-stage company engaged in research and development of integrated thermal containers, sold 3.4 million units (each unit consisting of one share of common stock and one separable warrant for one share of common stock with an exercise price of $8.25 and an expiration date of May 12, 2001) at a price of $5.50 per unit (with $5.40 allocated to the stock and $.10 allocated to the warrant). The warrants were redeemable at the option of the issuer, upon 30 days prior notice, at a price of $.05 per warrant at any time after the price of the common stock exceeded $11.00 per share for 20 consecutive trading days during the 30 day period prior to the date of notice.

A company can also issue *put warrants* on its common stock. A holder of a put warrant exercises the warrant by conveying a specified quantity of the issuer's stock back to the issuer and receives in return a specified sum of money. See "Financial Engineering 1.0," *New York Times*, November 22, 1998, sec. 3, p. 1, for examples of put warrants issued by technology companies.

tractually specified fraction γ of the common stock of the issuer, where $0 \leq \gamma < 1$, by paying the contractually specified aggregate exercise price E.[3] If there are N_s shares of stock outstanding at time T, the warrant holders will receive N_w shares of new stock following exercise of the warrants, where N_w satisfies the equation:

$$\gamma = \frac{N_w}{N_w + N_s} \tag{10.1}$$

γ is called the "dilution factor" of the warrants.[4]

We denote the value of the debt at time t as $V_1(t)$, the value of equity as $V_2(t)$, and the value of the warrants as $V_3(t)$.[5] The value of the firm, $W(t)$, is the sum of the values of the firm's securities: $W(t) = V_1(t) + V_2(t) + V_3(t)$.

Default and Bankruptcy

At time T creditors have a claim on the firm for payment of F. If the firm defaults it goes into bankruptcy. We assume that bankruptcy results in an instantaneous and costless liquidation of the assets of the firm and distribution of the proceeds according to the absolute priority rule. Creditors are paid the entire proceeds of the liquidation up to the amount F and stockholders receive any remaining residual balance. Warrant holders receive nothing, because they have no claim on the firm other than their right to purchase stock.

The Contingent Value of the Debt, Equity, and Warrants at Time T

In view of our assumptions regarding (1) default and bankruptcy and (2) the warrant holders' option to purchase stock, we can specify how the value of the firm will be apportioned among creditors, shareholders and warrant holders when the debt matures and the warrants expire.

---

3. We assume that the warrants expire at the same time the debt matures, and that they can not be exercised prior to expiration, to avoid the analytical complexity of changes in corporate asset and capital structures at multiple points in time. If the warrants can be exercised prior to expiration, a competitive market equilibrium may be characterized by sequential exercise and the price and exercise characteristics of the warrants will be affected by whether warrant holders can coordinate their actions, by the investment and disbursement policies of the issuer, and by the presence in the warrant contract of "anti-dilution" provisions intended to protect warrant holders from losses attributable to discretionary corporate actions. See Emanuel (1983), Constantinides (1984), and Spatt and Sterbenz (1988).

4. Galai and Schneller (1978) emphasize the importance of dilution, and compare warrants to conventional, nondilutive call options written by somebody other than the issuer of the underlying stock. See also Lauterbach and Schultz (1990).

5. This follows our convention (see the second paragraph of section 2.1) of denoting more senior securities with a lower index number. Equity is senior to the warrants in the sense that equity may have positive value even if the warrants are worthless, but the warrants cannot have value if the equity is worthless.

If the value of the firm is less than F, the debt is worth the value of the firm and the stock and warrants are worthless. If the value of the firm exceeds F, creditors are paid F and the balance of the terminal value of the firm, $W(T) - F$, is divided between the shareholders and the warrant holders. The details of the division depend on whether or not the warrant holders exercise their call option.

If the warrant holders do not exercise their call option, their warrants expire worthless and the stock is worth $W(T) - F$. If, on the other hand, the warrant holders exercise their option to purchase stock, they will pay (to the firm) the aggregate exercise price E and receive in return new stock giving them a fraction γ of the total outstanding stock of the firm. Following redemption of the debt and exercise of the warrants, the firm will be capitalized entirely with common stock and it will have an aggregate value of $W(T) - F + E$. The former warrant holders hold a fraction γ of the stock, worth $\gamma \cdot (W(T) - F + E)$, and the original shareholders hold the balance of the stock, worth $(1 - \gamma) \cdot (W(T) - F + E)$. It follows that immediately *prior* to exercise at time T, the warrants will be worth the difference between (1) the value of the stock that will be received upon exercise, $\gamma \cdot (W(T) - F + E)$, and (2) the cost of exercise, E, or $\gamma \cdot (W(T) - F + E) - E$. This implies that the warrant holders will choose to exercise their warrants if $\gamma \cdot (W(T) - F + E)$ is greater than E, or if $W(T)$ exceeds $F + (\gamma^{-1} - 1) \cdot E$.

The contingent value of the firm's debt, equity and warrants at time T can be summarized in tabular form as

	$W(T) < F$	$F \leq W(T) <$ $F + (\gamma^{-1} - 1) \cdot E$	$F + (\gamma^{-1} - 1) \cdot E \leq W(T)$
$V_1(T)$	$W(T)$	F	F
$V_2(T)$	0	$W(T) - F$	$(1 - \gamma) \cdot (W(T) - F + E)$
$V_3(T)$	0	0	$\gamma \cdot (W(T) - F + E) - E$

or as

$$V_1(T) = \min[W(T), F] \tag{10.2a}$$

$$V_2(T) = \min[\max[0, W(T) - F], \max[0, (1 - \gamma) \cdot (W(T) - F + E)]] \tag{10.2b}$$

$$V_3(T) = \max[0, \gamma \cdot (W(T) - F + E) - E] \tag{10.2c}$$

Figure 10.1 shows a graphical representation of the terminal contingent security values.

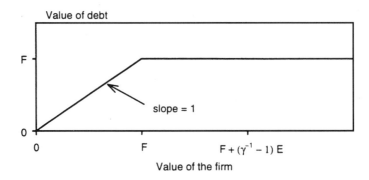

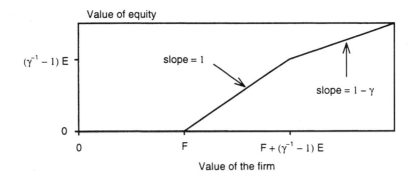

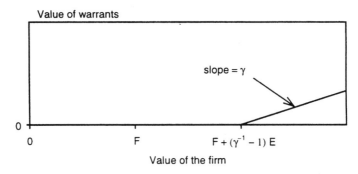

Figure 10.1
Contingent value of debt, equity, and warrants at time T

10.2   The Valuation Problem

We assume there exists a set of three functions, f_1, f_2, and f_3, with two arguments: time and the value of the firm, such that the value of the ith security at time t can be calculated as

$$V_i(t) = f_i(W(t), t), \qquad i = 1, 2, 3 \tag{10.3}$$

The valuation problem is identifying the forms of these contingent value functions.

10.3   Solving the Valuation Problem

We have already solved the valuation problem in the special case of $t = T$. From equations (10.2a, b, c) we have

$$f_1(W, T) = \min[W, F] \tag{10.4a}$$

$$f_2(W, T) = \min[\max[0, W - F], \max[0, (1 - \gamma) \cdot (W - F + E)]] \tag{10.4b}$$

$$f_3(W, T) = \max[0, \gamma \cdot (W - F + E) - E] \tag{10.4c}$$

We can complete the identification of f_i by describing an algorithm for computing the value of $f_i(W^*, t^*)$ for any value of t^* less than T and for any positive value of W^*.

The problem of computing $f_i(W^*, t^*)$ is similar to the valuation problem stated at the beginning of section 3.3. Both problems concern a firm capitalized with three classes of securities, where the value of the firm evolves as a lognormal random walk. The only difference is the specification of the terminal conditions: compare equations (10.4a, b, c) with equations (3.4a, b, c). Thus it suffices to specify here the terminal conditions of equations (10.4a, b, c) for a discrete time–discrete state approximation to the lognormal random walk.

We discretize time by dividing the interval between t^* and T into K subintervals of length Δt and defining a sequence of $K + 1$ discrete points in time:

$$t_k = t^* + (k - 1) \cdot \Delta t, \qquad k = 1, 2, \ldots, K + 1 \tag{10.5}$$

and we discretize the value of the firm by defining an array of prospective values: $W_{j,k}$ for $j = 1, 2, \ldots, k$ and $k = 1, 2, \ldots, K + 1$, where the natural logarithm of $W_{j,k}$ is defined as

$$\ln[W_{j,k}] = \ln[W^*] + (k - 1) \cdot \mu \cdot \Delta t + (2 \cdot j - k - 1) \cdot \sigma \cdot \Delta t^{1/2},$$

$$j = 1, 2, \ldots, k; \ k = 1, 2, \ldots, K + 1 \tag{10.6}$$

We denote the value of the ith security at time t_k when the value of the firm is $W_{j,k}$ as $V_{j,k,i}$.

Constructing the $V_{j,k,i}$ Terms for $k = K+1$

The terminal conditions, namely the values of $V_{j,K+1,i}$ for $j = 1, 2, \ldots,$ $K+1$, follow from our specification of the consequences of default and bankruptcy and the warrant holders' option to purchase stock.

If the value of the firm at time t_{K+1} is $W_{j,K+1}$ and if $W_{j,K+1}$ is less than F, the firm will default and creditors will receive all of the bankruptcy distribution. If $W_{j,K+1}$ exceeds F, creditors will be paid in full. This implies that

$$V_{j,K+1,1} = \begin{cases} W_{j,K+1} & \text{if } W_{j,K+1} < F \\ F & \text{if } F \leq W_{j,K+1} \end{cases} \tag{10.7}$$

If the value of the firm at time t_{K+1} is less than F, the firm will default and stockholders will receive nothing. If the value of the firm exceeds F but is less than $F + (\gamma^{-1} - 1) \cdot E$, the stock will be worth $W_{j,K+1} - F$ because the warrant holders will not exercise their call option. If the value of the firm exceeds $F + (\gamma^{-1} - 1) \cdot E$, the stock will be worth $(1 - \gamma) \cdot (W_{j,K+1} - F + E)$ because the warrant holders will exercise their option. Thus we also have

$$V_{j,K+1,2} = \begin{cases} 0 & \text{if } W_{j,K+1} < F \\ W_{j,K+1} - F & \text{if } F \leq W_{j,K+1} < F + (\gamma^{-1} - 1) \cdot E \\ (1-\gamma) \cdot (W_{j,K+1} - F + E) & \text{if } F + (\gamma^{-1} - 1) \cdot E \leq W_{j,K+1} \end{cases}$$
$$\tag{10.8}$$

Finally, the warrants will expire unexercised unless the value of the firm exceeds $F + (\gamma^{-1} - 1) \cdot E$, in which case the warrants are worth $\gamma \cdot (W_{j,K+1} - F + E) - E$:

$$V_{j,K+1,3} = \begin{cases} 0 & \text{if } W_{j,K+1} < F + (\gamma^{-1} - 1) \cdot E \\ \gamma \cdot (W_{j,K+1} - F + E) - E & \text{if } F + (\gamma^{-1} - 1) \cdot E \leq W_{j,K+1} \end{cases}$$
$$\tag{10.9}$$

From this point, the algorithm for computing $f_i(W^*, t^*)$ continues as in section 3.3 following equation (3.10).

10.4   Some Examples

It is instructive to examine some examples of contingent security pricing for a firm capitalized with debt, equity and warrants. We assume the U.S. Treasury yield curve is flat and stationary at $R_f = 0.10$, or 10% per annum. Except for the last example, we also assume that the face amount of the corporation's debt is $F = 134.986$ and that we are valuing the securities of the firm three years before the debt matures and the warrants expire. Ignoring the risk of default, the debt has a default-free value of 100.0. We further assume that the volatility of the value of the firm is $\sigma = 0.10$, or a volatility of 10% over one year.

Example A

The first example assumes the firm has *no* warrants in its capital structure, so the firm is capitalized with zero-coupon debt promising to pay 134.986 in three years and common stock that does not pay a dividend.

Figure 10.2 shows the contingent value of the debt (upper panel) and equity (lower panel).[6] We will use these contingent value functions as benchmarks for assessing the consequences of introducing warrants into the capital structure of the firm.

Example B

The second example assumes that the firm is capitalized with warrants with a dilution factor of $\gamma = 0.5$ and an exercise price of $E = 200.0$, as well as with debt and equity as in example A.

The contingent value of the debt is invariant with respect to the presence or absence of warrants in the capital structure of the firm, because the terminal condition for the value of the debt at time T does not depend on either γ or E (see equation 10.7).[7] Thus, the upper panel of figure 10.2 describes the contingent value of the debt in the present case as well as in the simpler case of example A.

The upper panel of figure 10.3 shows the contingent value of the warrants. The warrants are virtually worthless if the value of the firm is less than about 200, but they begin to acquire significant value as the value of the firm rises above 200. If the value of the firm exceeds 350, the value of the warrants increases by about 0.5 for every unit increase in the value of the firm. This reflects our assumption that $\gamma = 0.5$: the warrants are an option to acquire half of the stock of the firm.

The lower panel of figure 10.3 shows the contingent value of equity with a solid line. The dashed line shows what the stock would be worth in the absence of the warrants. The difference between the dashed line and the solid line reflects the reduction in the value of the stock attributable

6. The contingent value functions in figure 10.2 can be computed with the algorithm described in section 10.3 if we set $\gamma = 0$.

7. This is analogous to the observation in note 10 in chapter 3 that the contingent value of senior debt is invariant with respect to the structure of more junior claims.

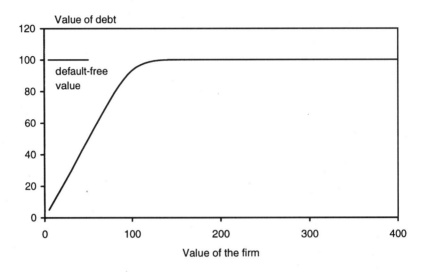

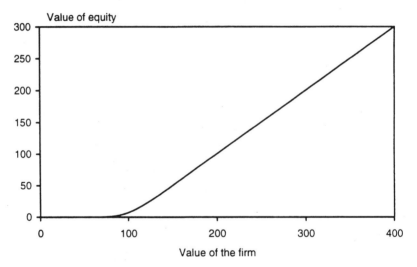

Figure 10.2
Contingent value of debt and equity three years before the debt matures in the absence of warrants in the capital structure of the firm

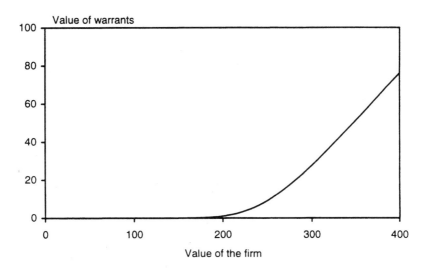

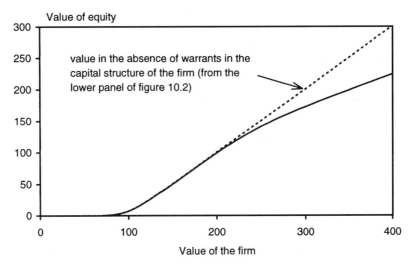

Figure 10.3
Contingent value of warrants and equity three years before the debt matures

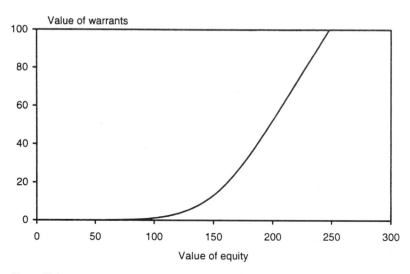

Figure 10.4
Value of warrants three years before the debt matures as a function of the value of equity

to the warrant holders' option to acquire half of the stock of the firm at a fixed price of 200.

The slope of the equity valuation function in the lower panel of figure 10.3 is (approximately) unity when the value of the firm is between 150 and 200 (where the debt is essentially free of credit risk but where the warrants have not yet begun to acquire any significant value) and it declines to 0.5 when the value of the firm exceeds 350 (where the warrants are deep-in-the-money). The latter region illustrates how warrants dilute the benefits that would otherwise go exclusively to shareholders when the firm prospers.

Warrant Value as a Function of Equity Value

Figure 10.4 shows the relationship between the value of the warrants and the value of the firm's equity. The relationship is similar to a conventional call option pricing structure, where the contingent value of a call option is represented as a function of the contemporaneous value of the underlying stock.[8]

Example C

The third example is similar to example B, except that we assume a warrant exercise price of $E = 100.0$ instead of 200.0.

---

8. It is *not* the relationship of Black and Scholes (1973) because the log of the value of the firm's equity does not evolve as a Gaussian random walk with constant volatility in the present model.

As shown in figure 10.5, reducing the exercise price of the warrants enhances the contingent value of the warrants and reduces the contingent value of equity. Observe, however, that the slope of the warrant valuation function and the slope of the equity valuation function at high values of the firm are not affected by the reduction in the exercise price; those slopes (at high values of the firm) are 0.5 in figure 10.5 as well as in figure 10.3.

Example D

The next example is also similar to example B, except that here we assume that the warrants are for 40% of the common stock of the firm, so that $\gamma = 0.4$, and that the warrant exercise price is $E = 133.33$.

As shown in figure 10.6, the lower dilution factor leads to lower contingent warrant values and higher contingent equity values. In addition the slope of the warrant valuation function rises only to 0.4, and the slope of the equity valuation function falls only to 0.6, at high values of the firm.

Example E

The last example illustrates how the presence of warrants in the capital structure of the firm can affect the relationship between the value of the firm's debt and equity.

Consider first a firm capitalized with common stock and zero coupon debt promising to pay 271.828 in ten years, where the volatility of the value of the firm is $\sigma = 0.20$ (or 20% over one year). We assume the yield on Treasury debt is $R_f = 0.10$ (or 10% per annum), so the default-free value of the company's debt is 100.0. Figure 10.7 shows the contingent value of the debt (upper panel) and equity (lower panel).

Consider next the same firm when it has warrants with a dilution factor of $\gamma = 0.5$ and an exercise price of $E = 50.0$ as well as debt and equity in its capital structure. The warrants do not affect the contingent value of the debt, so the contingent value of the debt remains as in the upper panel of figure 10.7. However, the warrants dilute the value of the firm's equity. Figure 10.8 shows the contingent value of the warrants (upper panel) and the contingent value of equity (lower panel).

Figure 10.9 shows the value of the company's debt as an implicit function of the value of equity for the cases where the firm's capital structure includes (solid line) and excludes (dashed line) warrants. The value of the debt associated with an observed market value of equity is greater when there are warrants in the corporation's capital structure. This shift in the debt-equity cross value function occurs because the value of the debt is an increasing function of the value of the firm (see the upper panel in figure 10.7) and because the value of the firm imputed from any observed equity

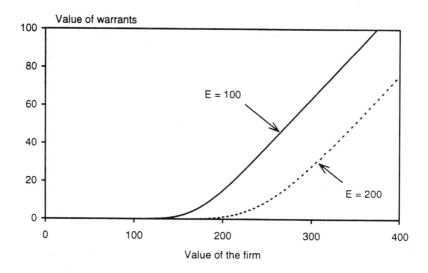

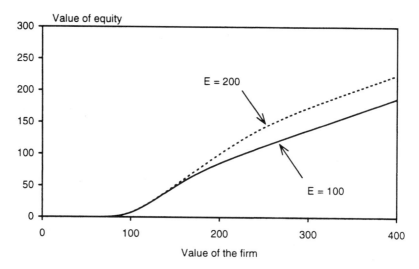

Figure 10.5
Contingent value of warrants and equity three years before the debt matures

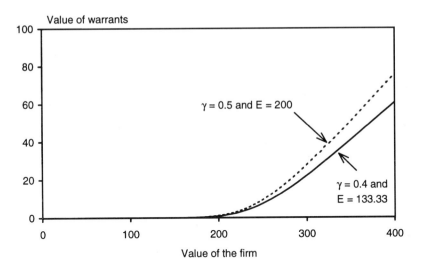

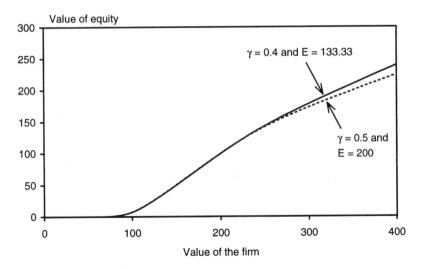

Figure 10.6
Contingent value of warrants and equity three years before the debt matures

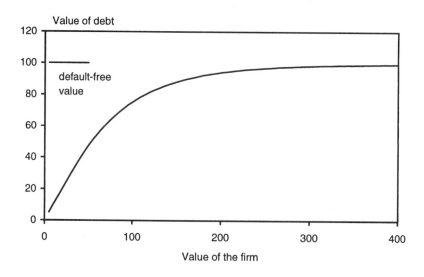

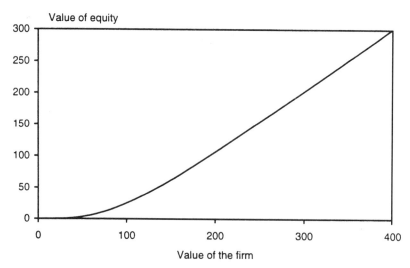

Figure 10.7
Contingent value of debt and equity ten years before the debt matures in the absence of
warrants in the capital structure of the firm

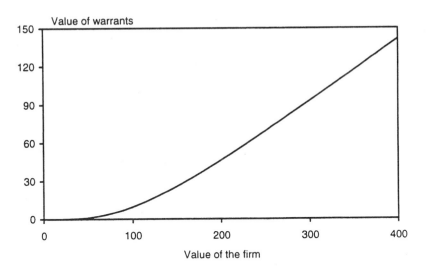

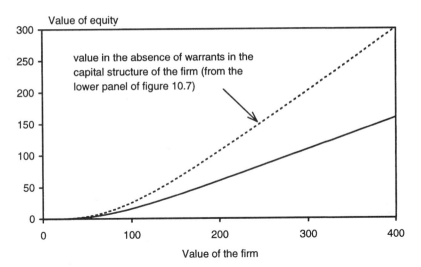

Figure 10.8
Contingent value of warrants and equity ten years before the debt matures

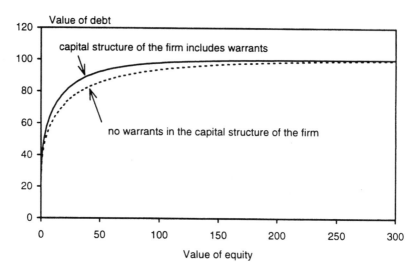

Figure 10.9
Value of debt ten years before maturity as a function of the value of equity

value will be higher if there are warrants in the corporation's capital structure (see the lower panel of figure 10.8).

This example illustrates the important proposition that assessing the relative values of debt and equity, and hedging debt with equity, can go awry if an analyst ignores warrants that dilute the value of equity at values of the firm where the debt bears appreciable credit risk.

10.5   Decomposing Convertible Debt into Warrants and Conventional Debt

Convertible debt is, in some cases, equivalent to a combination of warrants and nonconvertible debt.[9] Consider, for example, a firm capitalized with common stock and noncallable convertible zero-coupon debt. The debt promises to pay F when it matures at time T, and it can be converted into a fraction γ of the stock of the firm. As discussed in section 8.1, creditors will accept cash redemption if $W(T)$ is less than $\gamma^{-1} \cdot F$, and they will convert their debt to equity if $W(T)$ exceeds $\gamma^{-1} \cdot F$.

The creditors would be in an identical position if they held (1) conventional noncallable zero-coupon debt promising to pay F at time T and (2) warrants, where the warrants expire at time T and have a dilution factor of γ and an exercise price equal to the face amount of the debt. The

9. This equivalence was pointed out by Black and Scholes (1973), Merton (1973), and Galai and Schneller (1978).

creditors will be paid F if the firm avoids default at time T. They can keep this redemption payment, or they can exercise their warrants by conveying F back to the firm in return for a fraction γ of the common stock of the firm. Following the analysis in section 10.1, they will keep the cash redemption payment if $W(T)$ is less than $F + (\gamma^{-1} - 1) \cdot E$, or (since $E = F$) if $W(T)$ is less than $\gamma^{-1} \cdot F$. Conversely, they will exercise their warrants if $W(T)$ is greater than $\gamma^{-1} \cdot F$. Thus the convertible debt described in the preceding paragraph is equivalent to a combination of conventional debt promising to pay F at time T and warrants on a fraction γ of the stock of the firm with exercise price F.[10]

An Example

It may be helpful to illustrate the foregoing proposition with a numerical example. Consider a firm capitalized with common stock, noncallable nonconvertible debt promising to pay $F = 164.872$ in five years, and warrants expiring in five years with a dilution factor of $\gamma = 0.35$ and an exercise price of $E = 164.872$. We assume that $R_f = 0.10$ (or 10% per annum) and that the volatility of the value of the firm is $\sigma = 0.20$ (or a volatility of 20% over one year).

The top panel of figure 10.10 shows the contingent value of the debt with a dashed line and the aggregate contingent value of the debt and warrants with a solid line. The lower panel of the figure shows the contingent value of equity.

Recall now example A in section 8.4, where a firm is capitalized with common stock and non-callable zero coupon debt promising to pay $F = 164.872$ in five years and convertible into a fraction $\gamma = 0.35$ of the common stock of the firm. The contingent values of the convertible debt and equity appear in figure 8.6.

Inspection of the data used to construct the graphs in figures 8.6 and 10.10 reveals that the contingent value of the convertible debt in the upper panel of figure 8.6 is identical to the aggregate contingent value of the debt and warrants in the upper panel of figure 10.10. Similarly the contingent value of equity in the lower panel of figure 8.6 is identical to the contingent value of equity in the lower panel of figure 10.10. This illustrates the claim that the noncallable convertible debt is equivalent to a combination of noncallable nonconvertible debt and warrants.

10. The equivalence between noncallable convertible debt and a combination of noncallable nonconvertible debt and warrants does not extend to the case of *callable* convertible debt. Callable convertible debt is not exactly equivalent to any combination of callable nonconvertible debt and warrants because the warrants may remain outstanding when the issuer calls the debt for early redemption. A decision to call convertible debt results in either exercise or extinction of the embedded conversion option.

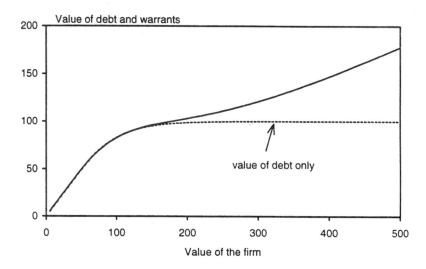

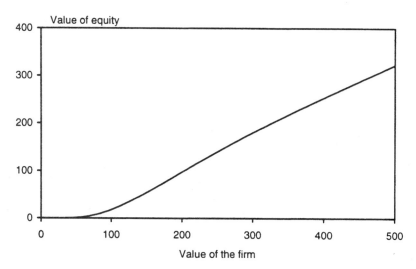

Figure 10.10
Contingent value of debt and warrants, and contingent value of equity, five years before the
debt matures

The Effect of a Change in Volatility on the Value of Convertible Debt

The ability to decompose convertible debt into a combination of conventional debt and warrants provides an opportunity to reexamine, from a different perspective, an issue addressed earlier: the effect of a change in the volatility of the value of the firm on the contingent value of convertible debt. (See example E in section 8.4.) Recall, from figure 8.12, that the contingent value of convertible debt is inversely related to the volatility of the value of the firm when the value of the firm is low, but that greater volatility enhances the contingent value of convertible debt when the value of the firm is higher. We would like to develop a deeper understanding of this behavior.

The convertible debt in figure 8.12 promises to pay $F = 164.872$ in five years and is convertible into 35% of the common stock of the firm. We remarked above that the debt can be decomposed into (1) conventional debt that promises to pay $F = 164.872$ in five years and (2) warrants that expire in five years and have a dilution factor of $\gamma = 0.35$ and an exercise price of $E = 164.872$.

Figure 10.11 shows the effect of a change in volatility on the contingent value of the conventional debt and warrants that together constitute the convertible debt in figure 8.12.[11] The upper panel of figure 10.11 shows that the contingent value of the warrants is an increasing function of the volatility of the value of the firm.[12] The effect of a change in volatility on the contingent value of the warrants is greatest when the value of the firm is between about 275 and 300. This is the value of the firm where the warrants are (approximately) at-the-money.[13]

The lower panel of figure 10.11 shows that greater volatility unambiguously reduces the contingent value of the conventional debt.[14] The effect of a change in volatility is greatest when the value of the firm is about 100,

---

11. As in example E in section 8.4, we assume that $R_f = 0.10$ (or 10% per annum).

12. The presence of warrants in the capital structure of the firm, like the presence of convertible debt, reduces the incentive for "asset substitution" (see note 14 in chapter 2 and note 12 in chapter 8).

13. The net exercise price of the warrants is $(1 - \gamma) \cdot E = (1 - 0.35) \cdot 164.872 = 107.167$. The present value of this net exercise price, discounted for five years at the 10% per annum yield on Treasury debt, is 65.0. An option to acquire 35% of the postredemption value of the firm is approximately at-the-money when 35% of the value of the securities representing the postredemption value of the firm is equal to the present value of the net exercise price, or when the value of the firm's stock and warrants is equal to about 185 (35% of $185 \approx 65$). The present value (computed at the 10% per annum yield on Treasury debt) of the firm's promise to pay creditors 164.872 in five years is 100. Adding this to the at-the-money value of the stock and warrants gives a total at-the-money value of the firm of about 285.

14. The effect of a change in volatility on the value of conventional debt was discussed in example C in section 2.6.

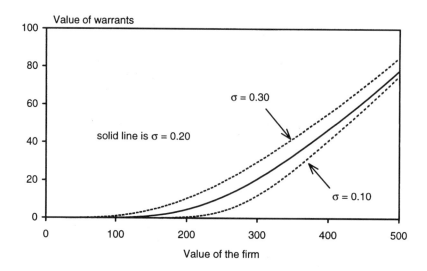

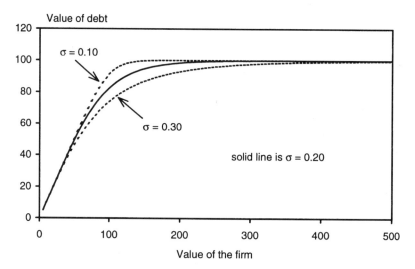

Figure 10.11
Contingent value of debt and warrants five years before the debt matures for various volatilities of the value of the firm

corresponding to the point at which the shareholders' option to redeem the debt is approximately at-the-money.[15]

It follows that the effect of a change in the volatility of the value of the firm on the value of convertible debt can be traced to the effect of two different and distinct options: the shareholders' option to redeem the debt and the creditors' option to convert the debt. Greater volatility of firm value enhances the value of the redemption option and thus reduces the value of the convertible debt.[16] The effect is greatest when the redemption option is at-the-money, or when the value of the firm is about 100. Greater volatility of firm value also enhances the value of the creditors' conversion option and thus increases the value of the convertible debt. This effect is greatest when the conversion option is at-the-money, or when the value of the firm is about 285. The value of the firm where the conversion option is at-the-money (285) exceeds the value of the firm where the redemption option is at-the-money (100), so greater volatility of firm value increases the value of convertible debt at higher values of the firm and reduces the value of the debt at lower values of the firm.

15. The shareholders' redemption option was discussed in section 2.2.

16. As discussed in section 2.2, creditors are short the redemption option, so greater option value reduces the value of the debt.

III PAYMENTS TO CREDITORS AT DIFFERENT TIMES

11 Multiple Debt Securities

The corporate capital structures examined in the preceding chapters exhibit an important common characteristic: all of the liabilities of the firm are payable at a single point in time. In four cases (chapter 2 on simple debt and equity, chapter 6 on callable debt, chapter 8 on convertible debt, and chapter 10 on warrants) the firm's liabilities were limited to a single issue of zero-coupon debt. In the fifth case (chapter 3 on senior and subordinated debt) the firm was capitalized with two issues of zero-coupon debt, but we assumed that both issues matured at the same time.

This chapter broadens the scope of contingent value analysis by supposing that the firm is obligated to make multiple payments to creditors at *different* times. Example 11.1 illustrates, with a strip of seven zero-coupon notes, the idea of multiple debt securities. To pose and analyze the valuation problem in as simple a context as possible, we examine a firm capitalized with just two issues of zero-coupon debt.[1]

11.1 Framework of the Analysis

We begin, once again, by describing the structure of the valuation problem.

Corporate Capital Structure

We assume that the firm is capitalized with three classes of securities: common stock and two issues of zero-coupon debt with different maturities. The stock cannot pay a dividend and cannot be repurchased by the firm until all of the debt has been redeemed.

The shorter term debt (the "short" debt) matures at time T_1 and promises to pay its face amount F_1 at maturity. It cannot be called for early redemption, and it cannot be converted to equity.

The longer-term debt (the "long" debt) matures at time T_2 (where $T_2 > T_1$) and promises to pay F_2 at that time. The indenture or loan agreement for the long debt provides that if the firm defaults on its promise to redeem the short debt at time T_1, the holders of the long debt have the right to accelerate the maturity of their debt and declare it immediately due and payable in the contractually specified amount D_2.[2] We

---

1. Chapter 12 examines the more complicated case where a firm has multiple liabilities payable at different times as a result of coupon-bearing debt in its capital structure.

2. This is an example of a cross-acceleration clause: the holders of the long debt can accelerate the maturity of their debt following default on a *different* obligation. Wruck (1991, p. 87) describes how the creditors of a financially distressed firm exercised their cross-acceleration options in 1988.

Example 11.1   A Series of Zero-Coupon Corporate Notes

In May 1982, Associated Dry Goods Corporation, a retailer that operated fifteen department store divisions, including Lord & Taylor in the eastern United States, Goldwaters in the southwest, and J. W. Robinson in California, sold a strip of seven zero-coupon notes:

Maturity date	Face value	Price (% of face value)	Yield (% per annum)
May 1, 1983	$15 million	86.638	15.000
May 1, 1984	$15 million	74.970	15.000
May 1, 1985	$15 million	65.100	14.875
May 1, 1986	$15 million	56.399	14.875
May 1, 1987	$15 million	49.145	14.750
May 1, 1988	$15 million	42.626	14.750
May 1, 1989	$110 million	37.702	14.450

Each of the notes ranked pari passu with the other notes. In the event of default, each note would (at the option of its holders) become immediately due and payable in an amount equal to the present value of the note, discounted back to the date of default using the original yield on the note (shown in the table above), compounded semiannually. Thus the accelerated redemption claim for the note maturing on May 1, 1988, following a default on November 1, 1984, would be computed as

$$\text{Redemption claim} = \frac{\$15 \text{ million}}{(1 + \frac{1}{2} \cdot 0.1475)^7} = \$9.115 \text{ million}$$

---

assume that the long debt is subordinated to the short debt and that it is noncallable and nonconvertible. (Section 11.7 examines two alternative cases: where the long debt ranks pari passu with the short debt and where it is senior to the short debt.)

We denote the value of the short debt at time t as $V_1(t)$, the value of the long debt as $V_2(t)$, and the value of equity as $V_3(t)$. The value of the firm is the sum of the values of the firm's securities: $W(t) = V_1(t) + V_2(t) + V_3(t)$.

Dynamic Evolution of the Value of the Firm

Following the discussion in section 1.4, we assume the natural logarithm of the value of the firm evolves up to time T_1 as a Gaussian random walk with mean change μ per annum and variance σ^2 per annum.

At time T_1 the firm is obligated to redeem the short debt. For expositional simplicity, we assume the firm liquidates assets and uses the proceeds to fund the redemption,[3] whereupon the value of the firm declines to $W(T_1) - F_1$.[4] (If $W(T_1) < F_1$, the firm defaults and goes into bankruptcy as described below.) Following redemption of the short debt, the natural logarithm of the value of the firm evolves from the *ex*-redemption value $\ln[W(T_1) - F_1]$ as a Gaussian random walk with an unchanged drift rate and volatility.[5]

Figure 11.1 illustrates the resulting evolution of the value of the firm: a conventional log normal random walk prior to and following time T_1, punctuated by a discontinuous decline of F_1 at time T_1.

3. This may not involve anything more complicated than selling liquid financial assets—such as Treasury bills—accumulated in anticipation of the redemption, but it could involve the sale of operating assets. See Lang, Poulsen, and Stulz (1995) for an analysis of debt redemption using proceeds from sales of operating assets, and see also the related studies by John and Ofek (1995) and Allen and McConnell (1998). Debt redemption with the proceeds from sales of operating assets by financially distressed firms has been examined by Shleifer and Vishny (1992) and Asquith, Gertner, and Scharfstein (1994). John, Lang, and Netter (1992) and Ofek (1993) report that firms experiencing financial decline also commonly sell assets and reduce leverage. The travails of Xerox Corporation in the fall of 2000 provides a recent example; see "Xerox to Post a Loss, Review Dividend," *Wall Street Journal*, October 3, 2000, p. A3, "Weakened Xerox Will Sell Assets to Strengthen Its Balance Sheet," *Wall Street Journal*, October 4, 2000, p. B6, "Xerox Slashes Its Dividend to Five Cents," *Wall Street Journal*, October 10, 2000, p. A3, "Xerox Plunges as Firm Taps Credit Line," *Wall Street Journal*, October 17, 2000, p. A3, and "Seeking Core-Business Survival, Xerox to Sell Many Operations," *New York Times*, October 25, 2000, p. C1.

Firms also fund debt redemption by selling new debt or (more rarely) equity. McCauley, Rudd, and Iacono (1999) describe equity offerings in the early 1990s, whose proceeds were used to retire maturing debt and reverse leveraged buyouts and recapitalizations undertaken in the late 1980s. As noted later in chapter 20, a more complete contingent value model would make the decision to finance debt redemption with sales of assets or new debt or new equity a matter for managerial discretion.

Several authors have examined the actions of a firm whose liquid assets may be insufficient to fund an immediately payable liability and whose operating assets are indivisible, including Bulow and Shoven (1978), White (1980, 1983, 1989, 1994), Kim, Ramaswamy, and Sundaresan (1993), Anderson and Sundaresan (1996), Mella-Barral and Perraudin (1997), and Mella-Barral (1999). Gertner and Scharfstein (1991) undertake a similar analysis assuming the firm has a nontransferable investment opportunity rather than indivisible operating assets.

4. Assuming equality of the redemption payment and the decline in the value of the firm is tantamount to assuming that the assets liquidated to fund redemption have a market value equal to their contribution to the value of the firm. Such assets lie on the boundary between assets with a positive net present value, whose liquidation would reduce the value of the firm by more than the proceeds derived form sale, and assets with a negative net present value, whose liquidation would generate proceeds in excess of their contribution to the value of the firm. (Quantum Chemical Corporation's decision in 1989 to sell one of its operating divisions and to use the proceeds to retire debt provides an example of the latter type of asset. The company remarked that the division "enjoys a commanding position in its . . . markets, but it is unrelated to the rest of our chemical business. We believe that it is worth substantially more to a strategic buyer than it can be to Quantum." Quantum Chemical Corporation 1988 Annual Report to Shareholders, p. 4. The circumstances surrounding Quantum's sale are discussed in section 17.1.)

5. The assumption that the parameters characterizing the evolution of the value of the firm remain unchanged at μ and σ^2 is tantamount to assuming that redemption of the short debt does not change the character of the firm's activities and only contracts the scale of those activities.

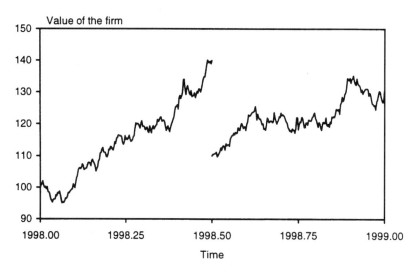

Figure 11.1
Evolution of the value of the firm from $W(t) = 100.0$ at time $t = 1998.00$ to time $t = 1999.00$, with a discontinuous decline of $F_1 = 30.0$ at time $T_1 = 1998.50$

Default and Bankruptcy

Default and bankruptcy can occur either at time T_1 or at time T_2.

At time T_1 the holders of the short debt have a claim on the firm for payment of F_1. If $W(T_1)$ is less than F_1, the firm cannot satisfy its contractual obligation and must default. The holders of the long debt exercise their option to accelerate the maturity of their debt and the firm goes into bankruptcy, where it faces a senior claim for F_1 from holders of the short debt and a subordinated claim for D_2 from holders of the long debt.

If $W(T_1)$ exceeds F_1 and the short debt is redeemed at time T_1 (we show in the appendix that the firm will not default voluntarily on redemption of the short debt), the long debt remains outstanding until time T_2. At T_2 the holders of the long debt have a claim on the firm for payment of F_2. If the firm does not meet this second contractual obligation, it defaults and goes into bankruptcy.

We assume that bankruptcy at either T_1 or T_2 results in an instantaneous and costless liquidation of the firm and distribution of the proceeds according to the absolute priority rule.

The Contingent Value of the Long Debt and Equity at Time T_2

When the long debt matures at T_2 the short debt has already been redeemed and the firm is capitalized with only the maturing long debt and equity. Our assumptions regarding default and bankruptcy imply that the contingent values of those securities can be described with terminal conditions analogous to the conditions stated at equations (2.3a, b):

$$V_2(T_2) = \min[W(T_2), F_2] \tag{11.1a}$$

$$V_3(T_2) = \max[0, W(T_2) - F_2] \tag{11.1b}$$

11.2   The Contingent Value of the Long Debt and Equity Prior to Time T_2 but Following Redemption of the Short Debt

At this point we have enough information to identify the contingent value of the long debt and equity prior to time T_2, assuming that the short debt has already been redeemed. This problem is identical to the problem examined in chapter 2: assessing the contingent values of the securities of a firm capitalized with common stock and a single issue of zero-coupon debt.

Let $g_2(W, t)$ denote the contingent value of the long debt at time t when the value of the firm is W, assuming that the short debt has been redeemed. Let $g_3(W, t)$ denote the contingent value of equity. The values of $g_2(W, t)$ and $g_3(W, t)$ can be computed with the algorithm described in section 2.4.[6]

Since we are assuming that the short debt has already been redeemed, the value of t cannot be less than T_1. Time $t = T_1$ is acceptable, but we have to be careful to interpret the expressions $g_2(W, T_1)$ and $g_3(W, T_1)$ to mean "the contingent value of the long debt and equity at time T_1 *immediately after* redemption of the short debt when the *ex*-redemption value of the firm is W."

11.3   The Contingent Value of the Short Debt, the Long Debt, and Equity at Time T_1

We can now identify how the value of the firm will be apportioned among creditors and stockholders when the short debt matures.

If $W(T_1)$ is less than F_1, the firm will default on redemption of the short debt, resulting in acceleration of the maturity of the long debt and liquidation in bankruptcy. The short (senior) creditors receive the full proceeds of the liquidation; the long (subordinated) creditors and stockholders receive nothing.[7]

---

6. The terminal contingent value functions follow from equations (11.1a, b): $g_2(W, T_2) = \min[W, F_2]$ and $g_3(W, T_2) = \max[0, W - F_2]$.

7. In this case the decision of the long creditors to accelerate is irrelevant: as subordinated creditors they get none of the proceeds of the bankruptcy liquidation. However, acceleration is important if the long debt is not subordinated (see the cases discussed in section 11.7).

Suppose, alternatively, that $W(T_1)$ exceeds F_1 and that the firm redeems the short debt at time T_1. The short debt will clearly be worth F_1, but what about the value of the long debt and equity?

If the value of the firm is $W(T_1)$ immediately *before* the short debt is redeemed, then the *ex*-redemption value of the firm will be $W(T_1) - F_1$. It follows that immediately *after* redemption of the short debt, the long debt will be worth $g_2(W(T_1) - F_1, T_1)$. Assuming that the markets do not allow opportunities for finite expected profits with arbitrarily small risk over arbitrarily short intervals of time, this implies that immediately *before* the redemption of the short debt the long debt will be worth the *same* amount: $g_2(W(T_1) - F_1, T_1)$. A similar argument shows that immediately before redemption of the short debt the equity will be worth $g_3(W(T_1) - F_1, T_1)$. Thus the contingent values of the firm's securities at time T_1 are

$$V_1(T_1) = \begin{cases} W(T_1) & \text{if } W(T_1) \leq F_1 \\ F_1 & \text{if } F_1 < W(T_1) \end{cases} \tag{11.2a}$$

$$V_2(T_1) = \begin{cases} 0 & \text{if } W(T_1) < F_1 \\ g_2(W(T_1) - F_1, T_1) & \text{if } F_1 < W(T_1) \end{cases} \tag{11.2b}$$

$$V_3(T_1) = \begin{cases} 0 & \text{if } W(T_1) \leq F_1 \\ g_3(W(T_1) - F_1, T_1) & \text{if } F_1 < W(T_1) \end{cases} \tag{11.2c}$$

An Example

It may be helpful to illustrate the foregoing contingent values with a numerical example.

Consider a firm capitalized with senior debt with face amount $F_1 = 82.436$ payable immediately, subordinated debt with face amount $F_2 = 135.914$ payable in five years (so that $T_2 = T_1 + 5.0$), and common stock. We assume that the U.S. Treasury yield curve is flat and stationary at $R_f = 0.10$ (or 10% per annum) and that the volatility of the value of the firm is $\sigma = 0.20$ (or a volatility of 20% over one year). Ignoring the risk of default, the long debt has a default free value of 82.436 (82.436 = 135.914 discounted for five years at the 10% per annum yield on Treasury debt).

Figure 11.2 shows the contingent value of the long debt (upper panel) and equity (lower panel) at time T_1. The value of the short debt is equal to the value of the firm if the value of the firm is less than $F_1 = 82.436$ and it is equal to F_1 if the value of the firm exceeds F_1.

Comment

The contingent value functions in equations (11.2a, b, c) and figure 11.2 are not terminal conditions because they do not express the contingent

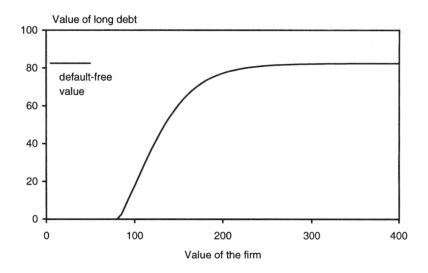

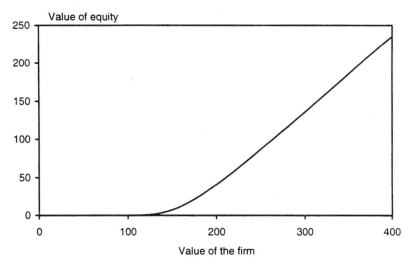

Figure 11.2
Contingent value of long debt and equity when the short debt matures at time T_1

values of the firm's long debt and equity at a "terminal" time when all of the contractual liabilities of the firm are extinguished. Rather, they are *transversality* conditions that characterize security values at the *boundary* —at time T_1—between two different capital structures: when the firm is capitalized with equity and two issues of zero-coupon debt and when (in the absence of default) it is capitalized with equity and a single issue of zero-coupon debt.

11.4   The Valuation Problem

We assume that there exists a set of three contingent value functions, f_1, f_2, and f_3, with two arguments: time and the value of the firm, such that the value of the ith security at time $t \le T_1$ can be calculated as

$$V_i(t) = f_i(W(t), t), \qquad i = 1, 2, 3 \tag{11.3}$$

The valuation problem is to identify the forms of these functions. (The problem of assessing the contingent values of the firm's securities at a time later than T_1 is a matter of valuing the securities of a firm capitalized with common stock and a single issue of zero-coupon debt. We addressed this problem in chapter 2.)

11.5   Solving the Valuation Problem

We have already solved the valuation problem in the special case of $t = T_1$. Let $\Phi(W)$ denote the indicator function:

$$\Phi(W) = \begin{cases} 1 & \text{if } W \le F_1 \\ 0 & \text{if } F_1 < W \end{cases} \tag{11.4}$$

so that $\Phi(W(T_1)) = 1$ indicates that the firm defaults on its obligation to pay F_1 at time T_1 and $\Phi(W(T_1)) = 0$ indicates that the firm fulfills its obligation. From equations (11.2a, b, c) we have

$$f_1(W, T_1) = \Phi(W) \cdot W + (1 - \Phi(W)) \cdot F_1 \tag{11.5a}$$

$$f_2(W, T_1) = (1 - \Phi(W)) \cdot g_2(W - F_1, T_1) \tag{11.5b}$$

$$f_3(W, T_1) = (1 - \Phi(W)) \cdot g_3(W - F_1, T_1) \tag{11.5c}$$

We complete the identification of f_i by describing an algorithm for computing the value of $f_i(W^*, t^*)$ for any value of t^* less than T_1 and for any positive value of W^*.

The problem of computing $f_i(W^*, t^*)$ is similar to the valuation problem stated at the beginning of section 3.3. Both problems concern a firm capitalized with three classes of securities, where the value of the firm evolves as a log normal random walk. The only difference is that here we have transversality conditions at time T_1 (equations 11.5a, b, c) and in chapter 3 we had terminal conditions at time T (equations 3.4a, b, c). Thus it suffices to restate equations (11.5a, b, c) for a discrete time–discrete state approximation to the evolution of the value of the firm.

We discretize time by dividing the interval between time t^* and time T_1 into K subintervals of length Δt and defining a sequence of $K + 1$ discrete points in time:

$$t_k = t^* + (k - 1) \cdot \Delta t, \qquad k = 1, 2, \ldots, K + 1 \tag{11.6}$$

Then we discretize the value of the firm by defining an array of prospective values of the firm:

$$\ln[W_{j,k}] = \ln[W^*] + (k - 1) \cdot \mu \cdot \Delta t + (2 \cdot j - k - 1) \cdot \sigma \cdot \Delta t^{1/2},$$

$$j = 1, 2, \ldots, k; \; k = 1, 2, \ldots, K + 1 \tag{11.7}$$

We denote the value of the ith security at time t_k when the value of the firm is $W_{j,k}$ as $V_{j,k,i}$.

Constructing the $V_{j,k,i}$ Terms for $k = K + 1$

The values of $V_{j,K+1,i}$ for $j = 1, 2, \ldots, K + 1$ follow from our specification of the consequences of default and redemption, respectively, of the short debt.

If the value of the firm at time $T_1 = t_{K+1}$ is less than F_1, the firm cannot avoid default and holders of the short (senior) debt receive all of the proceeds of the bankruptcy distribution. If the value of the firm exceeds F_1, the holders of the short debt will be paid in full. Thus we have

$$V_{j,K+1,1} = \begin{cases} W_{j,K+1} & \text{if } W_{j,K+1} \leq F_1 \\ F_1 & \text{if } F_1 < W_{j,K+1} \end{cases} \tag{11.8}$$

If the value of the firm is less than F_1 at time t_{K+1}, the long (subordinated) debt and the stock will be worthless. If the value of the firm exceeds F_1, the value of the long debt will be equal to what that debt will be worth immediately following redemption of the short debt. Equity is valued similarly. Thus[8]

---

8. As described in section 11.2, $g_2(W, t)$ is the value of the long debt, and $g_3(W, t)$ is the value of equity, at time t when the value of the firm is W and the firm is capitalized with only the long debt and equity.

$$V_{j,K+1,2} = \begin{cases} 0 & \text{if } W_{j,K+1} \leq F_1 \\ g_2(W_{j,K+1} - F_1, t_{K+1}) & \text{if } F_1 < W_{j,K+1} \end{cases} \tag{11.9}$$

and

$$V_{j,K+1,3} = \begin{cases} 0 & \text{if } W_{j,K+1} \leq F_1 \\ g_3(W_{j,K+1} - F_1, t_{K+1}) & \text{if } F_1 < W_{j,K+1} \end{cases} \tag{11.10}$$

From this point, the algorithm for computing $f_i(W^*, t^*)$ continues as in section 3.3 following equation (3.10).

11.6   An Example

It may be helpful to examine a numerical example of our valuation problem.[9] We assume that the U.S. Treasury yield curve is flat and stationary at $R_f = 0.10$ (or 10% per annum) and that the volatility of the value of the firm is $\sigma = 0.20$ (or a volatility of 20% over one year). As in the example at the end of section 11.3, the face amount of the short (senior) debt is $F_1 = 82.436$ and the face amount of the long (subordinated) debt is $F_2 = 135.914$. Say that we are here valuing the securities five years before the short debt matures and that the long debt matures five years after the maturity of the short debt, or ten years after the valuation date. Ignoring the risk of default, the short debt has a default-free value of 50.0 (50.0 = 82.436 discounted for five years at the 10% yield on Treasury debt) and the long debt also has a default-free value of 50.0 (50.0 = 135.914 discounted for ten years at the Treasury yield).

Figure 11.3 shows the contingent value of the short debt (upper panel) and long debt (solid line in the lower panel). The two securities have the same default-free value of 50.0, but the short debt is substantially more valuable when the value of the firm is less than 250 as a result of the seniority of that debt. Figure 11.4 shows (with a solid line) the contingent value of equity.

Comparison with the Case Where the Debt Securities Mature at the Same Time

It is instructive to compare the contingent values in figures 11.3 and 11.4 with the contingent values that result when the firm is capitalized with senior and subordinated zero-coupon debt that matures at the same time, so that $T_1 = T_2$, and that have the same default-free values of 50.0 on the valuation date.

Recall example A in section 3.4, where $F_1 = F_2 = 82.436$ and where we valued the debt and equity of the firm five years prior to the maturity of

---

9. See also the related analysis in Ho and Singer (1982, pp. 397–98).

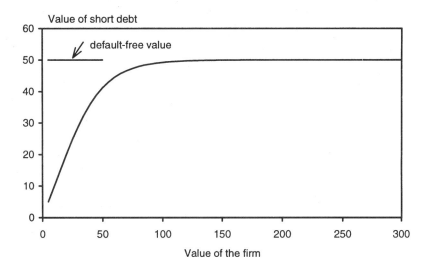

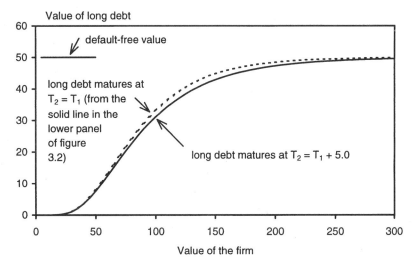

Figure 11.3
Contingent value of short debt and long debt five years before the short debt matures

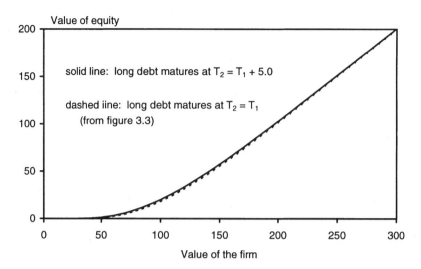

Figure 11.4
Contingent value of equity five years before the short debt matures

the two debt securities. In that case, as in the present example, each zero-coupon security has a default-free value of 50.0. The contingent values of the securities are shown with dashed lines in figures 11.3 and 11.4.

The upper panel of figure 11.3 shows that the contingent value of the senior debt is the same regardless of whether the junior debt matures contemporaneously with or later than the senior debt. (The dashed line is coincident with the solid line.)

However, the lower panel of figure 11.3 shows that the contingent value of the subordinated debt is greater if that debt matures contemporaneously with the senior debt than if it matures five years later. (The dashed line lies above the solid line.) A creditor is better off if she holds a subordinated claim with a face value of 82.436 (and a default-free value of 50.0) maturing in five years than if she holds a subordinated claim with a face value of 135.914 (and a default-free value of 50.0) maturing in ten years, because there is more uncertainty about the value of the firm in ten years than there is about the value of the firm in five years. This is another instance of the greater value of shorter maturity debt when the default-free value of the debt is held constant. (See also example D in section 2.6.)

Figure 11.4 shows that the contingent value of the equity of a firm capitalized with senior debt and longer term subordinated debt exceeds the contingent value of the equity of a firm capitalized with contemporaneously maturing debt with the same default-free values. This reflects the greater value of equity when a firm is capitalized with longer maturity debt (holding the default-free value of the debt constant). (See, again, example D in section 2.6.)

11.7   Alternative Assumptions on Seniority and Subordination

This section examines the consequences of relaxing the assumption that the long debt is subordinated to the short debt.

As in the preceding sections, we assume that the short debt promises to pay $F_1 = 82.436$ at T_1 and that the long debt promises to pay $F_2 = 135.914$ at T_2, where $T_2 = T_1 + 5.0$. The accelerated redemption claim of the long debt, $D_2 = 74.591$, is computed by discounting the face amount of that debt at a rate of 12% per annum $(F_2 \cdot \exp[-\rho \cdot (T_2 - T_1)] = 74.591$ when $F_2 = 135.914$, $\rho = 0.12$ and $T_2 - T_1 = 5.0)$. The U.S. Treasury yield curve is flat and stationary at $R_f = 0.10$ (or 10% per annum) and the volatility of the value of the firm is $\sigma = 0.20$ (or a volatility of 20% over one year).

When the Long Debt Ranks Pari passu with the Short Debt

Consider first the case where the long debt ranks pari passu with the short debt.

If the value of the firm at time T_1 is less than F_1, the firm will default on redemption of its short debt. Default triggers acceleration of the maturity of the long debt and that debt becomes immediately due and payable in the amount D_2. The short debt and the long debt rank pari passu with respect to each other, so creditors divide the proceeds of the ensuing bankruptcy liquidation on a pro rata basis: the holders of the short debt receive $W(T_1) \cdot F_1/(F_1 + D_2)$, and the holders of the long debt receive $W(T_1) \cdot D_2/(F_1 + D_2)$.

This implies that the transversality conditions in equations (11.2a, b) for the contingent values of the two classes of debt become

$$V_1(T_1) = \begin{cases} W(T_1) \cdot \dfrac{F_1}{F_1 + D_2} & \text{if } W(T_1) \le F_1 \\[2mm] F_1 & \text{if } F_1 < W(T_1) \end{cases} \tag{11.11a}$$

$$V_2(T_1) = \begin{cases} W(T_1) \cdot \dfrac{D_2}{F_1 + D_2} & \text{if } W(T_1) \le F_1 \\[2mm] g_2(W(T_1) - F_1, T_1) & \text{if } F_1 < W(T_1) \end{cases} \tag{11.11b}$$

The transversality condition for equity in equation (11.2c) is not affected by the change in the relative priorities of the short and long debt.

Figure 11.5 illustrates the transversality conditions of equations (11.11a, b). Observe that the contingent values of the short and long debt are *not* continuous functions of the value of the firm. If $W(T_1)$ is only slightly less than $F_1 = 82.436$, the firm will default and the two classes of creditors will divide the proceeds of liquidation. The short creditors will receive 52.5% of the proceeds ($F_1 = 52.5\%$ of $F_1 + D_2$ when $F_1 = 82.436$ and $D_2 = 74.591$), and the long creditors will receive the balance. Neither creditor class will be paid the full amount of its claims. However, if $W(T_1)$ is slightly greater than F_1, the short debt will be redeemed *in full* and the holders of the long debt will be left as creditors of a firm with negligible value. A marginal change in $W(T_1)$, from slightly less than F_1 to just a bit more than F_1, has a discontinuous effect on the value of both the short debt and the long debt.[10]

Except for modification of the transversality conditions stated in equations (11.8) and (11.9), the valuation algorithm described in section 11.5 is not affected by the change in the relative priorities of the short and long debt. The transversality condition for the short debt becomes

$$V_{j,K+1,1} = \begin{cases} W_{j,K+1} \cdot \dfrac{F_1}{F_1 + D_2} & \text{if } W_{j,K+1} \le F_1 \\ \\ F_1 & \text{if } F_1 < W_{j,K+1} \end{cases} \tag{11.12}$$

and the transversality condition for the long debt becomes

$$V_{j,K+1,2} = \begin{cases} W_{j,K+1} \cdot \dfrac{D_2}{F_1 + D_2} & \text{if } W_{j,K+1} \le F_1 \\ \\ g_2(W_{j,K+1} - F_1, t_{K+1}) & \text{if } F_1 < W_{j,K+1} \end{cases} \tag{11.13}$$

Figure 11.6 shows the contingent value of the short debt (with a solid line) and the long debt (with a dashed line) five years before the short debt matures. The two securities have the same priority in bankruptcy and the same default-free value of 50.0, but the short debt is materially more valuable than the long debt when the value of the firm is between 25 and 250. (The contingent value of equity is identical to the solid line in figure

---

10. As a practical matter, one may be skeptical of the proposition that when the value of the firm is just slightly greater than F_1, the managers of the firm will redeem the short debt in full and leave the long debt outstanding with negligible value, since this action leaves the long creditors so much worse off than if the firm had simply defaulted on the short debt and filed for bankruptcy. It may be more reasonable to specify a default threshold materially greater than F_1 in equations (11.11a, b). This issue did not arise in the model introduced in section 11.1 because that model assumed the long debt was subordinated to the short debt, so the transversality conditions for the short debt and the long debt were not discontinuous at F_1 (compare the lower panel of figure 11.5 with the upper panel of figure 11.2).

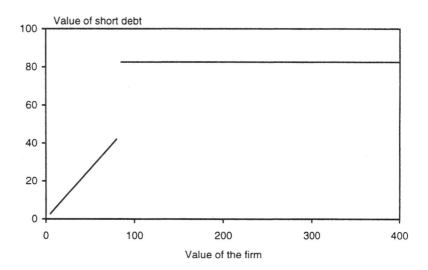

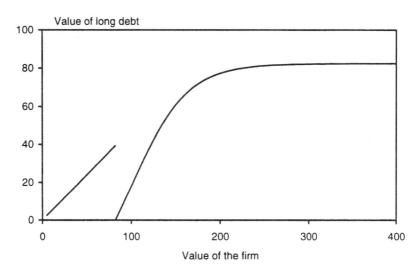

Figure 11.5
Contingent value of short debt and long debt when the short debt matures at time T_1 and when the short debt and the long debt rank pari passu with respect to each other

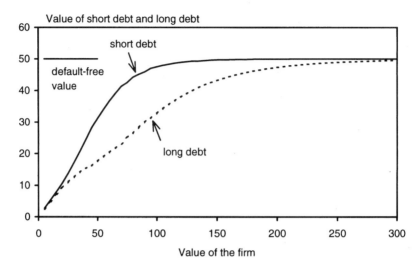

Figure 11.6
Contingent value of short debt and long debt five years before the short debt matures, when the short debt and the long debt rank pari passu with respect to each other

11.4 because the transversality condition for equity is invariant with respect to the relative priorities of the short and long debt.)

To appreciate the reason for the difference between the values of the short debt and the long debt when the value of the firm is between 25 and 250, it will be helpful to examine first the cases where the values of the debt securities are not very different: when the value of the firm is less than 25 and when it is more than 250. The securities have nearly the same value when the value of the firm is less than 25 because (1) default at time T_1 is a virtual certainty (assuming the risk neutral drift rate), (2) the securities rank pari passu with respect to each other, and (3) the bankruptcy claims of the two classes of creditors are similar ($F_1 = 82.436$ and $D_2 = 74.591$). The securities have nearly the same value when the value of the firm exceeds 250 because default is highly unlikely *either* at T_1 *or* at T_2 (assuming the risk neutral drift rate). Both securities are then valued at close to their default-free values of 50.0.

In the intermediate case, when the value of the firm is between 25 and 250, there is some nontrivial probability that the short debt will be paid in full at time T_1 but redemption of the long debt at time T_2 is not as likely. In this case the short debt is valued at a smaller discount from its contemporaneous default-free value than the long debt. In the more striking subcase where the value of the firm lies between 125 and 175, default at time T_1 is unlikely (so the value of the short debt is close to its default-free value) but redemption at time T_2 is far from certain (so the value of the long debt remains at a significant discount to the default-free value of that debt).

Chronological Subordination

The lower value of the long debt relative to the short-term debt in figure 11.6 reflects the "chronological" subordination of the long debt to the short debt. Holders of the short debt will be paid in full at time T_1 as long as the contemporaneous value of the firm exceeds F_1, even if this leaves the long debt virtually worthless.[11]

Figure 11.7 illustrates the notion that the long debt is chronologically subordinated to the short debt. The lower panel shows the contingent value of the long debt five years before the short debt matures when the long debt ranks pari passu with the short debt (solid line) and when it is subordinated to the short debt (dashed line). Observe the convergence of the pari passu value (solid line) and the subordinated value (dashed line) as the value of the firm increases above 50 and as it becomes increasingly unlikely that the firm will default at T_1—and hence increasingly likely that the holders of the short debt will be paid in full, regardless of how the holders of the long debt fare. At values of the firm above 125, the value of the long debt is hardly affected by whether it ranks pari passu with the short debt or is subordinated to that debt.[12]

When the Long Debt Is Senior to the Short Debt

Consider next the case where the short debt is subordinated to the long debt.[13]

If the value of the firm at time T_1 is less than F_1, the firm will default on redemption of its short debt.[14] Default triggers acceleration of the maturity of the long debt and that debt becomes immediately due and payable in the amount D_2. Since the long debt is senior to the short debt, the holders of the long debt receive all of the proceeds of the ensuing bankruptcy liquidation up to the aggregate amount of their claims. The holders of the short debt receive any residual proceeds. This implies that the transversality conditions for the two classes of debt for the discrete time binomial algorithm become

11. See, however, the reservations stated in note 10.

12. The significance of the chronological subordination of the long debt would be attenuated if, as suggested in note 10, the default threshold of the firm is materially greater than F_1.

13. See also the related analysis in Ho and Singer (1982, pp. 398–99).

14. For consistency with the preceding analyses in this chapter, we continue to denote the short debt with index number 1 and the long debt with index number 2, even though the long debt is now the more senior security.

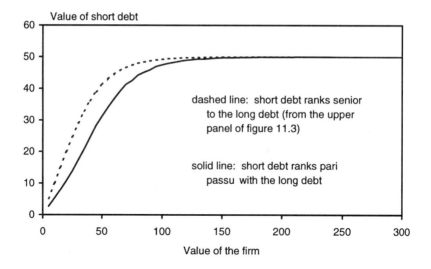

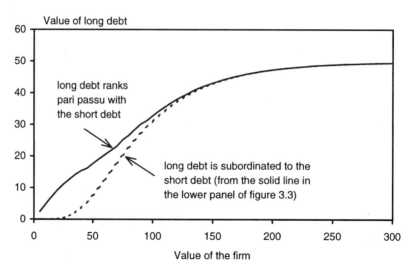

Figure 11.7
Contingent value of short debt and long debt five years before the short debt matures

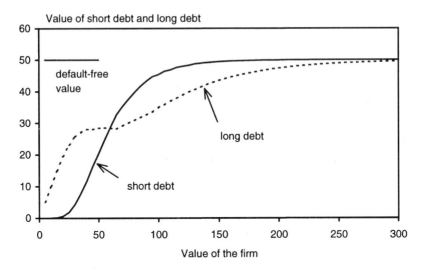

Figure 11.8
Contingent value of short debt and long debt five years before the short debt matures, when the long debt is senior to the short debt

$$V_{j,K+1,1} = \begin{cases} \max[0, W_{j,K+1} - D_2] & \text{if } W_{j,K+1} \leq F_1 \\ F_1 & \text{if } F_1 < W_{j,K+1} \end{cases} \tag{11.14}$$

and

$$V_{j,K+1,2} = \begin{cases} \min[W_{j,K+1}, D_2] & \text{if } W_{j,K+1} \leq F_1 \\ g_2(W_{j,K+1} - F_1, t_{K+1}) & \text{if } F_1 < W_{j,K+1} \end{cases} \tag{11.15}$$

Figure 11.8 shows the contingent value of the short debt (with a solid line) and the long debt (with a dashed line) five years before the short debt matures. The value of the long (senior) debt exceeds the value of the short (subordinated) debt when the value of the firm is less than about 65. This reflects the substantial likelihood of default at time T_1 and the seniority of the long debt.

Default in five years (at time T_1) becomes less likely as the value of the firm increases, so the value of the short debt rises towards the default-free value of that debt. The likelihood of default in ten years (at time T_2) also declines as the value of the firm increases, but it does not decline nearly as quickly. Hence the value of the long debt rises more slowly toward the default-free value of that debt. (In fact the value of the long debt is practically invariant with respect to the value of the firm at values of the firm around 60, because a higher value of the firm implies a lower probability of default on the short debt and so a lower probability that the seniority of the long debt will have any practical significance.) Figure 11.8 shows that the value of the short debt exceeds the value of the long debt when the value of the firm exceeds 65, even though the short debt is sub-ordinated to the long debt. This demonstrates that the chronological subordination of the long debt can be more important than the actual subordination of the short debt when the prospect of redemption of the short debt at time T_1 is not remote.

Appendix: Strategic Default on Redemption of the Short Debt

This appendix examines whether the managers of the firm, acting in the best interests of shareholders, might cause the firm to default voluntarily on redemption of the short debt at time T_1 even if the value of the firm exceeds the face amount of that debt.[15]

If $W(T_1)$ is greater than F_1 but less than $F_1 + D_2$, failure to redeem the short debt will leave the equity of the firm worthless because the value of the firm does not exceed the aggregate bankruptcy claims of its creditors. Suppose therefore that $W(T_1)$ exceeds $F_1 + D_2$. If the firm redeems the short debt, the equity will be worth the (positive) quantity $g_3(W(T_1) - F_1, T_1)$. If (1) the firm defaults, (2) the holders of the long debt accelerate the maturity of their debt, and (3) the firm goes into bankruptcy, the equity will be worth the (also positive) quantity $W(T_1) - F_1 - D_2$. Thus defaulting voluntarily would appear to enhance shareholder value when $W(T_1) - F_1 - D_2$ exceeds $g_3(W(T_1) - F_1, T_1)$.

When Strategic Default Enhances Shareholder Value

It is useful to think of defaulting voluntarily as roughly similar to exercis-ing a call option on the long debt at a call price of D_2. From the analysis in chapter 6 we know that a firm will not call debt for early redemption if the call price equals or exceeds the value of comparable default-proof debt. (See example B in section 6.4.) In the context of the present dis-cussion, the firm will not default voluntarily at time T_1 if D_2 equals or exceeds $F_2 \cdot \exp[-R_f \cdot (T_2 - T_1)]$.

However, if D_2 is less than $F_2 \cdot \exp[-R_f \cdot (T_2 - T_1)]$, there is a critical value of the firm such that if the value of the firm exceeds the critical

---

15. The notion that managers might cause a firm to default on a required payment, in the absence of an actual inability to make the payment, to maximize the value of equity was encountered earlier, in section 5.2. The incentive for strategic default arose because Chapter 11 blurs the absolute priority of creditors over shareholders or, as suggested by Anderson and Sundaresan (1996) and Mella-Barral and Parraudin (1997), because managers may be able to capture for shareholders some of the savings derived from negotiating privately with creditors to avoid a costly bankruptcy. As noted in section 11.1, the present analysis assumes bankruptcy is an instantaneous and costless process that results in distributions in accord with the absolute priority rule.

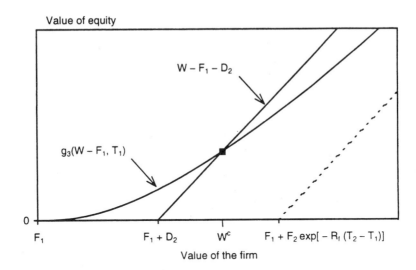

Figure 11.9
Critical value of the firm W^c

value, paying off the long debt immediately at a cost of D_2 is better for shareholders than leaving it outstanding until time T_2.[16] The critical value of the firm is the value of W^c that satisfies the equation

$$g_3(W^c - F_1, T_1) = W^c - F_1 - D_2 \qquad (A11.1)$$

As shown in figure 11.9, if $W(T_1)$ exceeds W^c, the value of the firm's equity conditional on default, acceleration and bankruptcy, $W(T_1) - F_1 - D_2$, exceeds the value of the equity conditional on redemption of the short debt, $g_3(W(T_1) - F_1, T_1)$.

Acceleration as a Contingent Option

The problem with the foregoing analysis is that holders of the long debt have the right, but do not have any obligation, to accelerate following default on the short debt. Before concluding that managers will default strategically if $W(T_1)$ exceeds W^c, we have to verify that holders of the long debt will actually choose to exercise their option to accelerate following default.

If $W(T_1)$ exceeds W^c and holders of the long debt accelerate following default on the short debt, the long debt will be worth D_2 because (as illustrated in figure 11.9) W^c is greater than the aggregate claims, $F_1 + D_2$, of the creditors of the firm.

16. This follows from the comment at the end of section 6.4.

Suppose, alternatively, that the holders of the long debt decide to abstain from accelerating. The firm may still petition for bankruptcy, but the holders of the long debt would doubtless complain that since the firm is preparing to pay $F_1 + D_2$ upon emergence from bankruptcy, filing following default on the smaller amount F_1 is an abuse of the bankruptcy process. Assuming that the supervising court dismisses the bankruptcy petition,[17] the short creditors can seek recovery on their claim for payment of F_1 in state court proceedings. Following recovery (and ignoring any litigation costs), the long debt will be worth $g_2(W(T_1) - F_1, T_1)$.

When $W(T_1)$ is greater than W^c, $g_2(W(T_1) - F_1, T_1)$ exceeds D_2,[18] so the holders of the long debt have no incentive to accelerate in circumstances where stockholders can benefit from strategic default. Strategic default will not consequently enhance shareholder value.

17. Courts dismiss bankruptcy petitions that are not filled "in good faith." See "Court Throws out SGL Filing Seeking Chapter 11 Protection," *Wall Street Journal*, January 6, 2000, p. B10 (reporting dismissal of a bankruptcy petition filed to gain bargaining leverage in civil antitrust litigation when the debtor could not show concrete harm from the litigation).

18. Since $W - F_1 - D_2$ exceeds $g_3(W - F_1, T_1)$ when W exceeds W^c (see figure 11.9), it follows that $W - F_1 - g_3(W - F_1, T_1)$ exceeds D_2 when W exceeds W^c. From the discussion of the adding up constraint in appendix B to chapter 2, we have that $g_2(W, t) + g_3(W, t) = W$ for all positive values of W and hence that $W - F_1 - g_3(W - F_1, T_1) = g_2(W - F_1, T_1)$ when W is greater than F_1. Thus $g_2(W - F_1, T_1)$ exceeds D_2 when W exceeds W^c.

12 Coupon-Bearing Debt

This chapter extends contingent value analysis to debt that promises to pay periodic coupons.[1] (Example 12.1 describes a coupon-bearing note issued by Marriott Corporation in 1992.) Analysis of coupon-bearing debt is important because most corporate debt promises to pay interest periodically, and also because it provides an opportunity to deepen our understanding of how transversality conditions describe what happens when a firm is obligated to make payments to creditors prior to the final maturity of its debt.

12.1 Framework of the Analysis

We begin by stating our assumptions regarding the capital structure of the firm, the dynamic evolution of the value of the firm, and the consequences of default and bankruptcy.

Corporate Capital Structure

We assume that the firm is capitalized with common stock and debt that promises to pay interest semiannually. The stock cannot pay a dividend and cannot be repurchased by the firm before the debt has been redeemed, and the debt is neither callable nor convertible.

The debt promises to pay an aggregate coupon C every six months up to and including maturity and promises to repay its aggregate principal P at maturity. (The annualized coupon rate is $2 \cdot C/P$. If $C = 6$ and $P = 100$, the coupon rate is 0.12, or 12% per annum.) We assume that the debt originally promised to make a total of n interest payments, at times $T_1, T_2, \ldots, T_n$, where T_1 is the date of the first payment, T_n is the maturity date of the debt, and $T_j = T_{j-1} + 0.5$ for $j = 2, 3, \ldots, n$. The indenture or loan agreement for the debt provides that if the issuer fails to make a coupon payment, the holders of the debt have the right to accelerate the maturity of their debt. Following acceleration the principal—as well as accrued interest—is immediately due and payable.[2] We assume that the firm liquidates assets to fund coupon payments.[3]

The value of the debt at time t is $V_1(t)$ and the value of equity is $V_2(t)$. The value of the firm, $W(t)$, is the sum of the values of the firm's securities: $W(t) = V_1(t) + V_2(t)$.

---

1. Geske (1977) provided the first contingent value analysis of coupon-bearing debt. See also Geske (1979).

2. The purpose of such an acceleration clause was noted in section 4.1.

3. Funding debt payments with the proceeds from asset sales was discussed in note 3 in chapter 11.

Example 12.1   A Coupon-Bearing Note

In the spring of 1992, Marriott Corporation issued $200 million principal amount of notes maturing on May 1, 2012, and paying interest at the rate of 10% per annum. Interest was to be paid semiannually, beginning on November 1, 1992, and concluding on May 1, 2012, so Marriott was obligated to make 40 interest payments of $10 million each ($10 million $= \frac{1}{2}$ of 10% of $200 million principal), as well as to repay the $200 million principal at maturity.

In the event of default the $200 million principal amount of the notes, as well as accrued interest since the last interest payment, would (at the option of the holders of the notes) become immediately due and payable.

Distinguishing *Ex*-payment Values from *Cum*-payment Values

At the time of a coupon payment prior to maturity—say the jth coupon, paid at time T_j, where $T_j < T_n$—the value of the debt, $V_1(T_j)$, and the value of the firm, $W(T_j)$, denote *cum*-payment values, or values that *include* the contemporaneous payment.

The value of the debt and the value of the firm decline by the amount C upon payment of the coupon. The value of the debt declines because a new buyer will not receive the coupon that has just been paid. If the debt was worth V_1^* immediately before the payment, it must be worth $V_1^* - C$ immediately after the payment. The value of equity does not exhibit any comparable discontinuous decline because stockholders do not receive a payment from the firm at time T_j. If the stock was worth V_2^* immediately before the coupon payment to creditors, then it must also be worth V_2^* immediately after the payment. The value of the firm declines by C because the value of the firm is the sum of the value of its debt (which declines by C) and the value of its equity (which is unaffected by the payment).

It will be useful to denote the *ex*-payment value of the firm at time t as $W^x(t)$ and to distinguish that value from the contemporaneous *cum*-payment value of the firm:

$$W^x(t) = W(t) - C, \qquad t \in \{T_1, T_2, \dots, T_{n-1}\} \tag{12.1a}$$

$$W^x(t) = W(t), \qquad t < T_n, t \notin \{T_1, T_2, \dots, T_{n-1}\} \tag{12.1b}$$

Equation (12.1a) says that at the time of a coupon payment, the *ex*-payment value of the firm differs from the *cum*-payment value by the amount of the payment. Equation (12.1b) says that the *ex*-payment value of the firm and the *cum*-payment value of the firm are identical at times other than the dates of the early coupon payments.

Dynamic Evolution of the Value of the Firm

Following the discussion in section 1.4, we assume the natural logarithm of the value of the firm evolves *up to* the time of the first coupon payment, and *between* subsequent payments, as a Gaussian random walk with mean change μ per annum and variance σ^2 per annum. The change in the log of the value of the firm over an interval of time that does not go over an interest payment date can written as

$$\ln[W(t + \Delta t)] - \ln[W^x(t)] = \mu \cdot \Delta t + \sigma \cdot \Delta t^{1/2} \cdot z \tag{12.2}$$

where the random variable z is normally distributed with mean zero and a variance of unity.

The change in the log of the value of the firm in equation (12.2) begins with the *ex*-payment value of the firm at time t and ends with the *cum*-payment value of the firm at time $t + \Delta t$. This convention ensures that the change in log value does not include a discontinuous drop attributable to a coupon payment at time t ($W^x(t)$ is the value of the firm at time t *following* any such payment) or at time $t + \Delta t$ ($W(t + \Delta t)$ is the value of the firm at time $t + \Delta t$ *before* any such payment).

Default and Bankruptcy

If the *cum*-payment value of the firm is less than C at time T_j for $T_j < T_n$, the firm can not satisfy its contemporaneous obligation to pay interest on its debt. The resulting default triggers acceleration of the maturity of the debt and gives creditors a claim for immediate repayment of principal (P) as well as payment of the missed coupon (C). Following default and acceleration, the firm goes into bankruptcy.

We assume that bankruptcy results in an instantaneous and costless liquidation of the firm and distribution of the proceeds according to the absolute priority rule. All of the proceeds go to the creditors (and the stockholders get nothing) because the creditors have a bankruptcy claim, $P + C$, in excess of the value of the firm (which, by hypothesis, is less than C).[4]

If the firm pays all of the early coupons, the debt will remain outstanding until maturity at time T_n. At that time creditors have a claim on the firm for payment of the last coupon and for repayment of principal. If

---

4. For reasons comparable to those stated in the appendix to chapter 11, we suppress the possibility that the firm might default strategically on its promise to pay a coupon in order to trigger acceleration of maturity and permit early redemption of the debt at its principal value. Such early redemption may benefit shareholders if the debt has a high coupon rate. Cox and Rubinstein (1985, p. 403) attribute to Scott Mason the observation that intermediate and long-term corporate bonds may commonly provide an *explicit* option for early redemption to avoid the bankruptcy costs associated with strategic default.

the firm defaults on this claim, it is liquidated and the proceeds distributed pursuant to the absolute priority rule. The terminal conditions describing the contingent value of the debt and equity are analogous to the conditions stated at equations (2.3a, b):

$$V_1(T_n) = \min[W(T_n), P + C] \tag{12.3a}$$

$$V_2(T_n) = \max[0, W(T_n) - P - C] \tag{12.3b}$$

Equity as a Compound Call Option

We observed in section 2.2 that when a firm is capitalized with common stock and zero-coupon debt, the stock can be thought of as a call option on the firm with a strike price equal to the face amount of the debt and an expiration date equal to the maturity date of the debt. The equity of a firm capitalized with coupon-bearing debt can be characterized in a related fashion.

Following payment of the coupon due at time T_{n-1}, the coupon-bearing debt has only a single remaining payment of $P + C$ due at time T_n. The stock is then tantamount to a call option on the firm with a strike price of $P + C$ and an expiration date of T_n.

Prior to payment of the coupon due at time T_{n-1} (but following payment of the coupon due at time T_{n-2}), the stock is comparable to a call option *on the call option described in the preceding paragraph*. If the firm pays the coupon due at time T_{n-1}, the stockholders get the right to decide whether to redeem the debt at time T_n and become the sole owners of the enterprise. Thus between T_{n-2} and T_{n-1} the stock is tantamount to an option (with strike price C and expiration date T_{n-1}) to acquire a call option on the firm, where the latter option has strike price $P + C$ and expiration date T_n. Similarly between T_{n-3} and T_{n-2} the stock is tantamount to an option (with strike price C and expiration date T_{n-2}) to acquire the foregoing option on an option. More generally, prior to payment of the coupon due at time T_{n-1} the stock can be characterized as a *compound* call option, or as a call option to acquire another call option.[5]

12.2   The Valuation Problem

We assume there exists a pair of functions, f_1 and f_2, with two arguments: time and the *cum*-payment value of the firm, such that the *cum*-payment value of the debt and equity at time $t \le T_n$ can be calculated as

---

5. Black and Scholes (1973, pp. 651–52) pointed out that the stock of a firm capitalized with coupon-bearing debt can be characterized as a compound option.

$$V_i(t) = f_i(W(t), t), \qquad i = 1, 2 \tag{12.4}$$

The valuation problem is to identify the forms of these two contingent value functions.

We have already solved the valuation problem in the special case of $t = T_n$. From equations (12.3a, b) we have

$$f_1(W, T_n) = \min[W, P + C] \tag{12.5a}$$

$$f_2(W, T_n) = \max[0, W - P - C] \tag{12.5b}$$

We want to extend these terminal contingent value functions backward in time, to times prior to the maturity of the debt.

12.3   Transversality Conditions at the Time of an Early Coupon Payment

In chapter 11 the liability of the firm for asynchronous debt redemptions led to transversality conditions at the maturity date of the shorter obligation (see equations 11.5a, b, c) as well as to terminal conditions at the maturity date of the longer obligation. In the present case the firm's coupon-bearing debt leads to transversality conditions at times $T_1, T_2, \ldots, T_{n-1}$ as well as to the terminal conditions at time T_n stated above. It will be useful to identify the transversality conditions before we begin to address the valuation problem.

At time T_j for $T_j < T_n$ the firm is contractually obligated to make its jth interest payment. It will default on the payment if the *cum*-payment value of the firm is less than C, in which case the *cum*-payment value of the debt will be equal to the value of the firm and the equity will be worthless. If the *cum*-payment value of the firm exceeds C, the firm liquidates assets and pays its creditors the required coupon.

Let $g_{i,j}(W^x)$ denote the *ex*-payment value of the ith security at time T_j when the *ex*-payment value of the firm is W^x. $g_{i,j}(W^x)$ is the limit of $f_i(W^x, t)$ as t approaches T_j from above:[6]

$$g_{i,j}(W^x) = \lim_{\varepsilon \downarrow 0} f_i(W^x, T_j + \varepsilon), \qquad i = 1, 2 \tag{12.6}$$

If the *cum*-payment value of the firm at time T_j is W and if $W > C$, then the *ex*-payment value of the firm is $W - C$ and the *ex*-payment values of the debt and equity are $g_{1,j}(W - C)$ and $g_{2,j}(W - C)$, respectively. The *cum*-payment value of the debt will be equal to the *ex*-

---

6. Note that, in general, $g_{i,j}(W^x)$ is not equal to the quantity $f_i(W^x, T_j)$. $f_i(W^x, T_j)$ denotes the *cum*-payment, rather than *ex*-payment, value of the ith security at time T_j when the *cum*-payment, rather than *ex*-payment, value of the firm is the quantity W^x.

payment value of the debt plus the contemporaneous coupon payment, or $g_{1,j}(W - C) + C$. Since the stock does not pay dividends, the *cum*-payment value of equity will be the same as the *ex*-payment value, or $g_{2,j}(W - C)$.

The foregoing remarks establish the transversality conditions for the debt and equity:

$$f_1(W, T_j) = \begin{cases} W & \text{if } W \le C \\ g_{1,j}(W - C) + C & \text{if } C < W \end{cases} \tag{12.7a}$$

$$f_2(W, T_j) = \begin{cases} 0 & \text{if } W \le C \\ g_{2,j}(W - C) & \text{if } C < W \end{cases} \tag{12.7b}$$

These conditions characterize the contingent values of the firm's securities at the boundary at time T_j between when the firm is capitalized with debt that has paid $j - 1$ coupons and promises to pay $n - j + 1$ additional coupons and when (in the absence of default) it is capitalized with debt that has paid j coupons and promises to pay $n - j$ additional coupons.

12.4   Solving the Valuation Problem

The valuation problem asks for the forms of the contingent value functions. We already know the forms of the functions at T_n from the terminal conditions of equations (12.5a, b). This section describes an algorithm for computing the value of $f_i(W^*, t^*)$ for any time t^* prior to time T_n and for any positive value of W^*. We begin by examining a simpler, up-to-the-next-coupon," problem and an algorithm for solving that problem.

An "Up-to-the-Next-Coupon" Problem

The "up-to-the-next-coupon" problem is to compute the value of $f_i(W^0, t^0)$ when $h - 1$ coupons have already been paid and t^0 lies between T_{h-1} and T_h $(T_{h-1} < t^0 < T_h)$, *assuming that we know the form of the contingent value function f_i at the time of the next coupon payment* (i.e., assuming we know, or can compute, the value of $f_i(W, T_h)$ for any positive value of W). This is a relatively simple problem because the firm does not make any coupon payments between t^0 and T_h.

We begin by dividing the interval between t^0 and T_h into K subintervals of length Δt so that $\Delta t = (T_h - t^0)/K$, and by defining a sequence of $K + 1$ discrete points in time:

$$t_k = t^0 + (k - 1) \cdot \Delta t, \qquad k = 1, 2, \ldots, K + 1 \tag{12.8}$$

We next specify that the value of the firm evolves as a binomial random walk over each of the K subintervals. Define an array $W_{j,k}$ for $j = 1, 2, \ldots, k$ and $k = 1, 2, \ldots, K + 1$:

$$\ln[W_{j,k}] = \ln[W^0] + (k - 1) \cdot \mu \cdot \Delta t + (2 \cdot j - k - 1) \cdot \sigma \cdot \Delta t^{1/2},$$

$$j = 1, 2, \ldots, k; \ k = 1, 2, \ldots, K + 1 \quad (12.9)$$

The value of the firm evolves through the array, beginning at $W_{1,1} = W^0$ at time $t_1 = t^0$. If the value of the firm is $W_{j,k}$ at time t_k, then the value of the firm at time t_{k+1} will be either $W_{j+1,k+1}$ (with probability $\frac{1}{2}$) or $W_{j,k+1}$ (with probability $\frac{1}{2}$). This binomial random walk is an approximation to the log normal random walk in equation (12.2).

Let $V_{j,k,i}$ denote the value of the ith security at time t_k when the value of the firm is $W_{j,k}$: $V_{j,k,i} = f_i(W_{j,k}, t_k)$. We compute the $V_{j,k,i}$ values using a recursion algorithm on k, beginning at $k = K + 1$ and proceeding backward to $k = 1$.

The values of $V_{j,K+1,i}$ for $j = 1, 2, \ldots, K + 1$ follow from the (known) form of the contingent value function at time T_h. Since $t_{K+1} = T_h$ (see equation 12.8), we have

$$V_{j,K+1,i} = f_i(W_{j,K+1}, T_h) \quad (12.10)$$

Consider now the problem of computing $V_{j,k,i}$ when $k < K + 1$. $V_{j,k,i}$ is the value of the ith security at time t_k when the value of the firm is $W_{j,k}$. The value of the firm will evolve over the subinterval from t_k to t_{k+1} to either:

1. $W_{j+1,k+1}$, where the ith security will be worth $V_{j+1,k+1,i}$, or

2. $W_{j,k+1}$, where the ith security will be worth $V_{j,k+1,i}$.

Assuming that the markets do not allow opportunities for riskless arbitrage profits, we have

$$V_{j,k,i} = h \cdot W_{j,k} + Q \quad (12.11)$$

where h and Q satisfy the equations

$$V_{j+1,k+1,i} = h \cdot W_{j+1,k+1} + Q \cdot e^{R_f \cdot \Delta t} \quad (12.12a)$$

$$V_{j,k+1,i} = h \cdot W_{j,k+1} + Q \cdot e^{R_f \cdot \Delta t} \quad (12.12b)$$

The foregoing algorithm can be applied recursively for $k = K, K - 1, \ldots, 1$, ending with the computation of $V_{1,1,i}$. Since $V_{1,1,i} = f_i(W_{1,1}, t_1) = f_i(W^0, t^0)$, this completes the computation of $f_i(W^0, t^0)$ for the case where the value of the firm evolves according to the discrete time binomial process. As Δt goes to zero the discrete time process converges to the continuous time Gaussian process of equation (12.2), and the value of $V_{1,1,i}$ converges to the value of $f_i(W^0, t^0)$ for the case where the value of the firm evolves according to that Gaussian process.

Remark

The same algorithm can be used when $t^0 = T_{h-1}$, but the value of $V_{1,1,i}$ must then be interpreted as the *ex*-payment value of the ith security at time T_{h-1} when the *ex*-payment value of the firm is W^0 :

$$V_{1,1,i} = g_{i,h-1}(W^0) \tag{12.13}$$

The ability to compute the *ex*-payment value of a security on a coupon payment date, contingent on the contemporaneous *ex*-payment value of the firm, is crucial for what follows.[7]

An Algorithm for Computing $f_i(W^*, t^*)$

Recall now the original problem: computing the value of $f_i(W^*, t^*)$. Assume that the debt has previously paid $h - 1$ coupons, so $T_{h-1} < t^* \leq T_h$.

Suppose that we have already identified the forms of the contingent value functions on the coupon payment dates. Then we can compute the value of $f_i(W, T_j)$ for any positive value of W and for any value of $j \in \{1, 2, \ldots, n\}$. If $t^* = T_h$, we can immediately compute $f_i(W^*, t^*)$ as $f_i(W^*, T_h)$. Alternatively, if time t^* is prior to time T_h so that $T_{h-1} < t^* < T_h$, we can compute $f_i(W^*, t^*)$ using the algorithm for the up-to-the-next-coupon problem with $W^0 = W^*$ and $t^0 = t^*$. It follows that identification of the forms of the contingent value functions on the coupon payment dates provides enough information to identify the forms of the contingent value functions on any other date.

A Recursion Algorithm for Identifying the Forms of the Contingent Value Functions on the Coupon Payment Dates

We can identify the forms of the contingent value functions on the coupon payment dates recursively, beginning at the maturity date of the debt and proceeding backward to the first coupon payment date.

When the debt matures at time T_n the contingent value functions are identical to the terminal conditions in equations (12.5a, b). Consider, therefore, the problem of identifying the form of $f_i(\cdot, T_j)$ assuming that we have already identified the form of $f_i(\cdot, T_{j+1})$.

From the transversality conditions in equations (12.7a, b), we can compute the value of $f_i(W, T_j)$ from the value of $g_{i,j}(W - C)$. As

---

7. The interpretation expressed in equation (12.13) is similar to the interpretation of $g_2(W, T_1)$ and $g_3(W, T_1)$ noted in the last paragraph of section 11.2.

pointed out in the text at equation (12.13), we can compute the value of $g_{i,j}(W - C)$ from the (already identified) form of the contingent value function $f_i(\cdot, T_{j+1})$, using the algorithm for the up-to-the-next-coupon problem with $W^0 = W - C$ and $t^0 = T_j$. Thus we can compute the value of $f_i(W, T_j)$ for an arbitrary value of W, and more generally, we can identify the form of the contingent value function $f_i(\cdot, T_j)$ from the form of the contingent value function $f_i(\cdot, T_{j+1})$. This recursive identification proceeds backward to $j = 1$. The appendix provides details on the construction.

12.5   An Example

It will be helpful to examine a numerical example of our contingent valuation algorithm.[8] We assume that the U.S. Treasury yield curve is flat and stationary at $R_f = 0.10$ (or 10% per annum) and that the volatility of the value of the firm is $\sigma = 0.20$ (or a volatility of 20% over one year).

We assume further that the debt pays interest at the rate of 10% per annum and has a principal value of $P = 101.963$, so the semiannual coupon payment is $C = 5.098$. Now suppose that we are valuing the debt fifteen years before it matures and that a coupon has just been paid, so there are thirty coupons remaining to be paid, including the coupon at maturity. The debt has a default-free value of 100.0. (The default-free value of the debt is the present value of the future payments of principal and interest, discounted at the continuously compounded rate R_f.)

Figure 12.1 shows the contingent value of the debt (upper panel) and equity (lower panel) of the firm. The general features of the contingent value functions are familiar from earlier analyses. When the value of the firm is less than about 50, the value of equity is negligible and the value of the debt is virtually identical to the value of the firm. This reflects the virtual certainty (assuming the risk neutral drift rate) of default on or before the maturity date of the debt. As the value of the firm increases above 50, the value of the debt rises and asymptotically approaches its default-free value. The value of equity rises as well, and converges to the difference between the value of the firm and the default-free value of the debt.

Do Coupon Payments Affect Debt Values?

The contingent value functions in figure 12.1 have the same general form as the contingent value functions in, for example, figure 2.11 for the secu-

---

8. See also the related analysis in Ho and Singer (1982, pp. 386–96).

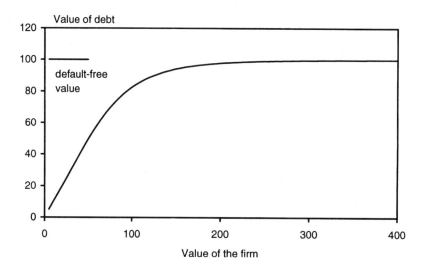

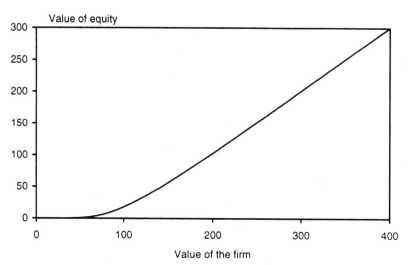

Figure 12.1
Contingent value of debt and equity fifteen years before the debt matures, when there are 30
coupons remaining to be paid

rities of a firm capitalized with common stock and *zero*-coupon debt. The functions are so similar that one might ask whether coupon payments matter for the contingent value of debt and equity?

In a superficial sense, coupon payments are obviously important: debt that promises to pay C semiannually, as well as P at maturity, is, certeris paribus, more valuable than debt that promises only to pay P at maturity. A more relevant comparison is between coupon-bearing debt and zero-coupon debt with the same default-free value and the same term to maturity.

Figure 12.2 shows (with dashed lines) the contingent value of the debt (upper panel) and equity (lower panel) of a firm capitalized with common stock and zero-coupon debt with a face value of 448.169 maturing in fifteen years. The zero-coupon debt has a default free value of 100.0. The solid lines reproduce the contingent value functions from figure 12.1.

The valuation functions in the upper panel of figure 12.2 show that when holding term to maturity and default-free value constant, coupon-bearing debt is more valuable than zero-coupon debt at every value of the firm. This is consistent with the proposition (from example D in section 2.6) that (holding default-free value fixed) the contingent value of shorter maturity debt exceeds the contingent value of longer maturity debt. Coupon-bearing debt with a default-free value of 100.0 maturing in fifteen years is more valuable than zero-coupon debt with the same default-free value maturing in fifteen years because the former debt makes some payments sooner (and does not make any payments later) than the latter debt.[9]

Conversely, the lower panel of figure 12.2 shows that ceteris paribus, the contingent value of the equity of a firm capitalized with coupon-bearing debt is lower than the contingent value of the equity of a firm capitalized with zero-coupon debt.

Appendix

This appendix provides computational details for constructing the contingent value functions for the firm's debt and equity on the coupon payment dates of the debt.

---

9. Similarly coupon-bearing debt with a sinking fund redemption requirement—where some principal must be repaid prior to final maturity—is, ceteris paribus, more valuable than bullet redemption coupon-bearing debt—where all principal is repaid at maturity—when the two securities have the same default-free value (Geske 1977). Analysis of sinking fund debt is, however, complicated by the option of the issuer to satisfy its sinking fund redemption requirements with open market purchases of the debt (Leader 1977; Laiderman 1980; Kalotay 1981; Ho and Singer 1984; Dunn and Spatt 1984; Ho 1985; Jones, Mason, and Rosenfeld 1984, 1985). The latter option can be valuable to the issuer, and it can reduce the market value of the debt if the debt has a low coupon rate.

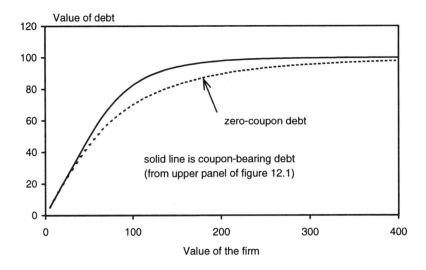

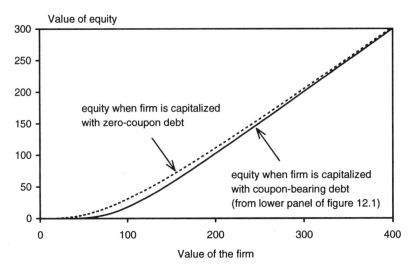

Figure 12.2
Contingent value of debt and equity fifteen years before the debt matures

The debt promises to pay interest semiannually. Divide the time interval between two consecutive payments into K subintervals of length $\Delta t = 0.5/K$. (The value of K need not be the same here as the value of K specified in the text preceding equation 12.8.)

Let $W_{\min}$ denote a value of the firm so low that the firm's equity is essentially worthless, and let $W_{\max}$ denote a value of the firm so high that the firm's debt is essentially default free. (We set $W_{\min} = 1$ and $W_{\max} = 2000$ for the numerical example in section 12.5.)

Next define a sequence of values of the firm, beginning with $W_1 = W_{\min}$,

$$\ln[W_{j+1}] = \ln[W_j] + \sigma \cdot \Delta t^{1/2}, \qquad j = 1, 2, \ldots, J \tag{A12.1}$$

where the terminal integer J is chosen so that $W_{J-1} < W_{\max} \leq W_J$.

Let $\Phi_{j,h,i}$ denote the *cum*-payment value of the ith security at time T_h (the time of the hth coupon payment) when the *cum*-payment value of the firm is W_j,

$$\Phi_{j,h,i} = f_i(W_j, T_h), \qquad i = 1, 2 \tag{A12.2}$$

We can use the values of $\Phi_{1,h,i}, \Phi_{2,h,i}, \ldots, \Phi_{J,h,i}$ to construct an approximation to the form of the ith contingent value function at time T_h.[10] Suppose, for example, that we want to compute $f_i(W, T_h)$ for some positive value of W, where $W_1 < W < W_J$.[11] Identify the integer $m \in \{1, 2, \ldots, J-1\}$ such that $W_m \leq W < W_{m+1}$, and compute the value of α that satisfies the equation

$$W = \alpha \cdot W_m + (1 - \alpha) \cdot W_{m+1} \tag{A12.3}$$

We can then approximate $f_i(W, T_h)$ as

$$f_i(W, T_h) = \alpha \cdot f_i(W_m, T_h) + (1 - \alpha) \cdot f_i(W_{m+1}, T_h) \tag{A12.4}$$

or, from the definition of $\Phi_{j,h,i}$ in equation (A12.2), as[12]

$$f_i(W, T_h) = \alpha \cdot \Phi_{m,h,i} + (1 - \alpha) \cdot \Phi_{m+1,h,i} \tag{A12.5}$$

Section 12.4 pointed out that identification of the forms of the contingent value functions on the coupon payment dates provides sufficient

---

10. The approximation error can be made arbitrarily small by reducing the size of Δt and consequently the spacing between $\ln[W_j]$ and $\ln[W_{j+1}]$ (see equation A12.1).

11. If $W \leq W_1$, the equity of the firm is essentially worthless and we can compute $f_1(W, T_h) = W$ and $f_2(W, T_h) = 0$. If $W \geq W_J$, the firm's debt is essentially default free. In that case we can compute $f_1(W, T_h)$ as the sum of the contemporaneous coupon payment C and the present value of the future payments of principal and interest on the debt, discounted at the rate R_f, and we can compute $f_2(W, T_h)$ as the difference between W and $f_1(W, T_h)$.

12. It would certainly be feasible to approximate $f_i(W, T_h)$ in equations (A12.4) and (A12.5) with, for example, a high-order spline.

information to identify the forms of those functions on any other date. Hence it suffices to compute the values of the $\Phi_{j,h,i}$ terms. We compute the terms recursively, beginning at $h = n$.

Constructing the $\Phi_{j,h,i}$ Terms for $h = n$

The values of $\Phi_{j,n,i}$ for $j = 1, 2, \ldots, J$ follow from the terminal conditions specified at equations (12.5a, b),

$$\Phi_{j,n,1} = f_1(W_j, T_n) = \min[W_j, P + C] \tag{A12.6a}$$

$$\Phi_{j,n,2} = f_2(W_j, T_n) = \max[0, W_j - P + C] \tag{A12.6b}$$

Computing the $\Phi_{j,h,i}$ Terms for $h < n$

Consider now the problem of computing $\Phi_{j,h,i}$ for $j = 1, 2, \ldots, J$ and for a value of h less than n, assuming that we already know the values of $\Phi_{j,h+1,i}$ for $j = 1, 2, \ldots, J$.

Based on the division of the interval between time T_h and time T_{h+1} into K subintervals, we can define a sequence of $K + 1$ points in time

$$t_k = T_h + (k - 1) \cdot \Delta t, \qquad k = 1, 2, \ldots, K + 1 \tag{A12.7}$$

Observe that $t_1 = T_h$ and that $t_{K+1} = T_{h+1}$.

We next specify that the value of the firm evolves as a binomial random walk over each of the subintervals. The change in the log of the value of the firm between t_k and t_{k+1} is

$$\ln[W(t_{k+1})] - \ln[W^x(t_k)] = \sigma \cdot \Delta t^{1/2} \cdot e_k, \qquad k = 1, 2, \ldots, K \tag{A12.8}$$

where e_k is a binomial random variable that can have the value $+1$ with probability $\frac{1}{2}$ and the value -1 with probability $\frac{1}{2}$.[13] If the ex-payment value of the firm is W_j at t_k, then the cum-payment value of the firm at t_{k+1} will be either W_{j+1} or W_{j-1}.

Define now an array $V_{j,k,i}$ for $j = 1, 2, \ldots, J$ and $k = 1, 2, \ldots, K + 1$. For values of $k > 1$, $V_{j,k,i}$ denotes the cum-payment value of the ith security at time t_k when the cum-payment value of the firm is W_j,

$$V_{j,k,i} = f_i(W_j, t_k), \qquad k > 1 \tag{A12.9}$$

For $k = 1$, $V_{j,k,i}$ denotes the ex-payment value of the ith security at time T_h when the ex-payment value of the firm is W_j,

---

13. We previously approximated the change in the log of the value of the firm over an interval of length Δt as $\mu \cdot \Delta t + \sigma \cdot \Delta t^{1/2} \cdot e_k$. However, as observed in appendix C to chapter 2, contingent value functions are invariant with respect to the drift rate μ. We here take advantage of that result and set μ equal to zero for computational simplicity.

$$V_{j,1,i} = g_{i,h}(W_j) = \lim_{\varepsilon \downarrow 0} f_i(W_j, T_h + \varepsilon) \tag{A12.10}$$

We will first show how to compute the $V_{j,k,i}$ terms recursively from $k = K + 1$ to $k = 1$, and then show that we can compute the $\Phi_{j,h,i}$ terms from the $V_{j,1,i}$ terms using the transversality conditions in equations (12.7a, b).

Constructing the $V_{j,k,i}$ Terms for $k = K + 1$

The values of $V_{j,K+1,i}$ follow from equations (A12.9), (A12.7), and (A12.2):

$$V_{j,K+1,i} = f_i(W_j, t_{K+1}) = f_i(W_j, T_{h+1}) = \Phi_{j,h+1,i}, \qquad j = 1, 2, \ldots, J \tag{A12.11}$$

Since, by hypothesis, we know the values of the $\Phi_{j,h+1,i}$ terms, we can construct the values of the $V_{j,K+1,i}$ terms.

Computing the $V_{j,k,i}$ Terms for $k < K + 1$

Assume now that we know $V_{j,k+1,i}$ for $j = 1, 2, \ldots, J$ and that we want to compute $V_{j,k,i}$ for $j = 1, 2, \ldots, J$. If j is greater than 1 and less than J, we compute $V_{j,k,i}$ from an arbitrage pricing argument.[14]

Over the subinterval from t_k to t_{k+1} the value of the firm will evolve to either

1. W_{j+1}, where the ith security will be worth $V_{j+1,k+1,i}$, or

2. W_{j-1}, where the ith security will be worth $V_{j-1,k+1,i}$.

Assuming the markets do not allow opportunities for riskless arbitrage profits, the value of the ith security at time t_k when the value of the firm is W_j must be

$$V_{j,k,i} = h \cdot W_j + Q \tag{A12.12}$$

where h and Q satisfy the equations

$$V_{j+1,k+1,i} = h \cdot W_{j+1} + Q \cdot e^{R_f \cdot \Delta t} \tag{A12.13a}$$

$$V_{j-1,k+1,i} = h \cdot W_{j-1} + Q \cdot e^{R_f \cdot \Delta t} \tag{A12.13b}$$

The foregoing algorithm can be applied recursively for $k = K, K-1, \ldots, 1$, ending with the computation of $V_{j,1,i}$ for $j = 1, 2, \ldots, J$.

---

14. If $j = 1$, then $W_j = W_{\min}$—see text at equation (A12.1)—and the equity of the firm is essentially worthless. Thus we can set $V_{1,k,1} = W_1$ and $V_{1,k,2} = 0$. If $j = J$, then $W_j \geq W_{\max}$, and the firm's debt is essentially default free. Thus we can set $V_{J,k,1}$ equal to the present value of the future payments of principal and interest on the debt, discounted at the rate R_f, and we can set $V_{J,k,2}$ equal to the difference between W_J and $V_{J,k,1}$.

Computing the $\Phi_{j,h,i}$ Terms from the $V_{j,1,i}$ Terms

Consider now the problem of computing $\Phi_{j,h,1}$. Since $\Phi_{j,h,1} = f_1(W_j, T_h)$, the transversality condition in equation (12.7a) implies that

$$\Phi_{j,h,1} = \begin{cases} W_j & \text{if } W_j \leq C \\ g_{1,h}(W_j - C) + C & \text{if } C < W_j \end{cases} \tag{A12.14}$$

It follows that we can compute the value of $\Phi_{j,h,1}$ if we can compute $g_{1,h}(W_j - C)$.

If $W_j - C$ is greater than W_1, we can compute the value of $g_{1,h}(W_j - C)$ by linear interpolation.[15] Identify the integer $m \in \{1, 2, \ldots, J-1\}$ such that $W_m \leq W_j - C < W_{m+1}$, and compute the value of α that satisfies the equation

$$W_j - C = \alpha \cdot W_m + (1 - \alpha) \cdot W_{m+1} \tag{A12.15}$$

We can then approximate $g_{1,h}(W_j - C)$ as

$$g_{1,h}(W_j - C) = \alpha \cdot g_{1,h}(W_m) + (1 - \alpha) \cdot g_{1,h}(W_{m+1}) \tag{A12.16}$$

or, from the definition of $V_{j,1,1}$ in equation (A12.10), as

$$g_{1,h}(W_j - C) = \alpha \cdot V_{m,1,1} + (1 - \alpha) \cdot V_{m+1,1,1} \tag{A12.17}$$

Consider next the problem of computing $\Phi_{j,h,2}$. Since $\Phi_{j,h,2} = f_2(W_j, T_h)$, the transversality condition in equation (12.7b) implies that

$$\Phi_{j,h,2} = \begin{cases} 0 & \text{if } W_j \leq C \\ g_{2,h}(W_j - C) & \text{if } C < W_j \end{cases} \tag{A12.18}$$

If $W_j - C$ is greater than W_1, we can compute the value of $g_{2,h}(W_j)$ by linear interpolation as described in the preceding paragraph.[16]

---

15. If $W_j - C$ is less than or equal to W_1, then $W_j - C$ is less than or equal to $W_{\min}$, and we can set $g_{1,h}(W_j - C) = W_j - C$.

16. If $W_j - C$ is less than or equal to W_1, then $W_j - C$ is less than or equal to $W_{\min}$, and we can set $g_{2,h}(W_j - C) = 0$.

13 Pay-in-Kind Bonds

A pay-in-kind (PIK) bond is a coupon-bearing bond with an option to pay interest with additional bonds instead of cash, or to pay interest "in kind." PIK bonds are interesting because they allow an issuer to exercise discretion over the timing of its cash disbursements.[1] Payments on PIK bonds thus provide a conceptual bridge between the rigid contractual obligations of conventional debt and the discretionary dividend payments of common stock.

This chapter examines the contingent valuation of PIK bonds. We begin with an illustrative example.

13.1 An Example of a PIK Bond

Consider a ten-year PIK bond, issued on December 15, 2000, and maturing on December 15, 2010, with an original principal value of $100 million and a coupon rate of 15% per annum, on which interest is paid semiannually on June 15 and December 15.

If the issuer pays all of the coupons in cash, it will disburse $7.5 million every six months from June 15, 2001, until December 15, 2010, inclusive ($7.5 million $= \frac{1}{2}$ of 15% of $100 million), and it will be obligated to repay $100 million principal on December 15, 2010. However, the issuer may choose to satisfy some of its interest obligations with bonds instead of cash.

Events on the First Coupon Payment Date

On June 15, 2001, the issuer has to make an initial interest payment of $7.5 million. It can satisfy this obligation in either of two ways: by disbursing $7.5 million in cash, or by issuing $7.5 million principal amount of additional PIK bonds. Choosing the second option means that immediately following the distribution of the additional bonds, the issuer will have $107.5 million principal amount of PIK debt outstanding.

Events on the Second Coupon Payment Date

Six months later, on December 15, 2001, the issuer will have to pay interest of *either* $7.5 million *or* $8.063 million, depending on whether the June 15 interest obligation was paid in cash or kind.

If the interest due on June 15 was paid in cash, the aggregate principal value of PIK debt remained at $100 million, and the issuer has to pay $7.5

---

1. Goodman and Cohen (1988, 1989), Opler (1993), and Tufano (1993) discuss the contribution of PIK bonds and other "reduced cash flow" securities (including zero-coupon bonds, increasing rate notes, and original issue discount bonds) to limiting the risk of early financial distress following a highly leveraged acquisition.

million interest on December 15. This obligation can be satisfied by paying $7.5 million in cash or by distributing $7.5 million principal amount of additional bonds. Choosing the second option means that the issuer will have $107.5 million principal amount of PIK debt outstanding immediately after December 15.

If the interest due on June 15 was paid in kind, the aggregate principal value of PIK debt increased to $107.5 million, and the issuer has to pay $8.063 million interest on December 15 ($8.063 million = $\frac{1}{2}$ of 15% of $107.5 million). This obligation can be satisfied by paying $8.063 million in cash or by distributing $8.063 million principal amount of additional bonds. Choosing the second option means that the issuer will have a total of $115.563 million principal amount of bonds outstanding immediately after December 15 ($115.563 million = $107.5 million + $8.063 million).

Following the second interest payment on December 15, 2001, the principal amount of PIK debt outstanding will be one of three values:

· $100 million (if the interest obligations on June 15, 2001 and December 15, 2001 were both paid in cash).

· $107.5 million (if one of the interest obligations was paid in cash and the other was paid in kind).

· $115.563 million (if both obligations were paid in kind).

Subsequent Events

Assuming that the pay-in-kind option does not terminate prior to the bond's maturity,[2] the process described above continues on each interest payment date through and including June 15, 2010.

Immediately following the nineteenth semiannual interest payment on June 15, 2010, the principal amount of PIK debt outstanding can be any one of twenty values, indexed conveniently with the integer η:

$\eta = 0$: $100 million principal amount of debt—if all nineteen obligations were paid in cash

$\eta = 1$: $107.5 million principal amount of debt—if one interest obligation was paid in kind and the other eighteen obligations were paid in cash

$\eta = 2$: $115.563 million principal amount of debt—if two interest obligations were paid in kind, where $115.563 million = $1.075^2 \cdot$ $100 million original principal value

$\vdots$

2. Table 1 of Goodman and Cohen (1989) exhibits the structure of ten PIK bonds issued by eight firms in 1986 and 1987. The pay-in-kind option remained alive throughout the life of two of the bonds.

$\eta = 19$: $395.149 million principal amount of debt—if all nineteen interest obligations were paid in kind, where $395.149 million $=$ $1.075^{19} \cdot \$100$ million original principal value

Starting from the base of $100 million original principal value, each payment in kind increases the principal amount of debt outstanding by 7.5%.

On the maturity date of the bonds on December 15, 2010, bondholders have a claim on the firm for repayment of principal and for interest on that principal for six months at the rate of 15% per annum. If the issuer previously made η interest payments in kind (where η is a member of the set $\{0, 1, 2, 3, \ldots, 19\}$), the creditors' claim is for principal of $1.075^{\eta} \cdot \$100$ million plus interest equal to 7.5% of that principal, or for a total of $1.075^{\eta+1} \cdot \$100$ million.

Comment

The foregoing example illustrates three important features of pay-in-kind debt.

First, the issuer of a PIK bond does not have a rigid contractual obligation to pay creditors specified amounts of money on specified dates: the issuer can satisfy an interest obligation by distributing additional bonds, and thereby postpone any cash disbursement. In addition the amount of interest required to be paid (in cash or kind) on a particular date depends on the earlier decisions of the firm. More interest will be due if the issuer decided to pay more interest in kind in the past.

These two features complicate identification of the transversality conditions linking the *cum*-payment and *ex*-payment values of the firm's securities on coupon payment dates. It is far from obvious how we can specify transversality conditions like those in equations (12.7a, b) when the interest required to be paid in cash is not a fixed number.

The third important feature of a PIK bond is the increase in the principal amount of the bond when the firm chooses to pay interest in kind. Unlike the analysis in chapter 12, we cannot specify ex ante the principal liability of the firm to its creditors. This complicates the identification of terminal conditions, analogous to equations (12.5a, b), for the contingent values of the firm's securities when the debt matures.

13.2   An Analytical Framework

The balance of this chapter examines the contingent valuation of securities issued by a firm capitalized, in part, with PIK debt. We begin by stating the assumptions of the analysis.

Corporate Capital Structure

We assume the firm is capitalized with common stock and a noncallable PIK bond that pays interest semiannually.[3] The stock cannot pay a dividend and cannot be repurchased by the firm until the bond has been redeemed.

The coupon rate on the bond is denoted R_c. If $R_c = 0.12$ (so the bond has a coupon rate of 12% per annum), and the principal amount of the bond outstanding immediately prior to an interest payment date is $250 million, the interest due is $15 million ($15 million $= \frac{1}{2}$ of 12% of $250 million).

We assume that the bond is issued with an original principal value of P and makes a total of n interest payments, at times $T_1, T_2, \ldots, T_n$, where T_1 is the date of the first payment, T_n is the maturity date of the bond, and $T_j = T_{j-1} + 0.5$ for $j = 2, 3, \ldots, n$. We assume that the firm liquidates assets if it chooses to pay interest in cash.

We denote the *cum*-payment value of the bond at time t as $V_1(t)$ and the value of the stock as $V_2(t)$. The *cum*-payment value of the firm is $W(t) = V_1(t) + V_2(t)$.

As in the preceding chapter, it will be useful to denote the *ex*-payment value of the firm at time t as $W^x(t)$. If the firm pays interest of C_j in cash at time T_j, the contemporaneous *ex*-payment value of the firm is

$$W^x(T_j) = W(T_j) - C_j, \qquad j = 1, 2, \ldots, n-1 \tag{13.1}$$

C_j is zero and $W^x(T_j) = W(T_j)$ if the firm pays interest in kind at time T_j. The *ex*-payment and *cum*-payment values are identical at any time prior to maturity that is not a coupon payment date.

The value of the firm evolves up to the time of the first coupon payment, and between subsequent payments, as a log normal random walk with drift rate μ and variance σ^2 per annum.[4]

Default and Bankruptcy

For reasons comparable to those stated in the appendix to chapter 11, we suppress the possibility that the firm might default strategically on its promise to pay interest prior to maturity and assume that it will surely pay interest in kind if it chooses not to pay in cash. Thus there is no possibility that the firm will default prior to the maturity of the bond.

At time T_n bondholders have a claim on the firm for repayment of principal and for interest on that principal. If the firm defaults, it is liqui-

---

3. PIK bonds are usually callable (Goodman and Cohen 1989). We ignore the call option in order to focus attention on the PIK option.

4. See text at equation (12.2).

dated in an instantaneous and costless bankruptcy proceeding. The proceeds of the liquidation are distributed, to creditors and shareholders, according to the absolute priority rule.

13.3   A Notational Scheme for the Contingent Value Functions

Consider now the matter of describing the value of the ith security at time t as a function of the contemporaneous value of the firm.

We cannot express, as in earlier chapters (e.g., see equation 12.4), $V_i(t)$ as a function of only time and the value of the firm, because the principal amount of the PIK debt is not fixed and constant through time. The allocation of the value of the firm between creditors and shareholders is not, in general, independent of the principal amount of the debt, so we need to add the principal amount of the debt as a third variable affecting the contingent values of the firm's securities. This section develops a notational scheme for contingent debt and equity values by exploiting the dependence of the principal amount of the PIK debt on the interest paid in kind on earlier coupon payment dates.

The Principal Values of a PIK Bond

The PIK bond described in the preceding section was issued with an initial principal value of P, pays interest at the annualized rate R_c at times $T_1, T_2, \ldots, T_n$, and matures at time T_n.

Prior to the interest payment at T_1 the principal value of the bond is P. However, between T_1 and T_2 the principal amount of the debt can be either P or $P \cdot (1 + \frac{1}{2} R_c)$, depending on whether the firm paid the interest due at T_1 in cash, in which case the principal amount of the debt is P, or in kind, in which case the principal amount of the debt is $P \cdot (1 + \frac{1}{2} R_c)$. Similarly between T_2 and T_3 the principal amount of the debt can be P, $P \cdot (1 + \frac{1}{2} R_c)$, or $P \cdot (1 + \frac{1}{2} R_c)^2$, depending on whether the firm did not make any earlier interest payments in kind, made one payment in kind, or made both payments in kind.

More generally, the principal amount of PIK debt outstanding at any point in time can be expressed as $P \cdot (1 + \frac{1}{2} R_c)^\eta$, where the integer η is the number of earlier interest obligations paid in kind.

The Contingent Value Functions

We can express the dependence of $V_i(t)$ on the principal amount of PIK debt outstanding, as well as on time and the value of the firm, by introducing a *different and distinct* contingent value function for each possible principal amount of debt, or for each possible value of η in the expression

$P \cdot (1 + \frac{1}{2} R_c)^\eta$. That is, we can think of a contingent value function for the ith security when $\eta = 0$ and the principal amount of PIK debt is P, another (different) contingent value function for the case where $\eta = 1$ and the principal amount of debt is $P \cdot (1 + \frac{1}{2} R_c)$, and so on, to $\eta = n - 1$, where the principal amount of debt is $P \cdot (1 + \frac{1}{2} R_c)^{n-1}$. (The value of η cannot exceed $n - 1$, the number of interest payments prior to maturity.)

We assume that there exists a set of $2n$ contingent value functions, $f_{1,\eta}$ and $f_{2,\eta}$ for $\eta = 0, 1, 2, \ldots, n - 1$, with two arguments: time and the *cum*-payment value of the firm, such that the *cum*-payment value of the debt and equity at time $t \leq T_n$ when the *cum*-payment value of the firm is $W(t)$ and the *cum*-payment principal amount of PIK debt is $P \cdot (1 + \frac{1}{2} R_c)^\eta$, can be calculated as

$$V_i(t) = f_{i,\eta}(W(t), t), \qquad i = 1, 2 \text{ and } \eta = 0, 1, \ldots, n - 1 \qquad (13.2)$$

The sequence of contingent value functions $f_{i,0}, f_{i,1}, \ldots, f_{i,n-1}$ can be thought of as slices from a loaf of bread. If we want the contingent value of the ith security when the firm has made all previous interest payments in cash, we use the first slice and compute $V_i(t) = f_{1,0}(W(t), t)$. We compute with the second slice, $V_i(t) = f_{i,1}(W(t), t)$, if the firm previously satisfied exactly one coupon obligation by paying interest in kind, and we compute with the $\eta + 1$st slice, $V_i(t) = f_{i,\eta}(W(t), t)$, if the firm previously paid η interest obligations in kind.[5]

13.4   The Valuation Problem

The valuation problem is to identify the forms of the $2n$ contingent value functions specified in equation (13.2). Before we begin to describe a solution to the problem, it will be helpful to characterize the decision of the firm to pay interest in cash or kind prior to maturity, and to identify the transversality and terminal conditions for the debt and equity.

13.5   The Decision of the Firm to Pay Interest in Cash or Kind

The firm can pay interest in cash or in kind at each coupon payment date prior to maturity. This section characterizes the firm's *optimal* payment

---

5. For a specified value of t, the integer η must be an element of the set $\{0, 1, 2, \ldots, j - 1\}$ where j is the integer that satisfies the inequalities $T_{j-1} < t \leq T_j$. That is, if t lies between T_{j-1} and T_j, the bond has already made exactly $j - 1$ coupon payments (in cash or kind) and the principal amount of PIK debt outstanding must be an element of the set $\{P, P \cdot (1 + \frac{1}{2} R_c), P \cdot (1 + \frac{1}{2} R_c)^2, \ldots, P \cdot (1 + \frac{1}{2} R_c)^{j-1}\}$.

policy. Following the discussion in section 1.5, we assume that the firm always acts in the best interest of shareholders.

Suppose, at time T_j for $T_j < T_n$, that the *cum*-payment value of the firm is W and the *cum*-payment principal amount of PIK debt is $P \cdot (1 + \frac{1}{2} R_c)^\eta$ for some value of η in the set $\{0, 1, 2, \ldots, j-1\}$, so the firm has an obligation to make a contemporaneous interest payment of $I_\eta = \frac{1}{2} R_c \cdot P \cdot (1 + \frac{1}{2} R_c)^\eta$. The firm cannot avoid paying interest in kind if the value of the firm is less than I_η. However, the firm can take either of two actions if W exceeds I_η:

· It can pay interest in cash. The value of the firm will then fall to $W - I_\eta$, and the principal amount of PIK debt will remain at $P \cdot (1 + \frac{1}{2} R_c)^\eta$.

· It can pay interest in kind. The value of the firm will then remain at W and the principal amount of PIK debt will increase to $P \cdot (1 + \frac{1}{2} R_c)^{\eta+1}$.

The firm will pay in cash or kind to maximize the value of equity.

Let $g_{i,\alpha,j}(W^x)$ denote the *ex*-payment value of the ith security at time T_j when the *ex*-payment value of the firm is W^x and the *ex*-payment principal amount of PIK debt is $P \cdot (1 + \frac{1}{2} R_c)^\alpha$. The integer α must be an element of the set $\{0, 1, 2, \ldots, j\}$. $g_{i,\alpha,j}(W^x)$ is the limit of $f_{i,\alpha}(W^x, t)$ as t approaches T_j from above:[6]

$$g_{i,\alpha,j}(W^x) = \lim_{\varepsilon \downarrow 0} f_{i,\alpha}(W^x, T_j + \varepsilon), \qquad i = 1, 2 \tag{13.3}$$

If the firm pays interest of I_η in cash at time T_j when the *cum*-payment value of the firm is W and the *cum*-payment principal amount of PIK debt is $P \cdot (1 + \frac{1}{2} R_c)^\eta$, the *ex*-payment value of the firm will be $W - I_\eta$ and the *ex*-payment principal amount of debt will remain at $P \cdot (1 + \frac{1}{2} R_c)^\eta$. The *ex*-payment value of equity will be $g_{2,\eta,j}(W - I_\eta)$, and since shareholders do not receive a payment at time T_j, the *cum*-payment value of equity will also be $g_{2,\eta,j}(W - I_\eta)$. If the firm pays interest in kind, the *ex*-payment value of the firm will be W, the *ex*-payment principal amount of debt will be $P \cdot (1 + \frac{1}{2} R_c)^{\eta+1}$ and the *ex*-payment and *cum*-payment values of equity will be $g_{2,\eta+1,j}(W)$.

The firm pays interest in cash or kind to maximize the value of equity, so it will pay in cash if $g_{2,\eta,j}(W - I_\eta)$ exceeds $g_{2,\eta+1,j}(W)$, and it will pay in kind if the inequality runs in the opposite direction.

An Optimal Interest Policy Function

The foregoing results can be summarized with a set of functions describing the optimal interest policy of the firm. Let $C_{\eta,j}(W)$ denote the cash

---

6. Equation (13.3) is comparable to equation (12.6).

interest payment at time T_j when the *cum*-payment principal amount of PIK debt is $P \cdot (1 + \frac{1}{2}R_c)^\eta$ and the *cum*-payment value of the firm is W. Then

$$
C_{\eta,j}(W) = \begin{cases} 0 & \text{if } I_\eta \geq W \text{ or if } W > I_\eta \text{ and } g_{2,\eta,j}(W - I_\eta) \leq g_{2,\eta+1,j}(W) \\ I_\eta & \text{if } W > I_\eta \text{ and } g_{2,\eta,j}(W - I_\eta) > g_{2,\eta+1,j}(W) \\ & \eta = 0, 1, \ldots, j-1; \ j = 1, 2, \ldots, n-1 \quad (13.4) \end{cases}
$$

where $I_\eta = \frac{1}{2}R_c \cdot P \cdot (1 + \frac{1}{2}R_c)^\eta$.

The optimal interest policy in equation (13.4) is a step function. It will be in the best interest of shareholders to pay the bond's coupon in kind when the value of the firm is low; essentially "reborrowing" from bondholders what would otherwise be a cash payment, at a cost of R_c per annum, compounded semiannually. However, at higher values of the firm, where the risk of a future default is low, it may be more economical to distribute cash to bondholders.

The critical, or threshold, value of the firm—above which paying interest in cash maximizes the value of equity at time T_j when the *cum*-payment principal amount of PIK debt is $P \cdot (1 + \frac{1}{2}R_c)^\eta$—is the value of W^c that satisfies the equation[7]

$$
g_{2,\eta,j}(W^c - I_\eta) = g_{2,\eta+1,j}(W^c) \tag{13.5}
$$

13.6 Transversality Conditions

Having characterized the optimal interest policy of the firm, we can now identify the transversality conditions for the contingent values of the firm's securities.

Suppose that the *cum*-payment value of the firm is W at time T_j, where $T_j < T_n$, and the *cum*-payment principal amount of PIK debt is $P \cdot (1 + \frac{1}{2}R_c)^\eta$ for some value of η in the set $\{0, 1, 2, \ldots, j-1\}$, so the firm has an obligation to make a contemporaneous interest payment of $I_\eta = \frac{1}{2}R_c \cdot P \cdot (1 + \frac{1}{2}R_c)^\eta$. Since the firm does not make any payments to shareholders, and since the firm pays interest in cash or kind to maximize the value of equity, the transversality condition for the firm's equity can be expressed as

$$
f_{2,\eta}(W, T_j) = \begin{cases} g_{2,\eta+1,j}(W) & \text{if } W \leq I_\eta \\ \max[g_{2,\eta+1,j}(W), g_{2,\eta,j}(W - I_\eta)] & \text{if } I_\eta < W \end{cases} \tag{13.6}
$$

---

7. There will not be any finite value of W^c that satisfies equation (13.5) if the value of R_c is sufficiently low. In that case the firm will pay interest in kind regardless of the value of the firm.

The upper branch of the right-hand side of the expression says that if the firm is unable to pay interest in cash, then the *cum*-payment value of equity must be equal to the *ex*-payment value of equity assessed at the same value of the firm and a (larger) principal amount of debt that reflects the payment of interest in kind. The lower branch says that if the firm can pay interest in cash, the *cum*-payment value of equity must be equal to the *greater* of (1) the *ex*-payment value of equity assessed at the same value of the firm and a larger principal amount of debt that reflects payment of interest in kind and (2) the *ex*-payment value of equity assessed at an unchanged principal amount of debt and a (lower) value of the firm that reflects payment of interest in cash. This transversality condition is consistent with the optimal interest policy in equation (13.4).

The transversality condition for the PIK debt at time T_j is

$$f_{1,\eta}(W, T_j) = \begin{cases} g_{1,\eta+1,j}(W) & \text{if } W \le I_\eta \\ \min[g_{1,\eta+1,j}(W), g_{1,\eta,j}(W - I_\eta) + I_\eta] & \text{if } I_\eta < W \end{cases} \quad (13.7)$$

The upper branch of the right-hand side of the expression says that if the firm is unable to pay interest in cash, then the *cum*-payment value of the debt must be equal to the *ex*-payment value of the debt assessed at the same value of the firm and a (larger) principal amount of debt that reflects the payment of interest in kind. The lower branch says that if the firm can pay interest in cash, the *cum*-payment value of the debt must be equal to the *lesser* of (1) the *ex*-payment value of the debt assessed at the same value of the firm and a larger principal amount of debt that reflects payment of interest in kind and (2) the sum of (a) the *ex*-payment value of the debt assessed at an unchanged principal amount of debt and a value of the firm that reflects payment of interest in cash and (b) the cash interest payment. This transversality condition is consistent with the proposition that, when the firm is capitalized only with PIK debt and common stock, the firm chooses to pay interest in cash or kind to *minimize* the value of the debt.

13.7 Terminal Conditions

At time T_n the holders of the PIK debt have a claim on the firm for repayment of the principal amount of the debt and for payment of interest on that principal. If the firm previously made η interest payments in kind, the principal amount of PIK debt will be $P \cdot (1 + \frac{1}{2} R_c)^\eta$ and the interest will be $\frac{1}{2} R_c \cdot P \cdot (1 + \frac{1}{2} R_c)^\eta$, so the creditors will have a claim for $P \cdot (1 + \frac{1}{2} R_c)^{\eta+1}$.

In light of the assumptions on the consequences of default and bank-ruptcy specified in section 13.2, the terminal conditions for the contingent value of the debt and equity are

$$f_{1,\eta}(W, T_n) = \min[W, P \cdot (1 + \tfrac{1}{2} R_c)^{\eta+1}], \quad \eta = 0, 1, \ldots, n-1 \quad (13.8a)$$

$$f_{2,\eta}(W, T_n) = \max[0, W - P \cdot (1 + \tfrac{1}{2} R_c)^{\eta+1}], \quad \eta = 0, 1, \ldots, n-1 \quad (13.8b)$$

13.8 Solving the Valuation Problem

The valuation problem posed in section 13.4 asks for the forms of the contingent value functions $f_{i,\eta}$ for $i = 1$ and 2 and for $\eta = 0, 1, 2, \ldots, n - 1$. We already know the forms of the functions at time T_n from the terminal conditions of equations (13.8a, b). In this section we describe an algorithm for computing the value of $f_{i,\eta}(W^*, t^*)$ for any time t^* prior to time T_n and for any positive value of W^*. The first step is to specify and solve an "up-to-the-next-coupon" valuation problem.

The "Up-to-the-Next-Coupon" Problem

The up-to-the-next-coupon valuation problem is to compute the value of $f_{i,\nu}(W^0, t^0)$ when $h - 1$ coupons have already been paid and t^0 lies between T_{h-1} and T_h ($T_{h-1} < t^0 < T_h$, so ν is an element of the set $\{0, 1, 2, \ldots, h - 1\}$), *assuming that we know the form of the contingent value function $f_{i,\nu}$ at the time of the next coupon payment*, in other words, that we know (or can compute) the value of $f_{i,\nu}(W, T_h)$ for any positive value of W.

Computing $f_{i,\nu}(W^0, t^0)$ is virtually identical to the computation described at the beginning of section 12.4. Dividing the interval between t^0 and T_h into K subintervals of length Δt and defining a sequence of $K + 1$ points in time,

$$t_k = t^0 + (k - 1) \cdot \Delta t, \quad k = 1, 2, \ldots, K + 1 \quad (13.9)$$

we construct an array $W_{j,k}$, where the natural logarithm of $W_{j,k}$ is defined as

$$\ln[W_{j,k}] = \ln[W^0] + (k - 1) \cdot \mu \cdot \Delta t + (2 \cdot j - k - 1) \cdot \sigma \cdot \Delta t^{1/2},$$

$$j = 1, 2, \ldots, k; \ k = 1, 2, \ldots, K + 1 \quad (13.10)$$

Let $V_{j,k,i,\nu}$ denote the value of the ith security at time t_k when the value of the firm is $W_{j,k}$ and the firm has previously paid ν coupons in kind: $V_{j,k,i,\nu} = f_{i,\nu}(W_{j,k}, t_k)$. We compute the $V_{j,k,i,\nu}$ values using a recursion algorithm on k, beginning at $k = K + 1$ and proceeding backward to $k = 1$, where we have $V_{1,1,i,\nu} = f_{i,\nu}(W_{1,1}, t_1) = f_{i,\nu}(W^0, t^0)$.

The values of $V_{j,K+1,i,v}$ for $j = 1, 2, \ldots, K+1$ follow from the known form of the contingent value function at T_h:

$$V_{j,K+1,i,v} = f_{i,v}(W_{j,K+1}, T_h) \tag{13.11}$$

From this point, the algorithm continues as in section 12.4 following equation (12.10).

Remark

The same algorithm can be used when $t^0 = T_{h-1}$, but the value of $V_{1,1,i,v}$ is then interpreted as the *ex*-payment value of the ith security at time T_{h-1} when the *ex*-payment value of the firm is W^0 and the firm has paid v earlier coupons in kind: $V_{1,1,i,v} = g_{i,v,h-1}(W^0)$.

An Algorithm for Computing $f_{i,\eta}(W^*, t^*)$

Recall now the original problem: computing the value of $f_{i,\eta}(W^*, t^*)$. As was the case with the algorithm described in section 12.4, identification of the forms of the contingent value functions on the coupon payment dates provides enough information to identify the form of a contingent value function on any other date.[8] We can identify the forms of the contingent value functions on the coupon payment dates recursively, beginning at the maturity date of the PIK bond.

When the bond matures at time T_n the contingent value functions are the terminal conditions in equations (13.8a, b). Consider therefore the problem of identifying the form of $f_{i,\eta}(\cdot, T_j)$ for $T_j < T_n$ assuming that we have already identified the forms of $f_{i,\alpha}(\cdot, T_{j+1})$ for $\alpha = 0, 1, \ldots, j$.

From the transversality conditions in equations (13.6) and (13.7), we can compute the value of $f_{i,\eta}(W, T_j)$ from the values of $g_{i,\eta,j}(W - I_\eta)$ and $g_{i,\eta+1,j}(W)$. As pointed out in the remark following equation (13.11), we can compute the value of $g_{i,\eta,j}(W - I_\eta)$ from the (already identified) form of the contingent value function $f_{i,\eta}(\cdot, T_{j+1})$ using the algorithm for the up-to-the-next-coupon problem with $W^0 = W - I_\eta$, $t^0 = T_j$ and $v = \eta$. Similarly we can compute the value of $g_{i,\eta+1,j}(W)$ from the (already identified) form of the contingent value function $f_{i,\eta+1}(\cdot, T_{j+1})$ using the algorithm for the up-to-the-next-coupon problem with $W^0 = W$, $t^0 = T_j$ and $v = \eta + 1$. Thus we can compute the value of $f_{i,\eta}(W, T_j)$ for an arbitrary value of W. More generally, we can identify the form of the contingent value function $f_{i,\eta}(\cdot, T_j)$ from the forms of the contingent value

---

8. If the PIK bond has already paid $h - 1$ coupons and if t^* is prior to T_h so that $T_{h-1} < t^* < T_h$, we can compute $f_{i,\eta}(W^*, t^*)$ from the form of the contingent valuation function $f_{i,\eta}(\cdot, T_h)$ using the algorithm for the up-to-the-next-coupon problem with $W^0 = W^*$, $t^0 = t^*$ and $v = \eta$.

functions at time T_{j+1}. This recursive identification proceeds backward to $j = 1$. The appendix provides details of the construction.

13.9   An Example

This section examines several characteristics of the contingent value of the debt and equity of a firm capitalized with pay-in-kind debt. We suppose that the U.S. Treasury yield curve is flat and stationary at $R_f = 0.10$ (or 10% per annum) and that the volatility of the value of the firm is $\sigma = 0.20$ (or a volatility of 20% over one year).

We assume that the PIK bond pays interest semiannually (in cash or kind) at the rate of 12% per annum (so $R_c = 0.12$), that we are valuing the bond fifteen years before maturity, and that the bond has a contemporaneous principal value of $P = 88.318$. The bond would have a market value of 100.0 if market participants were certain that all thirty remaining coupons will be paid in cash and that the company will repay principal at maturity.

Figure 13.1 shows, with solid lines, the contingent value of the debt (upper panel) and equity (lower panel) of the firm. The dashed lines show what the securities would be worth if the company did not have the option to pay interest in kind.

When the value of the firm is less than about 30, the PIK option has negligible value. In this case the firm is unlikely (assuming the risk neutral drift rate) to redeem its debt at maturity—regardless of whether it pays interest in cash or kind—so the stock is virtually worthless and the value of the bond is equal to the value of the firm.

The PIK option also has negligible value when the value of the firm exceeds 300. In this case the firm is so well capitalized that it is unlikely (assuming the risk neutral drift rate) to ever pay interest in kind, and it is unlikely to fail to redeem its debt at maturity. The value of the bond is equal to the default-free value of a comparable coupon-bearing bond with no PIK option.

When the value of the firm is between about 50 and 250, the contingent value of the PIK bond is lower than the contingent value of a comparable coupon-bearing bond with no PIK option. As shown in the lower panel of figure 13.1, in this region shareholders derive value from the option to pay interest in kind.

The Optimal Interest Policy of the Firm

The first interest payment on the PIK bond comes due when the bond has 14.5 years remaining to maturity. Since the bond has an initial principal

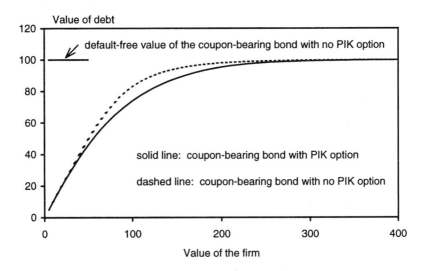

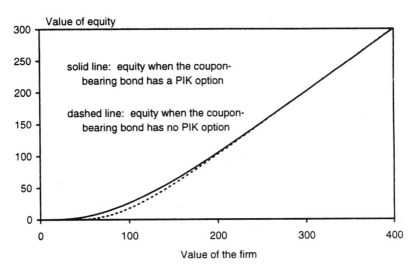

Figure 13.1
Contingent value of coupon-bearing debt and equity fifteen years before the debt matures

value of 88.318, the first interest obligation is for 5.299 (5.299 $= \frac{1}{2}$ of 12% of 88.318). The optimal interest policy of the firm is to pay the interest in cash if the contemporaneous *cum*-payment value of the firm exceeds 223.8 and to pay in kind if the *cum*-payment value of the firm is less than that critical value (223.8 is the value of W^c that satisfies equation (13.5) when $j = 1$ and $\eta = 0$).

The second interest payment comes due six months later, when the PIK bond has 14 years remaining to maturity. The interest obligation will be either 5.299 (if the first coupon was paid in cash) or 5.617 (if the first coupon was paid in kind, where 5.617 $= \frac{1}{2}$ of 12% of the sum of 88.318 and 5.299). If the interest obligation is 5.299, the optimal interest policy of the firm is to pay in cash if the *cum*-payment value of the firm exceeds 222.6 (222.6 is the value of W^c that satisfies equation (13.5) when $j = 2$ and $\eta = 0$). If the interest obligation is 5.617, the optimal policy is to pay in cash if the *cum*-payment value of the firm exceeds 236.1 (236.1 is the value of W^c that satisfies equation (13.5) when $j = 2$ and $\eta = 1$).

The top panel of figure 13.2 shows, for the first five interest payment dates, the critical values of the firm above which the optimal policy is to pay interest in cash. On any given payment date the critical value of the firm is an increasing function of the number of coupons previously paid in kind (indexed by the integer η) or, equivalently, of the contemporaneous principal amount of the PIK debt. Shareholders are better off if the firm pays interest with additional (risky) debt instead of (riskless) cash over a wider range of values of the firm the greater the firm's contemporaneous indebtedness. For a specified value of η—or, equivalently, for a specified amount of PIK debt—the critical value of the firm declines over time as the bond approaches maturity.

The bottom panel of figure 13.2 shows comparable critical values of the firm throughout the life of the bond for representative values of η.[9] The graph shows that the critical value of the firm is an increasing function of η (on any given coupon payment date) at all coupon payment dates and a declining function of time (at a specified value of η) for all values of η.

An Alternative Comparison

Figure 13.1 contrasted the contingent value of the PIK bond to the contingent value of an otherwise comparable coupon-bearing bond with no PIK option. The difference between the contingent values is the cost to bondholders (and the value to stockholders) of the firm's option to pay interest in kind.

---

9. The penultimate interest payment six months prior to maturity is the 29th payment, so the largest possible value of η at that time is $\eta = 28$.

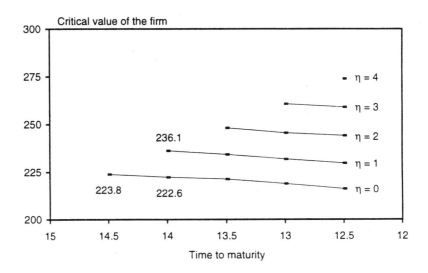

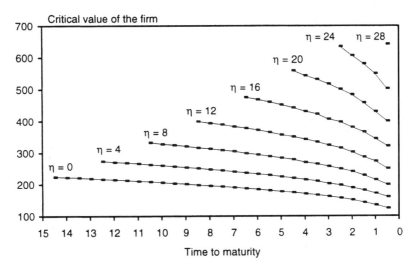

Figure 13.2
Critical values of the firm (above which the firm will pay interest on the PIK debt in cash)

We can also compare the contingent value of the PIK bond to the contingent value of a fifteen-year *zero-coupon* bond maturing at the same time as the PIK bond and promising to pay, at maturity, an amount equal to what the PIK bond would be obligated to pay if the PIK bond *never* made a cash interest payment prior to maturity. The difference between these contingent values measures the value to shareholders of the option to pay interest on the PIK bond in cash.

If the firm made all 29 interest payments prior to maturity in kind, the principal amount of PIK debt outstanding at maturity would be 478.541, because $(1 + \frac{1}{2} \cdot R_c)^{29} \cdot P = 478.541$ when $R_c = 0.12$ and $P = 88.318$. The interest on that principal would be 28.712 ($28.712 = \frac{1}{2}$ of 12% of 478.541), so the total liability of the firm to its creditors would be 507.253. The upper panel of figure 13.3 compares the contingent value of the fifteen-year PIK bond to the contingent value of a zero-coupon bond promising to pay 507.253 at maturity in fifteen years. (The default-free value of a promise to pay 507.253 in 15 years is 113.185 when the yield on Treasury debt is 10% per annum.) The value of the PIK bond is substantially lower than the value of the zero-coupon bond when the value of the firm exceeds 200. This follows because, at high values of the firm, the firm will choose to exercise its option to pay interest in cash to maximize the value of equity. (The lower panel of figure 13.3 shows how the option to pay interest in cash enhances the value of equity.) At values of the firm below 100, the firm is unlikely to make any interest payments in cash and the value of the PIK bond is comparable to the value of the zero-coupon bond.

A Joint Comparison

Figure 13.4 shows that the contingent value of the PIK bond is lower than (1) the contingent value of a comparable coupon-bearing bond with no PIK option *and* (2) the contingent value of a zero-coupon bond promising to pay 507.253 in fifteen years. This illustrates the value of the option to pay interest *either* in cash *or* in kind. The option to pay in cash (instead of being obligated to pay in kind) is most valuable when the value of the firm is high. The option to pay in kind (instead of being obligated to pay in cash) is most valuable at more modest values of the firm.

Appendix

This appendix provides computational details for constructing the contingent value functions for the firm's PIK debt and equity on the coupon payment dates of the debt.

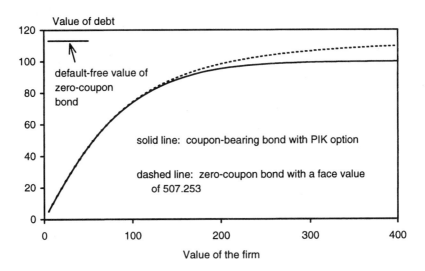

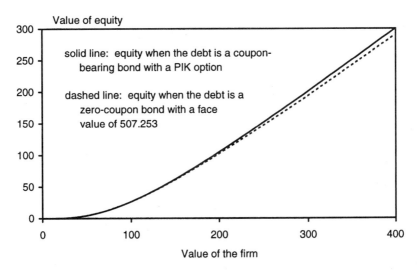

Figure 13.3
Contingent value of debt and equity fifteen years before the debt matures

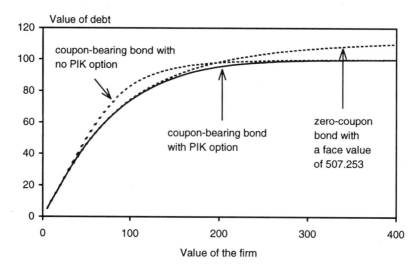

Figure 13.4
Contingent value of debt fifteen years before it matures

The PIK bond promises to pay interest (in cash or kind) semiannually. Divide the interval between consecutive interest payments into K subintervals of length $\Delta t = 0.5/K$. (The value of K need not be the same here as the value of K specified in the text preceding equation (13.9).)

Let $W_{\min}$ denote a value of the firm so low that the firm's equity is essentially worthless, and let $W_{\max}$ denote a value of the firm so high that the firm is virtually certain to repay principal at maturity. (We set $W_{\min} = 1$ and $W_{\max} = 2000$ for the numerical example in section 13.9.) Define a sequence of values of the firm, beginning with $W_1 = W_{\min}$ and proceeding recursively:

$$\ln[W_{j+1}] = \ln[W_j] + \sigma \cdot \Delta t^{1/2}, \qquad j = 1, 2, \ldots, J \qquad \text{(A13.1)}$$

where the terminal integer J is chosen so that $W_{J-1} < W_{\max} \leq W_J$.

Let $\Phi_{j,h,i,\eta}$ denote the *cum*-payment value of the ith security at time T_h (the time of the hth coupon payment) when the *cum*-payment value of the firm is W_j and the firm has paid η earlier coupons in kind:

$$\Phi_{j,h,i,\eta} = f_{i,\eta}(W_j, T_h) \qquad \text{(A13.2)}$$

We can approximate the form of $f_{i,\eta}(\cdot, T_h)$ with the values of $\Phi_{1,h,i,\eta}$, $\Phi_{2,h,i,\eta}, \ldots, \Phi_{J,h,i,\eta}$ using linear interpolation as outlined at equations (A12.3) to (A12.5) in the appendix to chapter 12.

Section 13.8 pointed out that identification of the forms of the contingent value functions on the bond's coupon payment dates provides sufficient information to identify the forms of those functions on any other date. Hence it suffices to compute the values of the $\Phi_{j,h,i,\eta}$ terms. We compute the terms recursively, beginning at $h = n$.

Constructing the $\Phi_{j,h,i,\eta}$ Terms for $h = n$

The values of $\Phi_{j,n,i,\eta}$ for $j = 1, 2, \ldots, J$ follow from the terminal conditions specified at equations (13.8a, b):

$$\Phi_{j,n,1,\eta} = f_{1,\eta}(W_j, T_n) = \min[W_j, P \cdot (1 + \tfrac{1}{2} R_c)^{\eta+1}] \tag{A13.3a}$$

$$\Phi_{j,n,2,\eta} = f_{2,\eta}(W_j, T_n) = \max[0, W_j - P \cdot (1 + \tfrac{1}{2} R_c)^{\eta+1}] \tag{A13.3b}$$

Computing the $\Phi_{j,h,i,\eta}$ Terms for $h < n$

Consider now the problem of computing $\Phi_{j,h,i,\eta}$ for $j = 1, 2, \ldots, J$ and for a value of h less than n, assuming that we already know the values of $\Phi_{j,h+1,i,\eta}$ and $\Phi_{j,h+1,i,\eta+1}$ for $j = 1, 2, \ldots, J$.

Based on the division of the interval between T_h and T_{h+1} into K subintervals, we can define a sequence of $K + 1$ points in time:

$$t_k = T_h + (k - 1) \cdot \Delta t, \qquad k = 1, 2, \ldots, K + 1 \tag{A13.4}$$

Observe that $t_1 = T_h$ and that $t_{K+1} = T_{h+1}$.

We approximate the evolution of the log of the value of the firm between T_h and T_{h+1} as a binomial random walk over each of the subintervals:

$$\ln[W(t_{k+1})] - \ln[W^x(t_k)] = \sigma \cdot \Delta t^{1/2} \cdot e_k, \qquad k = 1, 2, \ldots, K \tag{A13.5}$$

where the random variable e_k can have the value $+1$ with probability $\tfrac{1}{2}$ and the value -1 with probability $\tfrac{1}{2}$.[10] Thus, if the *ex*-payment value of the firm is W_j at time t_k, the *cum*-payment value of the firm at time t_{k+1} will be either W_{j+1} or W_{j-1}.

Define now an array $V_{j,k,i,\eta}$ for $j = 1, 2, \ldots, J$ and $k = 1, 2, \ldots, K + 1$. For values of $k > 1$, $V_{j,k,i,\eta}$ denotes the *cum*-payment value of the ith security at time t_k when the *cum*-payment value of the firm is W_j and the firm has paid η earlier coupons in kind:

$$V_{j,k,i,\eta} = f_{i,\eta}(W_j, t_k), \qquad k > 1 \tag{A13.6}$$

For $k = 1$, $V_{j,k,i,\eta}$ denotes the *ex*-payment value of the ith security at time T_h when the *ex*-payment value of the firm is W_j and the firm has paid η earlier coupons in kind:

---

10. As in the appendix to chapter 12 (see text at equation A12.8 and note 13 in chapter 12), we here take advantage of the observation, in appendix C to chapter 2, that contingent value functions are invariant with respect to the value of the drift rate μ and set μ equal to zero for computational simplicity.

$$V_{j,1,i,\eta} = g_{i,\eta,h}(W_j) = \lim_{\varepsilon \downarrow 0} f_{i,\eta}(W_j, T_h + \varepsilon) \qquad\qquad\qquad \text{(A13.7)}$$

We will first show how to compute the $V_{j,k,i,\eta}$ terms recursively from $k = K + 1$ to $k = 1$, and then show that we can use the transversality conditions in equations (13.6) and (13.7) to compute the $\Phi_{j,h,i,\eta}$ terms from the $V_{j,1,i,\eta}$ terms and the $V_{j,1,i,\eta+1}$ terms.

Constructing the $V_{j,k,i,\eta}$ Terms for $k = K + 1$

The values of $V_{j,K+1,i,\eta}$ follow from equations (A13.6), (A13.4), and (A13.2):

$$V_{j,K+1,i,\eta} = f_{i,\eta}(W_j, t_{K+1}) = f_{i,\eta}(W_j, T_{h+1}) = \Phi_{j,h+1,i,\eta}, \qquad j = 1, 2, \ldots, J \qquad \text{(A13.8)}$$

Since, by hypothesis, we know the values of the $\Phi_{j,h+1,i,\eta}$ terms, we can construct the values of the $V_{j,K+1,i,\eta}$ terms.

Computing the $V_{j,k,i,\eta}$ Terms for $k < K + 1$

Assume now that we know $V_{j,k+1,i,\eta}$ for $j = 1, 2, \ldots, J$ and that we want to compute $V_{j,k,i,\eta}$ for $j = 1, 2, \ldots, J$. If j is greater than 1 and less than J, we can compute $V_{j,k,i,\eta}$ from an arbitrage pricing argument.[11]

Over the subinterval from t_k to t_{k+1} the value of the firm will evolve from W_j to either W_{j+1} or W_{j-1}. Assuming that the markets do not allow opportunities for riskless arbitrage profits, the value of the ith security at time t_k, when the value of the firm is W_j and the firm has paid η earlier coupons in kind, must be

$$V_{j,k,i,\eta} = h \cdot W_j + Q \qquad\qquad\qquad \text{(A13.9)}$$

where h and Q satisfy the equations

$$V_{j+1,k+1,i,\eta} = h \cdot W_{j+1} + Q \cdot e^{R_f \cdot \Delta t} \qquad\qquad \text{(A13.10a)}$$

$$V_{j-1,k+1,i,\eta} = h \cdot W_{j-1} + Q \cdot e^{R_f \cdot \Delta t} \qquad\qquad \text{(A13.10b)}$$

The foregoing algorithm can be applied recursively for $k = K, K - 1, \ldots, 1$, ending with the computation of $V_{j,1,i,\eta}$ for $j = 1, 2, \ldots, J$.

Comment

The values of $V_{j,1,i,\eta+1}$ for $j = 1, 2, \ldots, J$ can be computed similarly from the $\Phi_{j,h+1,i,\eta+1}$ terms.

---

11. If $j = 1$, then $W_j = W_{min}$ and the equity of the firm is essentially worthless. In this case we can set $V_{1,k,1,\eta} = W_1$ and $V_{1,k,2,\eta} = 0$. If $j = J$, then $W_j \geq W_{max}$ and the firm's debt is essentially default free. In this case we can set $V_{J,k,1,\eta}$ equal to the default-free value of the bond, and we can set $V_{J,k,2,\eta}$ equal to the difference between W_J and $V_{J,k,1,\eta}$.

Computing the $\Phi_{j,h,i,\eta}$ Terms from the $V_{j,1,i,\eta}$ and the $V_{j,1,i,\eta+1}$ Terms

Consider now the problem of computing $\Phi_{j,h,i,\eta}$ for $i = 1$. Since $\Phi_{j,h,1,\eta} = f_{1,\eta}(W_j, T_h)$—see equation (A13.2)—the transversality condition in equation (13.7) implies that

$$
\Phi_{j,h,1,\eta} = \begin{cases} g_{1,\eta+1,h}(W_j) & \text{if } W_j \le I_\eta \\ \min[g_{1,\eta+1,h}(W_j), g_{1,\eta,h}(W_j - I_\eta) + I_\eta] & \text{if } I_\eta < W_j \end{cases} \quad \text{(A13.11)}
$$

where $I_\eta = \frac{1}{2} R_c \cdot P \cdot (1 + \frac{1}{2} R_c)^\eta$. It follows that we can compute the value of $\Phi_{j,h,1,\eta}$ if we can compute $g_{1,\eta,h}(W_j - I_\eta)$ and $g_{1,\eta+1,h}(W_j)$.

If $W_j - I_\eta$ is greater than W_1, we can compute the value of $g_{1,\eta,h}(W_j - I_\eta)$ by linear interpolation.[12] Identify the integer $m \in \{1, 2, \ldots, J - 1\}$ such that $W_m \le W_j - I_\eta < W_{m+1}$, and compute the value of α that satisfies the equation

$$
W_j - I_\eta = \alpha \cdot W_m + (1 - \alpha) \cdot W_{m+1} \quad \text{(A13.12)}
$$

We can then approximate $g_{1,\eta,h}(W_j - I_\eta)$ as

$$
g_{1,\eta,h}(W_j - I_\eta) = \alpha \cdot g_{1,\eta,h}(W_m) + (1 - \alpha) \cdot g_{1,\eta,h}(W_{m+1}) \quad \text{(A13.13)}
$$

or, from the definition of $V_{j,1,1,\eta}$ in equation (A13.7), as

$$
g_{1,\eta,h}(W_j - I_\eta) = \alpha \cdot V_{m,1,1,\eta} + (1 - \alpha) \cdot V_{m+1,1,1,\eta} \quad \text{(A13.14)}
$$

We can compute similarly the value of $g_{1,\eta+1,h}(W_j)$ from the $V_{j,1,1,\eta+1}$ terms.

Consider next the problem of computing $\Phi_{j,h,2,\eta}$. Since $\Phi_{j,h,2,\eta} = f_{2,\eta}(W_j, T_h)$, the transversality condition in equation (13.6) implies that

$$
\Phi_{j,h,2,\eta} = \begin{cases} g_{2,\eta+1,h}(W_j) & \text{if } W_j \le I_\eta \\ \max[g_{2,\eta+1,h}(W_j), g_{2,\eta,h}(W_j - I_\eta)] & \text{if } I_\eta < W_j \end{cases} \quad \text{(A13.15)}
$$

We can compute the value of $g_{2,\eta,h}(W_j - I_\eta)$ by linear interpolation from the $V_{j,1,2,\eta}$ terms as described in the preceding paragraph, we can compute similarly the value of $g_{2,\eta+1,h}(W_j)$ by linear interpolation from the $V_{j,1,2,\eta+1}$ terms, and we can use those values to compute $\Phi_{j,h,2,\eta}$ as in equation (A13.15).

This algorithm can be applied recursively for $h = n - 1, n - 2, \ldots, 1$, leading to the computation of all of the $\Phi_{j,h,i,\eta}$ terms.

---

12. If $W_j - I_\eta$ is less than or equal to W_1, then $W_j - I_\eta$ is less than or equal to $W_{\min}$, and we can set $g_{1,\eta,h}(W_j - I_\eta) = W_j - I_\eta$.

IV

DIVIDENDS AND OTHER DISCRETIONARY DISTRIBUTIONS TO SHAREHOLDERS

14 Dividend-Paying Stock

This chapter examines the contingent valuation of securities issued by a firm capitalized, in part, with common stock that pays a cash dividend.

All of the analyses in the preceding chapters assumed that the firm could neither pay a dividend nor repurchase its stock until all of the firm's debt had been redeemed—or, in the case of convertible debt, converted into stock. This strong assumption simplified the analyses because, prior to chapter 11, it allowed us to avoid addressing the consequences of disbursements to securities holders prior to redemption of the corporation's debt. However, chapters 11 and 12 broadened the earlier analytical framework by supposing that the firm is obligated to make payments to *creditors* at different points in time, so there is not now any reason why we should not also examine dividend payments to *shareholders*.[1]

14.1 Framework of the Analysis

We begin, as before, by stating our assumptions regarding the capital structure of the firm and the consequences of default and bankruptcy.

Corporate Capital Structure

We assume the firm is capitalized with dividend-paying stock and coupon-bearing debt, and that it liquidates assets to finance both dividend payments and interest payments.

The debt promises to pay an aggregate coupon C every six months up to and including maturity, and promises to repay its aggregate principal P at maturity. We assume that the debt originally promised to make a total of n interest payments, at times $T_1, T_2, \ldots, T_n$, where T_n is the maturity date of the debt and $T_j = T_{j-1} + 0.5$ for $j = 2, 3, \ldots, n$. The indenture or loan agreement for the debt provides that if the issuer fails to make a coupon payment, the holders of the debt have the right to accelerate, so the principal of the debt becomes immediately due and payable.

The common stock is a claim on the residual value of the firm after the debt has been redeemed at time T_n. In addition the stock may pay a dividend to shareholders immediately after each interest payment prior to time T_n.[2]

---

1. We focus on dividend payments, but the analysis would not be different if the company repurchased stock in lieu of paying dividends. What matters is that the company distributes cash to its shareholders.

2. We assume a semiannual dividend following payment of interest on the debt for expositional simplicity. Assuming quarterly or annual dividends, and/or dividends paid at dates other than interest payment dates, would not lead to any materially different results. The stock may also pay dividends following redemption of the debt at time T_n, but any such dividends are irrelevant to the present analysis because they are paid after the shareholders have become the sole claimants to the earnings and assets of the firm.

We denote the *cum*-payment value of the debt at time t as $V_1(t)$ and the *cum*-payment value of equity as $V_2(t)$. The *cum*-payment value of the firm is the sum of the *cum*-payment values of the firm's securities: $W(t) = V_1(t) + V_2(t)$.

Corporate Dividend Policy

T_j is the time of the jth interest and dividend payment. We denote the aggregate dividend paid at time T_j as D_j, and we assume that the dividend is a function of the contemporaneous *cum*-payment value of the firm:[3]

$$D_j = D_j(W(T_j)), \qquad j = 1, 2, \ldots, n-1 \tag{14.1}$$

The function $D_j(\cdot)$ is such that $D_j(W)$ is less than $W - C$ for all values of W greater than C. As a result the firm never pays a dividend greater than its value net of the contemporaneous coupon payment. If $W(T_j)$ is less than C, then, as described below, the firm defaults and no dividend is paid.

The functions $D_1(\cdot), D_2(\cdot), \ldots, D_{n-1}(\cdot)$ represent the dividend policy of the firm.[4] The dividend policy functions are analogous to the interest policy functions identified at equation (13.4) describing cash coupon payments on a pay-in-kind bond. The latter functions were *derived* (in section 13.5) by identifying when paying interest on a PIK bond in cash is in the best interest of shareholders. Here we merely *assert* the existence of the dividend policy functions and defer until chapter 15 the question of whether the functions can be derived as a consequence of managerial efforts to maximize the value of equity.

***Ex*-payment Values**

At time T_j the firm pays C to its creditors and $D_j(W(T_j))$ to its shareholders. Following the payments, the value of the debt and equity decline by corresponding amounts. The *ex*-payment values of the securities are

---

3. Specifying D_j as a function of only the value of the firm is not as restrictive as it might appear. The specification includes cases where dividends are a function of a variable that itself depends on the value of the firm—such as the value of the firm's equity. See example A in section 14.5.

4. This terminology follows the observation of Marsh and Merton (1987, p. 11n. 10) that "the term 'dividend policy' refers to the contingent schedule or plan for future dividend payments." Lease, John, Kalay, Loewenstein, and Sarig (2000, p. 1) define dividend policy similarly as "the payout policy that management follows in determining the size and pattern of cash distributions to shareholders over time." Merton (1973, p. 155n. 24) distinguishes between "knowing future dividends and dividend policy. With the former, one knows, currently, the actual amounts of future payments while, with the latter, one knows the conditional future payments, conditional on (currently unknown) future values, such as the stock price."

$$V_1^x(T_j) = V_1(T_j) - C, \qquad j = 1, 2, \ldots, n-1 \tag{14.2a}$$

$$V_2^x(T_j) = V_2(T_j) - D_j(W(T_j)), \qquad j = 1, 2, \ldots, n-1 \tag{14.2b}$$

The value of the firm is the sum of the values of the securities issued by the firm. Therefore at time T_j the value of the firm declines by $C + D_j(W(T_j))$ and the *ex*-payment value of the firm is

$$W^x(T_j) = W(T_j) - C - D_j(W(T_j)), \qquad j = 1, 2, \ldots, n-1 \tag{14.3}$$

The *ex*-payment value of the firm is identical to the *cum*-payment value of the firm at any time other than a payment date.

Default and Bankruptcy

If the *cum*-payment value of the firm is less than C at time T_j for $T_j < T_n$, the firm can not satisfy its contemporaneous obligation to pay interest on its debt. The resulting default triggers acceleration of the maturity of the debt and gives creditors a claim for immediate repayment of principal as well as for payment of the missed coupon.[5]

Following default and acceleration, the firm goes into bankruptcy. We assume that bankruptcy results in an instantaneous and costless liquidation of the assets of the firm and distribution of the proceeds according to the absolute priority rule. Creditors have a senior claim on the firm in excess of the value of the firm (which, by hypothesis, is less than C) and thus receive all of the proceeds of the liquidation.

If the firm pays the first $n-1$ coupons, the debt will remain outstanding until maturity at time T_n. Creditors then have a claim on the firm for payment of the last coupon and for repayment of principal. If the firm defaults on this claim it is liquidated and the proceeds distributed pursuant to the absolute priority rule.

14.2 The Valuation Problem

We assume that there exists a pair of functions, f_1 and f_2, with two arguments: time and the *cum*-payment value of the firm, such that the *cum*-payment value of the debt and equity at time $t \le T_n$ can be calculated as

$$V_i(t) = f_i(W(t), t), \qquad i = 1, 2 \tag{14.4}$$

---

5. For reasons comparable to those stated in the appendix to chapter 11, we suppress the possibility that the firm might default strategically on its promise to pay a coupon prior to maturity.

The valuation problem is to identify the forms of these contingent value functions.

In the special case of time $t = T_n$ our assumptions regarding default and bankruptcy imply that

$$f_1(W, T_n) = \min[W, P + C] \tag{14.5a}$$

$$f_2(W, T_n) = \max[0, W - P - C] \tag{14.5b}$$

We want to extend these terminal contingent value functions backward in time, to times prior to the maturity of the debt.

14.3 Transversality Conditions

At time T_j for $T_j < T_n$, the firm is contractually obligated to make an interest payment, and it may make a dividend payment. The payments lead to transversality conditions analogous to those described in section 12.3.

If the *cum*-payment value of the firm at time T_j is less than C, the firm will default on its interest obligation, the *cum*-payment value of the debt will be equal to the value of the firm and the stock will be worthless. If the *cum*-payment value of the firm exceeds C, the firm liquidates assets and pays its creditors the required coupon.

Let $g_{i,j}(W^x)$ denote the *ex*-payment value of the ith security at time T_j when the *ex*-payment value of the firm is W^x. (As in equation 12.6, $g_{i,j}(W^x)$ is the limiting value of $f_i(W^x, T_j + \varepsilon)$ as ε goes to zero from above.) If the *cum*-payment value of the firm at time T_j is W, and if W is greater than C, then, as described at equation (14.3), the *ex*-payment value of the firm is $W - C - D_j(W)$. The *ex*-payment values of the debt and equity will be $g_{1,j}(W - C - D_j(W))$ and $g_{2,j}(W - C - D_j(W))$, respectively. The *cum*-payment value of the debt will be equal to the *ex*-payment value of the debt plus the contemporaneous coupon payment, or $g_{1,j}(W - C - D_j(W)) + C$. The *cum*-payment value of equity will be equal to the *ex*-payment value of equity plus the contemporaneous dividend payment, or $g_{2,j}(W - C - D_j(W)) + D_j(W)$. Thus the transversality conditions for the debt and equity are

$$f_1(W, T_j) = \begin{cases} W & \text{if } W \leq C \\ g_{1,j}(W - C - D_j(W)) + C & \text{if } C < W \end{cases} \tag{14.6a}$$

$$f_2(W, T_j) = \begin{cases} 0 & \text{if } W \leq C \\ g_{2,j}(W - C - D_j(W)) + D_j(W) & \text{if } C < W \end{cases} \tag{14.6b}$$

14.4   Solving the Valuation Problem

The valuation problem posed in section 14.2 asks for the forms of the contingent value functions f_1 and f_2. We already know the forms of the functions at time T_n from the terminal conditions of equations (14.5a, b). The value of $f_i(W^*, t^*)$ for any positive value of W^* and for any time t^* prior to T_n can be computed with an algorithm virtually identical to the algorithm described in section 12.4. The only change is that we have to modify the transversality conditions to account for dividend payments to shareholders—compare equations (14.6a, b) with equations (12.7a, b). The appendix to this chapter provides details.

14.5   Some Examples

The numerical examples in this section illustrate the contingent valuation of securities issued by a firm capitalized with dividend-paying stock. We assume the yield on U.S. Treasury debt is constant at $R_f = 0.10$ (or 10% per annum) and that the volatility of the value of the firm is $\sigma = 0.20$ (or a volatility of 20% over one year).

The firm is capitalized with debt that pays interest at the rate of 10% per annum and has a principal value of $P = 101.963$, so the semiannual coupon payment is $C = 5.098$. Suppose that we are valuing the debt and equity of the firm fifteen years before the debt matures and that a coupon has just been paid, so there are thirty coupons remaining to be paid. Ignoring the risk of default, the debt has a default-free value of 100.

Example A

The first example assumes the firm pays a semiannual dividend equal to 5% of the contemporaneous value of equity:

$$D_j(W) = 0.05 \cdot f_2(W, T_j), \qquad j = 1, 2, \ldots, n - 1 \tag{14.7}$$

Figure 14.1 shows, with solid lines, the contingent value of the debt (upper panel) and equity (lower panel) of the firm. The dashed lines show what the securities would be worth if the firm paid no dividends to its shareholders. The policy of paying a regular dividend enhances the value of equity, and reduces the value of the debt, when the value of the firm is above about 50. It has virtually no effect when the value of the firm is low, the stock is (very nearly) worthless and dividends are (consequently) negligible.

The dividend policy specified in equation (14.7) also has virtually no effect on debt and equity values at very high values of the firm.

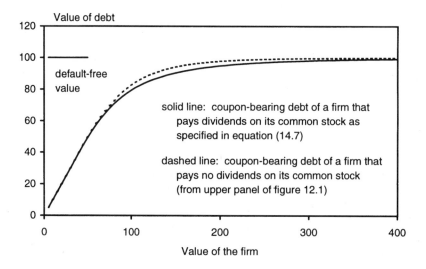

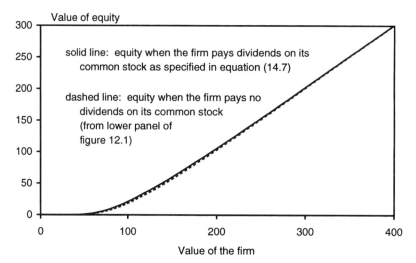

Figure 14.1
Contingent value of debt and equity fifteen years before the debt matures

As the value of the firm increases, the value of the debt asymptotically approaches the default-free value of the debt and the value of equity approaches the difference between the value of the firm and the default-free value of the debt, regardless of whether or not the firm pays the dividend prescribed in equation (14.7).

The consequences of the dividend policy in equation (14.7) are not difficult to understand. Dividends are funded by liquidating assets that would otherwise be available to satisfy future claims of creditors. Paying dividends cannot make the debt more valuable and, excluding the case of negligible leverage, will make it less valuable.[6] The reduction in the value of the debt due to prospective dividend payments is matched by a corresponding increase in the value of equity.

Example B

The second example assumes that subject to one caveat, the firm pays a fixed dividend of 0.75 every six months, regardless of the value of the firm and regardless of the value of the firm's equity. (The exception is that the firm pays no dividend if the value of the firm is less than 25% of the principal value of its debt. This precludes the possibility that the firm might pay a dividend in excess of its value net of the contemporaneous interest payment to creditors.) The dividend policy function is

$$D_j(W) = \begin{cases} 0.00 & \text{if } W < 0.25 \cdot P \\ 0.75 & \text{if } W \geq 0.25 \cdot P, \ j = 1, 2, \ldots, n-1 \end{cases} \tag{14.8}$$

Figure 14.2 shows, with solid lines, the contingent value of the debt (upper panel) and equity (lower panel) of the firm. The dashed lines show what the securities would be worth if the firm paid no dividends to its shareholders. As in example A the policy of paying a regular dividend reduces the value of the debt and enhances the value of equity. However, it has a diminishing effect on debt and equity values as the value of the firm increases above 100.

Comment

The preceding examples demonstrate that the contingent value of debt and equity is not invariant with respect to the decision of the firm to pay dividends to its shareholders. A comparison of the two examples suggests that contingent debt and equity values also depend on the *details* of the dividend policy of the firm.

Figure 14.3 shows (with a solid line) the contingent value of the firm's debt when the firm pays a (nearly) constant dividend, as in equation

6. See similarly Lease et al. (2000, pp. 75–78)

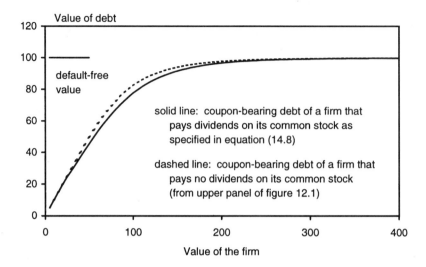

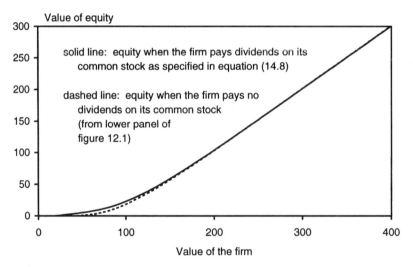

Figure 14.2
Contingent value of debt and equity fifteen years before the debt matures

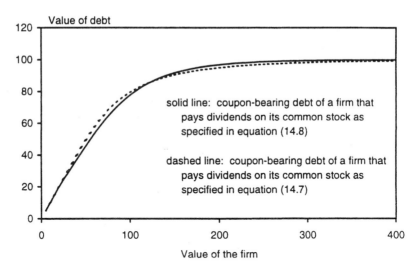

Figure 14.3
Contingent value of debt fifteen years before the debt matures, for two alternative dividend policies

(14.8), and also shows (with a dashed line) the contingent value of the debt when the corporation pays a dividend proportional to the value of equity, as in equation (14.7). The (nearly) constant dividend has a greater effect on the value of the debt when the value of the firm is less than about 125, and it has a smaller effect when the value of the firm exceeds 125. This follows because the (nearly) constant dividend leads to relatively larger dividend payments when the value of the firm (and hence the value of equity) is low, and to relatively smaller payments when the value of the firm and the value of equity are high.

Appendix

The algorithm for computing the value of $f_i(W^*, t^*)$ for any positive value of W^* and for any time t^* prior to T_n is, with one exception, identical to the algorithm described in section 12.4 and the appendix to chapter 12. The exception is that we have to accommodate the change in the transversality conditions from equations (12.7a, b) to equations (14.6a, b) by replacing equation (A12.14) with

$$\Phi_{j,h,1} = \begin{cases} W_j & \text{if } W_j \le C \\ g_{1,h}(W_j - C - D_h(W_j)) + C & \text{if } C < W_j \end{cases} \tag{A14.1}$$

and by replacing equation (A12.18) with

$$\Phi_{j,h,2} = \begin{cases} 0 & \text{if } W_j \leq C \\ g_{2,h}(W_j - C - D_h(W_j)) + D_h(W_j) & \text{if } C < W_j \end{cases} \qquad \text{(A14.2)}$$

In some cases the dividend policy of the firm may be an indirect function of the value of the firm, and we may not initially know the forms of the $D_h(\cdot)$ functions. Equations (A14.1) and (A14.2) have to be modified in such cases. For example, suppose that the dividend paid at time T_h is a known function, denoted $\varphi_h(\cdot)$, of the value of the equity of the firm,[7] so that

$$D_h(W) = \varphi_h(f_2(W, T_h)) \qquad \text{(A14.3)}$$

This equation says that the dividend paid at time T_h depends on the value of the firm because (1) the dividend depends on the value of the firm's equity (through the function $\varphi_h(\cdot)$) and because (2) the value of the firm's equity depends on the value of the firm (through the contingent value function $f_2(\cdot, T_h)$). Since we do not initially know the form of $f_2(\cdot, T_h)$, we also do not initially know the form of $D_h(\cdot)$.

For the case where $D_h(\cdot)$ is as described in equation (A14.3), equation (A14.2) would be replaced by an implicit equation for $\Phi_{j,h,2}$:

$$\Phi_{j,h,2} = \begin{cases} 0 & \text{if } W_j \leq C \\ g_{2,h}(W_j - C - \varphi_h(\Phi_{j,h,2})) + \varphi_h(\Phi_{j,h,2}) & \text{if } C < W_j \end{cases} \qquad \text{(A14.4)}$$

Similarly equation (A14.1) would become

$$\Phi_{j,h,1} = \begin{cases} W_j & \text{if } W_j \leq C \\ g_{1,h}(W_j - C - \varphi_h(W_j - \Phi_{j,h,1})) + C & \text{if } C < W_j \end{cases} \qquad \text{(A14.5)}$$

where we here make use of the adding up constraint that $\Phi_{j,h,1} + \Phi_{j,h,2} = W_j$.

---

7. See example A in section 14.5, where $\varphi_h(x) = 0.05 \cdot x$.

15 Optimal Dividend Policy

The preceding chapter examined the contingent value of the securities issued by a levered firm that pays dividends on its common stock. The dividend policy of the firm was characterized by a sequence of *exogenously specified* functions that relate the dividend paid on a particular date to the contemporaneous value of the firm.[1] However, corporate dividend policy is discretionary with the management of a firm and should be identified *endogenously*, in a manner analogous to the identification of discretionary policies for early redemption of debt and for interest payments on pay-in-kind bonds: as a consequence of managerial efforts to maximize the value of equity.[2]

This chapter derives the optimal dividend policy of a firm in the context of a conventional contingent value model and compares that policy to observed corporate behavior. We find a material difference between the dividend policy that maximizes the value of equity and observed dividend policies, and we conclude that conventional contingent value models do not have an internal structure sufficiently rich to support a derivation of the dividend policy of the firm based on maximization of shareholder value.

15.1 An Unconstrained Optimal Dividend Policy

Consider first the problem of identifying the optimal dividend policy of the firm when there are no constraints on payments to shareholders. For simplicity, we retain the analytical framework specified in section 14.1: the firm is capitalized with debt that promises to pay a coupon C every six months (at times $T_1, T_2, \ldots, T_n$) and to repay principal P at maturity at time T_n, as well as equity that may pay a dividend immediately after each interest payment. For reasons that will become clear shortly, we can assume that we have already derived the optimal dividend policy functions at times $T_2, T_3, \ldots, T_{n-1}$ and that we have identified the contingent value functions for the debt and equity for values of t greater than T_1. What remains is to identify the optimal dividend policy at time T_1.

The Optimal Dividend at Time T_1

Assuming that managers act in the best interest of shareholders, the firm will pay a dividend D_1 at time T_1 to maximize the *cum*-payment value of equity.

---

1. See text at equation (14.1) and the examples in section 14.5.

2. Marsh and Merton (1987, p. 11n. 10) observe that "a dividend policy is ... much like the state-contingent functions for optimal control variables, which are derived from the solution of a stochastic dynamic control programming problem." Corporate policies for early redemption of debt were derived in chapters 6 and 8. Policies for paying interest on PIK bonds were derived in chapter 13.

Given the dividend payment D_1, the *cum*-payment value of equity is

$$V_2(T_1) = g_{2,1}(W(T_1) - C - D_1) + D_1 \tag{15.1}$$

where $g_{2,1}(W(T_1) - C - D_1)$ is the *ex*-payment value of equity at T_1 when the *ex*-payment value of the firm is $W(T_1) - C - D_1$. The marginal benefit to shareholders of an increase in D_1 is

$$\frac{dV_2}{dD_1} = 1 - g'_{2,1}(W(T_1) - C - D_1) \tag{15.2}$$

where $g'_{2,1}(\cdot)$ is the derivative of $g_{2,1}(\cdot)$. The *ex*-payment value of equity increases at less than a dollar-for-dollar rate with the *ex*-payment value of the firm (because a larger *ex*-payment value of the firm enhances the *ex*-payment value of the debt as well as the *ex*-payment value of equity), so $g'_{2,1}(W(T_1) - C - D_1)$ is less than unity for all positive values of $W(T_1) - C - D_1$. Equation (15.2) shows that dV_2/dD_1 is then positive for all values of D_1 (up to the limiting value of $W(T_1) - C$), so the *cum*-payment value of equity is a *monotonically increasing* function of D_1: shareholders are better off with an extra dollar in their own pockets than if the firm retains the dollar.[3] It follows that the firm, acting in the best interest of shareholders, will pay the largest dividend possible at T_1; that is, it will pay $W(T_1) - C$.

More particularly, in the absence of any restrictions on dividend payments, the *cum*-payment value of equity is maximized by *liquidating the firm at the first opportunity and paying the proceeds to shareholders*, leaving creditors holding claims on an empty shell.[4]

Comment

The optimal dividend policy at time T_1 has a striking implication: regardless of the firm's contractual obligations to creditors, the firm will make only the first payment on its debt.[5] Immediately following that payment the firm is liquidated and the proceeds paid to shareholders.

---

3. Lease, John, Kalay, Loewenstein, and Sarig (2000) observe (p. 77) that shareholders are better off with a larger dividend because "they receive the full dividend payment, yet the value of their equity claim falls by less than the full dividend as the bondholders share some of the dividend's effect on the value of the firm," and (p. 76) that "dividends are a means to transfer a firm's assets from the common pool shared by all the security holders of the firm to the exclusive ownership of the shareholders."

4. This optimal dividend policy was noted by Black and Scholes (1973, p. 651) and Black (1976, p. 7). It is the reason why, in the beginning of this section, we did not worry about the details of the optimal dividend policy at times $T_2, T_3, \ldots, T_{n-1}$. In fact the firm will not survive to make any payments after T_1.

5. The firm will not make even the first payment if a dividend can be paid earlier than T_1.

This is, of course, grossly inconsistent with observed corporate behavior. We consider in the next section one reason why companies are not usually observed behaving as predicted by the model.

15.2   Contractual Restrictions on Dividend Payments

Bond indentures and corporate loan agreements commonly contain a covenant limiting the ability of the obligor to pay dividends to its shareholders.

As described by Smith and Warner (1979), Kalay (1982), and Manning and Hanks (1990, pp. 105–12), the most frequently encountered form of the covenant limits a dividend payment to not more than the contemporaneous value of a "reservoir," defined as

$$R = \sum E + \sum S - \sum D + F \tag{15.3}$$

where

· $\sum E$ is the cumulative net earnings of the firm since a "peg date" usually set to the beginning of the fiscal quarter or year in which the debt is incurred,

· $\sum S$ is the aggregate proceeds derived from sales of new equity since the peg date,

· $\sum D$ is the cumulative dividends paid since the peg date ($\sum D$ also includes cash paid to repurchase stock), and

· F is the contractually specified initial size of the reservoir (usually called the "dip") on the peg date.[6]

The reservoir is "filled" by earnings and sales of stock and "drained" by losses, stock repurchases, and dividend payments. If the value of R prior to a payment is positive, the firm cannot pay a dividend in excess of that positive value. If the value of R is zero or negative, the firm cannot pay any dividend at all.[7] (However, the firm is not required to pay a "negative dividend," or to issue new stock, if the value of R is negative.)

6. The dip is most often set at a level somewhat in excess of one year's earnings (Kalay 1982).

7. Other covenants to limit dividends are discussed in American Bar Foundation (1971, pp. 401–21). Dividend payments can also be limited by state corporation law (Berle and Means (1932, pp. 133 and 146–48), Clark (1986, pp. 610–25), and Manning and Hanks (1990); see also *Randall v. Bailey*, 23 N.Y.S.2d 173 (1940), 288 N.Y. 280 (1942), where a trustee sued the directors of a bankrupt enterprise for approving a dividend alleged to have been paid in violation of New York State corporation law), fraudulent conveyance law (Clark 1986, pp. 40–52 and 86–90), and indirectly by contractual provisions requiring maintenance of net worth and/or working capital above specified levels and maintenance of leverage below a specified level (Kalay 1982, pp. 228–32).

The practical significance of a contractual restriction on dividend payments is clear: creditors can lend money to a corporation, or purchase its debt, without worrying that managers will liquidate the firm at the first opportunity and pay out the proceeds to shareholders.[8]

15.3   The Constrained Optimal Dividend Policy of the Firm

A dividend covenant limits the exercise of discretion by the managers of a firm. This section examines the problem of identifying the optimal dividend policy of a firm, and the contingent value of the debt and equity of the firm, when dividends are contractually limited. We begin by identifying the optimal dividend payment at time T_{n-1}.

The Optimal Dividend Payment at T_{n-1}

T_{n-1} is the date of the last interest and dividend payment prior to the maturity of the debt, so the dividend policy of the firm does not affect the contingent value of the firm's debt and equity after T_{n-1}. The form of $f_i(\cdot, t)$ for $t > T_{n-1}$ can be identified from the terminal conditions in equations (14.5a, b) using the algorithm described in chapter 2. The *ex*-payment contingent values of the firm's debt and equity at $T_{n-1}, g_{i,n-1}(\cdot)$ for $i = 1$ and 2 can be identified from the form of $f_i(\cdot, t)$ for $t > T_{n-1}$. ($g_{i,j}(W^x)$ is the limiting value of $f_i(W^x, T_j + \varepsilon)$ as ε goes to zero from above.)

Given the dividend D_{n-1} paid at T_{n-1}, the *cum*-payment value of equity is

$$V_2(T_{n-1}) = g_{2,n-1}(W(T_{n-1}) - C - D_{n-1}) + D_{n-1} \qquad (15.4)$$

The firm will pay the dividend that maximizes the *cum*-payment value of equity. The marginal benefit to shareholders of an increase in D_{n-1} is

$$\frac{dV_2}{dD_{n-1}} = 1 - g'_{2,n-1}(W(T_{n-1}) - C - D_{n-1}) \qquad (15.5)$$

The derivative $g'_{2,n-1}(W(T_{n-1}) - C - D_{n-1})$ is less than unity for all positive values of $W(T_{n-1}) - C - D_{n-1}$,[9] so dV_2/dD_{n-1} is always positive and the *cum*-payment value of equity is a monotonically increasing function of D_{n-1}. Managers, acting in the best interest of shareholders, will pay the largest possible dividend.

8. John and Kalay (1982) provide a theoretical analysis of optimal dividend constraints. Consistent with observed behavior, their model shows that bond indentures and loan agreements should not prohibit all dividend payments and that (as discussed at the end of the next section) firms will not always pay the maximum dividend allowed.

9. A larger *ex*-payment value of the firm enhances the *ex*-payment value of the debt as well as the *ex*-payment value of equity.

When dividends are limited by the covenant described in section 15.2, D_{n-1} cannot exceed the contemporaneous *cum*-payment size of the dividend reservoir, denoted $R(T_{n-1})$. The payment also cannot exceed the value of the firm following the payment of interest, $W(T_{n-1}) - C$, so it cannot exceed the lesser of the two constraints, or $\min[W(T_{n-1}) - C, R(T_{n-1})]$. However, since the firm is not forced to pay a "negative dividend" if $R(T_{n-1})$ is negative, we can express the optimal dividend payment at time T_{n-1} as

$$D_{n-1} = \max[0, \min[W(T_{n-1}) - C, R(T_{n-1})]] \tag{15.6}$$

The crucial feature of equation (15.6) is that the optimal dividend depends on the contemporaneous size of the dividend reservoir as well as the contemporaneous value of the firm. This is an important difference from the form of the dividend policy function postulated in chapter 14 (see equation 14.1, where the payment was assumed to depend only on the contemporaneous value of the firm).

The *Cum*-payment Value of Debt and Equity at T_{n-1}

If the *cum*-payment value of the firm at time T_{n-1} exceeds C, the *cum*-payment values of the firm's debt and equity depend on their *ex*-payment values, as well as on the contemporaneous interest and dividend payments. It follows from equation (15.6) that the *cum*-payment values of the debt and equity can expressed as

$$V_1(T_{n-1}) = g_{1,n-1}(W(T_{n-1}) - C - \max[0, \min[W(T_{n-1}) - C, R(T_{n-1})]]) + C \tag{15.7a}$$

$$V_2(T_{n-1}) = g_{2,n-1}(W(T_{n-1}) - C - \max[0, \min[W(T_{n-1}) - C, R(T_{n-1})]])$$
$$+ \max[0, \min[W(T_{n-1}) - C, R(T_{n-1})]] \tag{15.7b}$$

Equations (15.7a, b) demonstrate that when dividend payments are contractually limited, the *cum*-payment value of the debt and equity at time T_{n-1} cannot be expressed as a function of only the contemporaneous *cum*-payment value of the firm. The *cum*-payment values of those securities will also depend on the contemporaneous size of the dividend reservoir. A larger reservoir may permit a larger dividend payment, enhancing the *cum*-payment value of equity and reducing the *cum*-payment value of the debt.

The *Cum*-payment Value of Debt and Equity between T_{n-2} and T_{n-1}

Consider now the problem of assessing the value of the debt and equity at some time t^0 in the interval between T_{n-2} and T_{n-1} when the value of the firm is W^0. Since we know the values of the securities at time T_{n-1} contingent on the value of the firm and the value of the dividend reservoir—see equations (15.7a, b)—it might appear that this valuation problem is not materially different from the "up-to-the-next-coupon" problem examined in section 12.4.

However, at time t^0 we do not know what the dividend reservoir will turn out to be at time T_{n-1}. We probably know the current size of the reservoir, $R(t^0)$, and we know that (assuming the company does not sell any new equity or repurchase any outstanding equity) the size of the reservoir will rise or fall on a one-for-one basis with earnings recorded over the interval from t^0 to T_{n-1}. However, we do not know what those earnings will be, so we also do not know what $R(T_{n-1})$ will be. More particularly, we cannot satisfy the assumption in the "up-to-the-next-coupon" problem that the *cum*-payment values of the firm's securities at time T_{n-1} do not depend on any unpredictable variables other than the contemporaneous *cum*-payment value of the firm. It follows that we cannot compute the values of the securities at time t^0 with the arbitrage pricing algorithm used (in section 12.4) to solve the "up-to-the-next-coupon" problem.[10]

Comment

Since we can not identify the forms of the contingent value functions in the interval between T_{n-2} and T_{n-1}, we cannot identify the forms of the *ex*-payment contingent value functions $g_{1,n-2}(\cdot)$ and $g_{2,n-2}(\cdot)$. Without $g_{1,n-2}(\cdot)$ and $g_{2,n-2}(\cdot)$, we cannot undertake a derivation of the optimal dividend payment at time T_{n-2} comparable to the derivation of the expression for D_{n-1} in equation (15.6), and we cannot assess the *cum*-payment values of the firm's securities at time T_{n-2}. More generally, the recursive algorithm for identifying the contingent value functions breaks down.

A Conjecture on the Constrained Optimal Dividend Policy of the Firm

Although we cannot undertake a formal derivation of the optimal dividend payments prior to time T_{n-1}, it is reasonable to conjecture that the optimal strategy is to distribute to shareholders the largest possible dividend on each payment date.[11] In this case the dividend policy of the firm will be reflected in functions of the form of equation (15.6):

---

10. We could introduce into the valuation model the size of the dividend reservoir as a second random variable, comparable to the aggregate value of the firm, and attempt to value the debt and equity contingent on the pair of variables. However, the size of the dividend reservoir is not the price of a traded claim, and we would have no way of constructing the replicating positions (analogous to the positions underlying equations 12.11 and 12.12a, b) required by the arbitrage pricing algorithm. This problem also appeared when we examined, in section 5.2, the problem of incorporating violations of the absolute priority rule into the specification of a contingent value model.

11. See similarly Lease et al. (2000, p. 79).

$$D_j = \max[0, \min[W(T_j) - C, R(T_j)]], \qquad j = 1, 2, \ldots, n-1 \qquad (15.8)$$

Each dividend payment will deplete the dividend reservoir at the time of the payment (assuming that the value of the reservoir is less than the value of the firm net of the contemporaneous interest payment), so we should not observe the firm maintaining through time any significant capacity for paying future dividends.

Whether Contractual Limitations on Dividends Are Binding

The notion that a firm will always choose to pay out the maximum dividend allowed by the covenants on its debt is appealing, but it conflicts with observed corporate behavior. Kalay (1982) reports that the dividend reservoir of a typical firm fluctuates around a level equal to about 12% of the value of the firm. Many firms appear unwilling to exploit to anywhere close to the maximum their option to pay dividends to shareholders.[12]

15.4   Conclusion

A conventional contingent value model does not appear to have an internal structure sufficiently rich to support a derivation of the dividend policy of the firm based on maximization of shareholder value, because it leads inexorably to a policy of paying out the largest possible dividend. Incorporating a contractual limitation on dividend payments precludes the unsettling result that a levered firm cannot exist, but we are still left without an endogenous explanation for why a firm may choose to pay out materially less than the largest dividend permitted by the covenants on its debt.

---

12. Kalay (1982) conjectures that a company may choose to maintain its dividend reservoir at a significant positive level to avoid the prospect that it will one day be forced to invest in projects with a negative net present value because it is restricted from paying a dividend at that time.

Kalay (1982, p. 225) and John and Kalay (1982, p. 468) note that firms with greater leverage maintain relatively smaller reservoirs. This is consistent with the proposition (discussed by Smith and Warner 1979, p. 135, citing Kalay 1979) that it is relatively more costly for a more highly levered firm to maintain a significant reservoir because the shareholders of such a firm have more to gain from an extra dollar of dividends: the derivative on the left-hand side of equation (15.5) is a declining function of the value of the firm and hence an increasing function of the firm's leverage. Conversely, the shareholders of a modestly levered firm have less to gain from an extra dollar of dividends, so the marginal cost of maintaining a significant reservoir is smaller. Lease et al. (2000, p. 78) observe similarly that. "... the incentive for shareholders to pay dividends is stronger when their firm's leverage is high than when it is low."

Kalay's empirical findings on corporate dividend policy should not be interpreted to mean that contractual limitations on dividend payments are never binding. DeAngelo and DeAngelo (1990) found that more than half of a sample of firms in protracted financial distress reduced or omitted dividend payments because dividend covenants were either binding or close to binding. They concluded that contractual limitations on dividend payments are an important determinant of the dividend policy of a distressed firm.

16 Empirical Characteristics of Corporate Dividend Policy

The analysis in chapter 15 demonstrated that in the context of a conventional contingent value model of corporate securities prices, we cannot derive a reasonable representation of corporate dividend policy from the assumption that managers act to maximize shareholder value. An alternative approach, and the approach pursued in this chapter, is to identify the dividend policy of a firm from the observed behavior of the firm.[1] Section 16.1 examines corporate policies for regular dividends, and section 16.2 examines special dividends. Special dividends are dividends specifically labeled as "special" or "extra" and are usually paid on an irregular basis. Regular dividends are all other, unlabeled, dividends and are almost always paid on a periodic, usually quarterly, basis. Distinguishing between the two categories is important because a company behaves differently when it is deciding whether to pay one or the other type of dividend.

Dividend payments are not the only way a company can distribute cash to its shareholders. Over the last fifteen years, stock repurchases have become an increasingly important alternative. Ikenberry, Lakonishok, and Vermaelen (1995, p. 182) observe that "Towards the end of the 1980's, the dollars involved in repurchases [became] nearly half the amount paid as dividends." Section 16.3 examines corporate policies for stock repurchases.

16.1 Regular Dividends

This section addresses the problem of identifying, from the observed behavior of a firm, the policy of the firm for paying regular cash dividends.

Dividends as a Function of Earnings

Lintner (1956) provided the earliest empirical specification of corporate dividend policy.[2] On the basis of interviews with managers at 28 large industrial corporations he made two key observations.

First, net earnings is the single most important variable affecting the level of dividends. Managers use earnings to set dividend rates because earnings are understandable and readily visible to shareholders, analysts and employees. Lintner observed (p. 101) that "a [dividend] policy geared to considerations other than earnings would have to be explained and justified first on one thing and then on another. Even if there were a per-

---

1. In addition to the literature cited below, this chapter has benefited from the overview of dividend policy by Lease, John, Kalay, Loewenstein, and Sarig (2000). Frankfurter and Wood (1997) offer a broad historical appraisal of the evolution of dividend policy.

2. See also Lintner (1953) and Brittain (1966). The continuing usefulness of Lintner's specification is demonstrated by Baker, Farrelly, and Edelman (1985), Benzarti, Michaely, and Thaler (1997), and DeAngelo and DeAngelo (2000, pp. 168–72).

fectly consistent underlying rationale to such a policy, it would be difficult to explain in simple, understandable and persuasive terms, and would probably seem erratic, ad hoc, or 'academic'."

Lintner's second observation is that managers focus special attention on the decision to *change* an existing dividend rate (commonly expressed in units of dollars or cents per share of stock) and avoid changes that might have to be reversed in a year or two. Lintner noted that this leads to a pattern of lagged partial adjustments of dividends to increases in earnings.

Lintner did not claim that factors other than earnings and the existing dividend rate are unimportant. He noted specifically the episodic significance of, for example, bond covenants limiting dividend payments, the need to redeem maturing debt, and the need to rebuild cash balances and working capital. However, he argued (p. 101) that "a prudent foresighted management will always do its best to plan ahead ... to avoid getting into ... uncomfortable situations where dividends *have* to be cut substantially below those which the company's previous practice would lead stockholders to expect on the basis of current earnings."

Lintner reported that two thirds of the firms in his sample had a specific policy regarding the target, or desired, ratio of dividends to earnings, as well as a specific policy regarding the speed of adjustment to the target level. All but two of the remaining firms acted as if they had such policies. For most of the firms in his sample, the process of setting dividends as a function of earnings was so firmly established that dividend decisions preceded capital budgeting and working capital decisions. This implies that managers view dividends as a quasi-fixed charge on earnings and that working capital, capital expenditures, and external financing bear the brunt of fluctuations in earnings.

Although Lintner identified payout ratios and adjustment speeds as the most important proximate determinants of corporate dividend policy, he also noted that those characteristics are the result of a more fundamental effort by managers to maximize shareholder value. He observed (p. 104) that "the different target pay-out ratios and adjustment rates in the various companies reflected a large number of different factors in the companies' experience, objectives, and pattern of operations. In some cases management had weighed and in some manner 'balanced out' these considerations at some time in the earlier history of the company; in most companies a growing body of experience and precedents ... became more rationalized and formalized in a reasonably fixed and definite policy." Lintner reported a wide variation *across firms* in the choice of a target dividend-earnings ratio and a speed of adjustment to the target level, but little variation *through time* in either the target ratio or the adjustment speed for any particular firm. He found that the two policy parameters depend on

- the growth prospects of the industry within which the firm operates and the growth and earnings prospects of the firm itself,
- the pattern of cyclical variation in capital investment opportunities,
- the pattern of fluctuations in working capital requirements and availability of internal funds,
- management's view of the relative importance to shareholders of ordinary income versus capital gains, and
- the target ratios and adjustment speeds adopted by competitors.

He concluded that the operating environments of different firms have an important effect on target ratios and adjustment speeds, even though they have little additional effect on dividends once those two policy parameters are established.

A Model of Dividends as a Function of Earnings

Lintner proposed a simple model to make his observations on corporate dividend policy more concrete.

Let E_y denote the earnings of a firm during year y. The target level of dividends to be paid in year y might be expressed as

$$D_y^* = r \cdot E_y \tag{16.1}$$

where r is the target dividend-earnings ratio with a value between zero and unity.[3]

The adjustment of actual dividends to the target level might be written as

$$D_y - D_{y-1} = \theta \cdot (D_y^* - D_{y-1}) \tag{16.2}$$

where D_y denotes dividends paid during year y and θ is a speed of adjustment coefficient that also lies between zero and unity. Equation (16.2) implies that dividends will increase from year $y - 1$ to year y if D_y^* is greater than D_{y-1}, but that the magnitude of the increase will be less than the discrepancy between the target payment and the payment in year $y - 1$. The increase can thus be characterized as a "partial" adjustment.[4]

---

3. Equation (16.1) makes the not entirely palatable assumption that the firm knows the earnings that it will record over a fiscal year at the time it establishes the target dividend rate for the year. It may be more satisfactory to assume that $D_y^* = r \cdot E_{y-1}$. See similarly Marsh and Merton (1987, p. 10) and Kao and Wu (1994, p. 49 n. 3).

4. Lintner (1956, p. 107) proposed that the model in equation (16.2) should also include a constant term. Fama and Babiak (1968) found such a term statistically insignificant.

Substituting the expression for target dividends from equation (16.1) into equation (16.2) gives the dividend model

$$D_y = \theta \cdot r \cdot E_y + (1 - \theta) \cdot D_{y-1} \qquad (16.3)$$

If earnings remain constant at $\bar{E}$, dividends will converge over time to the target level $r \cdot \bar{E}$. Thus the model reflects a complete adjustment of dividends to the target level in the long run as well as a partial adjustment in the short run.[5]

Several authors have estimated the coefficients of the model in equation (16.3). Lintner (1956, pp. 102–103) reported that, on average, the firms in his sample adopted a target dividend–earnings ratio of 0.5 and a speed of adjustment coefficient between 0.2 and 0.5. Fama and Babiak (1968, table 2, panel D) reported an average payout ratio of 0.5 and an average speed of adjustment coefficient of 0.3 for a sample of 392 firms using annual data from 1947 to 1964.[6]

Comment

The utility of equation (16.3) in a conventional contingent value model is limited because corporate earnings are not the price of a traded claim.

To appreciate the significance of this observation, consider incorporating equation (16.3) into the valuation model described in chapter 14 so that dividends become a function of earnings. This will make debt and equity values a direct function of earnings and invalidate the assumption,

---

5. The model in equation (16.3) is not a uniquely appropriate specification of corporate dividend policy. Other models that exhibit (a) a pattern of short-run partial adjustments of dividends to earnings and (b) convergence of the actual dividend–earnings ratio to the target ratio in the long run may serve equally well. See, for example, the specifications in Fama and Babiak (1968) and Marsh and Merton (1987). In addition a firm may revise its dividend semiannually or quarterly. Laub (1970, cited in Watts 1973, pp. 194–95) reports that 35% of changes in regular corporate dividends occur *during* a fiscal year (see also Laub 1976 and Watts 1976).

6. Rozeff (1982a, b) found that the dividend–earnings ratio of a firm is lower the greater the growth rate of the firm (suggesting that firms with more attractive investment opportunities pay out relatively less cash) and that it is lower the greater the beta coefficient of the firm's equity. The latter result supports the proposition that dividend payments are quasi-fixed charges that can be substitutes for fixed interest expenses, because firms with high beta coefficients are typically more highly leveraged. See also Jensen, Solberg, and Zorn (1992).

Rozeff (1982a, b) further found that the dividend–earnings ratio of a firm is greater (a) the lower the fraction of equity owned by insiders and (b) the greater the total number of shareholders. Citing Jensen and Meckling (1976), he attributes this to the use of dividends to reduce the agency costs of outside equity. The role of dividends in reducing agency costs is discussed further in Easterbrook (1984) and Jensen (1986). Additional empirical results bearing on the issue are reported by Jensen, Solberg, and Zorn (1992) (the dividend–earnings ratio of a firm is greater the lower the fraction of equity owned by insiders) and Agrawal and Jayaraman (1994) (on average, an unlevered firm has a higher dividend-earnings ratio than a levered firm). Alli, Khan, and Ramirez (1993) also examined the cross-sectional determinants of dividend–earnings ratios.

Table 16.1
An example of dividends computed from the model of equation (16.3)

Year (y)	Earnings[a] (E_y)	Dividends[b] (D_y)
$y^* - 3$	\$100 million	\$40 million[c]
$y^* - 2$	100	40
$y^* - 1$	100	40
y^*	175[d]	58
$y^* + 1$	100	47.2
$y^* + 2$	100	42.9
$y^* + 3$	100	41.2
$y^* + 4$	100	40.5
$y^* + 5$	100	40.2

a. Assumed for purposes of the example.
b. Computed from equation (16.3) assuming $r = 0.4$ and $\theta = 0.6$, except for year $y^* - 3$.
c. Assumed for purposes of the example.
d. Includes an extraordinary item of \$75 million.

in equation (14.4), that the only variables affecting the value of a security are the aggregate value of the issuing firm and time.[7] More generally, it leads to a breakdown of the recursive algorithm for identifying contingent value functions.[8] The problem cannot be cured by expanding the arguments of the valuation function in equation (14.4) to include earnings, because the dynamic evolution of earnings cannot be replicated with securities traded in the market.

A Criticism

The dividend model in equation (16.3) can also be criticized for incorporating (from equation 16.1) the notion that the target dividend depends on current earnings.

Suppose, for example, that a corporation has stable earnings of \$100 million per year, a target dividend-earnings ratio of $r = 0.4$ and a speed of adjustment coefficient of $\theta = 0.6$. As shown in the first several lines of table 16.1, its dividends will be about \$40 million per year.

Now suppose that in year y^* the company records an extraordinary gain of \$75 million in addition to its ordinary earnings of \$100 million but that earnings subsequently return to the rate of \$100 million per year. It is doubtful that the company will pay dividends in years y^* and thereafter as computed with equation (16.3) and as shown in table 16.1:

7. Debt and equity values will depend directly on earnings because, from the transversality conditions in equations (14.6a, b), the *cum*-dividend values of the firm's securities depend on anything that affects dividends.

8. The reason for the breakdown is identical to the reason stated in section 15.3 for the breakdown of the algorithm when a dividend payment depends on the size of a dividend reservoir specified in a restrictive covenant.

increasing dividends sharply in year y^* and then reducing them back toward $40 million. As Lintner specifically observed, managers avoid dividend changes that might have to be reversed within a year or two. The more likely response is that the company will choose to maintain its annual dividend at $40 million because earnings net of the extraordinary gain are unchanged. (As described in section 16.2, the company could choose to distribute some or all of the $75 million as a special dividend.)

The foregoing example suggests that a target dividend might be better specified as a function of recent earnings net of extraordinary and non-recurring items or, even better, as a function of prospective "permanent" earnings. This leads to the idea that the regular dividend payments of a firm might be represented as a function of the firm's stock price rather than as a function of its earnings.

Dividends as a Function of Stock Prices

Marsh and Merton (1987) were the first to propose that dividends might be represented as a function of stock prices.

The authors observed that the market value of equity can be viewed as the present value of the anticipated future earnings of a firm. Let α denote the discount rate per annum, and let $V_e(t)$ denote the market value of equity at time t. We can then define the "permanent earnings" of the firm at time t as the level of annual earnings $E^P(t)$ which, when capitalized at rate α, gives the contemporaneous value of equity:

$$V_e(t) = \int_t^\infty E^P(t) \cdot e^{-\alpha \cdot (s-t)} \cdot ds \tag{16.4}$$

so that

$$E^P(t) = \alpha \cdot V_e(t) \tag{16.5}$$

The value of equity, and hence the measure of permanent earnings in equation (16.5), incorporates whatever might be known to market participants about prospective cyclical, seasonal and extraordinary fluctuations in earnings.

Marsh and Merton supposed that the target level of dividends to be paid in year y is set in year $y - 1$ as a function of permanent earnings at the end of year $y - 2$:

$$D_y^* = r \cdot E_{y-2}^P \tag{16.6}$$

Letting V_y denote the ex-dividend value of equity at the end of year y, equation (16.5) implies that $E_{y-2}^P = \alpha \cdot V_{y-2}$, so the target level of dividends in year y becomes

$$D_y^* = r \cdot \alpha \cdot V_{y-2} \tag{16.7}$$

The authors specified a model of short-run dividend changes in terms of the change in the natural logarithm of dividends (or, equivalently, in terms of the dividend growth rate[9]) using an adjustment process more complex than the simple specification of equation (16.2):

$$\ln[D_y] - \ln[D_{y-1}] = \bar{g} + \lambda \cdot \left\{ \ln\left[\frac{E_{y-1}^{\mathrm{p}}}{E_{y-2}^{\mathrm{p}}}\right] - m_{y-2} \right\} + \theta \cdot [\ln[D_y^*] - \ln[D_{y-1}]] \tag{16.8}$$

where $\bar{g}$ is the unconditional expected rate of growth of dividends and m_{y-2} is the expected (in year $y - 2$) rate of growth of permanent earnings from year $y - 2$ to year $y - 1$. The second term on the right-hand side of the equation reflects a dividend adjustment in response to a rate of growth in the permanent earnings of the firm from year $y - 2$ to year $y - 1$ different from what had been anticipated.

Using $D_y^* = r \cdot \alpha \cdot V_{y-2}$ from equation (16.7) and assuming that the unexpected rate of growth in the permanent earnings of the firm is

$$\ln\left[\frac{E_{y-1}^{\mathrm{p}}}{E_{y-2}^{\mathrm{p}}}\right] - m_{y-2} = \ln\left[\frac{V_{y-1} + D_{y-1}}{V_{y-2}}\right] - \alpha \tag{16.9}$$

the dividend adjustment model of Marsh and Merton becomes

$$\ln[D_y] = \bar{g} + \lambda \cdot \left\{ \ln\left[\frac{V_{y-1} + D_{y-1}}{V_{y-2}}\right] - \alpha \right\}$$
$$+ \theta \cdot \ln[r \cdot \alpha \cdot V_{y-2}] + (1 - \theta) \cdot \ln[D_{y-1}] \tag{16.10}$$

Lambert, Lanen, and Larcker (1989, table 1) estimated the coefficients of a variant of the model for a sample of 197 firms, using 20 years of data for each firm over an aggregate interval from 1927 to 1980. They report an average estimated value of θ of about 0.45, and their results imply an average long-run target level of annual dividends equal to about 6% of stock value. Kao and Wu (1994, table 2) estimated the coefficients of a quarterly version of the model for a sample of 454 firms, using data from 1965 to 1986. They report a mean estimated value of θ of about 0.3 (the equivalent adjustment coefficient for an annual model would be somewhat larger), and their results imply an average target ratio of quarterly dividends to stock value of about 1%. Michaely, and Vila (1996, p. 481)

---

9. The change in log dividends $\ln[D_y] - \ln[D_{y-1}]$ is approximately equal to the dividend growth rate $(D_y - D_{y-1})/D_{y-1}$ because $\ln[D_y/D_{y-1}]$ is approximately equal to $(D_y/D_{y-1}) - 1$.

and Benzarti, Michaely, and Thaler (1997, p. 1013) report comparable average ratios of dividends to stock values.

Other Factors Affecting Dividend Payments

Specifying the dividend policy of a firm as a function of the value of equity eliminates the problem that arises when dividends are specified as a function of a variable that is not the price of a traded claim. However, it ignores two important, albeit episodic, determinants of dividend policy: the distinctly different reaction of managers to weak earnings compared to outright losses, and the effect of restrictive covenants in loan agreements and bond indentures. It also ignores the possibility that managers might elect to change the dividend payments of a firm to signal new information about expected future earnings or to expropriate wealth from creditors.

Dividend Policies of Firms with Weak Earnings and Firms in Financial Distress

Research reported by DeAngelo and DeAngelo (1990) and DeAngelo, DeAngelo, and Skinner (1992) supports the proposition that companies are reluctant to reduce dividends in the absence of losses but that they cut dividends promptly and dramatically at the onset of financial distress and continue to cut dividends in the face of prolonged distress.[10]

The dividend model in equation (16.10) does not reflect this difference in the reaction of managers to outright losses compared to weak earnings. Thus it will understate dividends paid by a firm with reduced earnings that nevertheless chooses to maintain its dividend. Similarly it will overstate dividends paid by a more distressed firm that dramatically reduces its dividend, and it fails to reflect the possibility that a firm might eliminate its dividend in the face of severe distress.[11]

Modifying the model to reflect the different reaction of managers to weak earnings and losses is not a trivial undertaking. Aggressive reaction to losses suggests that the target dividend in equation (16.6) depends on contemporaneous actual earnings when those earnings are negative, as well as on prospective permanent earnings, and that the speed of adjustment coefficient rises when current earnings are negative (so the adjustment to a lower target occurs more rapidly). On the other hand, the reluctance of

10. See also Ofek (1993).

11. The dividend model in equation (16.10) has to be modified when a company suspends its dividend because the natural logarithm of zero is not a finite quantity. See Kao and Wu (1994, p. 59).

managers to reduce dividends in the face of weak but positive earnings suggests that the adjustment coefficient falls when earnings are weak but positive. These characteristics mean that dividends are not invariant with respect to earnings and thus reintroduce the problem of dependency on a variable that is not the price of a traded claim.

Restrictive Covenants

Section 15.2 described dividend reservoirs and the use of such reservoirs in covenants restricting dividend payments. The model in equation (16.10) does not distinguish between firms with ample reservoirs and firms with substantially depleted or negative reservoirs. It may consequently overstate dividends paid by firms with depleted reservoirs. Conversely, we might estimate an artificially low target payout ratio if we estimate the coefficients of the model using data from a period when a firm's dividends are restricted. The estimated model will understate future dividends if those future dividends are not similarly restricted, either because subsequent earnings or stock sales replenish the reservoir or because the debt protected by the restrictive covenant has been redeemed.[12]

Dividend Changes and Management Signaling

A substantial literature has accumulated over the past three decades documenting the reaction of stock prices to dividend changes. Empirical evidence shows that, on average, the price of a company's stock rises (falls) when the company announces a dividend increase (decrease).[13] This suggests that dividend announcements convey new information to market participants.

The positive correlation between changes in dividends and changes in stock prices is widely attributed to a "signaling" phenomenon.[14] The essential elements of the phenomenon are as follows:

12. See, for example, the plan of Silgan Corp. to eliminate a dividend covenant by calling and refinancing its senior subordinated notes. "Morgan Stanley LBO Begins Refinancing in Private Mart," *Investment Dealers Digest*, April 27, 1992, p. 14. See also Prospectus for Silgan Holdings, Inc. $15\frac{1}{4}\%$ Senior Subordinated Reset Debentures due 2004, dated June 23, 1989, pp. 12, 50, and 92.

13. See Pettit (1972), Charest (1978), Aharony and Swary (1980), Brickley (1983), Asquith and Mullins (1983, 1986), Healy and Palepu (1988), Kao and Wu (1994), and Michaely, Thaler, and Womack (1995).

14. See, for example, Bhattacharya (1979), Kalay (1980), Miller and Rock (1985), John and Williams (1985), and Lease et al (2000, ch. 7). Lang and Litzenberger (1989), following Jensen (1986), attribute the positive correlation to the distribution to shareholders of free cash flow by firms with limited value-enhancing investment opportunities. Howe, He, and Kao (1992) and Denis, Denis, and Sarin (1994) challenge that interpretation. Koch and Shenoy (1999) provide evidence in support.

• Equity investors value stable dividends and discount the stock price of a firm that varies its dividend widely over a short interval of time.[15]

• Managers seeking to maximize shareholder wealth are consequently reluctant to increase dividends unless they have confidence that future earnings will be strong enough to sustain the increase, and they are reluctant to reduce dividends if they believe that weak earnings are only temporary.

• Managers have better information about the future prospects of a firm than other market participants; that is, there is an "information asymmetry" between managers and the market.[16]

• An unexpected dividend increase (decrease) is therefore a signal to investors that better-informed managers are unexpectedly more optimistic (pessimistic) than the market about the future earnings of a firm; that is, it conveys new information to market participants.

• Upon receipt of the new information, market participants revise their appraisal of the aggregate value of the firm and the value of the firm's equity.[17] Thus stock prices rise (fall) when dividends are increased (decreased) unexpectedly.[18]

Some commentators are uncomfortable with the notion of management signaling because it seems to allow managers to trick the market by raising dividends even when they do not have any reasonable basis for believing that future earnings will be stronger than the market expects.[19] However, the higher stock price that would follow a spurious dividend increase can only be a transient phenomenon that evaporates as subsequent earnings

---

15. Lintner (1956, p. 99) noted "the belief on the part of many managements that most stockholders prefer a reasonably stable [dividend] rate and that the market puts a premium on stability or gradual growth in rate...."

16. The most direct support for the proposition that there is an information asymmetry between managers and other market participants is the empirical evidence that managers earn abnormal returns trading in the stock of the firms that they manage. See Jaffee (1974), Finnerty (1976), and Seyhun (1986); see also Yermack (1997).

17. Ofer and Siegal (1987) find that changes in forecasts of future corporate earnings published by securities analysts are positively correlated with unexpected dividend changes.

18. However, as discussed in Lease et al. (2000, pp. 106–108 and 112–14), several analysts have noted that, in some cases, an unexpected dividend increase may convey *adverse* information about the prospects of a firm (e.g., a decline in the availability of projects with positive net present value) so that the value of equity *falls* upon announcement of the dividend increase. Although these appear to be atypical cases (on average, stock prices rise in the wake of dividend increases), they support the proposition that interpreting the information conveyed by a dividend change may require additional data. See Ambarish, John, and Williams (1987) and John and Mishra (1990).

19. Brudney (1980) and Fischel (1981) discuss whether managers should be required to disclose the basis for their dividend decisions—either in general or in cases where a failure to disclose would leave market participants with a false impression of the prospects of the firm.

are reported and are seen to be weaker than anticipated on the basis of the previously increased dividend and as dividends are restored to a more appropriate (lower) level. The resulting volatility of dividends leads to stock prices lower than would have been the case had dividends not been first increased and then decreased.[20] Thus a manager seeking to maximize the value of equity over the long run has no incentive to resort to tricks.

Signaling new information with dividend changes cannot be incorporated readily into a conventional contingent value model for two related reasons. First, conventional models do not exhibit information asymmetries. There is no representation of management's view of the value of a firm and its prospective earnings distinct from the view of the market as a whole.

Second, the models do not allow for dividend changes that convey information to market participants. Future dividends may not be known with certainty and payments may vary over time—as in example A in section 14.5, where dividends are contingent on the contemporaneous value of equity—but the forms of the policy functions used to set the payments (the $D_j(\cdot)$ functions in equation 14.1) are assumed to be known to all market participants, and the values of the arguments of a policy function are assumed to be known at the time the function is evaluated to set the size of a payment: see the discussion of transversality conditions in the text preceding equations (14.6a, b). Thus every dividend is exactly what the market expects the moment before it is announced and disbursed. (For analytical simplicity the model in chapter 14 eliminated the interval between announcement and payment of a dividend.)

Dividend Changes and Wealth Transfers

The management signaling hypothesis asserts that a dividend change conveys information about the prospective earnings of a firm. Some analysts have suggested that dividend changes might alternatively or additionally convey information about a change in the dividend policy of the firm, and that dividend changes can lead to wealth transfers between shareholders and creditors.[21] (It is crucial to distinguish here between a dividend change stemming from a change in a *variable* like expected future earnings and a dividend change stemming from a change in the dividend *policy* of the firm.)

---

20. Asquith and Mullins (1986, p. 35, citing Charest 1978) point out that the decline in the price of a stock following a dividend decrease is, on average, larger than the rise in price that follows an increase, and conclude that dividend volatility tends to have a net depressing effect on stock prices.

21. See, for example, Galai and Masulis (1976) and Smith and Warner (1979).

To appreciate the mechanics of wealth transfer, suppose that market participants initially believe a company is highly unlikely to pay a dividend before its debt has been redeemed. The value of the firm's debt and equity might then vary with the value of the firm as shown by the dashed lines in figure 14.1.

Suppose next that management announces unexpectedly that it will begin to pay a semiannual dividend equal to 5% of the value of the firm's stock. The contingent value functions will shift to the solid lines in figure 14.1. Assuming that the aggregate value of the firm remains unchanged, the value of equity will rise on the announcement of the new dividend policy and the value of the debt will fall, leading to a transfer of wealth from creditors to stockholders. More generally, the wealth transfer hypothesis asserts that increases (decreases) in dividends lead to higher (lower) stock prices—and lower (higher) bond prices—because a dividend change conveys information about a change in the dividend policy of the firm.

The management signaling and wealth transfer hypotheses have identical implications for the reaction of stock prices to dividend changes, but contrary implications for the reaction of debt prices. (The management signaling hypothesis implies that an unexpected dividend increase should lead to an increase in the price of the company's debt, because the value of the debt is, like the value of equity, an increasing function of the aggregate value of the firm; see the upper panels in figures 14.1 and 14.2.) Several analysts have taken note of this asymmetry and have attempted to assess which of the two phenomena is more important by examining how bond prices react to dividend changes.

Woolridge (1983) and Handjinicolaou and Kalay (1984) found that bond prices are unaffected by dividend increases and fall following dividend decreases. The latter authors concluded that on average, dividend increases convey positive information on the prospective earnings of the firm *and also* signal a more aggressive dividend policy. The *net* effect on bond prices is approximately equal to zero, so managers are able to capture for shareholders *all* of the increase in value associated with greater prospective earnings. Handjinicolaou and Kalay also concluded that managers who reduce dividends as a result of weaker earnings do not, on average, lower them enough to provide an offsetting benefit to bondholders, so the loss in value associated with the prospect of lower future earnings is born by creditors as well as stockholders.

More recently Dhillon and Johnson (1994) have reported that, on average, bond prices fall following (1) unusually large (greater than 30%) increases in dividends and (2) the initiation of dividend payments by firms that did not previously pay dividends, and that they rise following (3) unusually large reductions in dividends and (4) the suspension of dividend payments. Their results suggest that on balance, wealth transfer may be more important than management signaling in the context of unusually large dividend changes. (Dhillon and Johnson do not address why managers sometimes reduce dividends so sharply as to benefit creditors at the expense of shareholders.)

The studies by Handjinicolaou and Kalay, Woolridge, and Dhillon and Johnson support the proposition that dividend changes convey information about dividend policy as well as about prospective earnings. Debt and equity values do not always move in the same direction following a change in dividends. However, the possibility that managers might alter unexpectedly the dividend policy of a firm can not be incorporated into a conventional contingent value model, because a conventional model assumes that dividend policy is fixed and known.

Summary

The preceding survey of corporate dividend policy suggests that we might model (approximately) the regular dividend payments of a firm as a function of the value of the firm's equity. The form of the function can be estimated from historical data and the resulting dividend policy function can be incorporated into a contingent value model, as in example A in section 14.5.

However, this approach is far from ideal. It does not account for the effect of restrictive dividend covenants and the different reaction of managers to weak earnings compared to losses, and it cannot reflect the conveyance of new information about prospective earnings. Additionally, since it can only provide a representation of the *historic* dividend policy of the firm, it has limited utility when changing circumstances prompt a firm to *change* its dividend policy.

16.2   Special Dividends

Casual examination of corporate dividend histories reveals that some companies sometimes make cash payments to shareholders labeled as "special" or "extra" dividends. Brickley (1983) reports that U.S. firms paid about one thousand special dividends annually between 1969 and 1979. The median size of a special dividend was about half of the most recent regular dividend. Similar statistics are reported by Jayaraman and Shastri (1988). This section describes the role of special dividends in the dividend policy of a firm and assesses whether they can be incorporated into the specification of a contingent value model.

Some Examples

It may be helpful to preface the discussion with some examples of special dividends.

Aluminum Company of America (Alcoa)

Figure 16.1 exhibits the history of dividends and earnings for Alcoa from 1974 to 1993. The solid bars in the upper panel show payments of regular quarterly dividends. The open bars show additional payments labeled as special dividends.

Observe that Alcoa disbursed only three special dividends over the sample interval and that the two largest were paid immediately following a year during which the company enjoyed exceptionally strong earnings. This suggests that each special dividend was a payment to shareholders of part of the exceptional component of earnings recorded during the preceding year.

This conjecture is supported by the formal dividend policy adopted by Alcoa in early 1989, when it paid its first special dividend of $1.12 per share. As stated in Alcoa's 1988 Annual Report to Shareholders:

Alcoa's objective is to pay common stock dividends at rates competitive with other investments of equal risk and consistent with the need to reinvest earnings for long-term growth. To support this objective, Alcoa pays a base quarterly dividend and *an additional dividend linked directly to Alcoa's financial performance.* The base quarterly dividend is 40 cents per common share. The additional dividend is 30% of Alcoa's annual earnings over $6.00 per share. (Emphasis added)

This statement shows that each special dividend was intentionally labeled as "special" to reflect the fact that it was based on actual historical earnings rather than on management's assessment of expected future earnings.

Corning

Figure 16.2 exhibits the history of dividends and earnings for Corning, Inc. from 1974 to 1993. The figure shows that the company paid a special dividend three times in four years between 1988 and 1991, during an interval of unusually strong earnings. This is similar to the pattern of dividends and earnings for Alcoa, although Corning had no formal policy for paying special dividends.

Asarco

Figure 16.3 shows dividends and earnings for Asarco from 1974 to 1993. Observe the unusually strong earnings in 1979 and 1980, the large special dividend paid at the end of 1979, and the multiple special dividends paid in 1980.

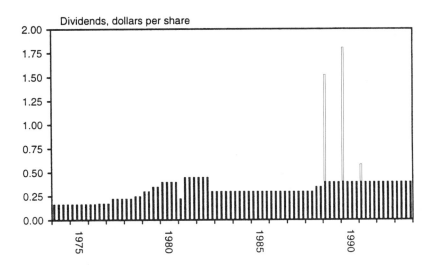

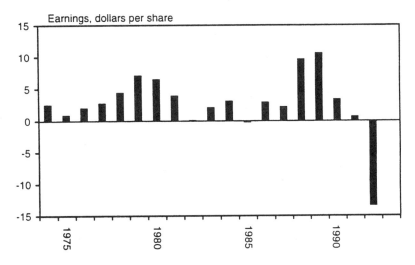

Figure 16.1
Aluminum Company of America, dividends and earnings per share, 1974 to 1993, adjusted for stock splits prior to December 31, 1993

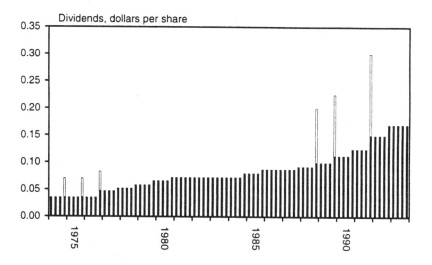

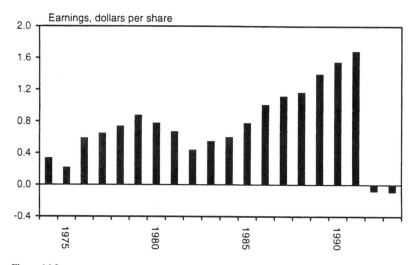

Figure 16.2
Corning, Inc. dividends and earnings per share, 1974 to 1993, adjusted for stock splits prior
to December 31, 1993

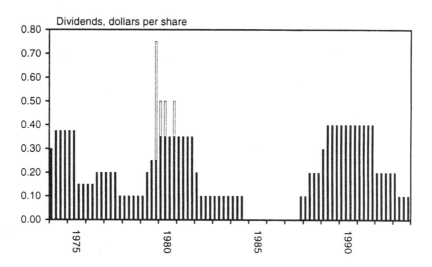

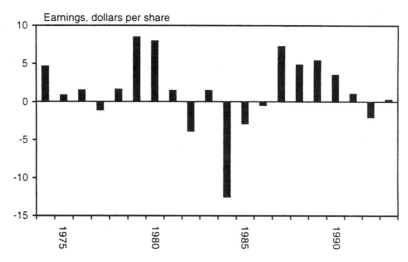

Figure 16.3
Asarco, Inc. dividends and earnings per share, 1974 to 1993

Asarco recorded either weak earnings or losses in the early and mid-1980s. This led the company to reduce its regular dividend twice (in the first and second quarters of 1982) and finally to omit its regular dividend altogether (in the fourth quarter of 1984). When earnings recovered in 1987, the company chose to restore—and subsequently increase—its regular dividend and did not pay any special dividends.

The Determinants of a Special Dividend Payment

No analyst has undertaken a study of special dividends as extensive as Lintner's study, describing qualitatively how managers go about deciding whether to pay a special dividend, and then specifying and estimating a quantitative model of their behavior. However, the preceding examples suggest that the timing and size of a special dividend depends on the recent earnings of the firm and, in particular, on earnings in excess of a threshold level. (Alcoa's dividend policy states explicitly that 30% of earnings in excess of $6.00 per share will be paid out as a special dividend.)

The link between special dividends and historical earnings contrasts with the case of regular dividends, which appear to be determined primarily by prospective earnings. The difference implies that the size of a special dividend is unlikely to be as closely linked to the price of a company's stock as the size of a regular dividend, and explains why companies take the trouble to label some dividend payments as "special." If a company distributed a one-time cash payment to shareholders without labeling it a special dividend (and thus made the payment in the form of an increased regular dividend), market participants might conclude that the company's managers had revised upward their appraisal of future earnings. The resulting stock price increase would be more than reversed in the following quarter, when the company fails to repeat the higher payout. By labeling the one-time payment a special dividend, the company avoids misleading the market—and the company's managers and shareholders avoid the penalties associated with poor dividend management skills.

Incorporating Special Dividends into a Contingent Value Model

There are two reasons for incorporating special dividends into the specification of a contingent value model: they are far from trivial in terms of both frequency and amount, and some corporations have, or appear to have, a policy of distributing a portion of unusually strong earnings as a special dividend to shareholders. Market participants can be expected to recognize that such a policy works to the advantage of shareholders and to the disadvantage of creditors, and they can be expected to value the debt and equity of the issuers accordingly. Ignoring special dividends may lead to overstated debt values and understated equity values.

Accepting the argument that special dividends *should* be incorporated into a contingent value model raises the question of *how* they can be incorporated. Special dividends cannot be lumped together with regular dividends because special dividends appear to depend on actual past earnings rather than prospective future earnings. As noted above, it seems reasonable to hypothesize that the timing and size of a special dividend can be represented as a function of earnings in excess of some threshold level. The problem with this approach is that earnings are not the price of a traded claim. Even if we can specify successfully the special dividend policy of a firm, we will be unable to incorporate that specification into a conventional contingent value model.[22]

16.3 Stock Repurchases in Open Market Transactions

Stock repurchases can be a substitute for cash dividends. For example, in 1994 FPL Group Inc. announced that it would cut its regular dividend by about one third—saving $144 million per year—and that it would also initiate a program to repurchase about $90 million of stock each year for three years.[23]

Most stock repurchases are accomplished through open market transactions.[24] This section describes open market repurchases and assesses whether they can be incorporated into the specification of a contingent

---

22. Special dividend payments are also subject to whatever constraints may be imposed by dividend covenants in the firm's bond indentures and loan agreements. Those covenants treat all dividends identically and do not distinguish between regular dividends and special dividends.

23. "FPL Group to Slash Dividend by 32%, Plans Repurchase to Boost Share Price," *Wall Street Journal*, May 10, 1994, p. A7.

Executive stock option programs give managers a personal financial incentive to substitute stock repurchases for cash dividends. Ceteris paribus, the price *per share* of a company's stock will be higher if the company pays out $1 million by repurchasing stock than if it pays out the same money in the form of a dividend, because the number of shares outstanding after the disbursement will be smaller in the former case. Lambert, Lanen, and Larcker (1989) report that on average, dividend payments fall short of the level predicted by the model of Marsh and Merton (1987) following adoption of an executive stock option plan. Smith and Watts (1992) report a negative cross-sectional correlation between dividend yield and option-based executive compensation.

24. Ikenberry, Lakonishok, and Vermaelen (1995) report that 90% of the dollar value of all share repurchases announced between 1985 and 1993 were to be completed through open market transactions. Stock is also repurchased through fixed price and Dutch-auction tender offers, transferable put rights, and targeted repurchases. See Masulis (1980b), Dann (1981), Vermaelen (1981), Bradley and Wakeman (1983), Dann and DeAngelo (1983), Kale, Noe, and Gay (1989), and Comment and Jarrell (1991).

value model. We begin by describing the mechanics and characteristics of a repurchase program.

Mechanics of a Repurchase Program

A company typically initiates a stock repurchase program with a public announcement that its board of directors has authorized the program. The announcement usually discloses either the "targeted" number of shares that the company intends to repurchase or the aggregate dollar amount of the program. The announcement may also indicate the time frame over which the repurchases are expected to occur.

Following announcement of a repurchase program, the company will begin to repurchase its stock in conventional transactions through one or more brokers or dealers. The company exercises virtually complete control over the pace of the repurchases.[25] It can accelerate or reduce the pace from time to time, or completely stop.

An open market repurchase program is a flexible device for distributing cash to shareholders that entails few of the public disclosures associated with cash dividends. A company is not obligated to complete a stock repurchase program as originally announced. It can choose to purchase more or less stock, or no stock, and it may expend more or less money. Additionally it is not required to announce periodically the status of a repurchase program, including how many shares have been repurchased or how much has been expended since initiation of the program, and it is not required to announce the completion or abandonment of a program.

Characteristics of a Repurchase Program

Two characteristics of stock repurchase programs have been examined in the literature: the behavior of the price of a stock around the time of an announcement of a repurchase program for the stock, and the execution of a repurchase program following announcement.

From a sample of 1,157 announcements of stock repurchase programs between 1985 and 1988, Comment and Jarrell (1991) found that on average, the price of a stock outperformed the market by about $2\frac{1}{2}\%$ upon announcement of a repurchase program for the stock. They also found

25. Rule 10b-18 (17 C.F.R. 240.10b-18) of the Securities and Exchange Commission specifies how the transactions can be conducted to avoid a charge of market manipulation. To take advantage of the "safe harbor" provided by the rule, purchases (exclusive of purchases in large block transactions) on any given day cannot exceed 25% of the average daily trading volume during the preceding four weeks and must be executed through a single broker or dealer. No purchases can be executed in the opening transaction in the stock or in the last half hour of trading, and purchases can not be made at a price in excess of the last independent transaction price or in excess of the current independent bid price for the stock.

that the price reaction is an increasing function of the ratio of targeted shares to total shares outstanding.

Stephens and Weisbach (1998) examined the execution of 450 repurchase programs announced between 1981 and 1990.[26] They found that on average, firms repurchased (over an interval of three years following announcement) between 74% and 82% of the shares originally targeted. (The targeted size of an average program amounted to about 7% of the issuer's stock.) The behavior of individual firms differed widely: 10% of the firms bought less than 5% of the shares originally targeted, 57% bought more than the number of shares targeted, and 30% bought more than twice the number of shares targeted. The pace of repurchase activity during a fiscal quarter was positively related to corporate cash flow during the quarter and inversely related to the return on the stock during the preceding quarter (so that a firm typically accelerates its repurchases following a decline in the price of its stock).

Stephens and Weisbach also found that market participants have some ability to forecast the volume of future stock repurchases at the time a repurchase program is announced. They report that the stock price reaction to announcement of a program is an increasing function of the fraction of shares *actually repurchased* during the two years following announcement and is independent of the initially targeted fraction of shares when actual repurchases are assumed to be known. (Actual repurchases serve as a proxy for the market's expectation—at the time of an announcement—of future repurchases.) They observe that the apparent influence of the announced size of a program on the stock price "is due only to the correlation between announced size and the market's expectations of the firm's actual repurchases."[27]

The Information Content of an Announcement of a Stock Repurchase Program

The increase in the price of a stock following announcement of a program to repurchase the stock suggests that the announcement conveys valuable information to market participants. There is, however, some dispute about the nature of the information conveyed by the announcement.

Management Signaling

Some analysts conjecture that the information conveyed by an announcement of a stock repurchase program is management's belief that the stock

---

26. Their sample did not include programs announced in the fourth quarter of 1987, following a sharp break in stock prices in October of that year. Netter and Mitchell (1989) examined repurchase programs announced in the wake of the 1987 market break.

27. Stephens and Weisbach (1998, p. 327).

is undervalued at the existing market price and that repurchasing some of the "cheap" stock is in the best interests of shareholders.[28]

The positive correlation found by Stephens and Weisbach (1998) between the increase in the price of a stock following announcement of a repurchase program and the market's expectation of the quantity of stock to be repurchased (proxied by the quantity of stock actually repurchased) is consistent with the management signaling interpretation. Managers are more likely to repurchase more stock if the stock is more deeply undervalued or if they are more confident of their assessment of the stock's undervaluation, so the announcement of a repurchase program that is expected to lead to more repurchases conveys more positive information.

There are, however, two problems with the management signaling interpretation. First, a firm is not obligated to complete an announced repurchase program. It is well known that many programs are not completed—and that some lead to hardly any repurchases—and there is no evidence that a manager suffers a penalty if his firm fails to complete an announced program. The absence of any penalization of managers who would disseminate a false signal, namely who would announce a repurchase program in the absence of any belief that a stock is undervalued and in the absence of any intent to actually repurchase stock, implies that mere announcement of a repurchase program is not a particularly credible signal that a company's stock is undervalued.

The second problem with the management signaling interpretation is that a substantial fraction of American corporations have initiated stock repurchase programs. Ikenberry and Vermaelen (1996, p. 25) observe that one out of every four companies in the S&P 500 index initiated a repurchase program in 1994 and remark that "... the notion that so many managers of ... closely monitored firms would find their stock undervalued at the same point in time seems unlikely."

A Free Option

Ikenberry and Vermaelen (1996) suggest that announcement of a stock repurchase program is tantamount to a statement by the firm that it is *prepared* to repurchase its stock *if* the stock becomes undervalued *in the future*. The increase in the price of the stock following the announcement reflects the value to shareholders of owning stock in a company where better-informed managers are prepared to buy the stock if it becomes undervalued but are not committed to buying the stock when it is fairly

---

28. This was cited as important by respondents to the survey reported in Wansley, Lane, and Sarkar (1989). Ofer and Thakor (1987) provide a unified analysis of signaling with both dividends and repurchases.

priced or overvalued. This interpretation suggests why so many firms have chosen to announce stock repurchase programs: the firms are publicizing that they are prepared to exercise an option that can enhance the value of their stock.[29] Ikenberry and Vermaelen support their interpretation with empirical evidence that the reaction to an announcement of a repurchase program is stronger when the potential for mispricing is greater: when the market value of the firm exhibits greater volatility and a lower correlation with the "true" value of the firm.

The Determinants of Stock Repurchases

Incorporating stock repurchases into a contingent value model requires that we specify the determinants of the timing and size of the repurchases. The preceding discussion suggests that information asymmetries play an important role in determining the timing and amount of repurchases. Both the management signaling and free option interpretations rely on the notion that a corporation will repurchase stock when its managers, on the basis of their superior information, believe the stock is undervalued.

The timing and amount of stock repurchases is influenced by other factors as well. Stephens and Weisbach (1998) point out the significance of fluctuations in corporate cash flow for repurchase activities. Their results suggest that some firms may use stock repurchases to distribute to shareholders cash that cannot be invested within the firm to enhance the value of equity. Repurchases may be especially attractive for this purpose because repurchases can be varied widely without significant public notice and without the adverse consequences of a comparably volatile dividend policy.[30]

Additionally a commonly cited reason for stock repurchases is to offset stock sold pursuant to exercise of executive and employee stock options.[31] This influence on the pace of a corporation's repurchases has not been examined in the literature, but it is consistent with the notion that companies use discretionary stock repurchases to distribute (to shareholders) cash for which they have no productive use.

29. Announcing an open market stock repurchase program may not be entirely without cost. Such programs increase the risk to market makers and other market participants that when they sell stock they may be selling "cheap" to a buyer (the issuer) with superior information. Barclay and Smith (1988) suggested that this leads to wider bid–ask spreads in secondary market trading and hence to a higher required rate of return on equity and a lower stock price. A more recent study by Miller and McConnell (1995) presents contrary evidence.

30. Corporations virtually never disclose how much stock they have repurchased, at what times and at what prices. Stephens and Weisbach (1998) discuss the difficulty of identifying stock repurchase activity from publicly available information.

31. Baker, Gallagher, and Morgan (1981) and Wansley, Lane, and Sarkar (1989).

Finally, it is important to observe that restrictive dividend covenants treat stock repurchases identically with dividends,[32] so the timing and amount of stock repurchases can be affected by the presence and stringency of such covenants.

Incorporating Stock Repurchases into a Contingent Value Model

Conventional contingent value models do not appear to be capable of supporting a functional representation of stock repurchases because they do not reflect information asymmetries between corporate managers and other market participants. In addition variables likely to be important to the decision to repurchase stock, such as corporate cash flow, the exercise of executive and employee stock options, and the constraints of restrictive dividend covenants, are not prices of traded claims.

16.4   Conclusions

The dividend policy of a firm can be incorporated into a contingent value model if dividends can be expressed as a function of the value of the firm or, more generally, of the prices of traded claims. The review in section 16.1 suggests that regular dividends can be represented (approximately) as a function of the value of equity. The surveys in the subsequent sections suggest that it will be difficult to incorporate policies for special dividends and stock repurchases.

32. Smith and Warner (1979) and Kalay (1982).

17 Leveraged Recapitalizations

The discussion in section 16.2 characterized a special dividend as a discretionary payment to shareholders funded from unusually strong earnings. In some cases, however, a company may choose to pay a special dividend funded with proceeds from a sale of new debt, or to pay a *leveraged* special dividend.[1] This chapter examines leveraged special dividends and a variety of related transactions, denoted generally as "leveraged recapitalizations." We begin by describing a concrete example.

17.1 The Leveraged Special Dividend of Quantum Chemical Corporation

In late 1988 Quantum Chemical Corporation ("Quantum") was a moderately large chemical company capitalized with $580 million in current liabilities, $1.3 billion of long-term debt rated BBB− by Standard & Poor's Corporation ("S&P") and Baa3 by Moody's Investors Services, Inc. ("Moody's"), and 22.8 million shares of common stock with a market price of $88 per share and an aggregate value of $2 billion.[2]

On Wednesday, December 28, 1988, Quantum announced that it would pay a special cash dividend of $50 per share to its common shareholders on January 10, 1989—a dividend equal to almost 60% of the preannouncement price of the stock.[3] The distribution was to be funded initially with a short-term loan that would later be refinanced with proceeds from a sale of longer term debt.

This section describes the economic incentive for Quantum's leveraged special dividend, the financing of the dividend, and the reaction of market participants. We begin with a brief description of Quantum's business operations.[4]

---

1. A company can also make a special payment to shareholders funded with proceeds from a sale of operating assets or from a sale of some of the stock of a subsidiary corporation, that is, from an equity "carve-out." However, such payments appear to be relatively rare. Lang, Poulsen, and Stulz (1995) examined a sample of 93 asset sales that occurred between 1984 and 1989 and found that the proceeds were reinvested in the firm in 57% of the cases and used to pay down debt in 38% of the cases. The authors identified only two cases (Culbro Corp. and Union Carbide) where the proceeds were used to pay a special dividend. In three additional cases (Allied Signal, Federal Mogul, and Koppers) the proceeds were used to repurchase stock. Allen and McConnell (1998) examined a sample of 186 carve-outs that occurred between 1978 and 1993. They were able to identify the use of the proceeds in 167 cases and found that the proceeds were reinvested in either the parent company or the subsidiary in 57% of the 167 cases and used to reduce debt in 39% of the cases. The proceeds were distributed to parent company shareholders in only 7 cases.

2. Quantum Chemical Corporation 1988 Annual Report to Shareholders, pp. 24 and 26.

3. "Quantum Chemical's Recapitalization to Include Special $50-a-Share Payout," *Wall Street Journal*, December 29, 1988, p. A2.

4. See Bower (1986), Bozdogan (1989), and Lane (1993) for discussions of restructuring in the chemical industry during the 1980s, and see also "Investors Take Note: The Push to Enhance Value," *Chemical Week*, February 8, 1989, pp. 21–24, and "Financial Services: Chemical Deals Get Fewer, Friendlier, and Smaller," *Chemical Week*, May 30, 1990, pp. 17–23.

Table 17.1
Quantum Chemical Corporation's net income ($ millions)

	1986	1987	1988
Operating income			
Petrochemicals	93	318	711
Energy	96	118	113
Corporate expenses and other	−35	−85	−64
	154	351	760
Interest expenses	−63	−82	−116
Provision for income taxes	−52	−142	−258
Other	37	125	−3
Net income	76	252	383

Source: "Consolidated Statement of Income" and "Information by Segment," from 1988 Annual Report to Shareholders.

Quantum's Business Operations

At the end of 1988 Quantum divided its principle business activities into two segments: petrochemicals and retail distribution of propane fuel. Petrochemical operations, conducted in the USI Division, consisted primarily of the production and sale of two thermoplastic polymers—polyethylene and polypropylene—and the production of the requisite ethylene and propylene feedstocks. Quantum's second operating division, the Suburban Propane Division, was a major retailer of propane fuel to residential customers. It had 1.2 million customers in 44 states, located primarily on the east and west coasts.

Table 17.1 shows Quantum's net income in 1986, 1987, and 1988. The most significant feature is the explosive growth in operating income attributable to petrochemical operations, increasing from $93 million in 1986 to $711 million in 1988. The growth resulted from a rapidly expanding demand for thermoplastic polymers after mid-1985. The rising demand bumped up against industry capacity constraints in late 1986 and 1987 and triggered unusually large product price increases and increases in operating income.[5]

The astounding profitability of the USI Division led Quantum to undertake several initiatives during 1988. In April the company announced a three year, $1.3 billion capital investment program intended to expand its polymer production capacity.[6] Over the course of 1988 Quantum also

5. Part of the increase in Quantum's petrochemical operating income from 1986 to 1987 was attributable to an increase in shipments following its acquisition of Enron Chemical Company in November 1986. Petrochemical shipments did not change materially from 1987 to 1988. Quantum Chemical Corporation 1988 Annual Report to Shareholders, pp. 20–21.

6. Quantum Chemical Corporation 1988 Annual Report to Shareholders, p. 3.

repurchased 7.4 million shares of common stock at a total cost of $656 million. The repurchases (offset in part by the issuance of stock to Quantum's employee stock ownership plans, ESOPs, and the sale of stock through the company's employee stock option program) reduced the outstanding stock of the company from 29.8 million shares at the end of 1987 to 22.8 million shares at the end of 1988.[7]

During 1988 Quantum additionally sold new long-term debt with an aggregate principal value of $700 million in three separate offerings:

· January 1988: $300 million of 10.50% sinking fund debentures due January 15, 2018.

· June 1988: $200 million of 11.00% sinking fund debentures due July 1, 2018.

· September 1988: $200 million of 10.875% sinking fund debentures due October 1, 2018.

The company used the proceeds to retire other long-term indebtedness and to finance a portion of its capital expenditures and stock repurchases.[8]

Why Quantum Decided to Pay a Leveraged Special Dividend

At the end of 1988 Quantum was enjoying remarkable profitability but the market price of its stock was not rising commensurately. From the end of 1986 to the end of 1988 the price of the stock only doubled—from $42.625 per share on December 31, 1986, to $88.50 on December 27, 1988—while its net income increased fivefold—from $76 million to $383 million. (Over the same interval the S&P 500 stock price index increased about 14%, from 242.17 to 276.83.) The combination of strong earnings and lagging stock prices was evident at other chemical companies and was attributed to investor concern that earnings in the chemical industry were at or near a cyclical peak and that the boom would soon end as new production capacity came on line.[9]

Believing that the stock was undervalued, Quantum's management decided to increase indebtedness substantially and to use the proceeds to pay a special cash dividend to its shareholders.[10] Broadly stated, the company would capitalize and pay out immediately a portion of the

7. Quantum Chemical Corporation 1988 Annual Report to Shareholders, pp. 26 and 38.

8. Quantum Chemical Corporation 1988 Annual Report to Shareholders, pp. 19 and 35.

9. "Heard on the Street: Payouts Become Crucial Weapon in Appeasement," *Wall Street Journal*, January 31, 1989, p. C1.

10. Even though it was unusually large, the special dividend was not prohibited by any covenants in the indentures for the three sinking fund debentures issued by Quantum in 1988.

exceptional profits it expected to earn from its petrochemical operations over the next several years.[11] Quantum's CEO said the dividend was intended to provide shareholders with the full value of their stock, which had gone "unrecognized" by the market.[12]

Concurrent with the announcement of the special dividend, Quantum disclosed that it would lend $172 million to its ESOPs so that the plans could purchase—on January 3, 1989—1.66 million shares of new stock from the company. Thus Quantum planned to pay an aggregate special dividend of $1.225 billion ($1.225 billion = $50 per share times a total of 24.5 million shares outstanding) on January 10, 1989.

Financing the Special Dividend

Quantum's special dividend was financed initially with a short term "bridge loan" for $1.233 billion. The loan accrued interest at the rate of 14% per annum, would mature on July 10, 1989, and would be extendible at Quantum's option for up to three additional 30-day periods, with the rate of interest on the loan increasing by 1% for each 30-day extension.[13]

Quantum refinanced the bridge loan from a variety of sources over the next five months. Its ESOPs repaid $83 million upon receipt of the special dividend on the recently acquired shares ($83 million = $50 per share times 1.66 million shares), and the company used the payment to reduce the principal balance on the bridge loan to $1.150 billion. In March 1989 Quantum sold $300 million of 12.50% senior subordinated notes maturing in 1999 and $500 million of 13% senior subordinated notes maturing in 2004 for aggregate proceeds of $772 million, and used all of the proceeds to reduce the principal balance on the bridge loan to $378 million.[14] The company reduced the principal balance by another $289 million using

11. The combination of strong earnings and lagging stock prices was also evident at companies involved in the production of aluminum and copper ("Heard on the Street: Payouts Become Crucial Weapon in Appeasement," *Wall Street Journal*, January 31, 1989, p. C1). As described in section 16.2, Alcoa also paid a special dividend in the beginning of 1989. However, Alcoa paid its (much more modest) special dividend out of actual past earnings and, unlike Quantum, did not borrow against expected future earnings. See similarly the $10 per share special dividend paid by Phelps Dodge in the second half of 1989 ("Phelps Declares Special Dividend of $10 a Share," *Wall Street Journal*, September 7, 1989, p. B10).

12. "Quantum Chemical's Recapitalization to Include Special $50-a-Share Payout," *Wall Street Journal*, December 29, 1988, p. A2.

13. Tufano (1993, p. 292) observes that it is not unusual for a bridge loan to provide for sharply higher interest rates as the price of extending the maturity of the loan.

14. The new senior subordinated notes were junior to most of Quantum's existing long-term debt, including the three sinking fund debentures sold in 1988 (Prospectus for Quantum Chemical Corporation 12.5% Senior Subordinated Notes Due 1999 and 13% Senior Subordinated Notes Due 2004, dated March 23, 1989, pp. 39–40).

Table 17.2
Prices of Quantum Chemical Corporation's debentures (% of principal value)

	Dec 23, 1988	Dec 30, 1988	Change
10.25% sinking fund debentures due Jan 15, 2018	95.66	86.16	−9.50
11% sinking fund debentures due Jul 1, 2018	100.88	90.38	−10.50
10.875% sinking fund debentures due Oct 1, 2018	99.63	89.25	−10.38

proceeds from the sale of an unrelated operating division in April 1989. The last $89 million was repaid with the proceeds from a sale of ESOP notes in June 1989.[15]

Market Reactions

The market in Quantum's common stock reacted favorably to the announcement of the special dividend. The stock closed at $107.125 per share on December 28, 1988, up 21% from the $88.50 closing price on December 27. (The stock subsequently dropped from $106.75 at the close of trading on January 10, 1989, to $56.625 when it began to trade *ex-dividend* on January 11.)

The bond market reacted sharply and negatively to the announcement of the credit-financed dividend. As shown in table 17.2, the market prices of the three sinking fund debentures issued in 1988 dropped about 10 points following the announcement.[16] S&P lowered its rating on Quantum's senior debt to BB− and Moody's downgraded the debt to Ba2, citing the "substantially more leveraged capital structure" of the company.[17]

17.2   The Economics of a Leveraged Recapitalization

A leveraged recapitalization is a distribution of cash to common shareholders financed with new debt. The distribution may be effected by a

15. Quantum Chemical Corporation 1988 Annual Report to Shareholders, p. 29 and 1989 Annual Report to Shareholders, pp. 18 and 19.

16. See also the allegation of the plaintiff in *Geren v. Quantum Chemical Corp.*, 832 F. Supp. 728 (S.D.N.Y. 1993) that the market price of Quantum's subordinated debt dropped 50% following announcement of the special dividend. Such debt was especially vulnerable because it ranked below the senior subordinated debt sold to refinance part of the original bridge loan.

17. "S&P Downgrades Ratings on Quantum Chemical," *Wall Street Journal and Dow Jones News Wire*, December 28, 1988, 1:45 PM and "Moody's Downgrades Quantum Chemical," *Wall Street Journal and Dow Jones News Wire*, January 20, 1989, 11:18 AM.

special dividend—as in the case of Quantum—but it can also be effected by repurchases of stock and by other means. (Appendix A describes how Colt Industries effected a credit-financed payment to its shareholders with an exchange and redemption of securities.) The term also denotes other similar transactions that lead to comparable distributions and increases in leverage, such as an exchange of new debt for outstanding equity or a pro rata distribution of new debt to common shareholders.[18] The terminology derives from the observation that a firm selling debt and distributing the proceeds to shareholders (or exchanging debt for equity, or distributing debt to shareholders) is increasing its leverage without restructuring its assets; that is, it is "recapitalizing" its existing operations.[19]

This section examines the economic incentives for a firm to undertake a leveraged recapitalization. We begin by describing how the transaction can mitigate the problem of free cash flow identified by Jensen (1986).

The Problem of Free Cash Flow

Free cash flow, defined by Jensen (1986, p. 323) as "cash flow in excess of that required to fund all projects that have positive net present values when discounted at the relevant cost of capital," cannot be deployed within a firm to enhance the value of the enterprise, so the most efficient use is to return it to shareholders as a dividend or with stock repurchases.[20] However, companies pay dividends and repurchase stock at the discretion of senior managers, and a manager may have a personal incentive to limit payments to shareholders in order to maintain or expand the

18. An exchange of new debt for outstanding equity is equivalent to a sale of the debt to existing shareholders and a contemporaneous repurchase of stock from the same shareholders funded with the proceeds of the debt sale. A pro rata distribution of new debt is equivalent to a pro rata sale of the debt to shareholders and a concurrent cash dividend payment funded with the proceeds of the debt sale.

The appendix to Denis and Denis (1993) gives brief descriptions of 39 proposed leveraged recapitalizations, 29 of which were completed. See also Kleiman (1988), the appendix to Gupta and Rosenthal (1991), and exhibit 1 in Handa and Radhakrishnan (1991). Individual leveraged recapitalizations are described in detail in Wruck (1994), *Colt Industries*, Harvard Business School Case Study 9-289-012 (1988); *Colt Industries, Inc.*, Harvard Business School Teaching Note 5-292-087 (1992); *FMC Corporation: A Recapitalization*, Harvard Business School Case Study 9-191-084 (1990); *FMC Corporation: A Recapitalization*, Harvard Business School Teaching Note 5-193-163 (1993); *Sealed Air Corporation's Leveraged Recapitalization (A)*, Harvard Business School Case Study 9-294-122 (1994); *Sealed Air Corporation's Leveraged Recapitalization (B)*, Harvard Business School Case Study 9-294-123 (1994); *Sealed Air Corporation's Leveraged Recapitalization (A) and (B)*, Harvard Business School Teaching Note 5-295-143 (1995); *USG Corporation*, Harvard Business School Case Study 9-027-052 (1996); and *USG Corporation*, Harvard Business School Teaching Note 5-297-093 (1997).

19. Masulis (1980a, 1983) emphasizes the significance of rearranging the capital structure of the firm without restructuring assets.

20. See also Lease, John, Kalay, Loewenstein, and Sarig (2000, pp. 29–30).

range of assets he controls. What is sometimes called "pyramid building" is especially likely if a manager's compensation is based on the idea that managers with control over more assets have greater responsibilities and therefore deserve greater compensation.[21]

The problem of free cash flow is the agency problem (Jensen and Meckling 1976; Stulz 1990) that a manager may choose to retain cash in an enterprise even when retention leads to investments that have negative net present values and that reduce the value of the firm.[22] Jensen (1986, p. 324) observes that the problem is likely to be especially important for companies that generate substantial cash flow but have limited growth prospects. The problem also appears when a firm fails to take advantage of an opportunity to sell an operating division or subsidiary at a price in excess of the operation's value to the enterprise,[23] or when it fails to terminate an activity that has a negative net present value in excess of the costs of closure.[24]

More subtly, the existence of free cash flow can reduce managerial incentives to run an enterprise efficiently. Wruck (1994, p. 196) points out that free cash flow "creates a comfortable cushion that is difficult to give up, and stunts any sense of urgency toward undertaking performance-improving actions."

Corporate managers commonly promise that they will run an enterprise efficiently and that they will pay out free cash flow as it appears,[25] but such promises sometimes lack credibility in light of managerial incentives to run larger businesses and to run them comfortably cushioned against

21. The managerial incentive to "build pyramids" and to prefer growth (of sales or assets) for its own sake is discussed in Baker and Smith (1998, pp. 8–18). See also Baumol (1962, 1967), Marris (1963, 1964), Coughlan and Schmidt (1985, p. 45), Benston (1985, pp. 67–71), Baker, Jensen, and Murphy (1988), Lang, Poulsen, and Stulz (1995), and Allen and McConnell (1998).

22. See, for example, the discussion of the negative net present value of exploration and development programs in the oil and gas industry in the late 1970s and early 1980s in McConnell and Muscarella (1985, pp. 418–19) and Jensen (1986, pp. 326–28).

23. In financing part of its leveraged special dividend by selling an operating division, Quantum noted that the division "enjoys a commanding position in its ... markets, but it is unrelated to the rest of our chemical business. We believe that it is worth substantially more to a strategic buyer than it can be to Quantum." Quantum Chemical Corporation 1988 Annual Report to Shareholders, p. 4. Harris and Raviv (1990) discuss the related case where a manager may choose to continue operating a firm even though liquidation is more beneficial to shareholders. See also Mehran, Nogler, and Schwartz (1998).

24. See the description of the value of closing (in 1984) the exploration and development program of Gulf Oil Corporation (a program with a negative net present value comparable to the total market value of Gulf's common stock) in *Gulf Oil Corporation—Takeover*, Harvard Business School Case Study 9-285-053 (1984) and *Gulf Oil Corporation—Takeover*, Harvard Business School Teaching Note 5-292-071 (1984).

25. The special dividend policy announced by Alcoa in early 1989 (see section 15.2) was an unusually explicit promise to pay out earnings that the firm could not reinvest efficiently.

distress. Accordingly market participants may come to discount the value of a firm for the risk that its managers are retaining cash and running the firm inefficiently.

Mitigating the Problem of Free Cash Flow with a Leveraged Recapitalization

A manager can make a credible commitment to pay out free cash flow by undertaking a leveraged recapitalization: by distributing new debt to shareholders, by exchanging new debt for outstanding equity, or by selling new debt and distributing the proceeds to shareholders. These actions create a credible commitment because they substitute *contractual* principal and interest obligations for *discretionary* dividend payments.[26] Leveraged recapitalizations can also be used to promote value-enhancing change in managerial behavior and to wring out operating inefficiencies (Jensen 1986, p. 324, and Wruck 1994).

Incentives to Undertake a Leveraged Recapitalization

A manager, acting on behalf of shareholders and anticipating that the existing operations and capital structure of a firm will generate significant future free cash flow, has at least three reasons for undertaking a leveraged recapitalization.

First, the value of the firm—and hence the value of the firm's equity—will increase with the reduction in the discount associated with the (reduced) risk of uneconomic retention of cash and inefficient operations.[27] Second, the value of the firm will be enhanced by the value of the tax shield associated with additional debt.[28] Third, a leveraged recapitalization can trigger a wealth transfer from creditors to stockholders.

---

26. Jensen (1986, p. 324). Stulz (1990) describes how a debt-financed dividend can enhance the value of a firm when managers would otherwise retain cash and invest beyond an efficient scale. (Jensen 1988, p. 852, had observed earlier that in a similar fashion, the debt issued in the leveraged buyout of RJR-Nabisco "prohibits RJR from continuing to squander its cashflows on the wasteful projects that it had undertaken prior to the buyout.") Harris and Raviv (1990) describe how a debt-financed dividend can enhance the value of a firm by increasing the likelihood of liquidation when managers would prefer to continue to operate the firm even though liquidation is more beneficial to shareholders. DeAngelo and DeAngelo (2000) note that dividend payments from a modestly leveraged firm can play a similar, albeit somewhat attenuated, role if the firm is controlled by a cohesive group of shareholders with a strong personal interest in such payments. See also the discussion of exchanges of new *preferred* stock for outstanding common stock in Pinegar and Lease (1986).

27. Stulz (1988) notes that a leveraged recapitalization may also increase the value of the firm by enhancing management's share of equity and increasing the premium that an outside bidder must offer in a takeover contest.

28. See Masulis (1980a, 1983); *Colt Industries, Inc.*, Harvard Business School Teaching Note 5-292-087 (1992), p. 4; Wruck (1994, pp. 164–65); and *Sealed Air Corporation's Leveraged Recapitalization (A) and (B)*, Harvard Business School Teaching Note 5-295-143 (1985), p. 7.

The Wealth Transfer Effect

The wealth transfer associated with a leveraged recapitalization is not difficult to understand.

Suppose, for simplicity, that announcement of a previously unanticipated leveraged special dividend has no effect on the aggregate value of the firm, and suppose also that the new debt to be issued by the firm will rank pari passu with the old debt. Since, by assumption, the value of the firm does not change following the announcement, and since the new debt will have the same priority as the old debt, the value of the old debt must fall when the recapitalization is announced—and the value of the firm's equity must rise by the same amount.[29] (The value of the old debt can fall—and the value of equity can rise—even if the new debt is subordinated to the old debt if market participants believe that the absolute priority rule may not be respected in the event of bankruptcy and that junior creditors may receive something even if more senior creditors are not paid in full; Masulis 1980a, 1983.)

Appendix B describes in more detail the mechanics of wealth transfer stemming from an unanticipated recapitalization.

Empirical Evidence

Masulis (1980a) examined the effect on debt and equity values of offers to exchange new debt for outstanding equity.[30] On average, over a sample of 85 exchange offers made between 1962 and 1976, the value of a firm's common stock increased 9.8% in excess of its expected value at the end of a two-day interval that included the announcement of the offer. The value of a firm's outstanding nonconvertible debt declined, on average, about 0.3%. The decline in debt value was greater (-0.8%) for debt whose covenants did not limit the issuance of additional debt of equal or greater seniority. It was smaller (-0.2%) for debt whose covenants prohibited the issuance of such debt.

These results are consistent with the proposition that managers undertake leveraged recapitalizations when the transactions enhance the value of the firm and that they typically structure the transactions to capture for shareholders all of the increase in value. The results also suggest that on average, leveraged recapitalizations lead to modest net wealth transfers

29. Following *completion* of the sale of the new debt and distribution of the proceeds to shareholders, the value of equity will fall from the post-announcement level by the value of the distribution, that is, by the value of the new debt that has entered the capital structure of the firm.

30. See also Masulis (1983) and the study by Pinegar and Lease (1986) of leverage-increasing exchanges of new preferred stock for outstanding common stock.

from creditors to shareholders. (Quantum's leveraged special dividend shows that in some cases the wealth transfer from creditors can be quite substantial. See similarly the wealth transfer associated with the leveraged recapitalization of Colt Industries described in appendix A.)

Leveraged Recapitalization as a Response to Control Threats

The mid- and late 1980s witnessed a string of unusually large leveraged recapitalizations, many of which were undertaken in response to a control threat to incumbent management or out of fear that such a threat could materialize in the near future. Appendix C discusses the view that these recapitalizations corrected distortions in equity values and corporate operations induced by misalignment of management and shareholder interests.

17.3   Leveraged Recapitalizations and the Contingent Value of Corporate Securities

We observed in chapter 15 that maximization of shareholder value in the context of a conventional contingent value model of corporate securities prices does not lead to a reasonable representation of the dividend policy of a firm, but we suggested in chapter 16 that the policy of a firm for paying regular dividends (as well as, possibly, special dividends funded from unusually strong earnings) might be identifiable from the historical behavior of the firm. In contrast, leveraged recapitalizations are rare events, and it seems unlikely that we can identify the policy of a firm regarding the timing and terms of a recapitalization by examining its historical behavior. We have to inquire more fundamentally into the economics of when a recapitalization might be in the best interest of shareholders. Any such inquiry requires analysis of the investment opportunities of the firm, the range of feasible financing instruments, the limitations imposed by bond covenants, and the prospect for expropriating wealth from existing creditors, as well as an assessment of how deeply the market might be discounting the value of the firm for the risk of uneconomic retention of cash and inefficient operations.[31]

Identifying whether a leveraged recapitalization is in the best interest of shareholders is hardly trivial, but incorporating a functional representation of recapitalization policy into a contingent value model may be even more difficult. We would have to specify transversality conditions linking the pre-recapitalization contingent values of the firm's securities to post-recapitalization values. The transversality conditions would reflect the

---

31. The case studies cited in note 18 illustrate how such analyses are undertaken in practice.

determinants of the decision to recapitalize and the terms of the recapitalization. This requires, however, a more detailed representation of the internal structure of the firm than is available in conventional models, where the firm is characterized by its aggregate value and a stochastic process describing the evolution of that value. In addition it is likely that at least some of the variables affecting the decision to recapitalize and the terms of a recapitalization will not be prices of traded claims. This would raise impediments to contingent valuation of the firm's securities comparable to those discussed in earlier chapters.

Leveraged Recapitalizations as a Source of Uncertainty

There is also reason to suspect that corporate policies for leveraged recapitalizations may be inherently difficult to identify. Empirical evidence shows that public announcement of a leveraged recapitalization leads, on average, to a significant increase in the value of equity and the value of the firm as a whole. This implies that on average, the announcements were not fully anticipated by market participants.[32] In particular, it suggests that a leveraged recapitalization is a discretionary managerial act with a significant element of unpredictability, in contrast to discretionary but more or less predictable corporate actions like early redemption of debt and payment of cash interest on a PIK bond.[33] Thus the process describing the evolution of the value of the firm may not be a simple lognormal random walk, but may include the prospect of a discontinuous jump (at the time a decision to recapitalize is announced).

Appendix A: The Leveraged Recapitalization of Colt Industries

In mid-1986 Colt Industries, Inc. ("Colt") was a moderately large manufacturer of aerospace, automotive, and industrial products, conservatively capitalized with $265 million of current liabilities, $340 million in long term debt, and 19.4 million shares of common stock with a market price of about $67 per share and an aggregate value of $1.3 billion. Its long-term debt consisted primarily of two securities—$150 million of 10.125%

32. Hite, Owers, and Rogers (1987, p. 250) make a similar observation regarding the ability of market participants to anticipate when managers might choose to liquidate a firm. Mehran, Nogler, and Schwartz (1998) report that the decision of a firm to liquidate is not perfectly predictable from publicly available information (p. 331 and table 3) and, on average, leads to an increase of 10 to 15% in the value of its equity (p. 335 and table 4).

33. The unpredictability of a leveraged recapitalization may arise because some variables that influence management's decision to recapitalize are not observable by market participants. For example, the decision of Quantum to pay a leveraged special dividend was, in part, the result of its managers' assessment of the likely persistence of high prices for thermoplastic polymers.

notes due in 1995 and $150 million of 11.25% debentures due in 2015—
that the company sold in late 1985. The debt was rated A+ by S&P and
A2 by Moody's. About 7% of its stock (1.3 million shares) was owned by
its employee retirement savings plan.[34]

On Sunday, July 20, 1986, Colt announced that it planned to recapitalize, paying out more than $1.5 billion to its common shareholders and
increasing indebtedness substantially.[35] This appendix describes Colt's
leveraged recapitalization and the reaction of market participants to the
announcement of the recapitalization.[36]

The Leveraged Recapitalization

The recapitalization was to take place in three stages:[37]

• Immediately prior to the effective date of the recapitalization, the company would exchange one one-hundredth of a share of a new issue of preferred stock, designated Series A Participating Preferred, for each share
of Colt common stock owned by the company's employee retirement
savings plan.

• On the effective date of the recapitalization, the company would exchange one share of new common stock and one one-hundredth of a share
of a second new issue of preferred stock, designated Series B Participating
Preferred, for each share of Colt common stock owned by its remaining
shareholders.

• Promptly after the exchanges described above, the company would
redeem each one one-hundredth of a share of Series B Participating Preferred for $85 in cash, and exchange one share of new common stock plus
additional shares of such stock with a market value of $85 for each one
one-hundredth of a share of Series A Participating Preferred.

As a result of the recapitalization, Colt would make a cash payment to its
common shareholders (other than the employee retirement savings plan)
of $85 per share—equal to more than 125% of the preannouncement
price of its stock—and its shareholders would retain "stub" stock (the

---

34. Colt Industries, Inc. 1985 Annual Report to Shareholders, pp. 25, 33, and 34 and Colt
Industries, Inc. Proxy Statement/Prospectus dated September 5, 1986 (hereafter, "Proxy/
Prospectus"), pp. 12 and 80.

35. "Colt Industries Plans to Recapitalize, Distributing over $1.5 Billion to Holders," *Wall
Street Journal*, July 21, 1986, p. 2.

36. Colt's recapitalization is also discussed in *Colt Industries*, Harvard Business School Case
Study 9-289-012 (1988), and *Colt Industries, Inc.*, Harvard Business School Teaching Note
5-292-087 (1992).

37. Proxy/Prospectus, p. 28.

new common stock) that analysts estimated would be worth between $10 and $15 per share.[38] In lieu of a cash payment to the savings plan, Colt would issue additional stub stock. It was expected that this would leave the savings plan with more than 30% of the stock of the company.[39]

Colt estimated that it would need $1.6 billion to finance the recapitalization. The company proposed to obtain $700 million from a term loan provided by a syndicate of bank lenders, $200 million from a revolving credit facility provided by the same group of lenders, $525 million from a new issue of senior subordinated debt, and $175 million from liquidating assets.[40]

Completion of the recapitalization was contingent on approval by a majority of Colt's common shareholders.[41] Approval by holders of the company's notes and debentures was not needed because the recapitalization was not prohibited by any of the covenants in the indentures for those securities.

Why Colt Recapitalized

Colt's CEO said the recapitalization was "selected as a means of maximizing shareholder value" and observed that it would provide shareholders with "an opportunity to receive a premium over historical prices for a portion of their [shares] while permitting [them] to retain a significant ongoing equity interest" in Colt.[42] The company had examined a variety of alternatives to recapitalization but concluded that "long-term shareholder values would be maximized through a recapitalization of the [company] that would create a more leveraged capital structure." Senior

38. Stub stock is discussed in "Stub Stocks Soar and Investors Latch onto the Trend," *Wall Street Journal*, August 18, 1989, p. C1.

39. "Colt Industries Plans to Recapitalize, Distributing over $1.5 Billion to Holders," *Wall Street Journal*, July 21, 1986, p. 2. Colt effected its recapitalization with new common stock and two series of preferred stock to comply with technical provisions of the law of the state in which it was incorporated (Proxy/Prospectus, p. 10).

40. Proxy/Prospectus, pp. 36–37. The term loan and borrowings under the revolving credit facility would rank pari passu with the company's existing long-term debt, including the 10.125% notes due in 1995 and the 11.25% debentures due in 2015. The senior subordinated debt would be junior to the term loan and borrowings under the revolving credit facility, as well as to most of the company's existing long term debt, including the notes due in 1995 and the debentures due in 2015. Proxy/Prospectus, pp. 37–46, and Prospectus for Colt Industries Inc. 12.5% Senior Subordinated Debentures Due 2001 dated September 30, 1986, pp. 57–58.

41. Colt held a special meeting of shareholders on September 29, 1986, and obtained the approval of more than 80% of the shares outstanding for the proposed recapitalization. "Colt Industries Holders Clear Recapitalization Plan," *Wall Street Journal*, September 30, 1986, p. 18.

42. "Colt Industries Plans to Recapitalize, Distributing over $1.5 Billion to Holders," *Wall Street Journal*, July 21, 1986, p. 2, and Proxy/Prospectus, p. 10.

managers believed the company's business could "support substantially more indebtedness than is presently outstanding...."[43]

Some market participants speculated that the recapitalization was intended to reduce the vulnerability of the modestly leveraged company to a hostile takeover. One portfolio manager remarked that "Something must have triggered this. Its too dramatic to be a random event." However, the company denied the speculation.[44]

Market Reactions

The market in Colt common stock reacted favorably to the proposed recapitalization. On Monday, July 21, 1986, the stock closed at $93.625 per share, an increase of 40% from the $66.75 closing price on Friday, July 18.

The bond market reacted sharply and negatively to Colt's plan. The yield on the company's bonds rose 200 basis points, from 9.5% per annum to 11.5%, as bond prices dropped as much as 20 points. One bond market participant characterized the recapitalization as "devastating." S&P downgraded Colt's public debt to B, citing the "very high financial risk" stemming from the recapitalization, and Moody's downgraded the debt to Ba2.[45]

The recapitalization became effective on Tuesday, October 7, 1986, concurrent with the closing on the bank loans, the sale of $550 million of 12.50% senior subordinated debentures due in 2001, and the payment to common shareholders (other than the employee retirement savings plan) of $85 per share. The price of the company's stock dropped from $96.75 at the close of trading on October 7 to $11.75 when the new stub stock began to trade on October 8.[46]

43. Proxy/Prospectus, pp. 6 and 10.

44. "Heard on the Street: Colt Industries Uses Novel Recapitalization That Sharply Boosts Debt to Lift Stock Price," *Wall Street Journal*, July 24, 1986, p. 53. See also "Credit Ratings: S&P, Moody's Review Various Debt Issues of Colt Industries, Inc.," *Wall Street Journal*, July 22, 1986, p. 45, and "Colt Says Financing for Recapitalization Has Been Arranged," *Wall Street Journal*, September 8, 1986, p. 36.

45. "Heard on the Street: Colt Industries Uses Novel Recapitalization that Sharply Boosts Debt to Lift Stock Price," *Wall Street Journal*, July 24, 1986, p. 53; "Heard on the Street: 'Recapitalizations' Are a Bonanza for Some, But Bondholders Can Take a Terrific Beating," *Wall Street Journal*, June 1, 1987, p. 53; "Credit Ratings: Colt Industries Inc. Senior Debt Lowered to Single-B by S&P," *Wall Street Journal*, September 4, 1986, p. 37; and "Credit Ratings: Colt Industries Gets Ratings Downgrade," *Wall Street Journal*, September 12, 1986, p. 47.

46. The retirement savings plan received 8.4 shares of stub stock for each share of common stock that it held prior to the recapitalization (8.4 shares = 1 share + 7.4 additional shares worth $85) and ended up with 38% of the stock of the company. The number of additional shares of stub stock distributed to the savings plan was computed as 7.4 shares = $85/$11.50 per share, where $11.50 was the median closing price of the stub stock over the first 15 trading days after October 7, 1986. Proxy/Prospectus, p. 2, and Colt Industries Inc. 1986 Annual Report to Shareholders, pp. 16–17.

Appendix B: The Mechanics of Wealth Transfer Stemming from an Unanticipated Leveraged Special Dividend

This appendix illustrates how an unanticipated leveraged special dividend can lead to a transfer of wealth from creditors to stockholders. We assume the U.S. Treasury yield curve is flat and stationary at a yield of $R_f = 0.10$ (or 10% per annum) and that the log of the value of the firm evolves as a Gaussian random walk with volatility $\sigma = 0.20$ (or 20% over one year).

Suppose that the firm is capitalized initially with a zero-coupon bond promising to pay 82.436 in five years and common stock that is not expected to pay a dividend before the bond has been redeemed. The dashed lines in figure 17.1 show the contingent value of the debt and equity of the firm.[47]

Now suppose that the firm sells new debt (ranking pari passu with the old debt) that also promises to pay 82.436 in five years and distributes the proceeds of the sale as a dividend to stockholders. The heavy solid lines in figure 17.1 show the contingent value of the old debt and the equity *following* the debt sale and dividend payment.[48] (The contingent value of the new debt is identical to the contingent value of the old debt, because the two issues have identical terms and equal priority.)

To understand the mechanics of wealth transfer, we have to examine carefully how the contingent values of the old debt and equity shift from the dashed lines to the heavy solid lines in figure 17.1.

Since the holders of the old debt do not receive a payment in connection with the recapitalization, the contingent value of that debt will shift from the dashed line to the solid line in the upper panel of figure 17.1 *immediately upon announcement* of the prospective transaction.

Also immediately upon announcement of the transaction, the contingent value of equity will shift from the dashed line in the lower panel of figure 17.1 to a function, shown with a thin solid line, that is the sum of

1. the contingent value of the equity following sale of the new debt and distribution of the proceeds to shareholders, namely the heavy solid line in the lower panel of the figure, and

2. the amount of the prospective dividend.

47. The dashed line in the upper panel of figure 17.1 is identical to the solid line in the upper panel of figure 3.2 for the reason noted in note 11 in chapter 3.

48. The solid line in the upper panel is identical to the dashed line in the upper panel of figure 3.2. The heavy solid line in the lower panel is identical to the contingent value function in figure 3.3.

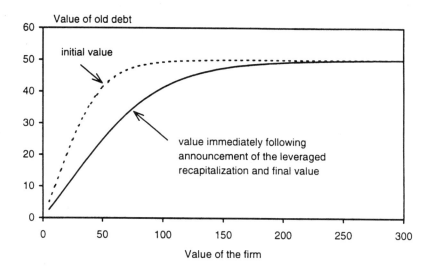

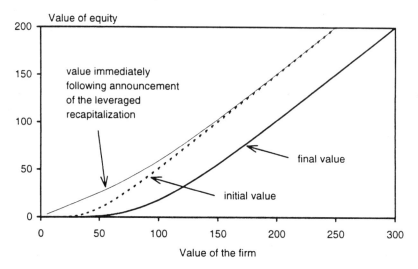

Figure 17.1
Wealth transfer from creditors to shareholders associated with an unanticipated leveraged special dividend

The amount of the prospective dividend is identical to the prospective value of the new debt, because all of the proceeds from the sale of that debt will be paid to shareholders. The function describing the contingent amount of the dividend is therefore identical to the contingent value function shown with a solid line in the upper panel of figure 17.1. (As noted above, the solid line in the upper panel describes the contingent value of the new debt as well as the contingent value of the old debt following announcement of the leveraged recapitalization.)

The announcement of the leveraged recapitalization transfers wealth from creditors to shareholders in the sense that the decline in the contingent value of the debt in the upper panel of figure 17.1 matches the rise in the contingent value of equity in the lower panel. Upon sale of the new debt and distribution of the proceeds to shareholders, the contingent value of equity will shift from the thin solid line to the heavy solid line in the lower panel of figure 17.1. This shift reflects the decline in the value of the stock when it begins to trade *ex*-dividend.

Appendix C: Control Threats and Large Leveraged Recapitalizations in the Middle and Late 1980s

Denis and Denis (1993) examined a sample of 39 firms that proposed exceptionally large leveraged recapitalizations between 1984 and 1988. They found that almost 90% of the proposals came at a time when incumbent management was threatened with a loss of control as a result of a proxy contest or hostile acquisition proposal.[49] This raises an important question: if firms undertake leveraged recapitalizations as a result of managers acting in the best interests of shareholders, why do we observe relatively few large recapitalizations undertaken in the absence of a control threat?

Large leveraged recapitalizations may have been undertaken primarily as takeover defenses because of a selection phenomenon. A manager whose personal interests are closely aligned with shareholder interests—as a result, for example, of the manager's ownership of stock and stock options—is unlikely to ignore the problem of free cash flow to the point

---

49. Fear that a control threat could materialize in the near future played a role in prompting the recapitalization of Colt industries (*Colt Industries*, Harvard Business School Case Study 9-289-012 (1988), and *Colt Industries, Inc.*, Harvard Business School Teaching Note 5-292-087 (1992)). The relationship between control threats and leveraged recapitalizations is also examined in *USG Corporation*, Harvard Business School Case Study 9-027-052 (1996); *USG Corporation*, Harvard Business School Teaching Note 5-297-093 (1997); *FMC Corporation: A Recapitalization*, Harvard Business School Case Study 9-191-084 (1990); and *FMC Corporation: A Recapitalization*, Harvard Business School Teaching Note 5-193-163 (1993). See also the study by Denis (1990) of 49 firms involved in a control contest sometime between 1980 and 1987 that paid out a special dividend or repurchased stock.

where her firm both becomes an attractive takeover target and would benefit from a significant recapitalization. Instead, the manager will address the problems of free cash flow and operating inefficiencies more or less continuously through time. She is likely to pay out free cash flow as it appears and to maintain the indebtedness of the firm at a level high enough to limit the prospect of future free cash flow and to keep operating inefficiencies from seeping in.[50] Such timely and continuous attention to shareholder interests will forestall the development of a discount in the market value of the firm (stemming from inefficient operations and uneconomic cash retention) that would make the firm an attractive takeover target. It will also make unnecessary the large distribution to shareholders and the abrupt change in capital structure that are the hallmarks of a large leveraged recapitalization.[51]

On the other hand, a manager whose interests are not closely aligned with shareholder interests may be relatively more sensitive to the significant personal costs of paying out free cash flow and maintaining indebtedness at an efficient level, including

· limitation of the range of assets controlled by the manager and hence of compensation based on management responsibilities,

· more stressful management responsibilities due to reduced operating slack, and

· a greater likelihood of financial distress and ensuing replacement.[52]

Such a manager may be reluctant to undertake a leveraged recapitalization except to shield himself from a more immediate threat of replacement.[53]

---

50. One fixed income analyst commented in the fall of 2000 that the increasing alignment of management and shareholder interests from stock and stock option grants in the 1990s had resulted in a "slow, leveraged recapitalization of corporate America" and transfer of risk to creditors. "Heard on the Street: Bond Players Warned Early about AT&T," *Wall Street Journal*, October 30, 2000, p. C1.

51. A systematic assessment of large leveraged recapitalizations undertaken in the absence of a control threat has not appeared in the literature. Wruck (1994) provides a case study of one such transaction.

52. These personal costs are noted by Lease et al. (2000, p. 84).

53. One fixed income portfolio manager commented that companies with little debt and a "sleepy management" were once a bondholder's dream because "you knew they wouldn't embark on anything reckless," but that they lost their appeal when in the mid-1980s they proved attractive as takeover candidates and liable to recapitalize in the course of defending themselves. "Heard on the Street: 'Recapitalizations' Are a Bonanza for Some, but Bondholders Can Take a Terrific Beating," *Wall Street Journal*, June 1, 1987, p. 53.

Stulz (1990, p. 13) points out the importance of the market for corporate control for promoting efficient capital structures: "... management could voluntarily issue debt ... to raise firm value so that shareholders do not tender their shares to a bidder that offers less than the firm is worth with the optimal amount of debt. Alternatively, a large shareholder could find it profitable to acquire shares to force management to issue the optimal amount of debt."

Empirical Evidence on the Characteristics of Firms That Undertake Large Leveraged Recapitalizations

Of the 39 firms identified by Denis and Denis (1993), 28 completed a proposed recapitalization and had publicly traded equity. The authors examined the characteristics of the 28 firms before and after their respective recapitalizations.

Prior to recapitalization, the authors found that on average, an announcement of a new investment—including an acquisition of another firm or an expansion of physical plant—resulted in a *decrease* in the price of the firm's stock and a *reduction* in shareholder wealth. Denis and Denis contrasted this with the observation of McConnell and Muscarella (1985) that an unexpected increase in corporate capital expenditures is typically associated with an increase in equity value. They concluded (Denis and Denis 1993, p. 230) that on average, the firms in their sample "misallocated resources through poor investment decisions in the years leading up to the [leveraged recapitalizations]." This conclusion is consistent with uneconomic cash retention and, more broadly, with a misalignment of management interests and shareholder interests.

Following completion of a leveraged recapitalization, the authors found that on average, the operating income of a firm increased (a result consistent with an improvement in operating efficiency), undistributed cash flow[54] declined (consistent with substantially larger interest obligations), and capital expenditures fell. They also found that post-recapitalization announcements of new investments were not, on average, associated with any significant change in the price of a firm's stock. They concluded that the reduction in capital expenditures following recapitalization was the result of a greater propensity to reject projects with a negative net present value.[55]

On average, over all 28 cases Denis and Denis found that the value of the firms' common stock appreciated about 32% relative to the market as a whole as a result of the leveraged recapitalizations.[56] This is consistent

---

54. Undistributed cash flow is operating income less interest, taxes and dividends.

55. Nine of the 28 firms encountered financial distress following their recapitalization and had to either restructure their debt privately or file for bankruptcy. In a subsequent study Denis and Denis (1995) found that the nine instances of distress resulted from industrywide problems, unexpectedly low proceeds from asset sales, and an adverse economic and regulatory environment.

56. Four of the 28 recapitalizations were announced in the absence of any control threat to incumbent management. On average, over these four cases the price of the firms' common stock appreciated about 14.5% relative to the market during a two-day interval that included the announcement of the proposed transaction.

The other 24 recapitalizations were undertaken in the context of a control threat. In these cases the price of a company's stock immediately prior to announcement of a proposed

with the proposition that managers undertake large leveraged recapitalizations when the transactions are beneficial to shareholders. In some cases managers acts voluntarily, but in many cases they are forced to act by the threat of a loss of control.

Gupta and Rosenthal (1991) found that on average, a large leveraged recapitalization also leads to a modest reduction in the value of a corporation's previously outstanding debt. This result supports the proposition that managers typically structure large leveraged recapitalizations to capture for shareholders all of the increase in the value of the firm generated by the transactions.

---

recapitalization may already reflect some anticipation by market participants that the company's managers would, as a defensive device, propose a recapitalization. (Gupta and Rosenthal 1991 report a 15.6% average increase in stock value associated with an announcement of a leveraged recapitalization when a firm in not already engaged in a contest for control, but only a 1.7% average increase in value when a firm is involved in such a contest.) To account for such anticipatory pricing, Denis and Denis computed the abnormal appreciation in stock price over an interval beginning immediately prior to the first indication of any "corporate control activity" and terminating when uncertainty about the outcome of the proposed transaction had been resolved.

The magnitude of the abnormal increase in the value of a firm's stock associated with a leveraged recapitalization was positively correlated with the magnitude of the subsequent reduction in the firm's capital expenditures. This is another indication that the reduction in capital expenditures following a leveraged recapitalization is a result of a greater propensity to reject investments with a negative net present value.

18 Spin-offs

The most familiar form of a corporate distribution to shareholders is cash: commonly as a dividend, but alternatively through stock repurchases. Sometimes, however, companies make distributions in other forms, including especially when they "spin off" the common stock of a subsidiary.

This chapter examines spin-offs and discusses whether they can be incorporated into a contingent value model of corporate securities prices. We begin with a brief introduction to the economics of a spin-off, and then describe a spin-off proposed by Marriott Corporation in 1992.

18.1 The Economics of a Spin-off

A spin-off occurs when a corporation distributes to its shareholders substantially all of the common stock that it owns in an operating subsidiary.[1] In the simplest case the parent company owns and distributes *all* of the subsidiary stock. The transaction partitions two businesses previously under common management into two separately managed businesses.[2]

Financial analysts have suggested a variety of motives for a firm to spin off an operating subsidiary.[3] First, a spin-off can reduce diseconomies of scale and scope, allowing the managers of the parent company to focus their attention on a narrower range of business activities and enhancing the authority and independence of the managers of the subsidiary.[4] This parallels the frequently expressed preference of investors and analysts for "pure plays," or for companies engaged in a single line of business with

---

1. Analysts usually exclude cases where a firm distributes some of the stock of a subsidiary but retains a controlling interest (e.g., the distribution of 42%—and retention of 58%—of the stock of Masco Industries by Masco Corp. in 1984, described in Cusatis, Miles, and Woolridge 1993, p. 295n. 3), as well as cases where a firm distributes stock in a firm that it did not previously control (e.g., the distribution of General Electric stock by Cyprus Mines in 1978, also described in Cusatis, Miles, and Woolridge 1993, p. 295n. 3).

2. Businesses can also be partitioned with a split-off: an exchange of stock of a subsidiary corporation for some of the outstanding stock of the parent; or with a split-up: a distribution of stock in two or more subsidiaries, followed by liquidation of the parent corporation (Siegel 1966; Jacobs 1967).

3. See Hite and Owers (1983), Schipper and Smith (1983), Miles and Rosenfeld (1983), Alexander, Benson, and Gunderson (1986), and Cusatis, Miles, and Woolridge (1993, 1994).

4. Alexander, Benson, and Kampmeyer (1984), Jain (1985), and John and Ofek (1995) observe that a firm can also reduce diseconomies of scale and scope, and increase its focus, by *selling* operating assets that are unrelated to its core business activities. A sell-off differs from a spin-off because it does not necessarily result in any distribution to shareholders of the selling firm, because it severs the economic interest of the shareholders as well as the creditors of the selling firm in the assets that are sold, and because it generates a payment that must be reinvested, used to retire debt, or distributed to shareholders. Lang, Poulsen, and Stulz (1995) emphasize the significance of the method of disposition of the payment, but see also Slovin, Sushka, and Ferraro (1995).

relatively transparent operations and financial reports.[5] Additionally a spin-off gives the former subsidiary direct access to the capital markets, in lieu of competing with other divisions for capital allocations from a parent-owner. When Fluor Corporation announced in mid-2000 that it would spin off the common stock of its coal mining subsidiary and retain its engineering and construction operations, its CEO remarked that the two businesses "blended together haven't had the kind of clear focus that they can have by separating," and that they would operate more efficiently without the "distraction" of "an unrelated sister business vying for capital and management attention."[6]

Second, a spin-off facilitates diversity in the choice of capital structure and other contractual arrangements. For example, a stable business in a mature industry might be run efficiently with substantial leverage and/or a high dividend payout rate, while a rapidly growing and inherently more volatile business might be better capitalized with little debt and equity paying no more than a token dividend. Similarly the optimal mix of executive stock options and other forms of incentivizing compensation may vary from business to business. And in a related vein, the existence of separate markets for the common stock of the parent and subsidiary sharpens the focus of equity-based incentivizing compensation.[7]

Third, a spin-off facilitates mergers and other forms of asset reallocation by partitioning diverse business activities and reducing corporate

5. See, for example, "Hanson Spinoff Plans Haven't Raised Shareholder Value," *Wall Street Journal*, September 26, 1996, p. B4 (commenting that "ICI's biggest problem ... was that chemical analysts followed the company. They didn't understand the drug side of the business."); "U.S. Office Products Plans to Spin Off Four Operations," *Wall Street Journal*, January 14, 1998, p. B6 (commenting that "Wall Street loves a pure play ..."); "Cognizant, a D&B Spinoff, to Split in Two," *Wall Street Journal*, January 15, 1998, p. A3 (observing that "In the 1990s, 'pure plays' are in, and diversified companies are out."); and "And Then There Will Be Two," *New York Times*, October 13, 1998, p. C1 (quoting an investment banker as saying that "Analysts have difficulty understanding multi-industry companies.").

6. *Wall Street Journal*, June 8, 2000, p. A3. The article also reports that Fluor's managers considered selling the coal business but concluded that a spin-off was in the best interest of shareholders.

7. Schipper and Smith (1986) observe that a firm can also provide independent capital market access to a previously wholly owned subsidiary, as well as more focused incentive compensation, by selling to the public a portion of the common stock of the subsidiary in an equity carve-out. (See Allen 1998 for a case study.) A carve-out differs from a spin-off because it does not necessarily result in any distribution to shareholders of the parent firm, because the parent firm commonly retains a controlling interest in the subsidiary (thereby attenuating—but not eliminating—the benefit to the parent of lower diseconomies of scale and scope and the benefit to the subsidiary of an independent management), and because it generates a payment that must be reinvested, used to retire debt, or distributed to the shareholders of the parent firm. Allen and McConnell (1998) emphasize the significance of the method of disposition of the payment. Slovin, Sushka, and Ferraro (1995) suggest that a firm is more likely to spin off the stock of a subsidiary if it believes the stock will be undervalued by the market and that it will undertake an equity carve-out of the subsidiary's stock if it believes the stock will be overvalued.

complexity.[8] This allows assets to flow more freely to their most efficient uses and further enhances corporate focus on core competencies.[9]

Finally, Galai and Masulis (1976, p. 69) observe that a spin-off, like a cash dividend, can be a device for distributing valuable corporate assets to common shareholders, leading to a transfer of wealth from creditors to shareholders: "In effect, the stockholders have 'stolen away' a potion of the bondholders collateral since [the bondholders] no longer have any claim on the assets of the new firm."[10]

18.2 Marriott's 1992 Spin-off Proposal

In late 1992 Marriott Corporation ("Marriott") was one of the biggest lodging, food service, and facilities management companies in the world. The company was capitalized with $1.5 billion of current liabilities, $2.7 billion of long-term debt (rated BBB by S&P and Baa3 by Moody's), and 100 million shares of common stock with a market price of about $20 per share and an aggregate value of $2 billion. Two sons of the founder managed the company—as CEO and vice chairman of the board of directors, respectively—and more than 25% of the stock was owned by investors related to the founder.[11]

On Monday, October 5, 1992, Marriott announced that it planned to reorganize its lodging and facilities management operations and some of its food service operations into a new subsidiary corporation—to be named Marriott International, Inc. ("Marriott International")—and that it would distribute to its shareholders all of the common stock of the new

8. Klein, Rosenfeld, and Beranek (1991) observe that carve-outs may also facilitate asset reallocations. They note that carve-outs are transient arrangements, commonly followed either by a sell-off of the parent's remaining interest in the subsidiary's stock or by re-acquisition by the parent of the publicly held stock of the subsidiary, and they conjecture that carve-outs are used to "showcase" a subsidiary and to establish a market value for the parent's remaining equity in the subsidiary. Whether a carve-out is followed by a sell-off or a reacquisition depends on whether a potential buyer emerges and on whether the parties can agree on a price for the parent's remaining equity in the subsidiary.

9. See "New Life through Chemistry," *New York Times*, February 11, 1998, p. D1 (remarking of specialty chemical companies recently spun off from larger parents, "The signatures barely dry on their incorporation papers, they are already acquiring each other, swapping product lines and downsizing—in short, doing all the things that are the hallmarks of any stand-alone business.").

10. Hite and Owers (1983, p. 412) note, however, that spin-offs can be aggregated with cash dividends and stock repurchases for purposes of assessing compliance with covenants limiting distributions to shareholders, and remark that a spin-off is not appreciably more or less harmful to creditors than an equivalent cash dividend permitted by the existing reservoir of payable funds. See also Siegel (1966, pp. 557–58).

11. Marriott Corporation 1992 Annual Report to Shareholders, pp. 34, 38, and 52 and Parrino (1997, p. 242).

subsidiary. Marriott would retain its real estate properties and would be renamed Host Marriott Corporation ("Host Marriott"). This section describes the economic incentives for Marriott's spin-off proposal and the reaction of market participants.[12] We begin by describing Marriott's business operations at the end of 1992 in the context of the historical development of the company in the late 1980s and early 1990s.

Marriott in the Late 1980s and Early 1990s

At the end of 1992, Marriott divided its operations into two segments: Lodging and Contract Services.

The lodging business consisted of five major product lines:

• Marriott Hotels, Resorts, and Suites—193 full-service hotels, 18 larger convention hotels, 22 resort hotels, and 9 full-service suite hotels that offered combined living room–bedroom accommodations.

• Courtyard Hotels—207 moderate priced hotels.

• Residence Inns—179 hotels targeted to travelers who stay more than five consecutive nights.

• Fairfield Inns—118 economy lodging facilities aimed at budget conscious travelers.

• Marriott Ownership Resorts—21 projects in 7 resort locations offering vacation time-sharing facilities.[13]

"Decapitalization" was a key aspect of Marriott's approach to the lodging business.[14] The company sited, designed, and constructed hotels and then, in many (but not all) cases, sold the developed properties to investors while continuing to operate the facilities under long-term management agreements.

Marriott's contract service business consisted of three major product lines:

• Marriott Management Services—providing food and facilities management services.

12. The Marriott spin-off is also discussed in Parrino (1997), *Marriott Corporation (A)*, Harvard Business School Case Study 9-394-085 (1993); *Marriott Corporation (B)*, Harvard Business School Case Study 9-394-086 (1993); and *Marriott Corporation—Restructuring*, Harvard Business School Case Study 9-024-090 (1994).

13. Marriott Corporation 1992 10-K, pp. 6–10.

14. Marriott Corporation 1988 Annual Report to Shareholders, p. 4. See also "Who's News: Checchi Sees NWA as His Next Challenge, Alumnus of Marriott Is Called Smart but Abrasive," *Wall Street Journal*, April 24, 1989, p. B8, and "Discordant Note: For Bill Marriott, Jr., The Hospitality Trade Turns Inhospitable," *Wall Street Journal*, December 18, 1992, p. A1.

Table 18.1
Marriott Corporation's net income ($ millions)

	1987	1988	1989	1990	1991	1992
Operating income						
Lodging	264	298	132	239	325	338
Contract services	189	203	403	114	153	158
Corporate expenses	−75	−93	−107	−137	−111	−129
	378	408	428	216	367	367
Net interest expenses	−43	−96	−130	−136	−222	−217
Provision for income taxes	−148	−123	−117	−33	−63	−65
Discontinued operations	36	43	−4	0	0	0
Net income	223	232	177	47	82	85

Source: "Consolidated Statement of Income" from respective 10-Ks, except that data for 1987 and 1988 taken from 1989 10-K.

• Host/Travel Plaza—operating restaurants and related facilities at airports and on limited-access highway systems.

• Senior Living Services—14 owned and operated retirement communities and 2 retirement communities operated under management contracts.[15]

Table 18.1 shows Marriott's annual net income from 1987 to 1992. The important features of the table are the decline in net income in 1989 and 1990 and the low level of net income in 1991 and 1992. Both features can be attributed to a soft hotel real estate market in the late 1980s and early 1990s, to the recession in aggregate economic activity that began in mid-1990, and to the anemic recovery that began in the spring of 1991.

These external forces had three important consequences for Marriott. First, persistently weak hotel prices forced the company to choose between marking down offering prices on new properties—Marriott later observed that it became "difficult to sell hotels except at distressed prices"[16]—and retaining and operating its new hotels and absorbing the normal start-up costs. Marriott chose to reduce asset sales and to own as well as operate a growing fraction of hotels, and it consequently accepted relatively sluggish growth in operating income from lodging services.[17] Second, as shown in table 18.1, Marriott's net interest expenses rose dramatically as a result of the need to finance the hotel properties that it was retaining. Third,

15. Marriott Corporation 1992 10-K, pp. 12–13.

16. Marriott Corporation 1992 Annual Report to Shareholders, p. 2. See also Parrino (1997, p. 248).

17. Marriott Corporation 1990 Annual Report to Shareholders, p. 29, 1991 Annual Report to Shareholders, p. 3.

Table 18.2
Marriott Corporation's long-term debt, current liabilities, convertible subordinated debt, and convertible preferred stock ($ millions, year end)

	1987	1988	1989	1990	1991	1992
Long-term debt						
Secured notes	149	123	168	175	527	485
Senior unsecured notes	648	1,047	1,047	1,198	1,323	1,618
Debentures	250	250	250	250	250	250
Bank loans and commercial paper	1,207	1,232	1,396	1,780	676	175
Other notes	225	161	155	144	193	188
Capital lease obligations	66	75	64	61	62	37
Current portion of long-term debt	−46	−31	−30	−55	−52	−21
	2,499	2,857	3,050	3,553	2,979	2,732
Current liabilities	1,123	1,292	1,416	1,637	1,335	1,496
Convertible subordinated notes	0	0	0	0	210	228
Convertible preferred stock	0	0	0	0	200	200
	3,622	4,149	4,466	5,190	4,724	4,656

Source: "Consolidated Balance Sheet," "Consolidated Statement of Shareholders' Equity," and "Long-Term Debt" from respective 10-Ks.

the 1990–91 recession and subsequent anemic recovery contributed to a decline in operating income from contract services.

Table 18.2 shows selected elements of Marriott's capital structure from 1987 to 1992. The most striking feature is the increase in the sum of current liabilities and long-term debt from $3.6 billion at the end of 1987 to $5.2 billion at the end of 1990, an increase that provided the funds for Marriott's program of retaining its new hotels. The expansion in aggregate liabilities stemmed from roughly equal increases in current liabilities, senior unsecured notes, and bank loans and commercial paper.

In late September 1990 Marriott began to reduce its use of bank loans and commercial paper. The $1.6 billion reduction from the end of 1990 to the end of 1992 was financed by a $350 million increase in secured notes, a $420 million increase in senior unsecured notes, a sale in June 1991 of zero-coupon convertible subordinated notes for proceeds of $195 million,[18] a sale in December 1991 of $200 million of convertible preferred stock, and a reduction in total assets of about $500 million (primarily from a reduction in lodging assets).

At the end of 1992 Marriott had three classes of publicly traded securities (other than common stock) in its capital structure:

1. Senior unsecured debt, consisting of twelve series of senior notes with an aggregate principal value of $1.6 billion and one debenture with a principal value of $250 million (see table 18.3).

18. The convertible subordinated notes are described in example 8.1.

Table 18.3
Marriott Corporation's senior unsecured debt, October 1992

	Coupon rate	Maturity date	Principal amount	Issue date	Early redemption options
Series B Senior Notes	9.625%	Feb 1, 1996	$100 million	Feb 4, 1986	Callable at par on and after Feb 1, 1993
Series C Senior Notes	8.125	Dec 1, 1996	200	Dec 10, 1986	None
Series D Senior Notes	8.875	May 1, 1997	100	May 7, 1987	None
Debentures	9.375	Jun 15, 2007	250	Jun 18, 1987	Putable at par on Jun 15, 1997
Series E Senior Notes	9.875	Nov 1, 1997	150	Oct 30, 1987	Callable at par on and after Nov 1, 1994
Series F Senior Notes	9.125	Jan 15, 1995	100	Jan 26, 1988	Callable at par on and after Jan 15, 1993
Series G Senior Notes	8.375	Feb 1, 1994	100	Feb 8, 1988	None
Series H Senior Notes	8.75	May 9, 1993	100	May 9, 1988	None
Series I Senior Notes	9	May 24, 1995	100	May 24, 1988	None
Series J Senior Notes	9.125	Sep 1, 1993	150	Sep 4, 1990	None
Series K Senior Notes	10.25	Jul 18, 2001	125	Jul 18, 1991	None
Series L Senior Notes	10	May 1, 2012	200	Apr 29, 1992	None
Series M Senior Notes	9.5	May 1, 2002	200	May 5, 1992	None

2. Zero-coupon convertible subordinated notes with a face amount of $675 million (carried at a book value of $228 million at the end of 1992).

3. Convertible preferred stock with a liquidation preference of $200 million.

Figure 18.1 shows the behavior of the price of Marriott common stock between 1990 and late 1993. The heavy solid line shows the stock price prior to the announcement (in early October 1992) of the planned spin-off of Marriott International. The dashed line shows the stock price following the announcement.

The upper panel of figure 18.2 shows the yield on a representative senior unsecured note. The heavy solid line shows yields prior to the October 1992 spin-off announcement and the dashed line shows yields following the announcement. The thin solid line shows the yield on a comparable U.S. Treasury note. The lower panel of figure 18.2 shows the spread between the yield on the Marriott note and the yield on the Treasury note.

Prior to the 1992 spin-off announcement, the most striking feature of figures 18.1 and 18.2 is the steep decline in the price of Marriott's stock during the third quarter of 1990 and the sharp break in the price of its debt that began in late September 1990. The price declines were associated with a growing recognition among market participants of the depressed state of the lodging market and the sharp contraction in demand for travel-related services following the initiation of hostilities in the Persian

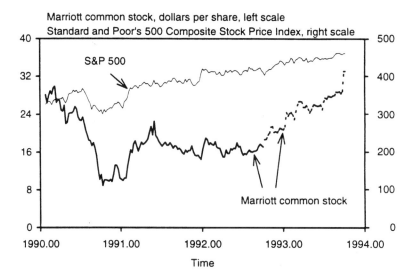

Figure 18.1
Price of Marriott common stock and value of Standard and Poor's 500 Composite Stock Price Index

Gulf in August 1990.[19] Marriott reacted to the decline in the value of its debt and equity by announcing, on September 25, 1990, that it would delay or cancel construction starts on new facilities.[20] Capital expenditures for lodging assets fell sharply from about $1 billion annually in 1988 and 1989 to $256 million in 1991 and to $86 million in 1992.[21]

By mid-1991 the price of Marriott common stock had recovered to about $20 per share and the yield on its senior unsecured debt had declined to about 200 basis points over the yield on comparable Treasury issues. However, during the next fifteen months Marriott's stock price did not appreciate further, despite a rising stock market and a generally improving bond market. By early October 1992 the stock traded at only $17 per share—even though the yield spread on Marriott's senior un-

19. The bond market break started on Monday, September 24, 1990, when S&P announced that it had placed Marriott on CreditWatch for possible downgrading ("Marriott Corp. Sr. Debt on S&P CreditWatch," *Business Wire*, September 24, 1990). Marriott's senior unsecured debt was subsequently downgraded by S&P from A– to BBB on Friday, October 12, 1990 ("Credit Ratings: Marriott Senior Debt Downgraded by S&P," *Wall Street Journal*, October 15, 1990, p. C17), and by Moody's from A3 to Baa2 on Monday, October 22, 1990 ("Moody's Lowers Ratings of Marriott Corp.," *Reuters*, October 22, 1990).

20. "Marriott Cuts Back Capital Spending, Construction Starts," *Wall Street Journal*, September 26, 1990, p. A6.

21. Marriott Corporation 1989 10-K, p. 145, 1990 Annual Report to Shareholders, p. 2, 1990 10-K, p. 47, 1991 10-K, p. 46 and 1992 10-K, p. 52.

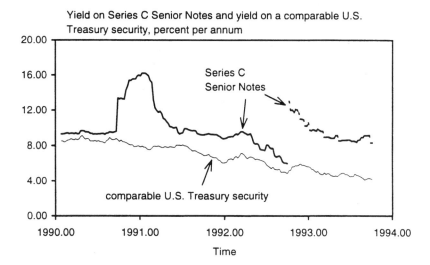

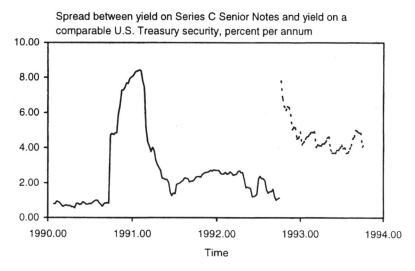

Figure 18.2
Yield on Marriott 8.125% Series C Senior Notes due December 1, 1996, and yield on comparable U.S. Treasury security

secured debt had narrowed to about 120 basis points over comparable Treasury issues.

Marriott's managers concluded that the stock was undervalued because investors had difficulty assessing the prospects of a company that both owned and managed lodging properties. They further concluded that the market would place a higher aggregate value on the businesses if they were separated from each other.[22]

The Spin-off Proposal

Marriott announced its spin-off plan on Monday, October 5, 1992. The key elements of the plan included

1. the reorganization of Marriott's lodging and facilities management businesses, and some of its food service operations, into Marriott International,

2. the distribution of all of the common stock of Marriott International to Marriott shareholders,

3. the retention of Marriott's hotel, resort and senior living real estate, its Host/Travel Plaza concessions, and most of its long-term debt by the renamed Host Marriott (Marriott International would have relatively little long-term debt),

4. contractual agreements between Marriott International and Host Marriott under which Marriott International would operate the hotels retained by Host Marriott, and

5. the opening of a $600 million line of credit from Marriott International to Host Marriott.[23]

The spin-off would separate what had previously been a single integrated business into two pure plays—one in lodging and facilities management, and the other in property ownership. Marriott's CEO stated that,

The division ... will enable us to advance our longstanding strategy of separating ownership of properties from management of operations. The transaction will permit Marriott International to focus its efforts on expansion of management businesses where individual opportunities require relatively small amounts of capital. Host Marriott will retain substantial fixed assets for longer-term opportunities in capital intensive businesses.... Under this plan, we seek to enable

---

22. *Marriott Corporation (A)*, Harvard Business School Case Study 9-394-085 (1993), p. 5, and *Marriott Corporation—Restructuring*, Harvard Business School Case Study 9-024-090 (1994), pp. 1–2.

23. Marriott Corporation 8-K dated September 29, 1992, and 8-K dated October 22, 1992.

shareholders to realize the inherent value of our management businesses more quickly while also giving them the potential over time to benefit from an upturn in real estate values.[24]

Most important, the partitioning would allow the new management company to use its operating income for expansion rather than debt service. The firm's CEO observed that "This frees up the management company to grow and gain market share. The management company has been very restrained; I think this lets the tiger out of the cage."[25]

Completion of the spin-off was contingent on approval by a majority of Marriott's common shareholders. Approval by holders of Marriott's senior unsecured debt and convertible subordinated notes was not needed because the spin-off was not prohibited by any of the covenants in the indentures for those securities.

Market Reactions

Marriott's common stock reacted favorably to the announcement of the spin-off. On the day of the announcement the stock closed at $19.25 (a gain of 12.4% from the $17.125 close on Friday, October 2, 1992) and on Friday, October 9, the stock closed at $18.625 (a net gain of 8.8% for the week—in contrast, the S&P 500 fell 1.9% over the same week). One equity analyst was quoted as saying that, "The sum of the parts is worth more than the whole." Another analyst estimated that the Host Marriott and Marriott International stock would be worth about $2 and $18 per share, respectively, and observed that the plan was "an attempt to segregate the healthy part of Marriott from the real estate laden and slow growth part. The costs of carrying that real estate have severely hampered Marriott's performance and prompted much lower earnings than otherwise might be the case."[26]

Marriott's senior unsecured debt reacted strongly and unfavorably to the spin-off announcement. As shown in the lower panel of table 18.4, between Friday, October 2, 1992, and Friday, October 9, spreads between yields on intermediate term Marriott notes and yields on comparable Treasury securities widened from about 125 basis points to between 650 and 750 basis points. The sharp rise in yields produced substantial price declines. Table 18.5 shows that prices on longer maturity issues fell by as

---

24. Marriott Corporation 8-K dated September 29, 1992.

25. "Marriott to Split Its Businesses into 2 Entities," *Wall Street Journal*, October 6, 1992, p. A3.

26. "Marriott to Split Its Businesses into 2 Entities," *Wall Street Journal*, October 6, 1992, p. A3.

Table 18.4
Yields on Marriott Corporation's noncallable senior unsecured notes and yield spreads to comparable U.S. Treasury issues

	Oct 2, 1992	Oct 9, 1992	Change
Yields			
Series C Senior Notes 8.125% due Dec 1, 1996	5.99%	12.98%	6.99%
Series D Senior Notes 8.875% due May 1, 1997	6.36	12.99	6.63
Series G Senior Notes 8.375% due Feb 1, 1994	4.62	10.95	6.33
Series H Senior Notes 8.75% due May 9, 1993	4.03	10.42	6.39
Series I Senior Notes 9% due May 24, 1995	5.31	11.98	6.67
Series J Senior Notes 9.125% due Sep 1, 1993	4.12	10.49	6.37
Series K Senior Notes 10.25% due Jul 18, 2001	7.36	13.00	5.64
Series L Senior Notes 10% due May 1, 2012	8.90	13.00	4.10
Series M Senior Notes 9.5% due May 1, 2002	7.88	13.00	5.12
Yield spreads to comparable U.S. Treasury issues			
Series C Senior Notes 8.125% due Dec 1, 1996	1.14%	7.80%	6.66%
Series D Senior Notes 8.875% due May 1, 1997	1.34	7.64	6.30
Series G Senior Notes 8.375% due Feb 1, 1994	1.29	7.30	6.01
Series H Senior Notes 8.75% due May 9, 1993	1.18	7.33	6.15
Series I Senior Notes 9% due May 24, 1995	1.22	7.57	6.35
Series J Senior Notes 9.125% due Sep 1, 1993	1.05	7.16	6.11
Series K Senior Notes 10.25% due Jul 18, 2001	1.16	6.51	5.35
Series L Senior Notes 10% due May 1, 2012	1.78	5.64	3.86
Series M Senior Notes 9.5% due May 1, 2002	1.52	6.36	4.84

Table 18.5
Prices of Marriott Corporation's debt and stock

	Oct 2, 1992	Oct 9, 1992	Change	Change in aggregate value
Debt (% of principal value)				
Series B Senior Notes 9.625% due Feb 1, 1996	101.80	91.14	−10.66	−$10.66 million
Series C Senior Notes 8.125% due Dec 1, 1996	107.75	84.75	−23.00	−46.00
Series D Senior Notes 8.875% due May 1, 1997	109.84	86.16	−23.68	−23.68
Debentures 9.375% due Jun 15, 2007	112.11	87.58	−24.53	−61.33
Series E Senior Notes 9.875% due Nov 1, 1997	110.02	88.69	−21.33	−32.00
Series F Senior Notes 9.125% due Jan 15, 1995	101.41	94.44	−6.97	−6.97
Series G Senior Notes 8.375% due Feb 1, 1994	104.78	96.89	−7.89	−7.89
Series H Senior Notes 8.75% due May 9, 1993	102.77	99.05	−3.72	−3.72
Series I Senior Notes 9% due May 24, 1995	108.97	93.42	−15.55	−15.55
Series J Senior Notes 9.125% due Sep 1, 1993	104.44	98.84	−5.60	−8.40
Series K Senior Notes 10.25% due Jul 18, 2001	118.48	85.83	−32.65	−40.81
Series L Senior Notes 10% due May 1, 2012	110.08	78.88	−31.20	−62.40
Series M Senior Notes 9.5% due May 1, 2002	110.78	81.16	−29.62	−59.24
				−378.65
Convertible subordinated notes due Jun 12, 2006	33.38	31.00	−2.38	−16.07
Stock ($ per share)				
Convertible preferred stock	62.75	58.13	−4.62	−18.48
Common stock	17.13	18.63	1.50	151.20
				−$262.00 million

much as 25% to 30% of principal value.[27] Promptly upon the announcement of the spin-off, Moody's lowered its rating on Marriott's senior
unsecured debt to Ba2 and S&P placed the company on CreditWatch.[28]

27. The decline in the value of Marriott's notes, debentures, convertible debt, and convertible preferred stock led to an aggregate decline of about $410 million in the market value of
Marriott's senior securities, an amount well in excess of the $150 million increase in the value
of the company's common stock. Parrino (1997, pp. 252–53) observes that "the fact that the
magnitude of the bondholder and preferred shareholder loss exceeds the common shareholder gain suggests that all of the shareholder gain resulted from a wealth transfer . . . ."

28. "Marriott to Split Its Businesses into 2 Entities," *Wall Street Journal*, October 6, 1992,
p. A3.

The reactions of individual bond buyers were consistent with the views of the rating agencies and the bond market as a whole. One fixed income portfolio manager remarked that "This was a shot from a rifle that nobody thought was loaded. It really is an outrage." Another manager characterized the announcement as a "slap in the face," and a third observed that "Marriott has taken a very tough approach to bondholders. It's a real burn-your-bridges approach." However, some portfolio managers recognized that the bond losses were, in the words of one, their "own fault," because they had bought bonds with covenants ranging from "slim to none."[29]

Marriott's Incentive to Restructure the Spin-off

Marriott responded to its unhappy creditors by observing that it had a fiduciary duty to stockholders that was constrained by the contractual obligations of the company to its bondholders but not otherwise balanced by any fiduciary duties to those creditors.[30] A spokesman for the company commented that, "We have a fiduciary obligation to stockholders, and this transaction is in the best interest of stockholders. Our obligation to bondholders is to make all the bond payments on time.... We plan to fulfill that obligation."[31]

Nevertheless, the strong reaction of creditors created a practical problem for the company: How would Host Marriott refinance its senior unsecured debt? As shown in table 18.3, Host Marriott would have to

29. "Marriott Plan Enrages Holders of Its Bonds," *Wall Street Journal*, October 7, 1992, p. C1, and "What Companies Will Follow Marriott and Trash Bondholders?" *Bloomberg Business News*, October 9, 1992.

The strong reaction of bondholders led to the resignation of First National Bank of Chicago as trustee on Marriott's senior unsecured debt and to the resignation of Merrill Lynch & Co. as an adviser to the company. See "Business Brief—Marriott Corp.: Banc One Affiliate is Named as Trustee for Senior Debt," *Wall Street Journal*, November 11, 1992, p. C15, "Marriott Bid to Split up Seems to Suffer Setback as Merrill Withdraws as Adviser," *Wall Street Journal*, November 18, 1992, p. A2; "Merrill Leaves as Adviser on Marriott Deal," *Washington Post*, November 18, 1992, p. F2; "Internal Rift Led Merrill Lynch to Quit as Marriott Adviser," *Wall Street Journal*, November 24, 1992, p. C1; and "Discordant Note: For Bill Marriott Jr., the Hospitality Trade Turns Inhospitable," *Wall Street Journal*, December 18, 1992, p. A1. See also "Marriott Spin-off Last Straw to Fed-up Corporate Bond Mart," *Investment Dealers' Digest*, October 12, 1992, p. 10, and Rosenberg (1993).

30. This is consistent with a long line of court cases holding that a company has no obligations to its creditors other than the contractual obligations arising out of a loan agreement or bond indenture. See *Harff v. Kerkorian*, 324 A. 2d 215 (1974), *Browning Debenture Holders' Committee v. DASA Corp.*, 560 F. 2d 1078 (1977); *Katz v. Oak Industries*, 508 A. 2d 873 (1986); *Simons v. Cogan*, 594 A. 2d 300 (1988); *Metropolitan Life Insurance Co. v. RJR Nabisco, Inc.*, 716 F. Supp. 1504 (1989); *Lorenz v. CSX Corp.*, 736 F. Supp. 650 (1990); and *Geren v. Quantum Chemical Corporation*, 832 F. Supp. 728 (1993).

31. "Marriott Plan Enrages Holders of Its Bonds," *Wall Street Journal*, October 7, 1992, p. C1.

redeem $1.1 billion of debt in the next five years.[32] Although Host Marriott would not be without alternative sources of financing—including mortgage financing, sales and leasebacks, and REITs[33]—it would be useful if the company either retained access to the market for publicly traded debt on reasonable terms or extended the maturities of its existing debt.

In December 1992 Marriott concluded that it would be in the best interest of its shareholders to explore with creditors the possibility of restructuring the spin-off. The appendix to this chapter describes the restructuring and completion of the Marriott spin-off.

18.3   Empirical Characteristics of Spin-offs

Empirical assessments of corporate spin-offs suggest that on average, announcement of a spin-off reveals new information that is favorable for shareholders. Additionally it appears that a spin-off is frequently part of a larger restructuring program intended to enhance the value of the firm and facilitate asset transfers among firms.

Hite and Owers (1983) examined the behavior of parent company stock prices around the time of 123 spin-off announcements between 1962 and 1981. On average, the price of a company's stock appreciated 3.3% in excess of the return on the market during a two-day interval that included the initial public announcement of a spin-off. Similarly Miles and Rosenfeld (1983) report an average announcement effect of 3.3% for a sample of 55 spin-offs between 1963 and 1980 and Schipper and Smith (1983) report an average announcement effect of 2.8% for a sample of 93 spin-offs between 1963 and 1981.[34]

The spin-offs examined by Hite and Owers (1983) varied widely in size. The value of the equity that was spun off relative to the *cum*-distribution value of the parent firm's equity ranged between 0.8% and 84.4%, with a median value of 6.6%. Larger spin-offs had a larger impact on the price of

---

32. The $1.1 billion consisted of $250 million of the series H and J notes maturing in 1993, $100 million of the series G notes maturing in 1994, $200 million of the series F and I notes maturing in 1995, $300 million of the series B and C notes maturing in 1996, and $250 million of the series D and E notes maturing in 1997.

33. Marriott Corporation 8-K dated October 22, 1992, exhibit 21, p. 15.

34. These abnormal returns are comparable to the average abnormal equity returns associated with announcements of asset sales: Jain (1985) reports 0.5%, Hite, Owers, and Rogers (1987) report 1.7%, John and Ofek (1995) report 1.5%, and Lang, Poulsen, and Stulz (1995) report 1.7%. They are also comparable to the average abnormal equity returns associated with announcements of equity carve-outs: Schipper and Smith (1986) report 1.8%, and Allen and McConnell (1998) report 1.9%.

the parent company's stock. The authors ordered the spin-offs in their sample by size and divided the ordered sample into two equal parts. The larger spin-offs had a median size of 19.9% of the *cum*-distribution value of the parent firm's equity and an average two-day announcement effect on equity values of 5.2%. The smaller spin-offs had a median size of 2.4% and an average announcement effect of only 0.8%. Miles and Rosenfeld (1983) and Schipper and Smith (1983) also found a positive relationship between the size of a spin-off and the effect of the spin-off announcement on the value of the parent firm's equity.

The Effect of a Spin-off on the Value of Debt

The effect of a spin-off on the value of corporate debt is not as firmly established as the effect on equity values. The Marriott episode suggests that for the reason pointed out by Galai and Masulis (1976), a spin-off can materially reduce the value of parent company debt. Nevertheless, Hite and Owers (1983) were unable to identify, from a small sample, any significant effect of a spin-off announcement on bond values. Schipper and Smith (1983) report comparable results for a similarly small sample.

There are at least three reasons why, on average, a spin-off may not impair the price of the parent company's debt. First, some spin-offs are so small that they are simply inconsequential for debt values. This is consistent with the observation that small spin-offs have a negligible effect on stock values. Second, a spin-off may be structured so that a well-capitalized parent company spins off a weak subsidiary that has borrowed in its own name. In this case the creditors as well as the shareholders of the parent company may benefit from the spin-off—at the expense of the creditors of the newly independent subsidiary.[35] Third, a spin-off may be structured to avoid impairing the interests of creditors because the parent does not want to damage its reputation in the credit markets.[36]

Although the available evidence suggests that on average, spin-offs do not lead to a significant decline in the value of a corporation's debt, there is also no evidence that debt values increase along with equity values. This implies that managers typically structure a spin-off to capture for shareholders all of the increase in the value of the firm associated with the spin-off.

35. See, for example, the discussion of the 1983 spin-off of Trans World Airlines, Inc. by Trans World Corporation in Alexander, Benson, and Gunderson (1986).

36. See, for example, the decision of B.A.T. Industries to refinance its public debt in connection with the spin-off of its tobacco operations, reported in "Doing Right by B.A.T. Bondholders," *New York Times*, October 26, 1997, sec. 3, p. 6. One analyst observed that "If you do borrow from the capital markets, it makes sense that your relationship with borrowers be as good as possible."

Spin-offs in the Context of Corporate Restructuring Programs and Asset Transfers

Cusatis, Miles, and Woolridge (1994) examined 161 spin-offs by 154 firms between 1965 and 1990. They found that on average, the value of a company's equity appreciated during the two years preceding a spin-off relative to the value of the stock of a similar company that did not undertake a spin-off.[37] They suggested (p. 104) that the superior antecedent performance stems from the fact that "... spinoffs are often part of a sequence of transactions in a larger ongoing program.... [By] the time many spinoffs are announced, the stock market has already anticipated the eventual improvements in operating performance that come out of this restructuring activity." The 1985 decision by General Mills to spin off the common stock of Kenner Parker Toys, Inc. and Crystal Brands, Inc.,[38] and the 1992 decision by Sears, Roebuck to sell 20% of the common stock of Dean Witter, Reynolds in an equity carve-out and then spin-off the remaining 80%,[39] illustrate the role of spin-offs in the context of larger restructuring programs.

In a related study, Cusatis, Miles, and Woolridge (1993) found that on average, the price of the stock of both a parent corporation and a spun-off subsidiary appreciated during the three years following a spin-off relative to the price of the stock of respectively similar companies that did not undertake a spin-off and were not spun off. They further found that both parents and spun-off subsidiaries were unusually likely to merge with, or be taken over by, another firm following a spin-off, and they identified such changes in control as an important source of the superior performance of both parents and subsidiaries following a spin-off. They concluded (p. 310) that "... spinoffs create value primarily by providing an efficient method of transferring control of corporate assets to acquiring firms. By splitting companies into separate businesses, spinoffs establish pure plays in the market, allowing bidders who are able to create more value to avoid the expense of taking over whole entities."

18.4   Spin-offs and the Contingent Value of Corporate Securities

Spin-offs, like leveraged recapitalizations, are rare events, so the policy of a firm regarding the timing and terms of a spin-off has to be identified

---

37. This contrasts with the findings reported by Alexander, Benson, and Kampmeyer (1984), Jain (1985), and Lang, Poulsen, and Stulz (1995) that asset sales are generally preceded by poor equity returns. Allen and McConnell (1998) find that equity carve-outs are not preceded by either unusually weak or unusually strong equity returns.

38. Donaldson (1990, 1991).

39. Gillan, Kensinger, and Martin (2000).

from a fundamental assessment of how a spin-off might enhance the value of equity, rather than from the historical behavior of the firm.

The broad determinants of whether a spin-off might be in the best interest of shareholders were noted in sections 18.1 and 18.3. They include the potential benefits of increased managerial focus and reduced diseconomies of scale and scope, greater diversity in the choice of capital structure and managerial compensation, reduced impediments to asset reallocations, the prospect for wealth transfers from creditors to shareholders, and limitations embedded in bond indentures and loan agreements. Incorporating even a few of these determinants into a contingent value model will require a more detailed representation of the operating structure of a firm than that exhibited in a conventional model. In addition the empirical evidence showing that spin-offs are not fully anticipated by market participants and lead to unexpected changes in stock prices suggests that spin-offs, like leveraged recapitalizations, are discretionary managerial acts with a significant element of unpredictability. The evolution of the aggregate value of the firm may therefore include the prospect of an unpredictable discontinuous jump at the time a spin-off is announced.

Appendix: Restructuring and Completing the Marriott Spin-off

Marriott revised its plan for spinning off Marriott International as a result of negotiations with its senior unsecured creditors between late December 1992 and early March 1993.[40] Marriott wanted any restructuring of the original plan to reduce the objections of creditors to the spin-off, deter litigation, and extend the maturities of its debt—thereby postponing the need to refinance that debt. The creditors wanted to enhance the market value and creditworthiness of their securities. This appendix describes how Marriott and its creditors accomplished their respective objectives.

It will be convenient to describe the restructured spin-off in two parts. The first is the basic plan for spinning off Marriott International. The second part consists of three related restructuring elements, including (1) a reorganization of Host Marriott, (2) an offer to exchange new debt, to be issued by an indirect subsidiary of the reorganized Host Marriott, for the outstanding senior unsecured debt of Marriott, and (3) a series of modifications to the basic spin-off plan, whose implementation was conditional

---

40. Rosenberg (1993) and Host Marriott Hospitality, Inc., Marriott Corporation and Marriott International, Inc. Prospectus and Consent Solicitation dated July 16, 1993 (hereafter, "Prospectus and Solicitation"), pp. 29–31.

on acceptance of the exchange offer and a prerequisite to consummation of the offer.

The Basic Plan

The basic plan for spinning off Marriott International provided that Marriott would reorganize its lodging and facilities management businesses, and some of its food service operations, into Marriott International, and that it would distribute the common stock of the new company on the basis of one share of the new company for each share of Marriott. The Host/Travel Plaza operations and most real estate properties would be retained by the renamed Host Marriott. Following the spin-off, Marriott International would manage the lodging properties and lease and operate the senior living facilities owned by Host Marriott.[41]

The basic plan further provided that Marriott International would assume responsibility for 90% of any payments to holders of Marriott's convertible subordinated notes. Host Marriott would call the notes for early redemption when requested by Marriott International (provided that Marriott International lent it funds for its share of any such redemption), and it would not call the notes for early redemption without the permission of Marriott International. Notes presented for conversion would receive 13.277 shares of Marriott International common stock and 13.277 shares of Host Marriott stock per $1,000 face amount of notes.[42] (This was consistent with the original conversion terms described in example 8.1: 13.277 shares of Marriott common stock per $1,000 face amount of notes.)

Balance Sheet Implications

The first column of table 18.6 shows the consolidated balance sheet of Marriott on March 26, 1993. The second column shows adjustments required to deconsolidate the assets and liabilities of Marriott International. (The deconsolidated assets and liabilities reappear in the first column of table 18.7.) The third column shows Marriott's balance sheet on March 26, 1993, using the equity method for accounting for its ownership of Marriott International.

The fourth column of table 18.6 shows adjustments to Marriott's balance sheet that would have been made on March 26, 1993, if the basic spin-off plan had become effective on that date. The distribution of Marriott International stock would have reduced Marriott's assets and equity

41. Marriott Corporation Proxy Statement dated June 19, 1993 (hereafter, "Proxy"), pp. 41–43.
42. Proxy, p. 44.

Table 18.6
Marriott Corporation/Host Marriott Corporation's consolidated balance sheet, March 26, 1993 ($ millions)

	Actual	Deconsolidation of assets, liabilities, and equity of Marriott International	Adjusted for equity accounting in Marriott International	Adjustments for and in connection with stock spin-off	Adjusted for stock spin-off and related items
Assets					
Current assets	1,631	−1,116	515	−194[c]	321
Property and equipment	3,461	−737	2,724	0	2,724
Investments in affiliates	459	−110	349	0	349
Intangible assets	445	−430	15	0	15
Marriott International	—	—	779	−779[a]	0
Notes receivable and other	575	−234	341	209[b]	550
	6,571		4,723	−764	3,959
Liabilities and equity					
Current liabilities	1,522	−1,099	423	−205[c]	218
Long-term debt	2,871	−370	2,501	−7[c]	2,494
Other long-term liabilities	446	−314	132	−2[c]	130
Convertible subordinated debt	232	0	232	0	232
Deferred income	177	−90	87	0	87
Deferred income taxes	472	25	497	0	497
Equity	851	0	851	$\left\{\begin{array}{c}-779^a\\209^b\\20^c\end{array}\right\}$	301
	6,571		4,723	−764	3,959

Source: Marriott Corporation Proxy Statement dated June 19, 1993, p. 70.
a. Represents spin-off of 100% of Marriott International common stock to Marriott stockholders.
b. Represents assumption by Marriott International of responsibility for 90% of the payments on Marriott's convertible subordinated debt.
c. Represents paydown of debt with available cash, adjustments to allocate outstanding drafts between Marriott International and Host Marriott and elimination of working capital for properties owned by Host Marriott to be managed by Marriott International.

by $779 million. Assumption by Marriott International of responsibility for 90% of the payments due on Marriott's convertible subordinated debt would have increased Marriott's assets and equity by $209 million.[43] The last column in table 18.6 shows what Host Marriott's balance sheet would have looked like on March 26, 1993, following the foregoing and other adjustments related to the basic spin-off plan.

The second column of table 18.7 shows adjustments to Marriott International's balance sheet that would have been made on March 26, 1993 if

43. The assumption of indebtedness was to be evidenced by a note issued by Marriott International to Host Marriott and hence would have increased Marriott's assets rather than reduced its liabilities.

Table 18.7
Marriott International's consolidated balance sheet, March 26, 1993 ($ millions)

	Assets, liabilities, and equity deconsolidated from Marriott's balance sheet	Adjustments for and in connection with stock spin-off	Adjusted for stock spin-off and related items
Assets			
Current assets	1,116	255[c]	1,371
Property and equipment	737	0	737
Investments in affiliates	110	0	110
Intangible assets	430	0	430
Notes receivable and other	259[a]	0	259
	2,652	255	2,907
Liabilities and equity			
Current liabilities	1,099	266[c]	1,365
Long-term debt	370	$\left\{\begin{array}{c}7^c\\209^b\end{array}\right\}$	586
Other long-term liabilities	314	2[c]	316
Deferred income	90	0	90
Equity	779	$\left\{\begin{array}{c}-209^b\\-20^c\end{array}\right\}$	550
	2,652	255	2,907

Source: Marriott Corporation Proxy Statement dated June 19, 1993, p. 60.
a. Reflects sum of $234 million reduction in notes receivable and $25 million increase in deferred income taxes on Marriott's balance sheet. See table 18.6, second data column.
b. Represents assumption by Marriott International of responsibility for 90% of the payments on Marriott's convertible subordinated debt.
c. Represents adjustments to allocate drafts between Marriott International and Host Marriott and working capital for properties owned by Host Marriott to be managed by Marriott International.

the basic spin-off plan had become effective on that date, and the third column shows what its balance sheet would have looked like following the spin-off.

The data in tables 18.6 and 18.7 indicate that consummation of the basic plan would have led to substantial leveraging of the assets that remained with Host Marriott. The ratio of the sum of long-term debt, other long-term liabilities and convertible subordinated debt to total assets was 0.54 for Marriott and would have been 0.72 for Host Marriott and 0.31 for Marriott International if the basic spin-off plan had become effective on March 26, 1993.

Obligations of Marriott International to Extend Credit to Host Marriott

The basic spin-off plan additionally provided for two loans from Marriott International to Host Marriott: Marriott International would provide up to $125 million of first mortgage financing for a convention center in Philadelphia, and it would provide a $600 million line of credit for speci-

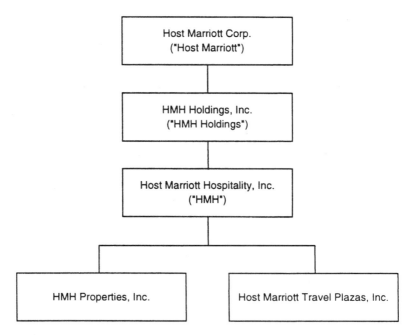

Figure 18.3
Contingent reorganization of Host Marriott

fied purposes, including construction expenditures and repayment of indebtedness. The line of credit would remain available through the end of 1999 and borrowings would carry a floating interest rate equal to the rate on Eurodollar time deposits plus 400 basis points.[44]

The Reorganization of Host Marriott

The first restructuring element was a contingent reorganization of Host Marriott's corporate structure. Conditional on acceptance and consummation of the exchange offer described below, the operating assets of Host Marriott would be reorganized as shown in figure 18.3. Most of the lodging properties and senior living facilities would be owned by a new indirect subsidiary, HMH Properties, Inc., and most of the food service properties would be owned by another new indirect subsidiary, Host Marriott Travel Plazas, Inc. Both operating subsidiaries would be owned by Host Marriott Hospitality, Inc. ("HMH"), which would in turn be owned by HMH Holdings, Inc. ("HMH Holdings"), a new direct subsidiary of Host Marriott.

44. Proxy, pp. 43 and 44.

The Exchange Offer

The second restructuring element was an offer to exchange new senior notes and debentures (to be issued by HMH), as well as Marriott common stock and (in two cases) cash, for Marriott's outstanding senior notes and debentures.

Table 18.8 summarizes the terms of the exchange offer.[45] With three exceptions, a creditor tendering a note or debenture with a principal value of $1,000 would receive

1. a new HMH note or debenture with (a) a principal value of $950.74, (b) a coupon rate 100 basis points higher, and (c) a maturity date four years later, and

2. common stock of Marriott valued at $49.26. (The Marriott stock would include the right to participate in the distribution of the Marriott International common stock.)

The exceptions were the Series F Senior Notes and the Series I Senior Notes, where the exchange offer provided for

1. a new HMH note with (a) a principal value of $456.35, (b) a coupon rate 100 basis points higher, and (c) a maturity date four years later,

2. common stock of Marriott valued at $23.65, and

3. $520 in cash,

and the Series L Senior Notes, where the maturity of the new notes would be five years *earlier* than the maturity of the old notes. Holders of the series F and I notes were offered a substantial amount of cash in exchange for materially extending the maturities of their notes from less than two years to more than five years. The reduction in the maturity of the series L notes was related to the long original maturity of those notes.

How the Exchange Offer Would Advance the Objectives of Marriott and Its Creditors

Consummation of the exchange offer would clearly advance one of Marriott's objectives: extending the maturity of its debt. In addition the offer provided that anyone tendering Marriott notes and/or debentures would be deemed to have consented to the distribution of Marriott International common stock by Marriott and to have waived any claims

---

45. The exchange offer did not apply to the Series G, H, and J Senior Notes. The series H and J notes matured in May 1993 and September 1993, respectively, prior to the anticipated spin-off, and would be retired by Marriott in the normal course of business. The series G notes matured early in 1994 and would be defeased prior to the spin-off. Prospectus and Solicitation, p. 35.

Table 18.8
Terms of the exchange offer

For each $1,000 principal amount of:	A holder would receive:
9.125% Series F Senior Notes due Jan 15, 1995	(a) $456.35 principal amount of HMH 10.125% Series F Senior Notes due Jan 15, 1999 (b) Marriott common stock valued at $23.65 (c) $520 cash
9% Series I Senior Notes due May 24, 1995	(a) $456.35 principal amount of HMH 10% Series I Senior Notes due May 24, 1999 (b) Marriott common stock valued at $23.65 (c) $520 cash
9.625% Series B Senior Notes due Feb 1, 1996	(a) $950.74 principal amount of HMH 10.625% Series B Senior Notes due Feb 1, 2000 (b) Marriott common stock valued at $49.26
8.125% Series C Senior Notes due Dec 1, 1996	(a) $950.74 principal amount of HMH 9.125% Series C Senior Notes due Dec 1, 2000 (b) Marriott common stock valued at $49.26
8.875% Series D Senior Notes due May 1, 1997	(a) $950.74 principal amount of HMH 9.875% Series D Senior Notes due May 1, 2001 (b) Marriott common stock valued at $49.26
9.875% Series E Senior Notes due Nov 1, 1997	(a) $950.74 principal amount of HMH 10.875% Series E Senior Notes due Nov 1, 2001 (b) Marriott common stock valued at $49.26
10.25% Series K Senior Notes due Jul 18, 2001	(a) $950.74 principal amount of HMH 11.25% Series K Senior Notes due Jul 18, 2005 (b) Marriott common stock valued at $49.26
9.125% Series M Senior Notes due May 1, 2002	(a) $950.74 principal amount of HMH 10.125% Series M Senior Notes due May 1, 2006 (b) Marriott common stock valued at $49.26
9.375% debentures due Jun 15, 2007	(a) $950.74 principal amount of HMH 10.375% debentures due Jun 15, 2011 (b) Marriott common stock valued at $49.26
10% Series L Senior Notes due May 1, 2012	(a) $950.74 principal amount of HMH 11% Series L Senior Notes due May 1, 2007 (b) Marriott common stock valued at $49.26

Source: Host Marriott Hospitality, Inc., Marriott Corporation, and Marriott International, Inc. Prospectus and Consent Solicitation dated July 16, 1993.

arising out of that distribution.[46] The exchange offer would thus advance Marriott's other objectives as well.

Consummation of the exchange offer would also be beneficial to the holders of Marriott's notes and debentures who choose to participate in the offer. The increase in coupon rates (in excess of the increases required to compensate creditors for their longer maturities) would enhance the market value of the debt, and a variety of redemption features, guarantees, pledges of collateral, and restrictive covenants on the new HMH notes would enhance the creditworthiness of the debt.[47]

Conditions for Consummation of the Exchange Offer

Consummation of the exchange offer was conditioned on two principle contingencies.

First, Marriott had to consummate the distribution of Marriott International common stock to its shareholders, and it had to consummate the modifications to the basic spin-off plan described below.

Second, at least 85% of the principal amount of *all* of the Marriott notes and debentures, and at least 51% of *each series*, had to be tendered for exchange.[48] The requirement for at least 85% of all of the notes and debentures ensured that Marriott would be able to complete the spin-off with the explicit consent of holders of a substantial majority of its senior unsecured debt. The requirement for at least 51% of each individual series was related to a provision in the exchange offer that anyone tendering Marriott securities would be deemed to have consented to an amendment to the indenture for the securities.[49]

Contingent Modifications to the Basic Plan

The third restructuring element was a set of contingent modifications designed generally to advance the objectives of creditors. Implementation of the modifications would be *contingent on* acceptance of the exchange offer by the required number of creditors and would be a *prerequisite to* consummation of the exchange offer, so the prospect of the modifications provided an added incentive for creditors to tender their bonds.

---

46. Prospectus and Solicitation, p. 6.

47. Prospectus and Solicitation, pp. 95–103.

48. Prospectus and Solicitation, cover page.

49. The amendment would eliminate a restriction on Marriott's ability to create liens on its assets without equally and ratably securing holders of the securities issued under the indenture—a covenant commonly referred to as a "negative pledge clause." Consent by holders of more than 50% of a series was needed to effect the amendment for the series. See, for example, Prospectus for Marriott Corporation Debt Securities dated January 10, 1986, pp. 5–7, accompanying the Prospectus Supplement for Marriott Corporation $9\frac{5}{8}$% Series B Senior Notes due February 1, 1996, dated January 28, 1986.

The contingent modifications had four principle components.[50] First, Marriott International would assume an additional $74 million of Marriott's indebtedness. Second, Marriott International would assume responsibility for drafts outstanding on January 1, 1993, relating to businesses to be conducted by Marriott International. Third, Marriott would transfer to Marriott International land with a book value of $42 million and related indebtedness of a comparable magnitude.

The fourth component of the modifications provided for substantial revisions in the $600 million line of credit from Marriott International: the line would be expanded to $630 million, the borrower would be HMH Holdings,[51] credit would be available until 2007, and interest in excess of 10.50% per annum would be deferred until maturity. In addition $200 million would be drawn by HMH Holdings contemporaneously with consummation of the exchange offer and would be used to repay other indebtedness, including the $104 million to be offered in exchange for the series F and I notes.

Balance Sheet Implications

Tables 18.9 and 18.10 show the implications of the exchange offer and contingent modifications for the balance sheets of Host Marriott and Marriott International, respectively, as of March 26, 1993. The tables indicate that the exchange offer and contingent modifications would advance the objectives of creditors by, inter alia, reducing Host Marriott's leverage. The ratio of the sum of long-term debt, other long-term liabilities, and convertible subordinated debt to total assets would have been 0.66 for Host Marriott and 0.40 for Marriott International if the exchange offer and contingent modifications had been consummated along with the basic spin-off plan on March 26, 1993.

Completion of the Spin-off

Marriott held its annual stockholders' meeting on July 23, 1993, and secured the approval of 85% of the shares voted for the restructured spin-off plan.[52] Thus, at a minimum, Marriott was prepared to consummate the basic plan.

50. Prospectus and Solicitation, pp. 33–36.

51. Drawdowns by HMH Holdings on the line of credit would be structurally subordinated to the claims of holders of the new HMH notes and debentures (but structurally senior to the claims of holders of the old Marriott notes and debentures) because HMH was to be a wholly owned subsidiary of HMH Holdings and because HMH Holdings was to be a wholly owned subsidiary of Host Marriott.

52. "Marriott Holders Approve Plan to Split Real Estate and Hotels, Making 2 Firms," *Wall Street Journal*, July 26, 1993, p. B4.

Table 18.9
Host Marriott Corporation's consolidated balance sheet, March 26, 1993 ($ millions)

	Pro forma per basic spin-off plan[a]	Adjustments for exchange offer and contingent modifications[b]	Adjusted for exchange offer and contingent modifications
Assets			
Current assets	321	−121[f]	200
Property and equipment	2,724	−42[e]	2,682
Investments in affiliates	349	0	349
Intangible assets	15	0	15
Notes receivable and other	550	0	550
	3,959	−163	3,796
Liabilities and equity			
Current liabilities	218	0	218
Long-term debt	2,494	−42[e] −44[d] −70[c] −208[f]	2,130
Other long-term liabilities	130	0	130
Convertible subordinated debt	232	0	232
Deferred income	87	0	87
Deferred income taxes	497	−14[e]	483
Equity	301	44[d] 70[c] 87[f] 14[e]	516
	3,959	−163	3,796

Source: Marriott Corporation Proxy Statement dated June 19, 1993, p. 70.
a. From the last column of table 18.6.
b. Does not include $200 million increase in long-term debt due to drawdown on line of credit from Marriott International and related $200 million decrease in long-term debt pursuant to the exchange offer and other paydowns.
c. Represents partial paydown of long-term debt with Marriott common stock pursuant to the exchange offer.
d. Represents net impact of additional debt to be assumed by Marriott International and 100 basis point increase in the coupon rate on the new HMH notes and debentures.
e. Represents transfer of land and related deferred taxes and debt to Marriott International.
f. Represents adjustments to allocate drafts between Marriott International and Host Marriott.

Marriott had launched its offer to exchange new HMH notes and debentures for its senior unsecured debt several days earlier. Shortly before the August 17 expiration date of the offer, it became clear that the minimum conditions for consummation might not be met: Marriott had received tenders accounting for only about 80% of the aggregate principal amount of the securities eligible for exchange. Following a short extension, the company was able to secure tenders of (1) 88% of the aggregate amount of notes and debentures eligible for exchange other than the Series F Senior Notes and the Series I Senior Notes and of (2) more than 51% of each individual series except the series F and I notes. By August 20

Table 18.10
Marriott International's consolidated balance sheet, March 26, 1993 ($ millions)

	Pro forma per basic spin-off plan[a]	Adjustments for exchange offer and contingent modifications	Adjusted for exchange offer and contingent modifications
Assets			
Current assets	1,371	−87[e]	1,284
Property and equipment	737	42[d]	779
Investments in affiliates	110	0	110
Intangible assets	430	0	430
Notes receivable and other	259	{ 200[b] −14[d] }	445
	2,907	141	3,048
Liabilities and equity			
Current liabilities	1,365	0	1,365
Long-term debt	586	{ 42[d] 74[c] 200[b] }	902
Other long-term liabilities	316	0	316
Deferred income	90	0	90
Equity	550	{ −14[d] −74[c] −87[e] }	375
	2,907	141	3,048

Source: Marriott Corporation Proxy Statement dated June 19, 1993, p. 60.
a. From the last column of table 19.7.
b. $200 million increase in notes receivable represents initial drawdown on line of credit by Host Marriott, funded with matched borrowing by Marriott International.
c. Represents additional debt assumed from Host Marriott.
d. Represents transfer of land and related deferred taxes and debt from Host Marriott.
e. Represents adjustments to allocate drafts between Marriott International and Host Marriott.

it had received tenders of only 46% of the series F notes and only 13% of the series I notes.[53]

On Monday, August 23, Marriott amended the conditions for consummating the exchange offer by dropping the requirement for 51% of the series F and I notes and by excluding those notes from the 85% minimum aggregate requirement.[54] At the end of August Marriott announced that

53. "Business Brief: Marriott Extends Bond-Swap Deadline as Lagging Response Delays Split-Up," *Wall Street Journal*, August 19, 1993, p. B4, and Host Marriott Hospitality, Inc., Marriott Corporation and Marriott International, Inc. Supplement to Prospectus and Consent Solicitation dated August 23, 1993 (hereafter, "Supplement to Prospectus and Solicitation"), p. 2.

54. Supplement to Prospectus and Solicitation, pp. 2–3. Marriott also announced that if it did not receive tenders of more than 50% of the series F notes it would call all of the untendered series F notes for early redemption prior to completion of the spin-off, and that if it did not receive tenders of more than 50% of the series I notes (which were not similarly callable), it would amend the indenture for the notes to provide that any series I notes remaining out-

the amended conditions had been satisfied and that the exchanges and so the prerequisite contingent modifications to the basic spin-off plan would be consummated.[55]

On Monday, October 11, 1993 (the last day of trading before the stock went *ex*-distribution), Marriott common stock closed at $33.25 per share. The following day Host Marriott common stock closed at $6.375 per share and Marriott International closed at $27.125.

---

standing would be secured equally and ratably with the new HMH securities (Supplement to Prospectus and Solicitation, p. 3). This change was required by the survival, in the absence of tenders of more than 50% of the series I notes, of the negative pledge clause in the indenture for those notes.

55. "Business Brief—Marriott Corp.: Minimum Tender Condition Is Met for Exchange Offer," *Wall Street Journal*, August 31, 1993, p. B3.

V ASSESSING THE METHODOLOGY

19 Empirical Tests of Contingent Value Models

We observed in chapter 1 that contingent claims analysis provides a methodology for valuing each slice of a corporation's capital structure from the aggregate value of the firm. The most direct test of the methodology is to compare the *model* values of different securities with the *market* values of the same securities.[1] In view of the efficiency of the capital markets, any material or systematic difference between model values and market values can be viewed as an indication of model failure.

This chapter summarizes the findings of five direct tests of the contingent value methodology.[2] Four of the studies indicate that the methodology materially and systematically undervalues common stock relative to more senior corporate claims or, equivalently, overvalues debt and other senior claims relative to common stock. All five studies report model estimates of security values that differ substantially from market values.

19.1 Jones, Mason, and Rosenfeld on Debt Values

Two papers by Jones, Mason, and Rosenfeld (1984, 1985) assess the empirical validity of contingent value models of corporate bond pricing. The first study examined a sample of 305 bonds issued by 27 firms. 129 of the bonds were subinvestment grade securities rated below BBB. The second study examined 163 investment grade bonds (rated BBB or higher) issued by 15 firms. Both studies examined bond prices monthly between January 1977 and January 1981.

The issuers included in the studies were selected for their relatively simple capital structures. The issuers had a small number of outstanding bonds, a low ratio of private debt to total capital,[3] a low proportion of short-term notes payable and capitalized leases to total capital, no convertible debt, no preferred stock, and a single class of common stock.

---

1. The methodology can also be tested by examining the assumptions embedded in a contingent value model, such as the characteristics of the distributions of cash and securities following bankruptcy (see section 4.6) and the decision of a firm to call debt for early redemption (see chapters 7 and 9).

2. See also McConnell and Schwartz (1986) (empirical assesment of the contingent value of a callable, putable, convertible zero-coupon bond, using the price of the issuer's stock as a state variable), Titman and Torous (1989) (empirical assesment of the contingent value of a nonamortizing, noncallable commercial mortgage, using the value of the mortgaged property as a state variable), Wei and Guo (1997) (empirical assesment of yields on Eurodollar time deposits maturing in one year or less), and Anderson and Sundaresan (2000) (empirical assessment of yield spreads on 30-year BBB industrial bonds). Brennan (1995, p. 17) has remarked on the paucity of empirical assessments of the methodology.

3. Private debt includes bank debt and debt privately placed with institutional lenders.

To compute bond values, the authors had to address several difficult modeling issues:[4]

· They assumed that U.S. Treasury yields would evolve with no uncertainty from the term structure existing on a given valuation date; that is, future Treasury yields were assumed to be identical to forward yields observed on the valuation date.

· They assumed that the firm could not issue any new debt until all existing debt had been redeemed.

· They assumed that all payments of principal and interest would be funded by liquidating assets.

· They assumed that a firm would not file for bankruptcy unless the value of the firm was less than a contemporaneously required payment to creditors.

· They assumed that bankruptcy is instantaneous and costless and results in distributions of cash and securities in accord with the absolute priority rule.

To compute the value of a bond with a contingent value model, an analyst must identify the value of the firm and the volatility of the value of the firm. In their 1984 paper, Jones, Mason, and Rosenfeld imputed the value of the firm from the market value of all publicly traded securities issued by the firm, and they inferred the volatility of the value of the firm from the historic volatility of the firm's stock and the leverage of the firm. In their 1985 paper, the authors imputed the value of the firm from the market value of the firm's stock, and they estimated the volatility of the value of the firm from the historic volatility of the imputed value of the firm.

Table 19.1 displays selected results from the 1984 study. The mean pricing error for investment grade debt was small (0.47% of market value), but the mean error for subinvestment grade debt was large and positive (10.05%).[5] Fluctuations around the mean errors were large in both subsamples—the standard deviations were 7.27% and 10.63%, respectively, and the mean absolute errors were 5.87% and 11.97%, respectively.

Table 19.2 displays selected results from the 1985 study of investment grade debt. The overall mean pricing error was modest (1.49%), but the

4. In addition to the assumptions noted in the text, Jones, Mason, and Rosenfeld paid close attention to the extremely difficult problem of valuing multiple issues of callable sinking fund debt when a sinking fund redemption requirement can be satisfied either with market repurchases or with a partial call for redemption at par. Valuation of sinking fund debt has also been examined by Leader (1977), Laiderman (1980), Kalotay (1981), Ho and Singer (1982, 1984), Dunn and Spatt (1984), Ho (1985), and Laber (1990).

5. The pricing error for a bond is the difference between model value and market value, expressed as a percent of market value.

Table 19.1
Selected results from Jones, Mason, and Rosenfeld (1984)

Partition of sample	Number of bonds	Mean error	Standard deviation of error	Mean absolute error
Full sample	305	4.52%	10.03%	8.45%
Investment grade	176	0.47	7.27	5.87
Subinvestment grade	129	10.05	10.63	11.97

Note: Error is measured as the difference between model value and market value and is expressed as a percentage of market value.

Table 19.2
Selected results from Jones, Mason, and Rosenfeld (1985)

Partition of sample	Number of bonds	Mean error	Standard deviation of error	Mean absolute error
Full sample	163	1.49%	7.14%	5.89%
Senior debt	147	0.83	7.01	5.70
Junior debt	16	7.51	5.23	7.63
Rated A or above	133	0.23	6.37	5.18
Rated below A	30	7.07	7.67	9.06
Firms with low volatility of value	40	0.96	6.11	5.27
Firms with high volatility of value	43	3.39	7.46	6.60

Note: Error is measured as the difference between model value and market value and is expressed as a percentage of market value.

variation around the mean error was large—a standard deviation of 7.14% and a mean absolute error of 5.89%. In addition the model systematically overvalued junior debt, lower rated debt, and debt issued by firms with more volatile values.

These results suggest that even in cases where the capital structure of the firm is relatively simple, a conventional contingent value model may not be capable of providing more than a rough indication of the value of a corporation's bonds. In addition a conventional model may not be capable of providing an unbiased assessment of bond value in those cases where such an assessment is of greatest interest: when the company has substantial operating risk and/or financial leverage and when its debt is not highly rated.

19.2   Ogden on Debt Values

Ogden (1987) examined the pricing of 57 bonds issued between 1973 and 1985 by companies with exceptionally simple capital structures. A selected bond had to represent at least 60% of the issuer's long-term debt, the total book value of other long-term debt could not exceed 20% of the book value of the issuer's equity, and the book value of the issuer's equity claims other than common stock (including preferred stock and warrants) could not exceed 10% of the book value of all equity claims.

Ogden assumed that corporate dividend payments would continue at the recently observed rate and, following Jones, Mason, and Rosenfeld, that

· U.S. Treasury yields would evolve with no uncertainty from the term structure existing on a given valuation date,

· a firm could not issue any new debt until all existing debt had been redeemed,

· all payments of principal, interest and dividends would be funded by asset liquidation,

· a firm would not file for bankruptcy unless the value of the firm was less than a contemporaneously required payment to creditors, and that

· bankruptcy is instantaneous and costless and results in distributions in accord with the absolute priority rule.

Ogden computed the value of the firm as the sum of the market value of the bond issued by the firm and the market value of the firm's common stock, and he inferred the volatility of the value of the firm from the historic volatility of the firm's stock and the leverage of the firm.

Using the computed value of the firm, Ogden identified the model value of the bond on the date it was issued by the firm, and then used that model value to compute a model bond yield (measured in percent per annum). He used the market value of the bond to compute a market yield. Subtracting from each of these yields the yield on a Treasury bond with a similar maturity gives the model and market yield premiums.

In the last step of his analysis Ogden regressed market yield premiums on model yield premiums:

$$
\begin{bmatrix} \text{Market} \\ \text{yield} \\ \text{premium} \end{bmatrix} = \underset{(0.175)}{1.042} + \underset{(0.102)}{0.925} \cdot \begin{bmatrix} \text{Model} \\ \text{yield} \\ \text{premium} \end{bmatrix}
$$

$$\text{Standard error of regression} = 0.906; \text{ Adjusted } R^2 = 0.594 \quad (19.1)$$

On the null hypothesis that the contingent value model provides accurate assessments of bond values and yields, the intercept coefficient should not be significantly different from zero, and the slope coefficient should not be significantly different from unity. The standard errors of the estimated coefficients are shown in parentheses below the coefficients.

The slope coefficient in equation (19.1) is not significantly different from unity, but the positive and statistically significant intercept suggests that Ogden's model produced downward biased estimates of market yields—or upward biased estimates of market prices—for the bonds in his sample. The standard error of the regression suggests that the model values were not particularly precise. Thus his results parallel the findings of Jones, Mason, and Rosenfeld.

19.3   King on Convertible Debt Values

King (1986) examined the pricing of 103 convertible bonds on March 31 and December 31, 1977.

To simplify his analysis, King excluded firms capitalized with preferred stock or with more than a single issue of convertible debt. He also assumed, in essence, that every firm in his sample had defeased all of its conventional debt, so for all practical purposes the firm was capitalized only with common stock and convertible debt.[6]

King further assumed that[7]

· the U.S. Treasury yield curve was flat and stationary at the level of yields on Treasury debt with a maturity comparable to the maturity of the convertible bond,

· corporate dividends would continue at the recently observed rate, and

· bankruptcy is instantaneous and costless and results in distributions in accord with the absolute priority rule.

The value of the firm was set at the sum of the market values of the firm's convertible debt and common stock. The volatility of the value of the firm was set at the historic volatility of the firm's stock.

King was able to obtain transaction prices for 50 convertible bonds on March 31, 1977, and for 71 bonds on December 31, 1977. On average, the difference between model values and market values was not significantly

---

6. King (1986, p. 55) noted: "The assumption that [the sum of the market values of the common stock and convertible bonds] follows a diffusion process does not allow the [conventional] debt to be affected by the same factors that influence the debt value of the convertible bonds. Essentially the [conventional] debt is viewed as riskless." King did not report whether the market prices of the conventional debt of the firms in his sample were close to their default-free values, as his assumption suggests.

7. In addition to the assumptions noted in the text, King noted that the firm could not issue any new debt until all existing debt had been redeemed, that all payments of principal, interest and dividends would be funded by asset liquidation, and that a firm would not file for bankruptcy unless the value of the firm was less than a contemporaneously required payment to creditors.

different from zero on either date. However, the standard deviation of the ratio of model value to market value was 0.072 on March 31, 1977, and 0.115 on December 31, 1977. Thus King's contingent value model did not lead to particularly precise convertible bond values on either date.

19.4   Ingersoll on Dual Fund Share Values

A dual purpose mutual fund is a special type of closed end investment company.[8] The assets of a dual fund consist of a diversified portfolio of stocks, bonds, and other financial instruments managed by a professional investment advisor. Unlike most closed end funds, however, a dual fund is capitalized with *two* classes of securities: common stock (usually called "capital shares") and preferred stock ("income shares").

The gross income of a dual fund (derived from interest and dividends on the fund's investments), less management fees and other expenses, is passed through to income shareholders as a dividend on their shares. Capital shareholders do not receive any dividends. Income shares also have a specified minimum annual dividend (but no maximum dividend), as well as a specified redemption date and redemption value. On the redemption date, income shareholders have a senior claim on the fund equal to the redemption value of their shares plus the cumulative shortfall (if any) of actual dividends below the minimum dividend. Capital shareholders receive the residual assets of the fund. Thus they are in the economic position of holding a call option on the assets of the fund, with an exercise price equal to the redemption value of the income shares (plus any shortfall in the dividends on those shares) and an expiration date equal to the redemption date of the income shares.

A dual fund is interesting in the context of assessing the validity of the contingent value methodology because it has the simplest possible nontrivial corporate capital structure (a conventional closed end fund has a trivial capital structure: it is capitalized entirely with common stock) and because it has no debt. Since there is no contractual obligation on which a dual fund can default, the valuation of dual fund shares does not depend on the characteristics of bankruptcy.

Ingersoll (1976) examined the values of income and capital shares issued by seven dual funds using weekly prices from May 1967 to December

---

8. See "Two for the Price of One," *Fortune*, February, 1967, p. 201; "Dual Purpose Fund Results," *Fortune*, August, 1967, p. 175; Shelton, Brigham, and Hofflander (1967); Gentry and Pike (1968); Johnston, Curley, and McIndoe (1968); "Another Look at Dual-Purpose Funds," *Fortune*, April, 1973, p. 25; Litzenberger and Sosin (1977a, b); Kumar, Philippatos, and Ezzell (1978); and Lemmon, Schallheim, and Zender (2000).

1973.[9] He assumed that the U.S. Treasury yield curve on a particular valuation date is flat and stationary at the contemporaneous median yield on Treasury bonds with more than fifteen years remaining to maturity, he computed the aggregate value of a fund as the sum of the market values of the fund's income and capital shares, and he estimated the volatility of the value of a fund directly from historically observed fluctuations in fund value.

Ingersoll also assumed that the annual dividend paid to income shareholders is a fixed fraction of the contemporaneous value of a fund, equal to the historically observed average fraction. The assumption of a proportional dividend is broadly consistent with the management incentives offered to dual fund investment advisors. Compensation contracts generally provided that an advisor would, over the course of a year, be paid the lesser of $\frac{1}{2}$% of the net asset value of a fund and one-sixth of the gross income of the fund.[10] This gave the advisor an incentive to allocate the fund's portfolio in a "balanced" fashion between income-producing assets, such as fixed income securities and stocks with high dividend–price ratios, and assets with greater potential for capital appreciation, such that gross annual income would equal about 3% of the net asset value of the fund (in which case one-sixth of gross income would be equal to $\frac{1}{2}$% of net asset value). Any less income would result in less compensation for the advisor. Any additional income would result in larger payments to income shareholders, reducing the net asset value of the fund (and hence the basis for future compensation) without producing any additional current compensation for the advisor.

Consistent with the findings of Jones, Mason, and Rosenfeld and of Ogden, Ingersoll reported that his model consistently and materially undervalued capital shares relative to income shares.

Ingersoll pointed out an important potential explanation for his empirical results. As explained in more detail below, the governance structure of a dual fund gives reason to believe that dividend payments to income shareholders might not be a fixed fraction of the value of a fund, but rather might increase as a fraction of fund value if fund value declines following the initial public offering price of the fund's securities.[11] Additionally the volatility of the value of the fund's asset portfolio might decline with the value of the portfolio. Ignoring these effects could lead

9. See also the study by Jarrow and O'Hara (1989) of "primes" and "scores," securities that are closely related to the income and capital shares of a dual fund.

10. Lemmon, Schallheim, and Zender (2000, p. 278).

11. See also Lemmon, Schallheim, and Zender (2000).

to model prices for capital shares relative to income shares lower than market price relationships if model prices are assessed during a period when, as in Ingersoll's sample, stock prices and dual fund asset values are low.

Corporate Governance and the Portfolio and Dividend Policies of a Dual Fund

The investment advisor that manages the asset portfolio of a dual fund is selected and monitored by the fund's board of directors. Capital shareholders generally elect the majority of the directors. However, if dividend arrearages on income shares grow to more than twice the minimum annual dividend, income shareholders become entitled to elect a majority of the board.[12] (Majority control reverts to the capital shareholders if and when the dividend arrearages are eliminated.) Prolonged failure of an investment advisor to generate income sufficient to pay the minimum dividend could therefore result in a change of control of the board and replacement of the advisor.

Over an interval like the late 1960s and early 1970s, when stock prices declined and dividend reductions were not uncommon, the threat of replacement gave dual fund investment advisors an incentive to generate gross income in excess of 3% of net asset value by shifting the composition of fund portfolios from "balanced" allocations towards allocations with relatively more income-producing securities. Consistent with this hypothesis, Ingersoll (1976, table 2) reports that the gross income of a typical dual fund averaged about $4\frac{1}{2}\%$ of net asset value over his sample period. The shift to relatively greater holdings of income producing securities, including especially fixed income securities, could be expected to lead to concomitantly lower volatility of fund value.

However, portfolio allocations emphasizing income rather than capital appreciation and characterized by relatively low volatility could not be expected to persist if stock prices and dividend payments were to rise. An investment advisor could then be expected to shift the composition of his fund's portfolio back toward a "balanced" allocation. This would result in a decline in the ratio of gross income (and hence dividends on income shares) to net asset value, as well as an increase in the volatility of the value of the fund.

Ingersoll's specification that the prospective dividend payout rate and volatility of a dual fund are fixed and equal to the historically observed payout rate and volatility, respectively, combined with observed dividend payout rates that were high (and volatilities of fund value that were low)

---

12. Lemmon, Schallheim, and Zender (2000, pp. 276–277).

relative to what they would have been with "balanced" portfolio allocations, may have led to an overstatement of prospective dividends and an understatement of prospective volatility. Either effect could account for the undervaluation of capital shares relative to income shares.

19.5   Two Sources of Model Failure

The studies by Ingersoll (1976), Jones, Mason, and Rosenfeld (1984, 1985), and Ogden (1987) suggest that contingent value models systematically undervalue common stock and overvalue more senior corporate claims. Two potential sources of this bias can be identified readily. Chapter 20 discusses a third source of model failure.

Violations of the Absolute Priority Rule

The first source of bias is the assumption that bankruptcy results in distributions of cash and securities in accord with the absolute priority rule. (This factor is not relevant for Ingersoll's study.)

Numerous studies have shown that shareholders frequently receive something at the conclusion of a large corporate bankruptcy even if creditors are not paid the full amount of their claims.[13] Other studies suggest that violations of the absolute priority rule do not come as a surprise to either creditors or shareholders.[14] Contingent value models thus understate bankruptcy distributions to shareholders and overstate distributions to creditors, and they can be expected to undervalue equity and overvalue debt prior to bankruptcy.

Section 5.2 examined how the prospect for violations of the absolute priority rule might be incorporated into the specification of a contingent value model.

Stochastic Evolution of Yields on U.S. Treasury Debt

The second source of bias is the assumption that yields on U.S. Treasury securities evolve with no uncertainty.

Suppressing uncertainty in the evolution of Treasury yields reduces the value of an option to redeem debt prior to maturity. This enhances the value of callable debt and reduces the value of equity issued by a firm capitalized with callable debt. (This factor is not relevant for Ingersoll's

---

13. Franks and Torous (1989), Weiss (1990), Eberhart, Moore, and Roenfeldt (1990), LoPucki and Whitford (1990), Eberhart and Sweeney (1992), and Betker (1995a).

14. Warner (1977a), Morse and Shaw (1988), Eberhart, Moore, and Roenfeldt (1990), Eberhart and Sweeney (1992), and Altman and Eberhart (1994).

study, which did not address the valuation of securities issued by a firm capitalized with callable debt.)

It is computationally burdensome, but feasible, to extend the contingent valuation of corporate securities to include stochastically evolving Treasury yields.[15]

15. See, for example, Brennan and Schwartz (1980), Titman and Torous (1989), Shimko, Tejima, and Deventer (1993), Kim, Ramaswamy, and Sundaresan (1993), Longstaff and Schwartz (1995), and Acharya and Carpenter (1999).

Chapter 19 summarized five empirical studies of corporate securities pricing. Four of the studies support the conclusion that contingent value analysis materially and systematically undervalues common stock relative to more senior corporate claims. Section 19.5 identified two potential sources of this model failure: failure to account for prospective violations of the absolute priority rule and failure to account for uncertainty in the evolution of yields on U.S. Treasury debt. This chapter describes a third potential source of model failure: failure to account for implicit management options embedded in the corporate form of organization.

20.1   The Structure of Contingent Value Models

Almost all contingent value models have two essential features:

· A description of how the price of a reference asset varies through time.

· A function describing how, at some terminal point in time, the price of a contingent claim varies with the price of the reference asset.

If market participants can construct, from the reference asset and default-proof debt, a portfolio whose future value replicates the future value of the contingent claim, then (in the absence of opportunities for riskless arbitrage profits) the present value of the portfolio must be identical to the present value of the contingent claim. This "arbitrage pricing" leads to a contingent value function describing the price of the contingent claim as a function of the price of the reference asset at times prior to the terminal time.

Contingent Value Models for Simple Corporate Securities

Contingent value models for simple corporate securities fit within the foregoing framework. For example, chapter 2 examined the case where a firm is capitalized with a single issue of zero-coupon debt and common stock that does not pay a dividend. We identified the reference asset as the firm as a whole, and we assumed that the value of the firm evolves as a lognormal random walk. Terminal value functions for the debt and equity were identified from a specification of the consequences of default and bankruptcy.

For present purposes, the most interesting characteristic of the model in chapter 2 is the absence of any description of the internal structure of the firm. The model does not identify either the operating characteristics or the investment opportunities of the firm. The firm may be operating efficiently, investing in projects with positive net present values, and divesting operations with negative net present values—or it may not; we know only that the aggregate value of the firm's securities evolves as a lognormal random walk, much like a child's wind-up toy.

Two Extensions

The model in chapter 2 can be extended in two important dimensions.

First, we can introduce debt with different priorities, as in chapter 3. Assuming that all of the firm's debt matures at the same time, this requires only a respecification of the terminal contingent value functions.

Second, we can introduce asynchronous liabilities stemming from debt that matures at different times (chapter 11) or from debt that promises to pay interest periodically before maturity (chapter 12). The analytical consequences of asynchronous liabilities are represented with transversality conditions describing the behavior of debt and equity values at the time a liability comes due.

Comment

The capital structure of a firm capitalized with debt with asynchronous payments and different priorities is certainly more complex than the simple capital structure examined in chapter 2, but the essential features of the models in chapters 2, 3, 11, and 12 are all quite similar to each other: a stochastic process describing the evolution of the value of the firm, coupled with terminal and transversality conditions derived from the firm's *contractual obligations*. In particular, none of the models exhibit any scope for discretion or decision making on the part of the company's management.

Debt with Embedded Options

Introducing debt with embedded options extends the conceptual framework of contingent value analysis in a third, distinctly different, dimension. Embedded options present opportunities for *alternative actions* by the firm. To price securities with such options, we have to identify the range of available actions, we have to say something about who chooses which action will be taken, and we have to say something about how the choice is made.

The simplest case is callable debt (chapter 6), where we assumed that the managers of the firm decide whether or not to call the debt and that they act to maximize the value of equity. Pricing pay-in-kind debt (chapter 13) is more complicated technically, because it involves relatively complex transversality conditions and families of contingent value functions, but it does not involve any decision making beyond managerial action to enhance shareholder value in the context of a series of binary choices. Pricing convertible debt (chapter 8) is more complicated conceptually because it requires analysis of creditor decisions to convert debt to common stock as well as the decision of the firm to call debt for early redemption.

Comment

It is important to note that the analyses in chapters 6, 8, and 13 are based on the same model of the firm as the analyses in chapters 2, 3, 11, and 12: the value of the firm is assumed to evolve between payments to creditors as a lognormal random walk. Since the value of the firm does not depend on the actions of its managers, the consequence—for the contemporaneous value of equity—of an action is exactly offset by the consequence of the action for the aggregate value of the balance of the firm's securities. Any benefit to shareholders of choosing one action in lieu of another comes at the expense of other claimants. The embedded options examined in chapters 6, 8, and 13 create opportunities for dividing the corporate pie in different ways, but they do not create any opportunities for expanding the overall size of the pie. Thus neglect of an embedded option to redeem a bond before its stated maturity date, or neglect of an issuer's option to pay interest on a PIK bond in cash or kind, leads to an understatement of the contingent value of equity and an overstatement of the aggregate contingent value of other claims.[1]

Other Contingent Claims with Embedded Options

Callable and convertible debt and pay-in-kind debt are not the only examples of contingent claims with embedded options. Pricing an American call option on dividend-paying stock, or an American put option on any stock, also requires an explicit appraisal of the circumstances that will lead a holder to exercise her option before expiration.[2] An analyst has to model when, prior to expiration, a decision to exercise enhances the value of the option relative to the value associated with a decision to continue to hold the option. Analysis of early exercise decisions is similarly important for valuing executive and employee stock options.[3] Passport options, a recently innovated over-the-counter derivative instrument, provide a more

---

1. The consequences of neglecting an issuer's option to redeem a bond before its stated maturity date are discussed at the end of example A in section 6.4 and at the end of example B in section 8.4. The consequences of neglecting an issuer's option to pay interest on a PIK bond in cash or kind are discussed in section 13.9.

2. Merton (1973, pp. 155 and 170–74).

3. Jennergren and Naslund (1993), Huddart (1994), Kulatilaka and Marcus (1994), Cuny and Jorion (1995), Huddart and Lang (1996), and Carpenter (1998).

complex example of a contingent claim with substantial embedded optionality.[4]

20.2   Implicit Management Options

Debt with embedded options introduces managerial discretion and decision making into contingent value models of corporate securities prices in a transparent, but relatively limited, form. In the case of callable debt the firm can call its debt or allow the debt to remain outstanding, and in the case of PIK debt the firm can pay interest in cash or in kind.

However, senior corporate managers exercise discretion over an enormous range of corporate actions, hardly any of which are provided for explicitly in any debt contract. Casual observation reveals that firms sometimes merge and sometimes acquire, sell, or spin off operating subsidiaries —and thereby change their business activities.[5] They alter, sometimes quite dramatically, their capital structures with exchange offers, with repurchases of common stock financed with new debt, and by paying out

4. Hyer, Lipton-Lifschitz, and Pugachevsky (1997). Garbade (1999) describes passport options and relates the pricing of such options to the issues discussed in this chapter.

5. Several authors, including Hite and Owers (1983), Schipper and Smith (1983), and Dennis and McConnell (1986), have observed that mergers and spin-offs are mirror images of each other: a merger combines two businesses previously operated separately and a spin-off partitions two businesses previously operated within a common structure. Recognizing the prospect of mergers in a contingent value model thus raises issues closely related to the issues encountered in recognizing spin-offs, including accounting for potential synergistic gains from combining assets and potential changes in corporate capital structure. (Melicher and Rush 1974, n. 7, observe that target shareholders in conglomerate mergers completed during the 1960s commonly received convertible preferred stock of the bidder in exchange for their common stock. Kim and McConnell 1977 report that conglomerate mergers in the 1960s typically led to increases in debt–equity ratios.)

Dodd (1980), Asquith (1983), and Asquith, Bruner, and Mullins (1983) assess the effect of merger announcements on the stock of bidder and target firms. All three studies report large average increases in the values of target stocks and either small increases or small decreases, on average, in the values of bidder stocks, suggesting significant synergistic gains—the bulk of which are captured by target shareholders. Hasbrouck (1985) and Palepu (1986) discuss the characteristics and predictability of acquisition targets.

The effect of mergers on the values of senior securities has been examined by Lewellen (1971) and Higgins and Schall (1975) (who point out a "co-insurance" effect that enhances the aggregate value of the debt of the merging firms and reduces the aggregate value of equity; see also the related analysis by Sarig 1985) and by Galai and Masulis (1976) and Kim and McConnell (1977) (who note that the co-insurance effect can be mitigated by greater leveraging of the merged enterprise). Additionally Asquith and Kim (1982) observe that the incentive—noted by Jensen and Meckling (1976)—for the shareholders of a levered firm to expropriate wealth from creditors by increasing the volatility of the value of the firm applies to mergers as well as to conventional investments (see also Galai and Masulis 1976). Dennis and McConnell (1986) report that the preferred stock and convertible securities of a target firm typically appreciate significantly at the time of a merger announcement (reflecting the prospect of redemption, exchange, or conversion on favorable terms), that the value of the conventional debt of a target does not, on average, change materially, and that the values of the senior securities of a bidder also do not change materially and significantly.

leveraged special dividends. They undertake investments financed with sales of new securities, they sell operating divisions and other assets and use the proceeds to redeem outstanding debt and to repurchase equity, and they decide whether to redeem maturing debt by selling new debt or equity or by selling assets. In an extreme case a firm can liquidate all of its assets and extinguish its capital structure.[6]

Each of these actions can be viewed as the exercise of an implicit management option to alter dynamically the asset and capital structure of the firm in the best interest of shareholders.[7] However, such actions are only rarely represented in contingent value models.[8]

Neglecting implicit management options in the specification of a contingent value model can have material consequences for the relative value of debt and equity. We noted earlier how neglect of an issuer's option to redeem a bond before its stated maturity date, or neglect of an option to pay interest on a PIK bond in cash or kind, leads to an understatement of the value of the issuer's equity (and an overstatement of the value of the bond) when management exercises the option in the best interest of shareholders. We might reasonably suppose that managers exercise their implicit options similarly.[9] Empirical evidence supports the proposition that managers typically undertake transactions such as leveraged recapitalizations (discussed in chapter 17) and spin-offs (see chapter 18) when

6. Corporate liquidation policies have been examined by Titman (1984), Hite, Owers, and Rogers (1987), Kim and Schatzberg (1987), Ghosh, Owers, and Rogers (1991), and Mella-Barral (1999). The frequency of liquidation declined dramatically after 1986 (Fleming and Moon 1995, table 1) as a result of a change in Federal tax law (Mehran, Nogler, and Schwartz 1998, pp. 322 and 324).

7. Many of the actions also be identified as "real options." See Dixit and Pindyck (1994), Trigeorgis (1996), and the works cited by Sundaresan (2000, pp. 1595–97).

In the early part of the nineteenth century, a corporation was chartered by an individual state legislative act that specified the business of the new enterprise in some detail. Any significant change in the business of the enterprise required the *unanimous* consent of all shareholders. Subsequently states adopted general incorporation laws that permitted incorporation "for any lawful business." This made it easier for a company to respond to changing business conditions and led to substantial delegation of the decision to change a line of business to senior officers and the board of directors. Berle and Means (1932, pp. 131, 135–36, and 140). See also the discussion of early requirements for *unanimous* shareholder consent for mergers and sales of assets in Berle and Means (1932, pp. 270–271).

8. Exceptions include Mello and Parsons (1992) (managerial discretion to close, reopen, or abandon a mine dynamically), Anderson and Sundaresan (1996), Mella-Barral and Perraudin (1997), Mella-Barral (1999) (managerial discretion to alter debt service dynamically when creditors have discretion to accept less than the originally promised debt service), and Leland (1998) (managerial discretion to alter operating risk dynamically). Mauer and Triantis (1994) examine a case where a manager can alter the production state and leverage of a firm dynamically, but they assume that debt covenants eliminate the conflict between the interests of creditors and the interests of shareholders by constraining the choice of operating policy and capital structure to that which maximizes the aggregate value of the firm.

9. Shleifer and Vishny (1997) discuss in detail whether and when this assumption is reasonable, and give examples where it is not well founded.

the transactions enhance the value of the firm, and typically structure the transactions to capture for shareholders all of the increase in value. It follows that neglecting implicit management options will lead to an understatement of the contingent value of a firm's equity and a concomitant overstatement of the relative value of its debt.

More generally, neglect of implicit management options may be a third source of the errors and biases reported in empirical studies of contingent security pricing.[10]

20.3   Improving the Representation of Implicit Management Options

Improving the representation of implicit management options in a contingent value model requires specification of a menu of discretionary corporate actions, methodologies for assessing whether a firm will undertake particular actions, and recognition of the role of debt covenants in constraining the actions of the firm.

A More Complete Menu of Discretionary Corporate Acts

Identifying the range of actions available to the holder of an option embedded in a debt security is relatively straightforward because the terms of the option are spelled out explicitly in a bond indenture or loan agreement. Identifying the range of actions associated with implicit management options is more difficult: managers have significant discretion with respect to mergers, acquisitions, capital investments, divestitures, spin-offs, sales of new securities, repurchases of outstanding securities, and dividend payments.

Specifying an implicit management option is further complicated by the accounting requirement that changes in assets must balance changes in liabilities and equity. A divestiture or equity carve-out cannot be considered in isolation; an analyst must also examine whether the proceeds are best used to repurchase or redeem debt, or to acquire other assets, or to

---

10. Anderson and Sundaresan (1996), Mella-Barral and Perraudin (1997), and Mella-Barral (1999) find that recognizing the possibility of strategic debt service can have a substantial effect on debt and equity values. Similarly Leland (1998) finds that recognizing the possibility of altering the operating risk of the firm can have a substantial effect on security values. See also the discussion of managerial discretion with respect to the allocation of the asset portfolio of a dual purpose mutual fund, and the implications of that discretion for dividend payments to income shareholders and the relative value of income and capital shares, at the end of section 19.4 and in Ingersoll (1976) and Lemmon, Schallheim, and Zender (2000). Mello and Parsons (1992) present a model of a levered firm where a shareholder-aligned manager exercises discretion with respect to whether a mine is closed, reopened, or abandoned, but they do not consider how exercise of the implicit management option alters the relative value of the debt and equity of the firm.

finance a distribution to shareholders.[11] Similarly a capital investment can be funded with the proceeds of an asset sale or with the proceeds of a sale of new debt or equity.

The Dimensionality Problem

Introducing implicit management options into a contingent value model presents a novel problem attributable to the high dimensionality of those options.

An option to call debt for early redemption is, at each point in time, a one-dimensional binary option: the debt is either called or it is left outstanding. In contrast, the dimension of the space of actions associated with exercise of an implicit management option may be quite large. Consider, for example, the option to recapitalize a firm with a leveraged special dividend payment. At each point in time management has to identify whether to undertake such a recapitalization, the size of the dividend, and how to finance the dividend. Clearly, the variety of securities that it might sell to finance the dividend is large. Similarly at any point in time a firm can contemplate merging with any of a large number of possible partners,[12] and it can contemplate acquiring, divesting, or spinning off operating subsidiaries in any of a large number of ways.[13]

The problem presented by the high dimensionality of implicit management options is analogous to the difference between tic-tac-toe and chess. Both games are finite games, but they are games of very different dimensionality. Grade school children commonly work out all the possible con-

---

11. See Lang, Poulsen, and Stulz (1995) and Allen and McConnell (1998).

12. See, for example, the extensive assessment of potential merger partners by General Electric Co. prior to its bid to acquire Honeywell International Inc. in October, 2000, and the expectation of market participants that United Technologies Corp. would seek other merger partners when its own bid to merge with Honeywell was displaced by General Electric's proposal. "Honeywell Becomes Acquisition Target," *Wall Street Journal*, October 20, 2000, p. A3; "2 Manufacturers Are Set to Merge in $40 Billion Deal," *New York Times*, October 20, 2000, p. A1; "General Electric Buying Honeywell in $45 Billion Deal," *New York Times*, October 23, 2000, p. A1, "On the Eve of Retirement, Jack Welch Decides to Stick Around a Bit," *Wall Street Journal*, October 23, 2000, p. A1; and "GE Move Flags Aerospace Consolidation," *Wall Street Journal*, October 24, 2000, p. A2.

13. See, for example, the alternative restructuring options available to AT&T Corp. in October 2000, described in "AT&T Proposes Long-Distance Spinoff," *Wall Street Journal*, October 4, 2000, p. A3; "Armstrong's Vision of AT&T Cable Empire Unravels on the Ground," *Wall Street Journal*, October 18, 2000, p. A1; "British Telecom, AT&T Abandon Services Merger, Discuss Options," *Wall Street Journal*, October 18, 2000, p. A18; "Heard on the Street: AT&T Wireless's Talks with Nextel Face Investor Static;" *Wall Street Journal*, October 18, 2000, p. C1; "AT&T Is Considering Four-Way Breakup;" *Wall Street Journal*, October 23, 2000, p. A3; "A Wounded Giant, AT&T Is Weighing a Split into 4 Parts," *New York Times*, October 23, 2000, p. A1; "AT&T's Board Mulls Breakup among Options," *Wall Street Journal*, October 24, 2000, p. A8; and "AT&T, in Pullback, Will Break Itself into 4 Businesses," *New York Times*, October 26, 2000, p. A1.

tingencies in tic-tac-toe and thereafter avoid losing even a single game. Chess is a different matter.

The high dimensionality of the space of implicit management actions means that we may be unable to identify exhaustively all of the actions that a corporation can take to alter shareholder wealth. It follows that we can hardly begin to think about how a company sorts through the set of feasible actions to identify those that *maximize* shareholder wealth. (Contrast this to the much simpler case of deciding whether or not to call a bond for early redemption. There are only two choices, so we can quickly move on to thinking about which to select.)

Assessing Whether to Undertake a Particular Action

Specifying a richer menu of discretionary corporate actions is not, by itself, sufficient to enhance the representation of implicit management options in a contingent value model; an analyst must also specify, for each action, how the firm decides whether to undertake the action.

The discussions of dividends and stock repurchases in chapter 16, leveraged recapitalizations in chapter 17, and spin-offs in chapter 18 suggest that providing a rational basis for many discretionary corporate acts will require a more detailed representation of the firm than that which appears in conventional contingent value models. A conventional model assumes that the state of the firm is summarized by an aggregate value that evolves through time as a lognormal random walk. It is unlikely that such a simple structure can support the decision of a firm to, for example, recapitalize. An analyst must also characterize the investment opportunities available to the firm and the likelihood that market participants are discounting the value of the firm for the risk of uneconomic retention of cash and inefficient operations. Similarly the decision of a firm to spin off an operating subsidiary will depend on how a spin-off might reduce diseconomies of scope and scale and enhance managerial focus on core competencies, as well as how it might facilitate value-enhancing asset transfers and diversity in corporate capital structures and in the design of executive compensation contracts.

Three Problems

Specifying a basis for deciding whether to undertake a discretionary corporate action leads to three significant stumbling blocks for the contingent valuation of corporate securities.

First, many corporate decisions depend on variables that are not prices of traded claims. Assessing how such variables affect corporate securities prices will be more difficult than, for example, assessing how the aggregate value of the firm affects the value of debt and equity in the simple pricing model presented in chapter 2.

Second, the observation that announcement of a significant corporate action frequently leads to material changes in securities prices implies that market participants did not fully anticipate the action. There is little reason to believe that analysts will be able to model corporate decision making with such precision that on the basis of publicly available information, no announcement of a corporate action ever comes as a surprise. However, any residual uncertainty about whether a firm might undertake a discretionary act is a source of risk that is likely to be reflected in the structure of securities prices.

Third, there is ample evidence that discretionary corporate actions commonly lead to change in the value of the firm as a whole, as well as to changes in the relative values of the securities issued by the firm. For example, the leveraged recapitalizations of Quantum Chemical (section 17.1) and Colt Industries (appendix A to chapter 17) led to increases in equity values that more than offset concurrent reductions in debt values. The initial announcement (in October 1992) of the spin-off of Marriott International (Section 18.2) led to a net reduction in the value of Marriott. The prospect that exercise of an implicit management option might alter the value of the firm is inconsistent with the specification of the evolution of the value of the firm in a conventional contingent value model.

Debt Covenants

The importance of debt covenants in the context of corporate securities pricing is evident from the descriptions of the spin-off of Marriott International and the leveraged recapitalizations of Quantum Chemical and Colt Industries. Bondholders suffered substantial losses in all three cases because the covenants on their bonds did not limit the issuer's ability to distribute cash or securities to stockholders.

Any significant expansion of the representation of implicit management options in a contingent value model will have to recognize the importance of covenants in constraining the actions of the firm and altering the net benefits to shareholders of alternative actions.[14] We should expect to find

---

14. See Jensen and Meckling (1976, pp. 337–39) (covenants chosen to maximize the value of the firm; costs of drafting, monitoring and compliance make numerous, detailed covenants undesirable, leaving room for exercise of managerial discretion), Kim, McConnell, and Greenwood (1977) (documenting losses to creditors and gains to shareholders from unanticipated formation of captive finance company, allowing a firm to issue new debt with greater effective seniority than old debt), Smith and Warner (1979) (identifying four sources of creditor-stockholder conflict: dividend payments, claim dilution (by issuing new debt of equal or higher priority), asset substitution, and underinvestment, and examining contractual devices to mitigate costs of the conflict by constraining actions of the firm), Kalay (1982)

that certeris paribus, the contingent value of debt with more and tighter covenants exceeds the contingent value of debt with fewer and looser covenants, because covenants limit corporate actions that might transfer wealth from creditors to shareholders.[15] Stated another way, errors and biases like those reported in the empirical studies described in chapter 19 may be smaller for firms subject to tight covenant restrictions, because the firms have more limited management options. A restrictive covenant can

---

(observed that covenants limit dividends financed with asset sales and sales of new debt, but do not limit dividends financed with sales of new equity; companies are permitted to, and typically do, maintain a dividend reservoir), Brennan and Schwartz (1984) (useful model of the firm would include description of (a) investment opportunities and financing alternatives available to the firm, (b) constraints imposed by debt covenants, and (c) managerial decision-making), Jensen and Smith (1985, pp. 111–12, 117–22), Dennis and McConnell (1986, pp. 180–81 and 184) (holders of nonconvertible debt may, on average, avoid loss of value when issuers merge because bond indentures frequently give creditors the right to veto a merger, thus limiting issuer incentives to advocate mergers that impair creditor interests), Malitz (1986) (covenants restricting dividend payments and the ratio of funded debt to tangible assets are more common the greater the leverage of the firm, consistent with the notion that the actions of managers of more leveraged firms taken to enhance the value of equity are more likely to impair debt values), Asquith and Wizman (1990) and Cook, Easterwood, and Martin (1992) (cross-sectional variation in covenants on bonds issued by firms subsequently acquired in leveraged buyouts correlated with cross-sectional variation in changes in bond prices upon announcement of the LBO and whether the bonds are called, defeased, tendered for, or remain outstanding following the LBO), Berkovitch and Kim (1990) (mitigation of incentives to overinvest and underinvest with covenants controlling seniority of new debt), and Opler (1993) (limiting costs of financial distress in leveraged buyouts with covenants forcing asset sales and payout of excess cash flow and limiting dividends).

See also the analyses of the difference (in terms of scope of covenants, monitoring, rene-gotiation, and discretionary enforcement) between (a) privately placed debt with con-centrated, static ownership and (b) public debt with dispersed, fluid ownership, in Zinbarg (1975) (privately placed debt typically has tighter covenants than public debt and is rene-gotiated frequently), Smith and Warner (1979) (value of the firm may be enhanced by financing with private debt with tight covenants that can be renegotiated easily, rather than with public debt with covenants that are looser because they cannot be renegotiated easily), Robertson (1988) (dispersed holders of public debt have a collective action problem in monitoring compliance of issuer with debt covenants), Berlin and Mester (1992) (optimal covenant restrictions become more severe, and the value of an option to renegotiate the covenants rises, as the creditworthiness of a prospective borrower declines), Carey, Prowse, Rea, and Udell (1993) (borrowers in the private placement market are more "information-problem-atic" than borrowers in the public debt market; they have relatively greater research and development expenses, relatively fewer fixed assets, and hence greater scope for the exercise of managerial discretion that could impair creditor interests; covenants on privately placed debt are tighter and renegotiations are more frequent), Kahan and Tuckman (1993) (obtaining creditor consent to amending covenants on public debt), Kahan and Tuckman (1996) (pri-vately placed debt has covenants that more tightly constrain managerial actions, covenants that can be triggered by deterioration in the creditworthiness of the firm, and covenants that facilitate monitoring by creditors), and Amihud, Garbade, and Kahan (1999, 2000) (pro-posal to faciliate monitoring, renegotiation, and efficient enforcement of public debt, and thereby encourage adoption of tighter covenants on such debt so that less creditworthy firms can borrow at lower cost in more liquid public debt markets).

15. Brauer (1983) describes two silver indexed bonds of the Sunshine Mining Company that—apart from a minor difference in maturity date—differ only with respect to their cov-enants limiting dividends to shareholders, and shows that the difference between the price of the bond with the more restrictive covenant and the price of the bond with the less restrictive covenant was, on average, positive.

also enhance the contingent value of debt (relative to what its contingent value would be in the absence of the covenant) because a firm may choose to redeem, repurchase, or defease the debt and eliminate the covenant in order to undertake an otherwise prohibited action.[16]

20.4 A Concluding Remark

Mason and Merton (1985, p. 25) observed that contingent value models of corporate securities prices are attractive because the "methodology takes into account the interactive effects of each of the securities [in the capital structure of a firm] on the prices of all of the others and insures a consistent evaluation procedure for the entire capital structure." However, the methodology demands that an analyst recognize not only the existing operating characteristics, capital structure, and contractual obligations of the firm but also the prospect for change attributable to managerial discretion and decision making. The importance of discretion is clear in the case of debt with embedded options. The challenge is to extend the analytical framework to include the role of discretion in the exercise of implicit management options.

16. See the discussion of unexpectedly early redemption of corporate debt in chapter 7, and see also the discussion in Brauer (1983, p. 16n. 9) of a decline in the difference between the prices of the Sunshine Mining bonds noted in the preceding note and a concurrent decline (attributable to a rise in interest rates and a fall in the price of silver) in the likelihood that the bond with the more restrictive covenant would be called for early redemption to eliminate the covenant. See "Carbide Plans Debt Buyback of $2.53 Billion," *Wall Street Journal*, November 5, 1986, p. 3, and "Union Carbide Corp. Holders Tender 96% of Some Debt Notes," *Wall Street Journal*, December 8, 1986, p. 17, for an example of repurchasing debt to eliminate a restrictive covenant. See the discussion in notes 45, 49, and 54 in chapter 18 for an example of a firm defeasing some debt and calling other debt to avoid a covenant.

References

Acharya, V., and J. Carpenter. 1999. Callable defaultable bonds: Valuation, hedging, and optimal exercise boundaries. Stern School of Business, New York University.

Aghion, P., O. Hart, and J. Moore. 1992. The economics of bankruptcy reform. 8 *Journal of Law, Economics, and Organization* 523.

Agrawal, A., and N. Jayaraman. 1994. The dividend policies of all-equity firms: A direct test of the free cash flow theory. 15 *Managerial and Decision Economics* 139.

Agrawal, A., and G. Mandelker. 1987. Managerial incentives and corporate investment and financing decisions. 42 *Journal of Finance* 823.

Aharony, J., and I. Swary. 1980. Quarterly dividend and earnings announcements and stockholders' returns: An empirical analysis. 35 *Journal of Finance* 1.

Aitchison, J., and J. Brown. 1957. *The Lognormal Distribution*. Cambridge: Cambridge University Press.

Alexander, G., P. Benson, and E. Gunderson. 1986. Asset redeployment: Trans World Corporation's spinoff of TWA. 15 *Financial Management* 50 (Summer).

Alexander, G., P. Benson, and J. Kampmeyer. 1984. Investigating the valuation effects of announcements of voluntary corporate selloffs. 39 *Journal of Finance* 503.

Allen, D., R. Lamy, and G. Thompson. 1987. Agency costs and alternative call provisions: An empirical investigation. 16 *Financial Management* 37 (Winter).

Allen, J. 1998. Capital markets and corporate structure: The equity carve-outs of thermo electron. 48 *Journal of Financial Economics* 99.

Allen, J., and J. McConnell. 1998. Equity carve-outs and managerial discretion. 53 *Journal of Finance* 163.

Alli, K., A. Khan, and G. Ramirez. 1993. Determinants of corporate dividend policy: A factorial analysis. 28 *The Financial Review* 523.

Altman, E. 1984. A further empirical investigation of the bankruptcy cost question. 39 *Journal of Finance* 1067.

Altman, E., and A. Eberhart. 1994. Do seniority provisions protect bondholders' investments? 20 *Journal of Portfolio Management* 67 (Summer).

Ambarish, R., K. John, and J. Williams. 1987. Efficient signaling with dividends and investments. 42 *Journal of Finance* 321.

American Bar Foundation. 1971. *Commentaries on Indentures*. American Bar Foundation, Chicago, IL.

Amihud, Y., K. Garbade, and M. Kahan. 1999. A new governance structure for corporate bonds. 51 *Stanford Law Review* 447.

Amihud, Y., K. Garbade, and M. Kahan. 2000. An institutional innovation to reduce the agency costs of public corporate bonds. 13 *Journal of Applied Corporate Finance* 114 (Spring).

Amihud, Y., and H. Mendelson. 1986. Asset pricing and the bid-ask spread. 17 *Journal of Financial Economics* 223.

Amihud, Y., and H. Mendelson. 1991a. Liquidity, maturity, and the yields on U.S. Treasury securities. 46 *Journal of Finance* 1411.

Amihud, Y., and H. Mendelson. 1991b. Liquidity, asset prices and financial policy. 47 *Financial Analysts Journal* 56 (November–December).

Amihud, Y., and H. Mendelson. 1996. A new approach to the regulation of trading across securities markets. 71 *New York University Law Review* 1411.

Amihud, Y., H. Mendelson, and B. Lauterbach. 1997. Market microstructure and securities values: Evidence from the Tel Aviv Stock Exchange. 45 *Journal of Financial Economics* 365.

Anderson, J., and P. Wright. 1982. Liquidating plans of reorganization. 56 *American Bankruptcy Law Journal* 29.

Anderson, R., and S. Sundaresan. 1996. Design and valuation of debt contracts. 9 *Review of Financial Studies* 37.

Anderson, R., and S. Sundaresan. 2000. A comparative study of structural models of corporate bonds yields: An exploratory investigation. 24 *Journal of Banking and Finance* 255.

Ang, J., and J. Chua. 1980. Coalitions, the me-first rule, and the liquidation decision. 11 *Bell Journal of Economics* 355.

Angbazo, L., J. Mei, and A. Saunders. 1998. Credit spreads in the market for highly leveraged transaction loans. 22 *Journal of Banking and Finance* 1249.

Asquith, P. 1983. Merger bids, uncertainty, and stockholder returns. 11 *Journal of Financial Economics* 51.

Asquith, P. 1995. Convertible bonds are not called late. 50 *Journal of Finance* 1275.

Asquith, P., and E. Kim. 1982. The impact of merger bids on the participating firms' security holders. 37 *Journal of Finance* 1209.

Asquith, P., and D. Mullins. 1983. The impact of initiating dividend payments on shareholders' wealth. 56 *Journal of Business* 77.

Asquith, P., and D. Mullins. 1986. Signalling with dividends, stock repurchases, and equity issues. 15 *Financial Management* 27 (Autumn).

Asquith, P., and D. Mullins. 1991. Convertible debt: Corporate call policy and voluntary conversion. 46 *Journal of Finance* 1273.

Asquith, P., and T. Wizman. 1990. Event risk, covenants, and bondholder returns in leveraged buyouts. 27 *Journal of Financial Economics* 195.

Asquith, P., R. Bruner, and D. Mullins. 1983. The gains to bidding firms from merger. 11 *Journal of Financial Economics* 121.

Asquith, P., R. Gertner, and D. Scharfstein. 1994. Anatomy of financial distress: An examination of junk-bond issuers. 109 *Quarterly Journal of Economics* 625.

Bab, A. 1991. Debt tender offer techniques and the problem of coercion. 91 *Columbia Law Review* 846.

Bagnani, E., N. Milonas, A. Saunders, and N. Travlos. 1994. Managers, owners, and the pricing of risky debt: An empirical analysis. 49 *Journal of Finance* 453.

Baird, D. 1986. The uneasy case for corporate reorganizations. 15 *Journal of Legal Studies* 127.

Baird, D. 1991. The initiation problem in bankruptcy. 11 *International Review of Law and Economics* 223.

Baird, D., and T. Jackson. 1988. Bargaining after the fall and the contours of the absolute priority rule. 55 *University of Chicago Law Review* 738.

Baird, D., and T. Jackson. 1990. *Cases, Problems and Materials on Bankruptcy*, 2nd ed. Boston: Little, Brown.

Baird, D., and R. Picker. 1991. A simple noncooperative bargaining model of corporate reorganizations. 20 *Journal of Legal Studies* 311.

Baker, G., and G. Smith. 1998. *The New Financial Capitalists: Kohlberg Kravis Roberts and the Creation of Corporate Value*. Cambridge: Cambridge University Press.

Baker, G., M. Jensen, and K. Murphy. 1988. Compensation and incentives: Practice vs. theory. 43 *Journal of Finance* 593.

Baker, H., G. Farrelly, and R. Edelman. 1985. A survey of management views on dividend policy. 14 *Financial Management* 78 (Autumn).

Baker, H., P. Gallagher, and K. Morgan. 1981. Management's view of stock repurchase programs. 4 *Journal of Financial Research* 233.

Baldwin, C., and S. Mason. 1983. The resolution of claims in financial distress: The case of Massey Ferguson. 38 *Journal of Finance* 505.

Barclay, M., and C. Holderness. 1989. Private benefits from control of public corporations. 25 *Journal of Financial Economics* 371.

Barclay, M., and C. Holderness. 1991. Negotiated block trades and corporate control. 46 *Journal of Finance* 861.

Barclay, M., and C. Holderness. 1992. The law and large-block trades. 35 *Journal of Law & Economics* 265.

Barclay, M., and C. Smith. 1988. Corporate payout policy. 22 *Journal of Financial Economics* 61.

Baumol, W. 1962. On the theory of the expansion of the firm. 52 *American Economic Review* 1078.

Baumol, W. 1967. *Business Behavior, Value and Growth*, rev. ed. New York: Harcourt, Brace.

Bebchuk, L. 1988. A new approach to corporate reorganizations. 101 *Harvard Law Review* 775.

Bebchuk, L., and A. Guzman. 1999. An economic analysis of transnational bankruptcies. 42 *Journal of Law & Economics* 775.

Benartzi, S., R. Michaely, and R. Thaler. 1997. Do changes in dividends signal the future or the past? 52 *Journal of Finance* 1007.

Bennett, P., K. Garbade, and J. Kambhu. 2000. Enhancing the liquidity of U.S. Treasury securities in an era of surpluses. 6 *Federal Reserve Bank of New York Economic Policy Review* 89.

Benston, G. 1985. The self-serving management hypothesis. 7 *Journal of Accounting and Economics* 67.

Bergström, C., and K. Rydqvist. 1992. Differentiated bids for voting and restricted voting shares in public tender offers. 16 *Journal of Banking and Finance* 97.

Berkovitch, E., and E. Kim. 1990. Financial contracting and leverage induced over- and under-investment incentives. 45 *Journal of Finance* 765.

Berle, A., and G. Means. 1932. *The Modern Corporation and Private Property*. London: Macmillan.

Berlin, M., and L. Mester. 1992. Debt covenants and renegotiation. 2 *Journal of Financial Intermediation* 95.

Betker, B. 1995a. Management's incentives, equity's bargaining power, and deviations from absolute priority in Chapter 11 bankruptcies. 68 *Journal of Business* 161.

Betker, B. 1995b. An empirical examination of prepackaged bankruptcy. 24 *Financial Management* 3 (Spring).

Bhagat, S. 1983. The effect of pre-emptive right amendments on shareholder wealth. 12 *Journal of Financial Economics* 289.

Bhagat, S., and J. Brickley. 1984. Cumulative voting: The value of minority shareholder voting rights. 27 *Journal of Law & Economics* 339.

Bhagat, S., and R. Jefferis. 1991. Voting power in the proxy process: The case of antitakeover charter amendments. 30 *Journal of Financial Economics* 193.

Bhattacharya, S. 1979. Imperfect information, dividend policy, and "the bird in the hand" fallacy. 10 *Bell Journal of Economics* 259.

Bhattacharyya, S., and R. Singh. 1999. The resolution of bankruptcy by auction: Allocating the residual right of design. 54 *Journal of Financial Economics* 269.

Black, F. 1976. The dividend puzzle. 2 *Journal of Portfolio Management* 5 (Winter).

Black, F., and J. Cox. 1976. Valuing corporate securities: Some effects of bond indenture provisions. 31 *Journal of Finance* 351.

Black, F., and M. Scholes. 1973. The pricing of options and corporate liabilities. 81 *Journal of Political Economy* 637.

Blain, P., and D. Erne. 1984. Creditor's committees under Chapter 11 of the United States Bankruptcy Code: Creation, composition, power and duties. 67 *Marquette Law Review* 491.

Booth, C. 1986. The cramdown on secured creditors: An impetus toward settlement. 60 *American Bankruptcy Law Journal* 69.

Boudoukh, J., and R. Whitelaw. 1991. The benchmark effect in the Japanese government bond market. 1 *Journal of Fixed Income* 52 (September).

Boudoukh, J., and R. Whitelaw. 1993. Liquidity as a choice variable: A lesson from the Japanese government bond market. 6 *Review of Financial Studies* 265.

Bower, J. 1986. *When Markets Quake: The Management Challenge of Restructuring Industry*. Boston: Harvard Business School Press.

Bozdogan, K. 1989. The transformation of the US chemicals industry. In *Working Papers of the MIT Commission on Industrial Productivity*, vol. 1. Cambridge: MIT Press.

Bradley, M. 1980. Interfirm tender offers and the market for corporate control. 53 *Journal of Business* 345.

Bradley, M., and M. Rosenzweig. 1992. The untenable case for Chapter 11. 101 *Yale Law Journal* 1043.

Bradley, M., and L. Wakeman. 1983. The wealth effects of targeted share repurchases. 11 *Journal of Financial Economics* 301.

Bradley, M., A. Desai, and E. Kim. 1983. The rationale behind interfirm tender offers. 11 *Journal of Financial Economics* 183.

Bradley, M., A. Desai, and E. Kim. 1988. Synergistic gains from corporate acquisitions and their division between the stockholders of target and acquiring firms. 21 *Journal of Financial Economics* 3.

Brauer, G. 1983. Evidence of the market value of me-first rules. 12 *Financial Management* 11 (Spring).

Brennan, M. 1995. Corporate finance over the past 25 years. 24 *Financial Management* 9 (Summer).

Brennan, M., and E. Schwartz. 1977. Convertible bonds: Valuation and optimal strategies for call and conversion. 32 *Journal of Finance* 1699.

Brennan, M., and E. Schwartz. 1978. Corporate income taxes, valuation, and the problem of optimal capital structure. 51 *Journal of Business* 103.

Brennan, M., and E. Schwartz. 1980. Analyzing convertible bonds. 15 *Journal of Financial and Quantitative Analysis* 907.

Brennan, M., and E. Schwartz. 1984. Optimal financial policy and firm valuation. 39 *Journal of Finance* 593.

Brenner, M., R. Eldor, and S. Hauser. 2001. The price of options illiquidity. 56 *Journal of Finance* 789.

Brickley, J. 1983. Shareholder wealth, information signaling and the specially designated dividend. 12 *Journal of Financial Economics* 187.

Brickley, J., S. Bhagat, and R. Lease. 1985. The impact of long-range managerial compensation plans on shareholder wealth. 7 *Journal of Accounting and Economics* 115.

Brickley, J., R. Lease, and C. Smith. 1988. Ownership structure and voting on antitakeover amendments. 20 *Journal of Financial Economics* 267.

Brigham, E. 1966. An analysis of convertible debentures. 21 *Journal of Finance* 35.

Brittain, J. 1966. *Corporate Dividend Policy*. Washington, DC: The Brookings Institution.

Broude, R. 1984. Cramdown and Chapter 11 of the bankruptcy code: The settlement imperative. 39 *Business Lawyer* 441.

Brudney, V. 1980. Dividends, discretion, and disclosure. 66 *Virginia Law Review* 85.

Bulow, J., and J. Shoven. 1978. The bankruptcy decision. 9 *Bell Journal of Economics* 437.

Burrough, B., and J. Helyar. 1990. *Barbarians at the Gate: The Fall of RJR Nabisco*. New York: Harper and Row.

Byrd, A., and W. Moore. 1996. On the information content of calls of convertible securities. 69 *Journal of Business* 89.

Campbell, C., L. Ederington, and P. Vankudre. 1991. Tax shields, sample–selection bias, and the information content of conversion-forcing bond calls. 46 *Journal of Finance* 1291.

Caouette, J., E. Altman, and P. Narayanan. 1998. *Managing Credit Risk: The Next Great Financial Challenge*. New York: Wiley.

Carey, M., S. Prowse, J. Rea, and G. Udell. 1993. The economics of private placements: A new look. 2 *Financial Markets, Institutions and Instruments* 1 (no. 3).

Carlson, J., and F. Fabozzi. 1992. *The Trading and Securitization of Senior Bank Loans.* Chicago: Probus.

Carpenter, J. 1998. The exercise and valuation of executive stock options. 48 *Journal of Financial Economics* 127.

Carpenter, J., and D. Yermack, eds. 1999. *Executive Compensation and Shareholder Value: Theory and Evidence.* Dordrecht: Kluwer Academic.

Cathcart, L., and L. El-Jahel. 1998. Valuation of defaultable bonds. 8 *Journal of Fixed Income* 65 (June).

Charest, G. 1978. Dividend information, stock returns and market efficiency—II. 6 *Journal of Financial Economics* 297.

Chou, A. 1991. Corporate governance in Chapter 11: Electing a new board. 65 *American Bankruptcy Law Journal* 559.

Clark, R. 1986. *Corporate Law.* Boston: Little, Brown.

Comment, R., and G. Jarrell. 1991. The relative signaling power of Dutch-auction and fixed price self-tender offers and open-market share repurchases. 46 *Journal of Finance* 1243.

Comment, R., and G. Schwert. 1995. Poison or placebo? Evidence on the deterrence and wealth effects of modern antitakeover measures. 39 *Journal of Financial Economics* 3.

Constantinides, G. 1984. Warrant exercise and bond conversion in competitive markets. 13 *Journal of Financial Economics* 371.

Coogan, P. 1982. Confirmation of a plan under the bankruptcy code. 32 *Case Western Reserve Law Review* 301.

Cook, D., and J. Easterwood. 1994. Poison put bonds: An analysis of their economic role. 49 *Journal of Finance* 1905.

Cook, D., J. Easterwood, and J. Martin. 1992. Bondholder wealth effects of management buyouts. 21 *Financial Management* 102 (Spring).

Coughlan, A., and R. Schmidt. 1985. Executive compensation, management turnover, and firm performance. 7 *Journal of Accounting and Economics* 43.

Cowan, A., N. Nayar, and A. Singh. 1990. Stock returns before and after calls of convertible bonds. 25 *Journal of Financial and Quantitative Analysis* 549.

Cox, J., and S. Ross. 1976. The valuation of options for alternative stochastic processes. 3 *Journal of Financial Economics* 145.

Cox, J., and M. Rubinstein. 1985. *Options Markets.* Englewood Cliffs, NJ: Prentice Hall.

Cox, J., J. Ingersoll, and S. Ross. 1985. A theory of the term structure of interest rates. 53 *Econometrica* 385.

Cox, J., S. Ross, and M. Rubinstein. 1979. Option pricing: A simplified approach. 7 *Journal of Financial Economics* 229.

Crabbe, L. 1991. Event risk: An analysis of losses to bondholders and "Super poison put" bond covenants. 46 *Journal of Finance* 689.

Crosbie, P. 1999. *Modeling Default Risk.* San Francisco, CA: KMV Corporation.

Cuny, C., and P. Jorion. 1995. Valuing executive stock options with endogenous departure. 20 *Journal of Accounting and Economics* 193.

Cusatis, P., J. Miles, and J. Woolridge. 1993. Restructuring through spinoffs: The stock market evidence. 33 *Journal of Financial Economics* 293.

Cusatis, P., J. Miles, and J. Woolridge. 1994. Some new evidence that spinoffs create value. 7 *Journal of Applied Corporate Finance* 100 (Spring).

Cutler, D., and L. Summers. 1988. The costs of conflict resolution and financial distress: Evidence from the Texaco-Pennzoil litigation. 19 *Rand Journal of Economics* 157.

Dammon, R., K. Dunn, and C. Spatt. 1993. The relative pricing of high-yield debt: The case of RJR Nabisco Holdings Capital Corporation. 83 *American Economic Review* 1090.

Dann, L. 1981. Common stock repurchases. 9 *Journal of Financial Economics* 113.

Dann, L., and H. DeAngelo. 1983. Standstill agreements, privately negotiated stock repurchases, and the market for corporate control. 11 *Journal of Financial Economics* 275.

Dann, L., and H. DeAngelo. 1988. Corporate financial policy and corporate control: A study of defensive adjustments in asset and ownership structure. 20 *Journal of Financial Economics* 87.

Das, S., ed. 1998. *Credit Derivatives*, New York: Wiley.

DeAngelo, H., and L. DeAngelo. 1985. Managerial ownership of voting rights: A study of public corporations with dual classes of common stock. 14 *Journal of Financial Economics* 33.

DeAngelo, H., and L. DeAngelo. 1989. Proxy contests and the governance of publicly held corporations. 23 *Journal of Financial Economics* 29.

DeAngelo, H., and L. DeAngelo. 1990. Dividend policy and financial distress: An empirical investigation of troubled NYSE firms. 45 *Journal of Finance* 1415.

DeAngelo, H., and L. DeAngelo. 2000. Controlling stockholders and the disciplinary role of corporate payout policy: A study of the Times Mirror Company. 56 *Journal of Financial Economics* 153.

DeAngelo, H., and E. Rice. 1983. Antitakeover charter amendments and stockholder wealth. 11 *Journal of Financial Economics* 329.

DeAngelo, H., L. DeAngelo, and D. Skinner. 1992. Dividends and losses. 47 *Journal of Finance* 1837.

Demsetz, H., and K. Lehn. 1985. The structure of corporate ownership: Causes and consequences. 93 *Journal of Political Economy* 1155.

Denis, D. 1990. Defensive changes in corporate payout policy: Share repurchases and special dividends. 45 *Journal of Finance* 1433.

Denis, D., and D. Denis. 1993. Managerial discretion, organizational structure, and corporate performance: A study of leveraged recapitalizations. 16 *Journal of Accounting and Economics* 209.

Denis, D., and D. Denis. 1995. Causes of financial distress following leveraged recapitalizations. 37 *Journal of Financial Economics* 129.

Denis, D., and J. Serrano. 1996. Active investors and management turnover following unsuccessful control contests. 40 *Journal of Financial Economics* 239.

Denis, D., D. Denis, and A. Sarin. 1994. The information content of dividend changes: Cash flow signaling, overinvestment, and dividend clienteles. 29 *Journal of Financial and Quantitative Analysis* 567.

Dennis, D., and J. McConnell. 1986. Corporate mergers and security returns. 16 *Journal of Financial Economics* 143.

Dhillon, U., and H. Johnson. 1994. The effect of dividend changes on stock and bond prices. 49 *Journal of Finance* 281.

Dixit, A., and R. Pindyck. 1994. *Investment under Uncertainty*. Princeton: Princeton University Press.

Dodd, P. 1980. Merger proposals, management discretion and stockholder wealth. 8 *Journal of Financial Economics* 105.

Dodd, P., and R. Leftwich. 1980. The market for corporate charters: "Unhealthy competition" versus federal regulation. 53 *Journal of Business* 259.

Dodd, P., and R. Ruback. 1977. Tender offers and stockholder returns. 5 *Journal of Financial Economics* 351.

Dodd, P., and J. Warner. 1983. On corporate governance: A study of proxy contests. 11 *Journal of Financial Economics* 401.

Donaldson, G. 1990. Voluntary restructuring: The case of General Mills. 27 *Journal of Financial Economics* 117.

Donaldson, G. 1991. Voluntary restructuring: The case of General Mills. 4 *Journal of Applied Corporate Finance* 6 (Fall).

Duffie, D., and K. Singleton. 1999. Modeling term structures of defaultable bonds. 12 *Review of Financial Studies* 687.

Dunn, K., and K. Eades. 1989. Voluntary conversion of convertible securities and the optimal call strategy. 23 *Journal of Financial Economics* 273.

Dunn, K., and C. Spatt. 1984. A strategic analysis of sinking fund bonds. 13 *Journal of Financial Economics* 399.

Easterbrook, F. 1984. Two agency-cost explanations of dividends. 74 *American Economic Review* 650.

Easterbrook, F. 1990. Is corporate bankruptcy efficient? 27 *Journal of Financial Economics* 411.

Easterbrook, F., and D. Fischel. 1983. Voting in corporate law. 26 *Journal of Law and Economics* 395.

Eberhart, A., and R. Sweeney. 1992. Does the bond market predict bankruptcy settlements? 47 *Journal of Finance* 943.

Eberhart, A., W. Moore, and R. Roenfeldt. 1990. Security pricing and deviations from the absolute priority rule in bankruptcy proceedings. 45 *Journal of Finance* 1457.

Elton, E., and T. Green. 1998. Tax and liquidity effects in pricing government bonds. 53 *Journal of Finance* 1533.

Emanuel, D. 1983. Warrant valuation and exercise strategy. 12 *Journal of Financial Economics* 211.

Engelmann, K., and B. Cornell. 1988. Measuring the cost of corporate litigation: Five case studies. 17 *Journal of Legal Studies* 377.

Epstein, D., S. Nickles, and J. White. 1993. *Bankruptcy*. Boulder, CO: West.

Fama, E. 1980. Agency problems and the theory of the firm. 88 *Journal of Political Economy* 288.

Fama, E., and H. Babiak. 1968. Dividend policy: An empirical analysis. 63 *Journal of the American Statistical Association* 1132.

Fama, E., and M. Jensen. 1983a. Separation of ownership and control. 26 *Journal of Law and Economics* 301.

Fama, E., and M. Jensen. 1983b. Agency problems and residual claims. 26 *Journal of Law and Economics* 327.

Finnerty, J. 1976. Insiders and market efficiency. 31 *Journal of Finance* 1141.

Fischel, D. 1981. The law and economics of dividend policy. 67 *Virginia Law Review* 699.

Fischer, E., R. Heinkel, and J. Zechner. 1989. Dynamic capital structure choice: Theory and tests. 44 *Journal of Finance* 19.

Fleming, M., and J. Moon. 1995. Preserving firm value through exit: The case of voluntary liquidations. *Federal Reserve Bank of New York Staff Reports*, no. 8.

Fortgang, C., and T. Mayer. 1990. Trading claims and taking control of corporations in Chapter 11. 12 *Cardozo Law Review* 1.

Francis, J., J. Frost, and J. Whittaker. 1999. *Handbook of Credit Derivatives*. New York: McGraw-Hill.

Frankfurter, G., and B. Wood. 1997. The evolution of corporate dividend policy. 23 *Journal of Financial Education* 16 (Spring).

Franks, J., and W. Torous. 1989. An empirical investigation of U.S. firms in reorganization. 44 *Journal of Finance* 747.

Franks, W., and W. Torous. 1992. Lessons from a comparison of US and UK insolvency codes. 8 *Oxford Review of Economic Policy* 70.

Franks, J., and W. Torous. 1994. A comparison of financial recontracting in distressed exchanges and Chapter 11 reorganizations. 35 *Journal of Financial Economics* 349.

Franks, J., K. Nyborg, and W. Torous. 1996. A Comparison of US, UK and German insolvency codes. 25 *Financial Management* 86 (Autumn).

Froot, K., and E. Dabora. 1999. How are stock prices affected by the location of trade? 53 *Journal of Financial Economics* 189.

Frost, C. 1992. Running the asylum: Governance problems in bankruptcy reorganizations. 34 *Arizona Law Review* 89.

Galai, D., and R. Masulis. 1976. The option pricing model and the risk factor of stock. 3 *Journal of Financial Economics* 53.

Galai, D., and M. Schneller. 1978. Pricing of warrants and the value of the firm. 33 *Journal of Finance* 1333.

Garbade, K. 1996. *Fixed Income Analytics*. Cambridge: MIT Press.

Garbade, K. 1999. Managerial discretion and the contingent valuation of corporate securities. 6 *Journal of Derivatives* 65 (Summer).

Gentry, J., and J. Pike. 1968. Dual funds revisited. 24 *Financial Analysts Journal* 149 (March–April).

Gerber, M. 1987. The election of directors and Chapter 11—The Second Circuit tells stockholders to walk softly and carry a big lever. 53 *Brooklyn Law Review* 295.

Gertner, R., and D. Scharfstein. 1991. A theory of workouts and the effects of reorganization law. 46 *Journal of Finance* 1189.

Geske, R. 1977. The valuation of corporate liabilities as compound options. 12 *Journal of Financial and Quantitative Analysis* 541.

Geske, R. 1979. The valuation of compound options. 7 *Journal of Financial Economics* 63.

Ghosh, C., J. Owers, and R. Rogers. 1991. The financial characteristics associated with voluntary liquidations. 18 *Journal of Business Finance and Accounting* 773.

Giammarino, R. 1989. The resolution of financial distress. 2 *Review of Financial Studies* 25.

Gillan, S., J. Kensinger, and J. Martin. 2000. Value creation and corporate diversification: The case of Sears, Roebuck & Co. 55 *Journal of Financial Economics* 103.

Gilson, S. 1989. Management turnover and financial distress. 25 *Journal of Financial Economics* 241.

Gilson, S. 1990. Bankruptcy, boards, banks and blockholders. 27 *Journal of Financial Economics* 335.

Gilson, S. 1991. Managing default: Some evidence on how firms choose between workouts and Chapter 11. 4 *Journal of Applied Corporate Finance* 62 (Summer).

Gilson, S., and M. Vetsuypens. 1993. CEO compensation in financially distressed firms: An empirical analysis. 48 *Journal of Finance* 425.

Gilson, S., K. John, and L. Lang. 1990. Troubled debt restructurings. 27 *Journal of Financial Economics* 315.

Goodman, L., and A. Cohen. 1988. Valuing deferred coupon debentures. Financial Strategies Group. Goldman, Sachs.

Goodman, L., and A. Cohen. 1989. Pay-in-kind debentures: An innovation. 15 *Journal of Portfolio Management* 9 (Winter).

Gordon, J. 1988. Ties that bond: Dual class common stock and the problem of shareholder choice. 76 *California Law Review* 1.

Gorton, G., and G. Pennacchi. 1995. Banks and loan sales: Marketing non-marketable assets. 35 *Journal of Monetary Economics* 389.

Green, R. 1984. Investment incentives, debt, and warrants. 13 *Journal of Financial Economics* 115.

Grossman, S., and O. Hart. 1980. Takeover bids, the free-rider problem, and the theory of the corporation. 11 *Bell Journal of Economics and Management Science* 42.

Grossman, S., and O. Hart. 1988. One share–one vote and the market for corporate control. 20 *Journal of Financial Economics* 175.

Grundfest, J. 1990. Subordination of American capital. 27 *Journal of Financial Economics* 89.

Gupta, A., and L. Rosenthal. 1991. Ownership structure, leverage, and firm value: The case of leveraged recapitalizations. 20 *Financial Management* 69 (Autumn).

Handa, P., and A. Radhakrishnan. 1991. An empirical investigation of leveraged recapitalizations with cash payout as takeover defense. 20 *Financial Management* 58 (Autumn).

Handjinicolaou, G., and A. Kalay. 1984. Wealth redistributions or changes in firm value: An analysis of returns to bondholders and stockholders around dividend announcements. 13 *Journal of Financial Economics* 35.

Harris, M., and A. Raviv. 1985. A sequential signaling model of convertible debt call policy. 40 *Journal of Finance* 1263.

Harris, M., and A. Raviv. 1988. Corporate governance: Voting rights and majority rules. 20 *Journal of Financial Economics* 203.

Harris, M., and A. Raviv. 1990. Capital structure and the informational role of debt. 45 *Journal of Finance* 321.

Harrison, J., and D. Kreps. 1979. Matingales and arbitrage in multiperiod securities markets. 20 *Journal of Economic Theory* 381.

Hasbrouck, J. 1985. The characteristics of takeover targets. 9 *Journal of Banking and Finance* 351.

Haugen, R., and L. Senbet. 1978. The insignificance of bankruptcy costs to the theory of optimal capital structure. 33 *Journal of Finance* 383.

Haugen, R., and L. Senbet. 1988. Bankruptcy and agency costs: Their significance to the theory of optimal capital structure. 23 *Journal of Financial and Quantitative Analysis* 27.

Hawkins, G. 1982. Essay on non-publicly issued debt: Revolving credit agreements and the pricing of privately placed debt. Ph.D. dissertation. Massachusetts Institute of Technology.

Healy, P., and K. Palepu. 1988. Earnings information conveyed by dividend initiations and omissions. 21 *Journal of Financial Economics* 149.

Henriques, D. 2000. *The White Sharks of Wall Street: Thomas Mellon Evans and the Original Corporate Raiders*. New York: Scribner.

Higgins, R., and L. Schall. 1975. Corporate bankruptcy and conglomerate merger. 30 *Journal of Finance* 93.

Hirshleifer, D., and S. Titman. 1990. Share tendering strategies and the success of hostile takeover bids. 98 *Journal of Political Economy* 295.

Hite, G., and J. Owers. 1983. Security price reactions around corporate spin-off announcements. 12 *Journal of Financial Economics* 409.

Hite, G., J. Owers, and R. Rogers. 1987. The market for interfirm asset sales: Partial sell-offs and total liquidations. 18 *Journal of Financial Economics* 229.

Ho, T. 1985. The value of a sinking fund provision under interest-rate risk. In E. Altman and M. Subrahmanyam, eds., *Recent Advances in Corporate Finance*. Homewood, IL: Richard D. Irwin.

Ho, T., and S. Lee. 1986. Term structure movements and pricing interest rate contingent claims. 41 *Journal of Finance* 1011.

Ho, T., and R. Singer. 1982. Bond indenture provisions and the risk of corporate debt. 10 *Journal of Financial Economics* 375.

Ho, T., and R. Singer. 1984. The value of corporate debt with a sinking-fund provision. 57 *Journal of Business* 315.

Holderness, C., and D. Sheehan. 1985. Raiders or saviors?: The evidence on six controversial investors. 14 *Journal of Financial Economics* 555.

Holderness, C., and D. Sheehan. 1988. The role of majority shareholders in publicly held corporations. 20 *Journal of Financial Economics* 317.

Hotchkiss, E. 1994. Investment decisions under Chapter 11 bankruptcy. Ph.D. dissertation. Stern School of Business, New York University.

Hotchkiss, E. 1995. Postbankruptcy performance and management turnover. 50 *Journal of Finance* 3.

Howe, K., J. He, and G. Kao. 1992. One-time cash flow announcements and free cash-flow theory: Share repurchases and special dividends. 47 *Journal of Finance* 1963.

Huddart, S. 1994. Employee stock options. 18 *Journal of Accounting and Economics* 207.

Huddart, S., and M. Lang. 1996. Employee stock option exercises. 21 *Journal of Accounting and Economics* 5.

Hull, J., and A. White. 1990. Pricing interest rate derivative securities. 3 *Review of Financial Studies* 573.

Hyer, T., A. Lipton-Lifschitz, and D. Pugachevsky. 1997. Passport to success. 10 *Risk* 127.

Iacono, F. 1997. Credit derivatives. In R. Schwartz and C. Smith, eds., *Derivatives Handbook*. New York: Wiley.

Ikenberry, D., and T. Vermaelen. 1996. The option to repurchase stock. 25 *Financial Management* 9 (Winter).

Ikenberry, D., J. Lakonishok, and T. Vermaelen. 1995. Market underreaction to open market share repurchases. 39 *Journal of Financial Economics* 181.

Ingersoll, J. 1976. A theoretical and empirical investigation of the dual purpose funds: An application of contingent-claims analysis. 3 *Journal of Financial Economics* 83.

Ingersoll, J. 1977a. A contingent-claims valuation of convertible securities. 4 *Journal of Financial Economics* 289.

Ingersoll, J. 1977b. An examination of corporate call policies on convertible securities. 32 *Journal of Finance* 463.

Jackson, T. 1986. *The Logic and Limits of Bankruptcy Law*. Cambridge: Harvard University Press.

Jacobs, R. 1967. The anatomy of a spin-off. 1967 *Duke Law Journal* 1.

Jaffe, J. 1974. Special information and insider trading. 47 *Journal of Business* 410.

Jaffee, D., and A. Shleifer. 1990. Costs of financial distress, delayed calls of convertible bonds, and the role of investment banks. 63 *Journal of Business* S107.

Jain, P. 1985. The effect of voluntary sell-off announcements on shareholder wealth. 40 *Journal of Finance* 209.

Jansson, S. 1981. The deep-discount bond fad. 15 *Institutional Investor* 69 (August).

Jarrell, G., and A. Poulsen. 1987. Shark repellents and stock prices: The effects of antitakeover amendments since 1980. 19 *Journal of Financial Economics* 127.

Jarrell, G., and A. Poulsen. 1988. Dual-class recapitalizations as antitakeover mechanisms: The recent evidence. 20 *Journal of Financial Economics* 129.

Jarrell, G., J. Brickley, and J. Netter. 1988. The market for corporate control: The empirical evidence since 1980. 2 *Journal of Economic Perspectives* 49.

Jarrow, R., and M. O'Hara. 1989. Primes and scores: An essay on market imperfections. 44 *Journal of Finance* 1263.

Jarrow, R., and S. Turnbull. 1995. Pricing derivatives on financial securities subject to credit risk. 50 *Journal of Finance* 53.

Jarrow, R., D. Lando, and S. Turnbull. 1997. A Markov model for the term structure of credit risk spreads. 10 *Review of Financial Studies* 481.

Jayaraman, N., and K. Shastri. 1988. The valuation impacts of specially designated dividends. 23 *Journal of Financial and Quantitative Analysis* 301.

Jennergren, L., and B. Naslund. 1993. A comment on "Valuation of executive stock options and the FASB proposal." 68 *Accounting Review* 179.

Jensen, G., D. Solberg, and T. Zorn. 1992. Simultaneous determination of insider ownership, debt, and dividend policies. 27 *Journal of Financial and Quantitative Analysis* 247.

Jensen. M. 1986. Agency costs of free cash flow, corporate finance, and takeovers. 76 *American Economics Review* 323.

Jensen, M. 1989. Active investors, LBOs, and the privatization of bankruptcy. 2 *Journal of Applied Corporate Finance* 35 (Spring).

Jensen, M. 1991. Corporate control and the politics of finance. 4 *Journal of Applied Corporate Finance* 13 (Summer).

Jensen, M. 1993. The modern industrial revolution, exit, and the failure of internal control systems. 48 *Journal of Finance* 831.

Jensen, M., and W. Meckling. 1976. Theory of the firm: Managerial behavior, agency costs and ownership structure. 3 *Journal of Financial Economics* 305.

Jensen, M., and K. Murphy. 1990a. Performance pay and top-management incentives. 98 *Journal of Political Economy* 225.

Jensen, M., and K. Murphy. 1990b. CEO incentives—It's not how much you pay, but how. 68 *Harvard Business Review* 138 (May–June).

Jensen, M., and R. Ruback. 1983. The market for corporate control: The scientific evidence. 11 *Journal of Financial Economics* 5.

Jensen, M., and C. Smith. 1985. Stockholder, manager, and creditor interests: Applications of agency theory. In E. Altman and M. Subrahmanyam, eds., *Recent Advances in Corporate Finance*. Homewood, IL: Richard D. Irwin.

John, K. 1993. Managing financial distress and valuing distressed securities: A survey and research agenda. 22 *Financial Management* 60 (Autumn).

John, K., and T. John. 1992. Coping with financial distress: A survey of recent literature in corporate finance. 1 *Financial Markets, Institutions and Instruments* 63.

John, K., and A. Kalay. 1982. Costly contracting and optimal payout constraints. 37 *Journal of Finance* 457.

John, K., and B. Mishra. 1990. Information content of insider trading around corporate announcements: The case of capital expenditures. 45 *Journal of Finance* 835.

John, K., and E. Ofek. 1995. Asset sales and increase in focus. 37 *Journal of Financial Economics* 105.

John, K., and J. Williams. 1985. Dividends, dilution and taxes: A signaling equilibrium. 40 *Journal of Finance* 1053.

John, K., L. Lang, and J. Netter. 1992. The voluntary restructuring of large firms in response to performance decline. 47 *Journal of Finance* 891.

Johnston, G., M. Curley, and R. McIndoe. 1968. Are shares of dual-purpose funds undervalued? 24 *Financial Analysts Journal* 157 (November–December).

Jones, E., S. Mason, and E. Rosenfeld. 1984. Contingent claims analysis of corporate capital structures: An empirical investigation. 39 *Journal of Finance* 611.

Jones, E., S. Mason, and E. Rosenfeld. 1985. Contingent claims valuation of corporate liabilities: Theory and empirical tests. In B. Friedman, ed., *Corporate Capital Structures in the United States*. Chicago: University of Chicago Press.

Kahan, M., and M. Klausner. 1993. Antitakeover provisions in bonds: Bondholder protection or management entrenchment? 40 *UCLA Law Review* 931.

Kahan, M., and B. Tuckman. 1993. Do bondholders lose from junk bond covenant changes? 66 *Journal of Business* 499.

Kahan, M., and B. Tuckman. 1996. Private versus public lending: Evidence from covenants. In J. Finnerty and M. Fridson, eds., *The Yearbook of Fixed Income Investing, 1995*. Burr Ridge, IL: Irwin.

Kaiser, K. 1996. European bankruptcy laws: Implications for corporations facing financial distress. 25 *Financial Management* 67 (Autumn).

Kalay, A. 1979. Corporate dividend policy: A collection of related essays. Ph.D. dissertation. University of Rochester.

Kalay, A. 1980. Signaling, information content, and the reluctance to cut dividends. 15 *Journal of Financial and Quantitative Analysis* 855.

Kalay, A. 1982. Stockholder–bondholder conflict and dividend constraints. 10 *Journal of Financial Economics* 211.

Kale, J., T. Noe, and G. Gay. 1989. Share repurchase through transferable put rights. 25 *Journal of Financial Economics* 141.

Kalotay, A. 1981. On the management of sinking funds. 10 *Financial Management* 34 (Summer).

Kalotay, A. 1984. An analysis of original issue discount bonds. 13 *Financial Management* 29 (Summer).

Kamara, A. 1994. Liquidity, taxes, and short-term treasury yields. 29 *Journal of Financial and Quantitative Analysis* 403.

Kamma, S., J. Weintrop, and P. Wier. 1988. Investors' perceptions of the Delaware Supreme Court decision in *Unocal v. Mesa*. 20 *Journal of Financial Economics* 419.

Kane, A., A. Marcus, and R. McDonald. 1984. How big is the tax advantage to debt? 39 *Journal of Finance* 841.

Kao, C., and C. Wu. 1994. Tests of dividend signaling using the Marsh-Merton model: A generalized friction approach. 67 *Journal of Business* 45.

Kashner, H. 1988. Majority clauses and non-bankruptcy corporate reorganizations— Contractual and statutory alternatives. 44 *Business Lawyer* 123.

Kim, E., and J. McConnell. 1977. Corporate mergers and the co-insurance of corporate debt. 32 *Journal of Finance* 349.

Kim, E., and J. Schatzberg. 1987. Voluntary corporate liquidations. 19 *Journal of Financial Economics* 311.

Kim, E., J. McConnell, and P. Greenwood. 1977. Capital structure rearrangements and me-first rules in an efficient capital market. 32 *Journal of Finance* 789.

Kim, I., K. Ramaswamy, and S. Sundaresan. 1993. Does default risk in coupons affect the valuation of corporate bonds? A contingent claims model. 22 *Financial Management* 117 (Autumn).

King, R. 1986. Convertible bond valuation: An empirical test. 9 *Journal of Financial Research* 53.

King, T., and D. Mauer. 2000. Corporate call policy for nonconvertible bonds. 73 *Journal of Business* 403.

Klee, K. 1979. All you ever wanted to know about cram down under the new bankruptcy code. 53 *American Bankruptcy Law Journal* 133.

Kleiman, R. 1988. The shareholder gains from leveraged cash-outs: Some preliminary evidence. 1 *Journal of Applied Corporate Finance* 46 (Spring).

Klein, A., J. Rosenfeld, and W. Beranek. 1991. The two stages of an equity carve-out and the price response of parent and subsidiary stock. 12 *Managerial and Decision Economics* 449.

Koch, P., and C. Shenoy. 1999. The information content of dividend and capital structure policies. 28 *Financial Management* 16 (Winter).

Kulatilaka, N., and A. Marcus. 1994. Valuing employee stock options. 50 *Financial Analysts Journal* 46 (November–December).

Kumar, P., G. Philippatos, and J. Ezzell. 1978. Goal programming and the selection of portfolios by dual-purpose funds. 33 *Journal of Finance* 303.

Kummer, D., and J. Hoffmeister. 1978. Valuation consequences of cash tender offers. 33 *Journal of Finance* 505.

Kwan, S., and W. Carleton. 1999. Financial contracting and the choice between private placement and publicly offered bonds. Economic Research Department, Federal Reserve Bank of San Francisco, November.

Laber, G. 1990. Bond covenants and managerial flexibility: Two cases of special redemption provisions. 19 *Financial Management* 82 (Spring).

Laiderman, R. 1980. The sinking fund bond game. 36 *Financial Analysts Journal* 33 (November–December).

Lambert, R., and D. Larcker. 1985. Golden parachutes, executive decision-making, and shareholder wealth. 7 *Journal of Accounting and Economics* 179.

Lambert, R., W. Lanen, and D. Larcker. 1989. Executive stock option plans and corporate dividend policy. 24 *Journal of Financial and Quantitative Analysis* 409.

Lambert, R., D. Larcker, and R. Verrecchia. 1991. Portfolio considerations in valuing executive compensation. 29 *Journal of Accounting Research* 129.

Lampkin, D. 1969. Convertible securities: Holder who fails to convert before expiration of the conversion period. 54 *Cornell Law Review* 271.

Lane, S. 1993. Corporate restructuring in the chemicals industry. In M. Blair, ed., *The Deal Decade*. Washington, DC: Brookings Institution.

Lang, L., and R. Litzenberger. 1989. Dividend announcements: Cash flow signaling vs. free cash flow hypothesis. 24 *Journal of Financial Economics* 181.

Lang, L., A. Poulsen, and R. Stulz. 1995. Asset sales, firm performance, and the agency costs of managerial discretion. 37 *Journal of Financial Economics* 3.

Laub, P. 1970. The dividend-earnings relationship: A study of corporate panel data. Ph.D. dissertation. University of Chicago.

Laub, P. 1976. On the informational content of dividends. 49 *Journal of Business* 73.

Lauterbach, B., and P. Schultz. 1990. Pricing warrants: An empirical study of the Black-Scholes model and its alternatives. 45 *Journal of Finance* 1181.

Leader, S. 1977. Playing the cat-and-mouse game in sinking fund bonds. 11 *Institutional Investor* 89 (April).

Lease, R., J. McConnell, and W. Mikkelson. 1983. The market value of control in publicly traded corporations. 11 *Journal of Financial Economics* 439.

Lease, R., J. McConnell, and W. Mikkelson. 1984. The market value of differential voting rights in closely held corporations. 57 *Journal of Business* 443.

Lease, R., K. John, A. Kalay, U. Loewenstein, and O. Sarig. 2000. *Dividend Policy: Its Impact on Firm Value*. Boston: Harvard Business School Press.

Lee, C. 1981. The pricing of corporate debt: A note. 36 *Journal of Finance* 1187.

Lehn, K., and A. Poulsen. 1991. Contractual resolution of bondholder-stockholder conflicts in leveraged buyouts. 34 *Journal of Law and Economics* 645.

Leland, H. 1994. Corporate debt value, bond covenants, and optimal capital structure. 44 *Journal of Finance* 1213.

Leland, H. 1998. Agency costs, risk management, and capital structure. 53 *Journal of Finance* 1213.

Leland, H., and K. Toft. 1996. Optimal capital structure, endogenous bankruptcy, and the term structure of credit spreads. 51 *Journal of Finance* 987.

Lemmon, M., J. Schallheim, and J. Zender. 2000. Do incentives matter? Managerial contracts for dual-purpose funds. 108 *Journal of Political Economy* 273.

Levy, H. 1983. Economic evaluation of voting power of common stock. 38 *Journal of Finance* 79.

Lewellen, W. 1971. A pure financial rationale for the conglomerate merger. 26 *Journal of Finance* 521.

Linn, S., and J. McConnell. 1983. An empirical investigation of the impact of "Antitakeover" amendments on common stock prices. 11 *Journal of Financial Economics* 361.

Lintner, J. 1953. The determinants of corporate saving. In W. Heller, ed., *Savings in the Modern Economy*. Minneapolis: University of Minnesota Press.

Lintner, J. 1956. Distribution of incomes of corporations among dividends, retained earnings, and taxes. 46 *American Economic Review* 97.

Litzenberger, R., and H. Sosin. 1977a. The structure and management of dual purpose funds. 4 *Journal of Financial Economics* 203.

Litzenberger, R., and H. Sosin. 1977b. The theory of recapitalizations and the evidence of dual purpose funds. 32 *Journal of Finance* 1433.

Long, J. 1974. Discussion. 29 *Journal of Finance* 485.

Longstaff, F., and E. Schwartz. 1995. A simple approach to valuing risky fixed and floating rate debt. 50 *Journal of Finance* 789.

Longstaff, F., and B. Tuckman. 1994. Calling nonconvertible debt and the problem of related wealth transfer effects. 23 *Financial Management* 21 (Winter).

LoPucki, L. 1982. A general theory of the dynamics of the state remedies/bankruptcy system. 1982 *Wisconsin Law Review* 311.

LoPucki, L. 1992. Strange visions in a strange world: A reply to Professors Bradley and Rosenzweig. 91 *Michigan Law Review* 79.

LoPucki, L., and W. Whitford. 1990. Bargaining over equity's share in the bankruptcy reorganization of large, publicly held companies. 139 *University of Pennsylvania Law Review* 125.

LoPucki, L., and W. Whitford. 1991a. Venue choice and forum shopping in the bankruptcy reorganization of large, publicly held companies. 1991 *Wisconsin Law Review* 11.

LoPucki, L., and W. Whitford. 1991b. Preemptive cram down. 65 *American Bankruptcy Law Journal* 625.

LoPucki, L., and W. Whitford. 1993a. Corporate governance in the bankruptcy reorganization of large, publicly held companies. 141 *University of Pennsylvania Law Review* 669.

LoPucki, L., and W. Whitford. 1993b. Patterns in the bankruptcy reorganization of large, publicly held companies. 78 *Cornell Law Review* 597.

Lys, T., and L. Vincent. 1995. An analysis of value destruction in AT&T's acquisition of NCR. 39 *Journal of Financial Economics* 353.

Malatesta, P., and R. Walkling. 1988. Poison pill securities: Stockholder wealth, profitability, and ownership structure. 20 *Journal of Financial Economics* 347.

Malitz, I. 1986. On financial contracting: The determinants of bond covenants. 15 *Financial Management* 18 (Summer).

Manne, H. 1965. Mergers and the market for corporate control. 73 *Journal of Political Economy* 110.

Manning, B., and J. Hanks. 1990. *Legal Capital*, 3rd ed. Westbury, NY: Foundation Press.

Marris, R. 1963. A model of the "managerial" enterprise. 77 *Quarterly Journal of Economics* 185.

Marris, R. 1964. *The Economic Theory of Managerial Capitalism*. New York: Free Press.

Mason, S., and R. Merton. 1985. The role of contingent claims analysis in corporate finance. In E. Altman and M. Subrahmanyam, eds., *Recent Advances in Corporate Finance*. Homewood, IL: Richard D. Irwin.

Marsh, B. 1985. *A Corporate Tragedy: The Agony of International Harvester Company*. New York: Doubleday.

Marsh, T., and R. Merton. 1987. Dividend behavior for the aggregate stock market. 60 *Journal of Business* 1.

Masulis, R. 1980a. The effects of capital structure change on security prices. 8 *Journal of Financial Economics* 139.

Masulis, R. 1980b. Stock repurchase by tender offer: An analysis of the causes of common stock price changes. 35 *Journal of Finance* 305.

Masulis, R. 1983. The impact of capital structure change on firm value: Some estimates. 38 *Journal of Finance* 107.

Mauer, D. 1993. Optimal bond call policies under transactions costs. 16 *Journal of Financial Research* 23.

Mauer, D., and A. Triantis. 1994. Interactions of corporate financing and investment decisions: A dynamic framework. 44 *Journal of Finance* 1253.

Mazzeo, M., and W. Moore. 1992. Liquidity costs and stock price response to convertible security calls. 65 *Journal of Business* 353.

McCauley, R., J. Ruud, and F. Iacono. 1999. *Dodging Bullets: Changing U.S. Corporate Capital Structure in the 1980s and 1990s*. Cambridge: MIT Press.

McConnell, J., and C. Muscarella. 1985. Corporate capital expenditure decisions and the market value of the firm. 14 *Journal of Financial Economics* 399.

McConnell, J., and E. Schwartz. 1986. LYON taming. 41 *Journal of Finance* 561.

McConnell, J., and H. Servaes. 1990. Additional evidence on equity ownership and corporate value. 27 *Journal of Financial Economics* 595.

McConnell, J., and H. Servaes. 1991. The economics of pre-packaged bankruptcy. 4 *Journal of Applied Corporate Finance* 93 (Summer).

Meeker, L., and O. Joy. 1980. Price premiums for controlling shares of closely held bank stock. 53 *Journal of Business* 297.

Megginson, W. 1990. Restricted voting stock, acquisition premiums, and the market value of corporate control. 25 *Financial Review* 175.

Mehran, H., G. Nogler, and K. Schwartz. 1998. CEO incentive plans and corporate liquidation policy. 50 *Journal of Financial Economics* 319.

Melicher, R., and D. Rush. 1974. Evidence on the acquisition-related performance of conglomerate firms. 29 *Journal of Finance* 141.

Mella-Barral, P. 1999. The dynamics of default and debt reorganization. 12 *Review of Financial Studies* 535.

Mella-Barral, P., and W. Perraudin. 1997. Strategic debt service. 52 *Journal of Finance* 531.

Mello, A., and J. Parsons. 1992. Measuring the agency cost of debt. 47 *Journal of Finance* 1887.

Merton, R. 1973. Theory of rational option pricing. 4 *Bell Journal of Economics and Management Science* 141.

Merton, R. 1974. On the pricing of corporate debt: The risk structure of interest rates. 29 *Journal of Finance* 449.

Merton, R. 1977. On the pricing of contingent claims and the Modigliani-Miller theorem. 5 *Journal of Financial Economics* 241.

Michaely, R., R. Thaler, and K. Womack. 1995. Price reactions to dividend initiations and omissions: Overreaction or drift? 50 *Journal of Finance* 573.

Michaely, R., and J. Vila. 1996. Trading volume with private valuation: Evidence from the ex-dividend day. 9 *Review of Financial Studies* 471.

Mikkelson, W. 1981. Convertible calls and security returns. 9 *Journal of Financial Economics* 237.

Mikkelson, W., and R. Ruback. 1985. An empirical analysis of the interfirm equity investment process. 14 *Journal of Financial Economics* 523.

Miles, J., and J. Rosenfeld. 1983. The effect of voluntary spin-off announcements on shareholder wealth. 38 *Journal of Finance* 1597.

Miller, A. 1971. How to call your convertibles. 49 *Harvard Business Review* 66 (May–June).

Miller, J., and J. McConnell. 1995. Open-market share repurchase programs and bid-ask spreads on the NYSE: Implications for corporate payout policy. 30 *Journal of Financial and Quantitative Analysis* 365.

Miller, M. 1986. Financial innovation: The last twenty years and the next. 21 *Journal of Financial and Quantitative Analysis* 459.

Miller, M., and K. Rock. 1985. Dividend policy under asymmetric information. 40 *Journal of Finance* 1031.

Mitchell, M., and K. Lehn. 1990. Do bad bidders become good targets? 98 *Journal of Political Economy* 372.

Mnookin, R., and R. Wilson. 1989. Rational bargaining and market efficiency: Understanding Pennzoil v. Texaco. 75 *Virginia Law Review* 295.

Monks, R., and N. Minow. 1995. *Corporate Governance*. Oxford: Blackwell.

Morck, R., A. Shleifer, and R. Vishny. 1988. Management ownership and market valuation. 20 *Journal of Financial Economics* 293.

Moritz, M., and B. Seaman. 1981. *Going for Broke: The Chrysler Story*. New York: Doubleday.

Morse, D., and W. Shaw. 1988. Investing in bankrupt firms. 43 *Journal of Finance* 1193.

Murphy, K. 1985. Corporate performance and managerial remuneration. 7 *Journal of Accounting and Economics* 11.

Nance, J. 1984. *Splash of Colors: The Self-destruction of Braniff International*. New York: Morrow.

Netter, J., and M. Mitchell. 1989. Stock-repurchase announcements and insider transactions after the October 1987 stock market crash. 18 *Financial Management* 84 (Autumn).

Nimmer, R., and R. Feinberg. 1989. Chapter 11 business governance: Fiduciary duties, business judgment, trustees and exclusivity. 6 *Bankruptcy Developments Journal* 1.

Ofer, A., and A. Natarajan. 1987. Convertible call policies. 19 *Journal of Financial Economics* 91.

Ofer, A., and D. Siegel. 1987. Corporate financial policy, information, and market expectations: An empirical investigation of dividends. 42 *Journal of Finance* 889.

Ofer, A., and A. Thakor. 1987. A theory of stock price responses to alternative corporate cash disbursement methods: Stock repurchases and dividends. 42 *Journal of Finance* 365.

Ofek, E. 1993. Capital structure and firm response to poor performance. 34 *Journal of Financial Economics* 3.

Ogden, J. 1987. Determinants of the ratings and yields on corporate bonds: Tests of the contingent claims model. 10 *Journal of Financial Research* 329.

Opler, T. 1993. Controlling financial distress costs in leveraged buyouts with financial innovations. 22 *Financial Management* 79 (Autumn).

Palepu, K. 1986. Predicting takeover targets. 8 *Journal of Accounting and Economics* 3.

Park, S., and M. Subrahmanyam. 1990. Option features of corporate securities. In S. Figlewski, W. Silber, and M. Subrahmanyam, eds., *Financial Options: From Theory to Practice*. Homewood, IL: Business One Irwin.

Parrino, R. 1997. Spinoffs and wealth transfers: The Marriott case. 43 *Journal of Financial Economics* 241.

Partch, M. 1987. The creation of a class of limited voting common stock and shareholder wealth. 18 *Journal of Financial Economics* 313.

Pettit, R. 1972. Dividend announcements, security performance, and capital market efficiency. 27 *Journal of Finance* 993.

Pinegar, J., and R. Lease. 1986. The impact of preferred-for-common exchange offers on firm value. 41 *Journal of Finance* 795.

Pitts, C., and J. Selby. 1983. The pricing of corporate debt: A further note. 38 *Journal of Finance* 1311.

Pound, J. 1987. The effects of antitakeover amendments on takeover activity: Some direct evidence. 30 *Journal of Law and Economics* 353.

Pound, J. 1988. Proxy contests and the efficiency of shareholder oversight. 20 *Journal of Financial Economics* 237.

Pound, J. 1989. Shareholder activism and share values: The causes and consequences of countersolicitations against management antitakeover proposals. 32 *Journal of Law and Economics* 357.

Pound, J. 1991. Proxy voting and the SEC: Investor protection versus market efficiency. 29 *Journal of Financial Economics* 241.

Radin, M. 1940. The nature of bankruptcy. 89 *University of Pennsylvania Law Review* 1.

Reich, R., and J. Donahue. 1985. *New Deals: The Chrysler Revival and the American System*. New York: Times Books.

Roberts, G., and J. Viscione. 1984. The impact of seniority and security covenants on bond yields: A note. 39 *Journal of Finance* 1597.

Robertson, S. 1988. Debenture holders and the indenture trustee: Controlling managerial discretion in the solvent enterprise. 11 *Harvard Journal of Law and Policy* 461.

Roe, M. 1983. Bankruptcy and debt: A new model for corporate reorganizations. 83 *Columbia Law Review* 527.

Roe, M. 1987. The voting prohibition in bond workouts. 97 *Yale Law Journal* 232.

Roe, M. 1990. Political and legal restraints on ownership and control of public companies. 27 *Journal of Financial Economics* 7.

Roe, M. 1993. Takeover politics. In M. Blair, ed., *The Deal Decade*. Washington, DC: Brookings Institution.

Roe, M. 1994. *Strong Managers, Weak Owners: The Political Roots of American Corporate Finance*. Princeton: Princeton University Press.

Rosen, K., and A. Rodriguez. 1982. Section 1121 and non-debtor plans of reorganization. 56 *American Bankruptcy Law Journal* 349.

Rosenberg, H. 1993. Marriott Corp.'s splitting headache. 27 *Institutional Investor* 42 (May).

Rosenthal, L., and C. Young. 1990. The seemingly anomalous price behavior of Royal Dutch/Shell and Unilever N.V./PLC. 26 *Journal of Financial Economics* 123.

Rozeff, M. 1982a. Growth, beta and agency costs as determinants of dividend payout ratios. 5 *Journal of Financial Research* 249.

Rozeff, M. 1982b. How corporations set their dividend payout ratios. 1 *Chase Financial Quarterly* 69.

Ruback, R. 1982. The Conoco takeover and stockholder returns. 23 *Sloan Management Review* 13 (Winter).

Ruback, R. 1983a. Assessing competition in the market for corporate acquisitions. 11 *Journal of Financial Economics* 141.

Ruback, R. 1983b. The Cities Service takeover: A case study. 38 *Journal of Finance* 319.

Ruback, R. 1988. Coercive dual-class exchange offers. 20 *Journal of Financial Economics* 153.

Rubinstein, M. 1995. On the accounting valuation of employee stock options. 3 *Journal of Derivatives* 8.

Ryngaert, M. 1988. The effect of poison pill securities on shareholder wealth. 20 *Journal of Financial Economics* 377.

Sanford, C. 1993. Financial markets in 2020. Paper delivered before the Federal Reserve Bank of Kansas City Economic Symposium, Jackson Hole, Wyoming. August.

Sarig, O. 1985. On mergers, divestments, and options: A note. 20 *Journal of Financial and Quantitative Analysis* 385.

Sarig, O., and A. Warga. 1989. Bond price data and bond market liquidity. 24 *Journal of Financial and Quantitative Analysis* 367.

Saunders, A. 2000. *Financial Institutions Management: A Modern Perspective*, 3rd ed. Boston: Irwin McGraw-Hill.

Schipper, K., and A. Smith. 1983. Effects of recontracting on shareholder wealth: The case of voluntary spin-offs. 12 *Journal of Financial Economics* 437.

Schipper, K., and A. Smith. 1986. A comparison of equity carve-outs and seasoned equity offerings: Share price effects and corporate restructuring. 15 *Journal of Financial Economics* 153.

Schwartz, E. 1977. The valuation of warrants: Implementing a new approach. 4 *Journal of Financial Economics* 79.

Seyhun, H. 1986. Insiders' profits, costs of trading and market efficiency. 16 *Journal of Financial Economics* 189.

Sharpe, W. 1978. *Investments*. Englewood Cliffs, NJ: Prentice-Hall.

Shelton, J., E. Brigham, and A. Hofflander Jr. 1967. An evaluation and appraisal of dual funds. 23 *Financial Analysts Journal* 131 (May–June).

Shimko, D., N. Tejima, and D. Van Deventer. 1993. The pricing of risky debt when interest rates are stochastic. 3 *Journal of Fixed Income* 58 (September).

Shleifer, A., and R. Vishny. 1986. Large shareholders and corporate control. 94 *Journal of Political Economy* 461.

Shleifer, A., and R. Vishny. 1992. Liquidation values and debt capacity: A market equilibrium approach. 47 *Journal of Finance* 1343.

Shleifer, A., and R. Vishny. 1997. A survey of corporate governance. 52 *Journal of Finance* 737.

Siegel, S. 1966. When corporations divide: A statutory and financial analysis. 79 *Harvard Law Review* 534.

Silber, W. 1991. Discounts on restricted stock: The impact of illiquidity on stock prices. 47 *Financial Analysts Journal* 60 (July–August).

Silver, A. 1981–82. Original issue deep discount bonds. 6 *Federal Reserve Bank of New York Quarterly Review* 18 (Winter).

Simons, K. 1993. Why do banks syndicate loans? *New England Economic Review of the Federal Reserve Bank of Boston* 45 (January–February).

Singh, A., A. Cowan, and N. Nayar. 1991. Underwritten calls of convertible bonds. 29 *Journal of Financial Economics* 173.

Slovin, M., M. Sushka, and S. Ferraro. 1995. A comparison of the information conveyed by equity carve-outs, spin-offs, and asset sell-offs. 37 *Journal of Financial Economics* 89.

Smith, B., and B. Amoako-Adu. 1995. Relative prices of dual class shares. 30 *Journal of Financial and Quantitative Analysis* 223.

Smith, C., and J. Warner. 1979. On financial contracting. 7 *Journal of Financial Economics* 117.

Smith, C., and R. Watts. 1982. Incentive and tax effects of executive compensation plans. 7 *Australian Journal of Management* 139.

Smith, C., and R. Watts. 1992. The investment opportunity set and corporate financing, dividend and compensation policies. 32 *Journal of Financial Economics* 263.

Spatt, C., and F. Sterbenz. 1988. Warrant exercise, dividends, and reinvestment policy. 43 *Journal of Finance* 493.

Stephens, C., and M. Weisbach. 1998. Actual share reacquisitions in open-market repurchase programs. 53 *Journal of Finance* 313.

Stevens, W. 1938. Voting rights of capital stock and shareholders. 11 *Journal of Business* 311.

Stulz, R. 1988. Managerial control of voting rights: Financing policies and the market for corporate control. 20 *Journal of Financial Economics* 25.

Stulz, R. 1990. Managerial discretion and optimal financing policies. 26 *Journal of Financial Economics* 3.

Sundaresan, S. 2000. Continuous-time methods in finance: A review and an assessment. 55 *Journal of Finance* 1569.

Tashjian, E., R. Lease, and J. McConnell. 1996. Prepacks: An empirical analysis of pre-packaged bankruptcies. 40 *Journal of Financial Economics* 135.

Tavakoli, J. 1998. *Credit Derivatives*. New York: Wiley.

Tehranian, H., and J. Waegelein. 1985. Market reaction to short-term executive compensation plan adoption. 7 *Journal of Accounting and Economics* 131.

Thatcher, J. 1985. The choice of call provision terms: Evidence of the existence of agency costs of debt. 40 *Journal of Finance* 549.

Titman, S. 1984. The effect of capital structure on a firm's liquidation decision. 13 *Journal of Financial Economics* 137.

Titman, S., and W. Torous. 1989. Valuing commercial mortgages: An empirical investigation of the contingent-claims approach to pricing risky debt. 44 *Journal of Finance* 345.

Trigeorgis, L. 1996. *Real Options*. Cambridge: MIT Press.

Tufano, P. 1993. Financing acquisitions in the late 1980s: Sources and forms of capital. In M. Blair, ed., *The Deal Decade*. Washington, DC: Brookings Institution.

Van Nuys, K. 1993. Corporate governance through the proxy process: Evidence from the 1989 Honeywell proxy solicitation. 34 *Journal of Financial Economics* 101.

Varma, R., and D. Chambers. 1990. The role of financial innovation in raising capital: Evidence from deep discount debt offers. 26 *Journal of Financial Economics* 289.

Vasicek, O. 1977. An equilibrium characterization of the term structure. 5 *Journal of Financial Economics* 177.

Vermaelen, T. 1981. Common stock repurchases and market signaling. 9 *Journal of Financial Economics* 139.

Vu, J. 1986. An empirical investigation of calls of non-convertible bonds. 16 *Journal of Financial Economics* 235.

Walking, R., and M. Long. 1984. Agency theory, managerial welfare, and takeover bid resistance. 15 *Rand Journal of Economics* 54.

Wansley, J., W. Lane, and S. Sarkar. 1989. Managements' view on share repurchase and tender offer premiums. 18 *Financial Management* 97 (Autumn).

Warga, A. 1992. Bond returns, liquidity, and missing data. 27 *Journal of Financial and Quantitative Analysis* 605.

Warner, J. 1977a. Bankruptcy, absolute priority, and the pricing of risky debt claims. 4 *Journal of Financial Economics* 239.

Warner, J. 1977b. Bankruptcy costs: Some evidence. 32 *Journal of Finance* 337.

Warner, J., R. Watts, and K. Wruck. 1988. Stock prices and top management changes. 20 *Journal of Financial Economics* 461.

Warren, E. 1992. The untenable case for repeal of Chapter 11. 102 *Yale Law Review* 437.

Watts, R. 1973. The information content of dividends. 46 *Journal of Business* 191.

Watts, R. 1976. Comments on "On the informational content of dividends." 49 *Journal of Business* 81.

Wei, D., and D. Guo. 1997. Pricing risky debt: An empirical comparison of the Longstaff and Schwartz and Merton models. 7 *Journal of Fixed Income* 8 (September).

Weisbach, M. 1988. Outside directors and CEO turnover. 20 *Journal of Financial Economics* 431.

Weiss, L. 1990. Bankruptcy resolution: Direct costs and violation of priority of claims. 27 *Journal of Financial Economics* 285.

Weiss, L., and K. Wruck. 1998. Information problems, conflicts of interest, and asset stripping: Chapter 11's failure in the case of Eastern Airlines. 48 *Journal of Financial Economics* 55.

White, M. 1980. Public policy toward bankruptcy: Me-first and other priority rules. 11 *Bell Journal of Economics* 550.

White, M. 1983. Bankruptcy costs and the new bankruptcy code. 38 *Journal of Finance* 447.

White, M. 1989. The corporate bankruptcy decision. 3 *Journal of Economic Perspectives* 129.

White, M. 1994. Bankruptcy, liquidation, and reorganization. In D. Logue, ed., *Handbook of Modern Finance*, 3rd ed. Boston: Warren, Gorham and Lamont.

Whittaker, J., and S. Kumar. 1996. Credit derivatives: A primer. In A. Konishi and R. Dattatreya, eds., *The Handbook of Derivative Instruments*, 2nd ed. Chicago: Irwin.

Wiggins, J. 1990. The relationship between risk and optimal debt maturity and the value of leverage. 25 *Journal of Financial and Quantitative Analysis* 377.

Williamson, O. 1975. *Markets and Hierarchies: Analysis and Antitrust Implications.* New York: Free Press.

Woolridge, J. R. 1983. Dividend changes and security prices. 38 *Journal of Finance* 1607.

Wruck, K. 1989. Equity ownership concentration and firm value: Evidence from private equity financings. 23 *Journal of Financial Economics* 3.

Wruck, K. 1990. Financial distress, reorganization, and organizational efficiency. 27 *Journal of Financial Economics* 419.

Wruck, K. 1991. What really went wrong at Revco? 4 *Journal of Applied Corporate Finance* 79 (Summer).

Wruck, K. 1994. Financial policy, internal control, and performance: Sealed Air Corporation's leveraged special dividend. 36 *Journal of Financial Economics* 157.

Yermack, D. 1995. Do corporations award CEO stock options effectively? 39 *Journal of Financial Economics* 237.

Yermack, D. 1997. Good timing: CEO stock option awards and company news announcements. 52 *Journal of Finance* 449.

Zinbarg, E. 1975. The private placement loan agreement. 31 *Financial Analysts Journal* 33 (July–August).

Zingales, L. 1995. What determines the value of corporate votes? 90 *Quarterly Journal of Economics* 1047.

Zwick, B. 1980. Yields on privately placed corporate bonds. 35 *Journal of Finance* 23.

Index

Absolute priority rule, 7, 21–22, 22n.3, 43
  as assumption, 79
  and bankruptcy-reform proposals, 96n.45
  in Chapter 7 cases, 83
  in Chapter 11 cases, 90–91
  and common stock, 89n.25
  and private recapitalizations, 109
  violations of, 91n.31, 99–103, 104, 117–23, 375
Acceleration of maturity, 79–80
  as contingent option, 231–32
"Act, the" (Bankruptcy Act of 1898), 81
Adding-up constraint, 44, 56–57
Aggregate risk, 5–6
Alignment of managerial behavior with shareholder interests, 12–16, 17n.31, 94n.39, 324
Aluminum Company of America (Alcoa), 304, 308, 318n.11
Arbitrage pricing, 39–44, 43, 377
Asarco, Inc., 304, 308
Asquith longitudinal study, 183–84
Asquith and Mullins cross-sectional study, 182–83, 184
Assessment
  of efficiency of corporate bond market with respect to violations of APR, 103
  of relative value, 3–4
  of risk, 5–6
  of whether to undertake particular action, 384–85
Asset stripping, 90n.29
Asset substitution, 50n.14, 168n.12
Asset transfers, and spin-offs, 351
Associated Dry Goods Corporation, 212

Bank loans, syndicated, 2, 106–107
Bankruptcy, 21–26, 79, 81–82
  and callable debt, 128–29
  Chapter 7 cases, 82–83
  Chapter 11 cases, 82, 83–96, 106n.62
  Chapter 11 cases (large corporate reorganizations), 97–104
  and convertible debt, 150–52
  costs of, 98–99, 111–17
  with coupon-bearing debt, 235–36
  and developments in corporate finance, 97n.46
  and dividend-paying stock, 275
  economic justification for, 79–81
  with multiple debt securities, 214–15
  with PIK bonds, 252–53
  and private recapitalization, 104–109
  proposals for reform of, 96n.45
  senior and subordinated debt in, 63, 64–67, 71
  and strategic default, 232
  and value of firm vs. value of debt, 45
  with warrants, 188–90
Bankruptcy Act (1898), 81
Bankruptcy Reform Act (1978), 81

Bargaining, in Chapter 11 bankruptcy cases, 93–96. *See also* Negotiations
Beta coefficient, and dividend-earnings ratio, 294n.6
Binomial random walk, 29
  and Gaussian random walk, 30, 41, 43, 60, 132
  technical condition on, 55
Binomial trees, x
Black, Fischer, ix, x
Black, Leon, 95n.41
Boards of directors, shareholders' right to replace, 14–15
Bond prices, and dividend changes, 302
Braniff International, 85n.15

Callable convertible zero-coupon note, 150
Callable debt, 127
  convertible, 179–86, 203n.10
  early redemption of, 131, 140, 142, 143–48
  and embedded options, 378, 380
  framework of analysis for, 127–29
  with partial call protection, 128n.3, 137–39
  with prohibitive call price, 161n.8
  valuation problem for, 129–42
Callable warrants, 187n.2
Call options
  equity as, 25–26, 153, 236
  and evolution of price of stock, 9
  with senior and subordinated debt, 65–67
  warrant as, 187
Capital structure of firm, 21
Carve-outs, 336n.7, 337n.8
Cash flow, free, 16n.30, 320–22
CEOs. *See also* Managers
  rate of departure or turnover of, 14n.21, 17n.31
  stock ownership by at time of bankruptcy, 102
Chapter 7 case in bankruptcy, 82–83
Chapter 11 case in bankruptcy, 83–86, 111
  bargaining in, 93–96
  and binding of dissenting creditors, 106n.62
  large corporate reorganizations under, 97–104
  operating in, 91–92
  outcome of, 96
  and private recapitalizations, 104–109
  reorganizing in, 86–91
Charter amendments, 16n.28
"Code, the," (Bankruptcy Reform Act of 1978), 81
Co-insurance effect, 380
Colt Industries, 325–28, 385
Constrained optimal dividend policy, 286–89
Constraint, adding-up, 44, 56–57
Contingency-free value of debt, 133n.10

Contingent claims
  corporate securities as, ix
  and corporate securities pricing, 1n.2
Contingent claims analysis, as area of
  inquiry, ix
Contingent claims methodology, vs.
  traditional methodology, 4n.10
Contingent option, acceleration as, 231–32
Contingent value (of securities). *See also* at
  Valuation problem
  and bankruptcy, 21–26, 79, 111n.2, 123
  (*see also* Bankruptcy)
  of debt, 45–47
  and default, 21–26
  of equity, 47
  of equity (senior-and-subordinated-debt
  example), 73–75
  of firm capitalized with common stock
  and single issue of zero-coupon debt, 21
  and leveraged recapitalizations, 324–25
  of multiple debt securities, 214–18
  of senior debt (example), 71
  and spin-offs, 351–52
  of subordinated debt (example), 71–73
  and violations of APR, 117–23
Contingent value analysis or model. *See
  also* at Valuation problem
  assumptions embedded in, 367n.1
  and bankruptcy, 375
  on callable convertible debt, 179
  on callable debt, 143
  on common stock, 127
  and debt with embedded options, 380–87
  and dividends, 283, 294, 301, 303, 308–
  309, 314 (*see also* Dividend policy)
  empirical tests of, 367–76
  methodology of, 387
  and model failure, 375–76, 377, 380–87
  and multiple debt securities, 211 (*see also*
  Multiple debt securities)
  structure of, 377–80
  uses of, 1n.3
Contingent value functions, 1
  and bankruptcy costs, 114–17
  and dividends, 295
  invariance of, 57–60, 267n.10
  notational scheme for, 253–54
  recursion algorithm for identifying forms
  of on coupon payment dates, 240–41
  three features of, 43–44
  and "up-to-the-next-coupon" problem,
  238–40, 258–59
  uses of, 1–6
  and valuation problem, 26–43, 56–57 (*see
  also* at Valuation problem)
  and violation of absolute priority rule, 118
Contingent value problem. *See* Contingent
  value analysis or model; at Valuation
  problem
Continuous time-continuous state model,
  9n.14

Contractual restrictions, on dividend
  payments, 285–86, 289, 298
Control threats
  and large leveraged recapitalizations
  (middle and late 1980s), 331–34
  leveraged recapitalization as response to,
  324
Conversion
  forced, 155, 179, 182–86
  voluntary, 155
Convertible debt, 149
  callable, 179–86, 203n.10
  and change in volatility, 205–207
  decomposition of (warrants and
  conventional debt), 202–207
  delays in calling for early redemption of,
  179–84
  and embedded options, 379
  examples of, 161–71
  vs. exchangeable, 185n.13
  framework for analysis of, 149–53
  with notice period for early redemption,
  171–77
  valuation problem for, 153–61
Convertible debt values, King on, 371–72
Convertible zero-coupon note, callable, 150
Corning, Inc., 304
Corporate acts, discretionary. *See*
  Discretionary corporate acts
Corporate control systems, 14n.26
Corporate dividend policy. *See* Dividend
  policy
Corporate governance
  assumption on, 12–17
  and portfolio and dividend policies of dual
  fund, 374–75
Corporate note, zero-coupon, 22, 129, 150,
  212
Corporate restructuring programs, and
  spin-offs, 351
Corporate securities, as contingent claims,
  ix
Corporate security values, and fluctuations
  in Treasury yields, 8
Costs, of bankruptcy, 98–99, 111–17
Coupon-bearing debt, 233
  framework for analysis of, 233–36
  with sinking fund redemption requirement,
  243n.9
  valuation problem on, 236–48
Covenant protection, 147
  and Marriott bondholders, 348
Covenants, importance of, 385–86, 385–
  86n.14. *See also* Debt covenants;
  Dividend covenants; Restrictive
  covenants
Cramdown, 89
  preemptive, 96n.45
Cross-acceleration clause, 80, 211n.2
Cross-sectional study by Asquith and
  Mullins, 182–83, 184

Cross valuation, 2, 47–48, 52
  for callable debty, 134–36
  with convertible debt, 163–64, 166
  with senior and subordinated debt, 75–77
Crystal Brands, Inc., 351
Cum-payment values
  under constrained optimal dividend policy, 287–88
  vs. ex-payment values, 234
  liquidation as maximizing, 284
  and transversality conditions, 257

Dean Witter, Reynolds, 351
Debt
  callable, 127–42 (*see also* Callable debt)
  contingent value of, 45–47 (*see also* Contingent value; at Valuation problem)
  with embedded options, 378–80, 387
  publicly traded, 107–108
Debt collection law, state, 80–81
Debt covenants, 385–87
Debtor in possession. *See* DIP
Debt prices, and management signaling or wealth transfer hypothesis, 302
Debt service, strategic, 382n.10
Debt value(s)
  convertible, 371–72
  effect of spin-off on, 350
  Jones, Mason, and Rosenfeld on, 367–69
  Ogden on, 369–71
Decapitalization, by Marriott, 338
Decision-control functions, vs. decision-management, 14n.26
Decision tree, for convertible debt, 157, 159–60
Decomposition, of convertible debt into warrants and conventional debt, 202–207
Default, 21–26, 81n.8
  and callable debt, 128–29
  and convertible debt, 150–52
  with coupon-bearing debt, 235–36
  and dividend-paying stock, 275
  with multiple debt securities, 214–15
  with PIK bonds, 252–53
  senior and subordinated debt in, 64–67
  strategic, 23n.4, 118, 230n.15, 230–32
  and value of firm vs. value of debt, 45
  with warrants, 188–90
Default-free value of debt, 45
Departure or turnover rate, of CEOs and other senior officers, 14n.21, 17n.31, 83n.12
Dimensionality problem, 383–84
DIP (debtor in possession), 83–84
  in reorganization, 86–87, 89–90
  and right to bring debtor out of Chapter 11 bankruptcy, 101n.51
  senior management of, 92n.34, 93–94
Disclosure of information, in private recapitalizations, 108

Discretionary corporate acts
  decision to undertake, 384–85
  menu of, 382–83
Discretization of time, 27–28
Dividend(s)
  as function of earnings, 291–96
  as function of stock prices, 296–98
  special, 291, 303–309, 315–19, 324, 329–31
Dividend changes
  Lintner on, 292
  and management signaling, 299–301
  and wealth transfers, 301–303
Dividend covenants, 285–86, 299, 309n.22, 314, 324
Dividend-earnings ratio, 294n.6
Dividend-paying stock, 273
  examples of, 277–82
  framework of analysis for, 273–75
  valuation problem for, 275–82
Dividend payments, contractual restrictions on, 285–86, 289, 309n.22, 314, 324
Dividend policy, 274, 274n.4, 291
  and contingent value model, 314
  of firms with weak earnings vs. firms in financial distress, 298–99
  optimal, 283–89
  for regular dividends, 291–303
  for special dividends, 303–309
Dividend reservoir, 285
  and cum-payment, 287–88, 288n.10
  and estimation of dividends, 299
  level of, 289, 289n.12
Drift rate, risk neutral, 45, 60–62
Dual fund share values, Ingersoll on, 372–75

Early coupon payment, transversality conditions at time of, 237–38
Early redemptiom
  of callable debt, 131, 140, 142, 143–48
  of convertible debt, 157, 159, 171–77, 179–84
Embedded options, debt with, 378–80, 387
Employee and executive stock options (EESOs), 187n.2
Equity
  as call option on firm, 25–26, 153, 236
  contingent value of, 47
Equity carve-out, 315n.1
E-II Holdings bankruptcy, 89n.26, 90n.28
Evolution of value of firm
  assumption on, 9–12
  discrete time-discrete state approximation to, 28–30
  and $W_{j,k}$ array, 34–36
Evolution of yields on U.S. Treasury debt, 375–76
Exchangeable bonds, 185n.13
Executive stock option programs, 309n.23

Ex-payment values, vs. cum-payment values, 234
Extraordinary actions, 92, 92n.33

Firm
capital structure of, 21
free cash flow of, 16ln.30, 320–22
Fluor Corporation, 336
Forced conversion, 155
failed, 179, 182–86
Foreclosure sales, 80
Free cash flow of firm, 16n.30, 320–22
Free-rider problem
in private recapitalization, 106
in takeover bids, 15n.27

Gaussian random walk, 212–13
and binomial random walk, 30, 41, 43, 60, 132
and value of firm, 9, 28
General Mills, 351
Growth rate of firm, and dividend-earnings ratio, 294n.6

Hedging, 4–5, 47–48, 52
with senior and subordinated debt, 75–77
Hostile takeovers, deterrents and defenses to, 16n.30

Implicit management options. See Management options, implicit
Incorporation laws, 381n.7
Information disclosure, in private recapitalizations, 108
Ingersoll on dual fund share values, 372–75
Intel Corporation, 184–86
Interest policy function, optimal, 255–56, 260, 262
Interest rates
and calling of debt, 127n.2
and early redemption, 145
International Business Machines Corporation, 184–86
International Harvester, 102n.53

Joint offering, 3n.8
Jones, Mason, and Rosenfeld on debt values, 367–69

Kenner Parker Toys, Inc., 351
King on convertible debt values, 371–72

Leveraged buyout (LBO), and early-redemption study, 146–48
Leveraged recapitalizations, 315
of Colt Industries, 325–28
and contingent value of corporate securities, 324–25
and control threats (mid and late 1980s), 324, 331–34
economics of, 319–24

and default, 81n.8, 333n.55
and Quantum special dividend, 315–19
wealth transfer from unanticipated instances of, 329–31
Leveraged special dividend, 315
of Quantum Chemical Corporation, 315–19, 324
Lintner's study on dividend policy, 291–94, 308
Liquidation(s)
through bankruptcy, 21–22, 64, 80
shareholders' right to vote on, 15–16
Liquidation of physical assets, and conversion of debt, 180
Liquidity, value of, 18n.32
Liquid public markets, 2
Lognormal random walk
characteristics of, 10–12
value of firm as, 379, 384
Long debt. See Multiple debt securities
Longitudinal study by Asquith, 183–84

McLean Industries bankruptcy, 84n.14
Maintenance and replacement fund, 128n.3
Management, sleepy, 332n.53
Management options, implicit, 377, 380–87
improving representation of, 382–87
Management signaling
and dividend changes, 299–301
stock repurchase program as, 311–12
Managerial behavior, mechanisms for aligning with shareholder interests, 12–16, 17n.31, 94n.39
Managerial discretion, 53, 378–82
Managerial wage contracts, 50n.14
Managers
assumption on behavior of, 12–17, 94n.39, 132–33
and free cash flow problem, 320–22
Marriott Corporation
callable covertible zero-coupon note issued by, 150
coupon-bearing note issued by, 234
and importance of debt covenants, 385
spin-off from, 337–49, 352–63
Mergers, and spin-offs, 380n.5
Merton, Robert, ix, x
Model failure, 375
from absolute priority rule violations, 375
and implicit management options, 377, 380–87
and yields on U.S. Treasury securities, 375–76
Multiple debt securities, 211
and alternative assumptions on seniority and subordination, 223–30
and contingent values, 214–18
framework of analysis for, 211–15
valuation problem for, 218–23

Negative pledge clause, 359n.49
Negotiations. *See also* Bargaining
  between managers and creditors, 230n.15
  in private recapitalization, 105–108
Notice period, for early redemption of
  convertible debt, 171–77, 180

Ogden on debt values, 369–71
Ontro, Inc., 187n.2
Open market transactions, stock
  repurchases in, 309–14
Optimal dividend policy, 283–89
Optimal interest policy function, 255, 260,
  262
Option, of debt redemption, 127. *See also*
  Callable debt
Option positions of stockholders and
  creditors. *See also* Call options
  with convertible debt, 153
  with senior and subordinated debt, 65–67
Options. *See* Call options; Contingent
  option; Embedded options; Management
  options, implicit; Passport options; Stock
  options
Ordinary course of business, actions taken
  in, 91–92

Passport options, 379–80
Pay-in-kind (PIK) bonds, 249
  analytical framework for, 251–53
  and computational details for constructing
    contingent value functions, 264–69
  and embedded options, 378–79, 380
  examples of, 249–51, 260–64
  valuation problem on, 254–60
Penny, J. C. Company, Inc., first zero-
  coupon corporate debt security from,
  22
Pennzoil-Texaco litigation, 85n.15, 93n.38
PIK bonds. *See* Pay-in-kind bonds
Pricing of corporate liabilities
  contingent claims approach to, 4n.10
  risk neutral, 41n.11
  traditional approach to, 4n.10
Pricing of corporate securities as contingent
  claims, 1n.2
Privately held securities, replication and
  problem of, 44
Private recapitalizations, as alternative to
  bankruptcy, 104–109
Probability, risk neutral, 41n.11, 61–62
Proxy contests, 15n.27, 179n.2
Publicly traded debt, restructuring of, 107–
  108
Put warrants, 187n.2

Quantum Chemical Corporation, 315–19,
  324, 385

Railroads, and piecemeal liquidation,
  81n.8

Random walk, lognormal, 10–12
Recapitalizations
  through bankruptcy, 22
  private, 104–109
  shareholders' right to vote on, 15
Recapitalizations, leveraged. *See* Leveraged
  recapitalizations
Recursion algorithm, 41, 43
Reduced cash flow securities, 249n.1
Reduced-form pricing models, x
Relative deviation, from APR, 100–102
Relative value, assessment of, 3–4
Reorganization, in Chapter 11 bankruptcy,
  86–91
Replication, and problem of privately held
  securities, 44
Repurchase of stock. *See* Stock repurchases
Restrictive covenants
  and dividends, 299, 309n.22
  early redemption to eliminate, 146–48
  as enhancing value of debt, 386–87
R_f, 8
Risk, concerning bankruptcy costs, 123
Risk assessment, 5–6
Risk-free interest rate, R_f, 8
Risk neutral drift rate, 45, 60–62
Risk neutral probability, 41n.11, 61–62

Scholes, Myron, ix, x
Sears, Roebuck, 351
Sell-offs, 335n.4
Senior officers, rate of departure of, 14n.21
Senior and subordinated debt, 63. *See also*
  Absolute priority rule
  alternative assumptions on, 223–30
  in Chapter 7 bankruptcy, 83
  framework for analysis of, 63–67
  and multiple debt securities, 215–16, 220,
    222
  valuation problem with, 63, 67
  valuation-problem examples with, 70–78
  valuation-problem solution with, 67–70
Shareholder(s)
  and absolute priority rule, 89n.25
  and dividend-paying stock, 273, 273n.1
Shareholder interests, mechanisms for
  aligning managerial behavior with, 12–
  16, 17n.31, 94n.39
Short debt. *See* Multiple debt securities
Short positions, 40n.10
Signaling phenomenon, dividend changes
  as, 299–301
Simple corporate securities, contingent
  value models for, 377–78
Sinking fund debt, callable, 368n.4
Sinking fund redemption requirement,
  coupon-bearing debt with, 243n.9
Sleepy management, 332n.53
Special dividends, 291, 315
  and dividend policy, 303–309
  leveraged, 315–19, 324, 329–31

Spin-offs, 335
  and contingent value of corporate
    securities, 351–52
  economics of, 335–37
  empirical characteristics of, 349–51
  Marriott's 1992 proposal for, 337–49,
    352–63
  and mergers, 380n.5
Split-off, 335n.2
Split-up, 335n.2
State corporation law, and dividend
    payments, 285n.7
State debt collection law, 80–81
Stockholders and stockholder committees,
    in Chapter 11 bargaining, 95–96
Stock options
  employee and executive (EESOs), 187n.2
  executive, 309n.23
Stock prices, and dividend changes, 299–
    303
Stock prices, dividends as function of, 296–
    98
Stock repurchases, 291
  in open market transactions, 309–14
  SEC rule on, 310n.25
Strategic debt service, 382n.10
Strategic default, 23n.4, 118, 230n.15
  on redemption of short debt, 230–32
Subordinated debt. See Senior and
    subordinated debt
Sunshine Mining Company, 386n.15,
    387n.16
Syndicated bank loans, restructuring of,
    106–107

Takeover bids, 15n.27
Taxes, assumptions on, 17–18
Terminal conditions, 22–24, 64–65, 112–13,
    118–23, 151–52, 188–90, 214–15, 235–
    36, 257–58
Terminal contingent value functions, 26
Texaco bankruptcy, 84n.14
Texaco-Pennzoil litigation, 85n.15, 93n.38
Time, discretization of, 27–28
Time in bankruptcy, for large corporate
    reorganizations, 97–98
Transactions costs, assumptions on, 17–
    18
Transfer of wealth. See Wealth transfers
Transversality conditions, 218
  and dividend policy, 276, 281, 287
  and leveraged recapitalization, 324–25
  and long debt pari passu with short debt,
    223–24
  and pay-in-kind bonds, 256–57
  at time of early coupon payment, 237–38
Treasury debt, stochastic evolution of yields
    on, 375–76
Treasury yields, 8
Trust Indenture Act (1939), 107

Turnover or departure rate, of CEOs and
    other senior officers, 14n.21, 17n.31

Uncertainty(ies), 123, 385
  leveraged recapitalizations as source of,
    325
  spin-offs as source of, 352
Unconstrained optimal dividend policy,
    283–85
Undertaking particular action, assessing of,
    384–85
Unexpectedly early redemption, 145
Unexpectedly late redemption, 144–45
"Up-to-the-next-coupon" problem, 238–40,
    258–59
U.S. Treasury debt, stochastic evolution of
    yields on, 375–76
U.S. Treasury yield curve, assumption on, 8

Valuation problem, 21, 26. See also at
    Contingent value
  assumptions of, 43
  numerical examples of, 44–53
  solution of, 26–43, 56–57
Valuation problem (callable debt), 129–30
  examples of, 133–42
  solution of, 130–33
Valuation problem (convertible debt), 153–
    54
  examples of, 161–71
  solution of, 154–61
Valuation problem (coupon-bearing debt),
    236–37
  and computational details for constructing
    contingent value function, 243–48
  example of, 241–43
  solution of, 238–41
  and transversality conditions at time of
    early coupon payment, 237–38
Valuation problem (dividend-paying stock),
    275–76
  examples of, 277–82
  solution of, 277
  and transversality conditions, 276
Valuation problem (multiple debt
    securities), 218
  example of, 220–23
  solution of, 218–20
Valuation problem (pay-in-kind bonds),
    254
  and decision of firm to pay interest in cash
    or kind, 254–57
  solution of, 258–60
  and terminal conditions, 257–58
  and transversality conditions, 256–57
Valuation problem (senior and
    subordinated debt), 63, 67
  examples of, 70–78
  solution of, 67–70
Valuation problem (warrants), 191

examples of, 192–202
solution of, 191–92
Value, relative, 3–4
Value of debt. *See* Debt value(s)
Value of firm, evolution of, 9–12, 28–30,
    212–14, 235
Value functions, contingent. *See* Contingent
    value functions
Volatility
  and subordinated debt, 77–78, 78n.12
  and value of convertible debt, 205–207
Voluntary conversion, 155
Voting rights, and takeover bids, 15n.27

Warrants, 187
  in decomposition of convertible debt, 202–
    207
  examples of, 192–202
  framework of analysis for, 187–90
  redeemable, 187n.2
  valuation problem with, 191–202
Wealth transfers
  and dividend changes, 301–303
  from early redemption, 133n.9
  from unanticipated leveraged special
    dividend, 329–31
$W_{j,k}$ array, 31–36, 57–58

Yield curve, U.S. Treasury, 8

Zero-coupon corporate note
  callable, 129
  callable convertible, 150
  first, 22
  series of, 212